Finland

Lapland
p202

West Coast &
Northern Ostrobothnia
p169

Tampere, the
Lakeland & Karelia
p126

Turku, the
South Coast &
Åland Archipelago
p79

⭐ Helsinki
p42

Paula Hotti, Angelo Zinna

CONTENTS

Plan Your Trip

The Journey Begins Here 4
Finland Map 6
Our Picks 8
Regions & Cities 20
Itineraries 22
When to Go 28
Get Prepared 30
The Food Scene 32
The Outdoors 36

The Guide

Helsinki 42
Find Your Way 44
Plan Your Days 46
City Centre, Kruununhaka & Katajanokka 48
Eira, Ullanlinna & Kaivopuisto 55
Punavuori, Kamppi & Hietalahti 61
Töölö, Kallio & Kaisaniemi 69
Places We Love to Stay 76

Turku, the South Coast & Åland Archipelago 79
Find Your Way 80
Plan Your Time 82
Turku 84
Beyond Turku 91
Mariehamn 94
Beyond Mariehamn 98
Hanko 103
Beyond Hanko 110

Porvoo 113
Beyond Porvoo 118
Places We Love to Stay 125

Tampere, the Lakeland & Karelia 126
Find Your Way 128
Plan Your Time 130
Tampere 132
Beyond Tampere 138
Saimaa Lakeland 141
Saimaa Lakeland Boat Trips 146
Beyond Saimaa Lakeland 149
Jyväskylä 152
Beyond Jyväskylä 156
Hämeenlinna 161
Beyond Hämeenlinna 161
Koli National Park 165
Beyond Koli National Park 165
Places We Love to Stay 167

West Coast & Northern Ostrobothnia 169
Find Your Way 170
Plan Your Time 172

Helsinki (p42)

Rauma 174
Beyond Rauma 178
Bonk 181
Vaasa 182
Beyond Vaasa 186
Oulu 190
Beyond Oulu 194
Oulanka National Park 197
Beyond Oulanka National Park 199
Places We Love to Stay 201

Lapland 202
Find Your Way 204
Plan Your Time 206
Rovaniemi 208
Beyond Rovaniemi 214
Inari 224
Siida 226
Beyond Inari 227
Kilpisjärvi 234
Places We Love to Stay 237

Reindeer-drawn sleigh

Oulanka National Park (p197)

Toolkit

Arriving 240
Getting Around 241
Money 242
Accommodation 243
Family Travel 244
Health & Safe Travel 245
Food, Drink & Nightlife ... 246
Responsible Travel 248
LGBTIQ+ Travellers 250
Accessible Travel 251
Finding Santa 252
Chasing Northern
Lights 253
Sauna Etiquette 254
Nuts & Bolts 255
Language 256

Storybook

A History of Finland
in 15 Places 260
Meet the Finns 264
The Sámi: Traditions
and Culture 266
The Many Sides
of Finnishness 268
Triumphs & Tragedies:
Nature Conservation
in Finland 270

Saimaa Lakeland (p141)

FINLAND
THE JOURNEY BEGINS HERE

When I moved back to Finland a couple of years ago after almost two decades of living and travelling abroad, the thing I had missed the most was the lakeside sauna at my parents' cottage, the big mugs of (rather weak) filter coffee and the pink and bluish hues of a brisk (read -20°C) winter's day. But above all, it was the calm pace of life and abundance of nature everywhere. Soon after settling back, I began working on my first Lonely Planet guidebook, which led me to dig deeper into my homeland's history. As a reward for my hard work, I saved the peaks of Koli National Park for last, sat down, and wondered why I had never been here before, even though the national landscape is etched into any Finnish psyche from our schoolbooks. Today, I'm a keen advocate of all-things-Finland, and happy to share my love for the country.

Paula Hotti

@retrotravels

Paula is a travel and murder mystery writer who has contributed to Lonely Planet's Finland and Scandinavia guidebooks and written about Scandinavia and her train travels for titles such as BBC Travel, DK Eyewitness, the Sunday Times and her blog retro-travels.com.

My favourite experience is slowly road-tripping through **Saimaa Lakeland** (p141), pausing to soak in the serene landscapes of shimmering lakes, savour local meals, or take a refreshing swim

WHO GOES WHERE

Our second writer and expert chooses the place which, for them, defines Finland.

Following Oskar van Leperen on the M/S *Leila* to the island of **Laitakari** (p214), off Kemi, gave me a chance to learn about the little-known history of Sea Lapland, the corner of the northern region facing the Gulf of Bothnia that flourished in the 19th century thanks to its wood industry. The abandoned island is a fascinating piece of industrial archeology. You can roam through the remnants of one of Europe's largest steam sawmills and the surrounding village that once housed 300 people, all absorbed by the lush vegetation.

Angelo Zinna

@angelo_zinna

Angelo is an Italian-Finnish journalist and photographer based in Florence.

CONTRIBUTING WRITERS

John Noble

@johnnoble11

John is a travel writer who has covered more than 20 countries for Lonely Planet. He loves being north of the Arctic Circle.

Barbara Woolsey

@xo_babxi

Barbara is a Filipina-Canadian writer telling stories about fascinating people, food and culture – when she's not penning guidebooks, find her DJing in Berlin clubs and beyond.

PLAN YOUR TRIP

Saimaa Lakeland
Catnap in a cottage between cycling trips and water adventures (p141)

Helsinki
Get inspired by brilliant designs, architecture and gastronomy (p42)

Hanko
Wander empty beaches from a scenic seaside retreat (p103)

Turku
Explore the harbour city's hot arts and design circuit (p84)

Jyväskylä
Discover the 'Athens of Finland' – campus life and creativity (p156)

Tampere
Get your glow-up in Finland's capital of sauna (p138)

Rauma
Eat, drink and shop 'til you drop in a historic timber town (p174)

LAND OF THE SÁMI

Over thousands of years, Sámi indigenous peoples have maintained an intimate knowledge of northern landscapes. They are spread across Norway, Sweden, Finland and Russia's Kola Peninsula, with around 4000 (speaking three different Sámi languages) residing in northern Lapland, considered the Sámi homeland in Finland. Get to know the modern Sámi through their cultural centres in Inari, their crafts and arts, and through experiencing contemporary Sámi lifestyles at their reindeer farms.

FROM LEFT: FOOTAGECLIPS/SHUTTERSTOCK ©, ZOUAVMAN LE ZOUAVE/WIKIMEDIA/CC BY-SA 3.0 ©, VW PICS/GETTY IMAGES ©

Reindeer Herding

Today, a significant percentage of Sámi are involved in reindeer husbandry. Herders keep track of their free-wandering stock with earmarks and GPS collars.

Homespun Treasures

Sámi handicrafts, recognised as indigenous art, range from the strikingSámi hats, to jewellery, silverware and more. Genuine handicrafts around Lapland carry the 'Sámi Duodji' logo.

Traditional Clothing

Sámi's beautiful embroidered costumes – patterned in red, blue and yellow – are now mostly worn on special occasions, yet are living, and deeply personal to, Sámi culture.

Tuula Airamo (p227) reindeer farm

BEST CULTURAL EXPERIENCES

Discover Sámi culture and history at the state-of-the-art ❶ **Siida** (p226) museum featuring exhibition halls and original buildings such as farmhouses and storage huts.

At the ❷ **Sámi Cultural Centre Sajos** (p224) cultural centre, visit the seat of Sámi Parliament and peruse the excellent Sámi Duodji crafts shop.

Explore Sámi life at ❸ **Tuula Airamo's** (p227) lakeside home. Feed reindeer, chat about folklore, and discover traditional handicraft from natural materials.

Learn about reindeer husbandry from Päivi and Samuli in their ❹ **Arkadia Reindeer Farm** (p216), where in winter sleigh-rides are possible.

Shop ❺ **Maahisen Tyvär** (p216) in Kemi keeps pre-Christian Sámi traditions alive with items such as drums once used for rituals, all made by the owner Annuka Ovaska.

Aurora borealis over Saariselkä (p229)

CHILLS & THRILLS

The Arctic winter's charm is undeniable. From frost-tipped trees to frozen lakes, Finland's northern wilderness sparkles once the temperatures drop. The best way to survive and thrive in subzero conditions? Bundling up and getting busy outdoors, from snow sports to spotting the aurora borealis (Northern Lights).

Snowed In

It's possible to spend the night in a room made of ice in one of Lapland's 'snow hotels'. If that's too hardcore, hit their ice bars instead.

Frosty Fun

Lapland is covered in snow for up to eight months a year, making for the ultimate snow-sports destination. From March, hours of daylight increase dramatically.

BEST ARCTIC WINTER EXPERIENCES

Explore some of the 150km of cross-country ski tracks around ❶ **Saariselkä** (p229), or hit the downhill slopes of the Ski Saariselkä resort.

Go on a winter sleigh ride at ❷ **Salla Wilderness Park** (p221), a 200-hectare area that is a home to about 60 reindeer.

Boost your chances of spotting the aurora borealis by booking a five-day tour with the Finnish-Sámi local family who run Aurora Holidays in ❸ **Utsjoki** (p232).

Cheer on reindeer and their skiing 'jockeys' at the ❹ **'Royal Reindeer Race'** (p228) in Inari.

Take the heat at Kemi's public ❺ **Satamakonttori** (p215) sauna, then head for a quick dip in the refreshingly cold Bay of Bothnia.

SAUNA CULTURE

Nothing is more integral to Finnish culture, psyche and wellbeing than the sauna. From fire-heated chimney saunas in rustic summer cottages, to modern electric versions in most homes, getting sweaty is an everyday ritual for the body and soul. With more than three million saunas around the country, there's no excuse not to sneak in a session.

Waterside Saunas

The best saunas are near water for you to jump in. Yes, the about-face from hot to cold is brutal, but that's just how it's done.

Sacred Ritual

For hundreds of years, saunas have been places in which to meditate, warm up, bathe and even give birth. Respect sauna etiquette (p254) accordingly.

Bundle Blunders

Sauna whisks (twig bunches) are called *'vihta'* in Finland's west and *'vasta'* in the east. Avoid making a cultural faux pas by using the right term.

BEST SAUNA EXPERIENCES

❶ **Kotiharjun Sauna** (p75), Helsinki's only original traditional public wood-fired sauna, dating back to 1928, is a winner for its atmosphere and optional scrub-down.

At ❷ **Löyly** (pictured; p59), on Helsinki's Hernesaari waterfront, go straight from an electric or traditional smoke sauna into the sea (or a winter ice hole).

Built and run by volunteers, Oulu's ❸ **Kesän Sauna** (p192) is a rare unisex bathing stop. Float in a wood-burning sauna sitting off the Oulujoki's northern bank.

Tampere's ❹ **Rajaportin sauna** (p137) is one of Finland's most famous public saunas, regularly heating up the photogenic Pispala neighbourhood since 1906.

At Helsinki 'scene spa' ❺ **Allas Sea Pool** (p51), go for a sauna, splash into Baltic seawater and catch events with DJs and full-moon, all-night nude swimming.

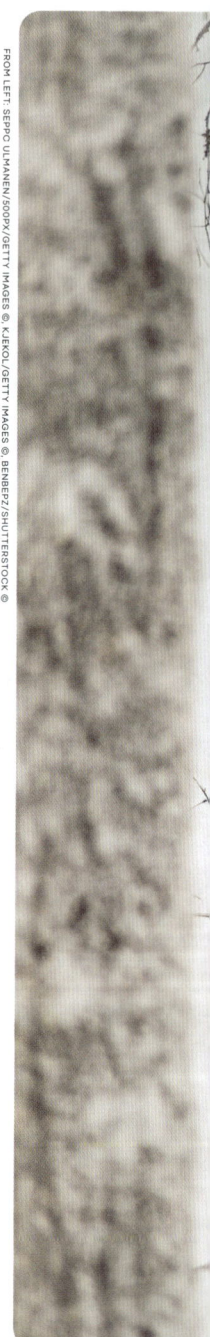

WILDLIFE WONDERS

Time and again, Finland has been recognised by environmental organisations for its conservation efforts – maintaining wonderful natural areas in which to experience wildlife. Dense forests and extensive coastlines are home to plentiful birdlife and myriad impressive mammals. Keep your eyes peeled for elk, foxes and wild swans, or take a dedicated wildlife tour in the east to spot bears, wolverines or the rare Saimaa ringed seal. Sustainable, ethical experiences keep animals, and their natural habitats, intact.

Seal Spotting

There remain only 400-odd endangered ringed seals (p144) in Saimaa Lakeland, though populations are rising. May is the most likely time to see them moulting on rocks.

Finland's Favourite

The brown bear (*Ursus arctos*) is Finland's national animal. See the bears in the northeast between mid-April and August (but for a little July gap during mating season).

Kuhmo Creatures

Kuhmo is Finland's best region for wildlife watching. Vast taiga forests run from here across Siberia, with Finland's highest number of bears and wolves roaming the border with impunity.

Lynx, Ranua Wildlife Park (p218)

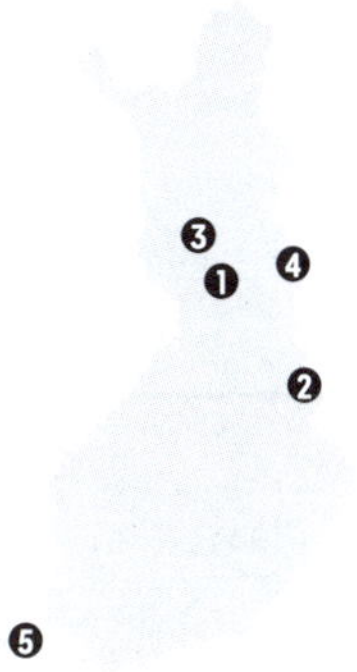

BEST WILDLIFE WATCHING EXPERIENCES

At ❶ **Ranua Wildlife Park** (p218), get a chance to see Finnish wildlife, including the brown bear, elk, lynx, wolverine, otter, Arctic fox, owls and eagles.

In Kuhmo, stay in one of ❷ **Bear Centre**'s (p165) big viewing cottages in marshland, looking out for bears and wolverines.

❸ **Lapland Welcome** (p219) is a well-known Rovaniemi-based tour operator with a focus on elk (moose) spotting and wilderness wildlife photography.

Watch for wild brown bears relaxing by a pond, as well as cheeky fish-eating ospreys, at the comfortable ❹ **Karhu-Kuusamo** (p199) hide.

Gaze at birdlife and wildlife on the vast nature trails of ❺ **Kumlinge** (p101) island. Look for cranes, roe deer, foxes and elk.

Kiasma (p51)

INSPIRING DESIGNS

Finnish design is a byword for quality, but it's not just the reliable excellence of the big-name brands that impresses. Helsinki's backstreets are fantastic for getting the creative juices flowing. Numerous ateliers and shops run the gamut from quirky to innovative, what-were-they-thinking and brilliant. Chances are you'll find something to stuff in your suitcase!

Design Hot Spot

The little settlement of Iittala Village, between Tampere and Hämeenlinna, is worth a half-day trip to discover its famous glass factory at the forefront of Finnish design.

Hit the Streets

Helsinki's Design District is a treasure trove of furniture, art, fashion, accessories and homewares. Discover hundreds of shops, studios and galleries mapped on its website (*designdistrict.fi*).

BEST HELSINKI EXPERIENCES FOR CREATORS

Helsinki's ❶ **Design Museum** (p63) looks at the roots of Finnish design in the nation's traditions and nature.

On ❷ **Korkeavuorenkatu** (p57) road in the Design District, you'll find vintage shops.

❸ **Lokal** (p63), a contemporary art gallery-cum-concept store, sells wares from local designers and artisans.

Stock up on sleek Finnish designs from well-known brands at the 'modernist shopping mall' ❹ **Lasipalatsi** (p61).

❺ **Kiasma** (p51) is a slick symbol of Helsinki's modernisation. The museum exhibits an eclectic collection of Finnish and international contemporary art and design.

SANTA'S LAPLAND

Situated right by the Arctic Circle, Rovaniemi is the 'official' terrestrial residence of Santa Claus. In the Finnish Lapland's capital, kitschy holiday cheer is an all-year affair with Christmas-themed attractions and accommodations. The centrepiece, of course, is Santa's 'official' village, where thousands of visitors, young and old, get to meet him every year.

365 Days a Year

The sprawling Santa Claus Village encompasses many Christmas-spirit experiences. Snowmobiling and ice sculpting run seasonally, but there's always a little action.

Meeting Mr Claus

Sitting on Santa's knee is the highlight. Or enjoy a tête-à-tête with Lapland's main man – a worldly, multilingual fellow. It's free, though photos with him aren't.

Happier Times

Rovaniemi was 90% destroyed by the Nazis in WWII. Today's cheesy Christmas cheer and booming tourism must be appreciated against this dark past.

BEST YEAR-ROUND CHRISTMAS EXPERIENCES

Visit the ❶ **Santa Claus Main Post Office** (pictured far left; p211) to send a postcard with Santa's 'official' stamp. Arctic Circle certificates are also available around Santa Claus Village.

Stay in the ❷ **Santa Claus Holiday Village** (p237), right at Santa's doorstep. The cute red cottages match the festive atmosphere around.

Enjoy a winter sport in summer, speeding down the 1km summer toboggan track at ❸ **Ruka** (p197), or dine in a log house worthy of Santa's home at Riipisen Riistaravintola.

Take a winter sleigh ride with Dasher and Dancer at ❹ **Santa Claus Village** (pictured left; p211), or accompany them on a summer forest walk.

Discover more about Santa's home in Rovaniemi at ❺ **Arktikum** (p208), a science centre on Lapland nature and the fascinating, arduous local history.

ELEGANT BUILDINGS

From great fires to wartime devastation, Finland is no stranger to reconstruction. Its architecture comprises an impressive pastiche of styles and influences across regions, reflecting periods from Swedish and Russian rule to postwar rebirth. Sleek, breathtaking modern architecture has been greatly influenced by Finnish architect Alvar Aalto's philosophy of beauty and functionality. Since the forest is ever-present in Finnish life, cottages and timber homes are designed to blend gloriously into natural landscapes, leaving feelings of awe and ease.

Going South

Turku, Finland's oldest city, holds the lion's share of historic buildings, and particularly medieval treasures. This is prime territory for exploring the region's past.

Living Artwork

Vanha Rauma is the Nordic region's largest wooden old town. Its 600 houses might be museum-worthy, but it's a lively area, active with residents and visitors alike.

Legacy of a 'Starchitect'

Aalto's democratic, practical view of architecture emphasised that it must be aesthetically pleasing yet serve the wellbeing of millions of citizens instead of a wealthy few.

Temppeliaukion Kirkko (Rock Church; p73)

BEST ARCHITECTURE-SPOTTING EXPERIENCES

Gape at ❶ **Helsinki's spectacularly diverse architecture** (p42)– from downtown art nouveau wonders to the Rock Church and Alto's magnum opus, Finlandia Hall.

Stroll ❷ **Rovaniemi's riverside** (p212) taking in 1960s and '70s Alto masterpieces and admiring an impressive era of rejuvenation after the town was razed in 1944.

Take in grand villas and Jugendstil stunners in ❸ **Hanko** (p103), a quiet seaside retreat and former spa for Russian nobility.

Roam around ❹ **Vanha Rauma** (p174) and its hundreds of 18th- and 19th-century wooden buildings. Introduce yourself – each one has its name above the door.

Go back to medieval times in ❺ **Turku** (p84), exploring the gloriously preserved cathedral and stone castle with its maze-like nooks and crannies.

PLAN YOUR TRIP OUR PICKS

Apocalyptica performing at Ruisrock (p87)

RHYTHMIC PARADISE

From chamber music to head-banging metal, Finland's music scene is among the world's richest. The output of quality Finnish musicians per capita is amazingly high (especially for a culture that's quite reserved offstage!). Summer is a medley of diverse music festivals, while winter is all about live bands in pubs and belting karaoke.

Summer Festivals

Packed into July, Finland's biggest music festivals, such as Savonlinna castle's month-long opera event (p141), Ruisrock (p87) and Pori's alt-music extravaganza (p179), draw famous artists and thousands-strong crowds.

Symphonic Chords

Finland's musical education is among the world's best. Finnish talent is a popular export to top overseas orchestras, and excellent classical-music festivals are held across the country.

BEST ON-STAGE EXPERIENCES

Legendary Helsinki rock venue ❶ **Tavastia** (p64) attracts up-and-coming local acts and bigger international groups, with a band almost every night.

East of Helsinki, Hamina celebrates military music in a fortress during the week-long ❷ **Hamina Tattoo** (p122). Uniformed bands perform in concerts and parades.

Bask in (five minutes' worth of) newfound fame by singing your favourite tune at one of ❸ **Turku's coolest karaoke bars** (p88).

Take in Inari's ❹ **'Nightless Night'** (p228) indigenous music festival and hear a full spectrum of Sámi music – traditional yoik chanting to rock, rap and more.

Find some gigs in Jyväskylä, where ❺ **cosy live-music pubs** (p153) and small stages host folk musicians and surprising jam sessions.

COTTAGE LIVING

Tucked away in Finland's forests and shores are half a million *kesämökkiä* (summer cottages), or *mökki* for short. Part holiday house, part sacred place, they are a spiritual home for the Finnish. Lakeland has abundant options, often boasting fishing piers and swimming beaches, but on islands and archipelagos. Scenic retreats are also everywhere.

Assorted Abodes

Pick your pleasure. The simplest rustic cabins have outside loos and water drawn from a well, while the most modern designer bungalows have every creature comfort.

Paddling Adventures

Rental cottages often come with a rowing boat that you can use free of charge to investigate the local lake and islands.

Steamy Tradition

There's no better sauna than a *mökki* one: the heat feels much gentler with their wood stoves. Dashing nude into the chilly lake is truly Finnish.

BEST MÖKKI EXPERIENCES

Stay in a shoreside hut, apartment or villa in Lake Saimaa's ❶ **Oravi village** (p143), a launching pad to the Kolovesi and Linnansaari national parks.

Take a ❷ **summer boat cruise** (p224) by a sacred Sámi island on the Inarijärvi in northern Lapland.

Relax in a wilderness hut on Finland's side of the ❸ **Three-Country Cairn** (p236), exploring the shores where Finnish, Norwegian and Swedish waters meet.

Get a taste for Finnish nature staying in a cottage in ❹ **Nuuksio National Park** (p53), close enough to Helsinki for a quick overnight stay.

Combine seaside cottage stays with island hops and hunting landscapes during Finland's best cycling adventure, the Turku ❺ **Archipelago Trail** (p92).

REGIONS & CITIES

Find the places that tick all your boxes.

Lapland

THE ARCTIC NORTH

The midnight sun, aurora borealis (Northern Lights) and awesome latitudes combine to cast a powerful spell. The sense of empty space, pure air and big skies is what's memorable here. Spend days sleighing, sledding, snowmobiling and reindeer-spotting. Head north to discover the ancestral home of the Sámi people.

p202

Lapland p202

West Coast & Northern Ostrobothnia

HARBOURS, BOATS, ISLANDS AND CITIES

Finland's west coast is a dreamy cache of historic wooden towns, sand-and-stone seaboard, and laidback islands. Northern Ostrobothnia, bordering Russia, offers remote national parks and some of the country's most abundantly beautiful scenery. With tumbling rivers, isolated lakes and dense forests, look no further for energetic alfresco escapes.

p169

Tampere, the Lakeland & Karelia

URBAN DISCOVERIES AND NATURE EXPERIENCES

Get in touch with nature – both in city centres and delightfully remote forests. With some 180,000 lakes, much of Finland is lakeland, but these parts boast the most glorious aqua. Discover trendy waterside haunts in Tampere and alfresco pursuits, from wildlife-spotting to hiking, eastwards to Kuhmo, near the Russian border.

p126

Helsinki

NORTHERN COOLNESS WITH A NEIGHBOURLY TWIST

Calling cool-hunters: Helsinki aims to inspire. Boulevards and backstreets overflow with marvellous architecture, hip gastronomy, and eye-catching design. Delight in impressive art and engineering, seaside beach life and exciting tastes from farm to forest. Here, in the capital of the 'world's happiest country', there's something for everyone.

p42

West Coast & Northern Ostrobothnia p169

Tampere, the Lakeland & Karelia p126

Turku, the South Coast & Åland Archipelago p79

✪ Helsinki p42

Turku, the South Coast & Åland Archipelago

ENDLESS ISLANDS, HISTORIC TOWNS AND COASTAL ALLURE

Discover Finland's seafaring southern charm and distinctive little port towns strung along the coast and archipelago. Unique historical features include captivating castles, fortresses and sailboats, plus former *bruk* (ironworks) buildings revamped for modern times. Get in touch with warm-hearted, Swedish-speaking islanders and their unique maritime traditions.

p79

ITINERARIES

Essential Suomi

Allow: 7 Days **Distance:** 957km

This greatest-hits list roves around the country's south and central regions. It features a little taster of everything: typical Finnish cities and coastal living across the seaside and lakes, plus some of the greatest historical sights the Nordics has to offer.

① HELSINKI ⏱ 2 DAYS

Kick things off in the capital, **Helsinki** (p42). The country's headliner is an electrifying urban space with world-renowned design and music scenes. Choose your own adventure with a spectacular ensemble of modern and stately architecture, stylish and quirky bars, and lavish spas embraced by Baltic Sea views. Your meals in Helsinki will be memorable – devour the 'new Suomi' epicurean scene in all its farmed and foraged glory.

② PORVOO ⏱ ½ DAY

Helsinki and **Porvoo** (p113) are a smart package deal. Finland's second-oldest city is a real charmer in its own right, though, famed for the enchanting wooden buildings stacked around its historic old town. Treat yourself to a fantastic lunch (Porvoo's gastronomy scene is currently the talk of Finland) and a few containers of local homemade sweets for the road.

③ SAIMAA LAKELAND ⏱ 1½ DAYS

Make your way eastwards to **Saimaa Lakeland** (p141), where the shiny bodies of water come in all cuts and shapes. Lake Saimaa, Finland's largest lake, has a solid pick of cute shorelines and abundant *mökki* (cottages) to call your sanctuary. The region offers epic drives and summer boat trips – a stop in Savonlinna, with its stunning medieval castle, is essential.

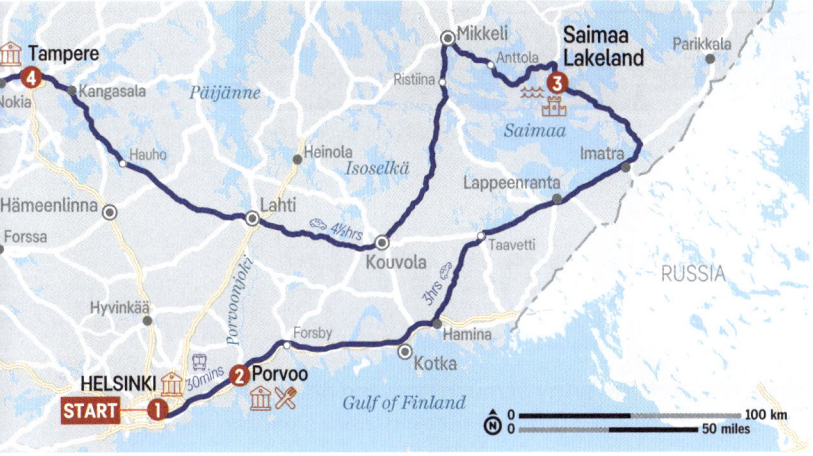

4
TAMPERE ⏱1 DAY

Loop west to **Tampere** (p138), where a groovy model of post-industrial regeneration awaits. Here, a peek into Finland's industrial origins is rounded out by the city's bohemian vibe and stunning lakescapes. Explore former fabric mills and warehouses revamped into gastronomy hot spots, eye-worthy shops and unconventional museums. If the weather's nice, take that coffee to go and sip it on the city-centre banks of the Tammerkoski rapids.

5
RAUMA ⏱1 DAY

Rauma's (p174) old-town district, Vanha Rauma, is the largest preserved Nordic wooden town. Your pleasure mission here is simply meandering the quaint streets of this UNESCO World Heritage site, popping into shops, perhaps a cosy cafe, and spying on artisans working in their small studios. Try to visit between Tuesday and Saturday, when everything's open and humming with life.

6
TURKU ⏱1 DAY

Cut southwards to **Turku** (p84). Finland's oldest city (and technically its original capital) is an essential Suomi 'hit parade' stop for its grand medieval seats, Swedish origin stories and showy harbour vistas. In this buzzy university city, you'll find plenty of action at live-music pubs, galleries and gratifying riverside restaurants. Not done exploring? Hop a ferry to the Åland islands from here.

FROM LEFT: RALAND/SHUTTERSTOCK ©, MIKKO LEMOLA/SHUTTERSTOCK ©, TRABANTOS/SHUTTERSTOCK ©

Ukko-Koli (p163), Koli National Park

ITINERARIES

Call of the Wild

Allow: 12 Days   **Distance:** 1420km

Finland's north is worthy of much time and affection. These upland beauties promise picture-perfect landscapes packed with sparkly waters, lush woodland and wildlife. Escape into nature or sample life in a tiny, forest-enclosed community. Tackle this route in a week – or better yet, two – to pack in more outdoor activities.

❶ KOLI NATIONAL PARK ⏱ 2 DAYS

Koli National Park (p165), Finland's most scenic turf, is a strong starter to getting wild in Suomi. Its 347m-high mountain inspired Finland's artistic National Romantic era. Do your own 'canvassing' of these rich primeval forests, whether hitting the hiking tracks (80km worth!), observing wildlife or strapping on a pair of snowshoes or skis.

❷ KUHMO ⏱ 2 DAYS

Head north to **Kuhmo** (p165), where brown-bear-watching is one of Finland's greatest wildlife experiences. Vast taiga forests, running from here across to Siberia, provide even more wildlife watching (wolves, lynx, wild reindeer, for example). Hike, swim and cycle to your heart's content.

⤴ *Detour: Discover Finland's 'capital of the north', Oulu (p190), where, depending on the season, the sun barely sets or rises. 3 hours.*

❸ OULANKA NATIONAL PARK ⏱ 2 DAYS

Cut even further north to **Oulanka National Park** (p197), where there's serious trekking to be done. The Karhunkierros (Bear's Ring) offers some of Finland's most breathtaking scenery. Part is manageable in a day, or you can also go canoeing or white-water rafting – and in winter, snowshoeing and cross-country skiing. At night, curl up in a wilderness hut.

ROVANIEMI ⏱ 2 DAYS

Head to **Rovaniemi** (p208), capital of Lapland, and a great base for outdoor activities. Get in direct communication with Arctic nature and become acquainted with northern climes: visit reindeer farms and husky kennels, forage berries and mushrooms in the forest, and search for wildlife such as elk. During winter, cross your fingers for clear skies to witness the aurora borealis (northern lights).

INARI ⏱ 2 DAYS

Inari (p224) is where unforgettable Arctic adventures take place. This tiny village in Lapland is a cultural capital for the Sámi. Prime yourself for guided nature tours, visits to reindeer farms and a cosy log-cabin stay. Get even more off the beaten track with a foray into the remote wilderness of Lemmenjoki and Urho Kekkonen national parks.

KILPISJÄRVI ⏱ 2 DAYS

Head up the 'arm' of Finland to remote **Kilpisjärvi** (p234). This is the highest village in the country. For a spectacular finale, take the boat to the remote border point where Finland meets both Norway and Sweden in the shadow of fearsome Norwegian mountains, then walk 11km back across electrifyingly beautiful Arctic wilderness.

Helsinki (p42)

ITINERARIES

Cities & Coasts

Allow: 7 Days   **Distance:** 661km

Finland's urban centres, though small, pack a big creative punch. Suomi cities are easy targets for cool-hunting, with thriving arts, music and design scenes. Seaside landscapes provide artisans with inspiration and also offer scenic performance venues. Let's face it, this itinerary may include pulling a late nighter or two.

❶ HELSINKI ⏱ 2 DAYS

Take a few days to sink your teeth into **Helsinki** (p42). Get your fix of Finland's distinctive brand of Nordic urban living through bold architecture, fascinating museums and the Design District's streets of boutiques. Get fired up on innovative, indulgent fine dining. Quirky (or just plain weird) bars, plus the Finnish tendency for really warming up after a few drinks, promise good times.

❷ HANKO ⏱ 1 DAY

Finland isn't just vast expanses of pristine wilderness. Small yet vibrant communities such as **Hanko** (p103) stock the country's southern areas, revealing a past forged by ironworks and foreign rule. Cherish this seaside escape with a stay in a former tsarist villa, a spa pampering and a dose of the port town's important wartime history. Catch a harbour sundowner before a pub evening.

❸ TURKU ⏱ 2 DAYS

Take in the social drinking scene in coastal **Turku** (p84) where locals lose that famous reserve after a *tuoppi* (half-litre glass) or two of beer. The city is full of original and offbeat bars boasting live music, boisterous karaoke and student life. At the market hall, a centuries-old fish-soup recipe cures any hangover, and will surely help for taking in Turku's wonderful arts and design circuit.

④
RAUMA ⏱ 1 DAY

Rauma (p174) deserves its UNESCO World Heritage status. Roam the streets and see where you can chat to neighbours across low-key cafes, shops, museums and artisans' workshops. Tune your ear into Rauman giäl, an old sailors' lingo that mixes up a host of languages still spoken here.

🗘 *Detour: Discover trendy Tampere (p138), where revived industrial buildings now house quirky museums, pubs and cafes. 2 hours.*

⑤
HÄMEENLINNA ⏱ ½ DAY

Turn away from the coast to **Hämeenlinna** (p161), Finland's oldest inland city. It's a wonderful place to recharge in quiet, picturesque surrounds. Don't miss the namesake castle. Hämeenlinna also makes an excellent pit stop between Helsinki and Tampere.

🗘 *Detour: Discover bustling student life and Aalto architecture in the 'Athens of Finland', Jyväskylä (p156). 2 hours.*

⑥
PORVOO ⏱ ½ DAY

Porvoo (p113) is an easy half-day's visit and a solid finish to your Finnish itinerary (it's less than 50km from Helsinki's airport). Stroll lovely cobbled lanes and riverside wooden warehouses lining the old town. Grab a last meal at one of its many up-and-coming gastronomic venues. Before you go, load up your luggage with chocolate boxes (the local speciality) and other handmade souvenirs.

WHEN TO GO

Gaze up at the aurora borealis (Northern Lights), or camp out in one of Scandinavia's sunniest spots. No matter the season, Finland delivers.

The Sámi have some 200 words for snow – hinting at the diversity of these climes. Inside the Arctic Circle, the Sámi's northern ancestral home sees extreme seasons, from 24-hour daylight to winter polar nights. Meanwhile, southern regions like Åland enjoy some of northern Europe's sunniest, mildest weather. Cities and villages, pristine parks and the lakes in between find their groove at different times of year.

Head north from March to April for the best shot at seeing the aurora borealis. From April, boat cruises and southern coastal festivals kick off. In October, ports get sleepy, but this is a fabulous quiet time at beaches and viewpoints.

Winters are prone to extreme conditions – in December, the Arctic sun never rises. Southern and central Finland are privy to downpours and six-hour windows of sunlight.

Saving on Accommodation

Prices don't vary much between seasons. During warmer months, campgrounds offer great budget stays, including caravans, cabins and often sauna facilities.

I LIVE HERE

SUMMER SOLSTICE

Helsinki-born artist Isabella Chydenius spent all her childhood summers in Hanko @isabellachydenius

Summer mornings start by deciding which beach to cycle to. Bellevue beach has shallow waters, with dunes for lounging by the warm sea and reading between ice-cream breaks. Although Hangö (Hanko) is famous for its beaches and villas, what's special to me are its large, round rocks and cliffs. They're warm to sit on in summer. Yet, they're still there, stable, holding me every time I return, offering the best seats to watch the sea.

Aurora borealis

BRIGHT DEAD OF NIGHT

The period of midnight sun – when the sun remains visible at midnight inside the Arctic Circle – runs from about mid-May to late July, bringing darkness down to five hours per night. In the far north, the sun doesn't set at all.

Weather through the Year in Helsinki

	JANUARY	FEBRUARY	MARCH	APRIL	MAY	JUNE

Avg. daytime max:	-2°C	-2°C	2°C	7°C	14°C	19°C
Days of rainfall:	10	7	7	7	6	7

AURORA BOREALIS QUESTS

In Lapland, October, November and March, between the hours of 9pm and 2am, are the best times to watch the aurora borealis dance. The region's ancient inhabitants believed the streaky skies were caused by a giant fox swishing its tail above the Arctic tundra.

Biggest Celebrations

Juhannus Midsommar (midsummer) is the most important annual celebration for Finns. The country shuts down as people head to cottages to celebrate the longest day of the year with bonfires and dancing. On the Åland islands, see villagers adorn maypoles in flowers (p102). 🌞 **June**

The **Savonlinna Opera Festival** (p141) is Finland's most famous festival. Month-long performances take place in the romantic covered courtyard of Olavinlinna Castle. 🌞 **July**

Join thousands of spectators at the **Ruisrock** (p87) rock festival on an island outside Turku. Line-ups are stacked with big acts. 🌞 **July**

In the weeks leading up to the Yuletide holidays, cobblestone town squares host traditional **Christmas markets** with wooden stands selling treats and decorations. Drink a *glögi* (hot punch). ❄ **December**

⭐ I LIVE HERE

WINTER PASTIME

Irene Kangasniemi designs jewellery and home decor from natural materials such as fish leather and reindeer antlers. She lives near Rovaniemi @kangasniemihornwork

Winters here are best when we have a lot of snow. The more snow, the better the berries are next summer. This time of year, I cook with my wood oven – it takes longer but tastes better. Moose meat with *rieska* (potato flatbread) is my favourite winter dish. Moose eat forest plants such as berries, grass, leaves...they are thankful for the winter, too.

Juhannus celebration

LUSH LAKE LIFE

The average Finn spends less than two days in a hotel each year, but several weeks in cottages. July is the busiest month on the coast and around lakes, as this is when Finns tend to enjoy their summer holidays.

Local Festivals & Celebrations

Head to Inari for the **'Royal Reindeer Race'** (p228), the grand finale of Finnish Lapland's reindeer-racing season over the frozen Inarijärvi. ❄ **March or April**

Traditionally a festival of students and workers, **Vappuaatto (May Day Eve)** followed by **Vappu (May Day)** mark the beginning of summer with plenty of sparkling wine and merrymaking by lakes and in parks. 🌱 **April to May**

In the southern port town of Naantali, **National Sleepyhead Day** is marked by villagers dousing each other with water and getting tossed out to sea. A lively carnival atmosphere includes dancing, live music, a bake-off and more. 🌞 **July**

The three-day **Skábmagovat** (p228) indigenous peoples' film festival holds screenings at an open-air snow theatre. It takes place in Lapland, in the Sámi capital of Inari. ❄ **January**

JULY	AUGUST	SEPTEMBER	OCTOBER	NOVEMBER	DECEMBER
☀	☀	☀	⛅	☁	❄
Avg. daytime max: 21°C	Avg. daytime max: 20°C	Avg. daytime max: 15°C	Avg. daytime max: 9°C	Avg. daytime max: 4°C	Avg. daytime max: 1°C
Days of rainfall: 7	Days of rainfall: 10	Days of rainfall: 9	Days of rainfall: 9	Days of rainfall: 11	Days of rainfall: 11

GET PREPARED FOR FINLAND

Useful things to load in your bag, your ears and your brain

Clothes

Casual attire Finns are masters of practicality. In the heart of Helsinki, fashion is sleek yet functional and minimalistic, with a penchant for textiles that are sustainable and long lasting. There's no need to pack lots of fancy clothes, especially when planning to spend time alfresco.

Comfy clothes Blend right in during warmer months with outfits that translate well from urban patio to *mökki* (summer cottage) such as comfy sandals and a light jacket. Sturdy walking shoes are a must.

Layers Pack for seasonal extremes. For northern climes, make sure you have items in which to bundle up, such as thermals, wool socks and other knitwear, windproof items and a puffy parka.

Manners

Finnish culture is rather polite and reserved. Finns believe in comfortable silences. There's no need to resuscitate conversations with small talk.

But, Finns love to have fun. It's not that Finns don't talk. Once they get a couple of pints in, that reserve tends to go out the window.

And they're known for quirky and dark humour. Self-deprecating jokes and well-timed jibes will be deeply appreciated.

Swimwear Don't forget your trunks and goggles. In saunas, swimwear is optional – bring flip-flops for showering.

📖 READ

Sisu: The Finnish Art of Courage (Joanna Nylund; 2018) Everything you need to know about the nation's defining, untranslatable trait and the desire for resilience.

Tales from Moominvalley (Tove Jansson; 1962) As a collection of short stories, this is one of the most beloved Moomin books in Finland and beyond.

A Frozen Hell: The Russo-Finnish Winter War of 1939–1940 (William R Trotter; 2013) Gripping historical account of Finland's fight to stay independent.

Kalevala (Elias Lönnrot; 1835) Finland's national epic, compiled from bard songs. It tells everything from the world's origins to how to home brew.

Words

'hei' (hay) is how you say 'hello' in Finnish.
'näkemiin' (na·ke·meen) means 'goodbye'.
'hyvää päivää' (hy·vah pai·vah) means 'good day'.
'hauska tavata' (hau·ska ta·va·ta) means 'nice to meet you'.
'kiitos (paljon)' (kee·tos (puhl·yon)) is 'thank you (very much)'.
Order in a restaurant by saying **'saisinko...'** (sai·sin·ko): 'I would like...'.
'pullon (olutta)' (pul·lon (o·lut·tuh)) is a bottle (of beer).
'(kupin) kahvia' ((ku·pin) kuh·vi·uh) is a cup of coffee.
'(kupin) teetä' ((ku·pin) tay·ta) is a cup of tea.
'kippis!' (kip·pis) means 'cheers!' In saunas, **'kauha'** (kau·ha) is the ladle, and the steam is called **'löyly'** (löy·ly).
'kalsarikännit' (kal·saree·kahn·it) is drinking at home with no pants or getting 'pantsdrunk'.

'sisu' (si·su) is a Finnish trait often translated as 'guts', or the resilience to survive prolonged hardship.
'kaamos' (kaa·mos) is a 'polar night'.
'tuliainen' (tu·li·ai·nen) is a gift you bring to someone's home, or a kitschy souvenir.
'bures' (pu·res; u is a long vowel) is how you say 'how are you, hello' when shaking hands in Northern Sámi.
And **'oaidnaleapmái'** (oa·y·dna-leap-may) means 'see you'.
'giitu' (ki·y·htu) is how you say 'thank you'.
'boazu' (po·a·tsu) is 'reindeer' in Northern Sámi; it's **'poro'** (po·ro) in Finnish.
'guovssahasat' (ku·ovs·sa·ha·saht) is 'Northern Lights' in Northern Sámi; it's **'revontulet'** (re·von·tu·let) in Finnish.
'Santa Claus' is **'Juovlastállu'** (juo·v·la·stal·lu) in Northern Sámi and **'Joulupukki'** (yo·loo·pu·ki) in Finnish.

▶ WATCH

The Unknown Soldier (Aku Louhimies; 2017) The third adaptation of Finland's most revered fictional novel about the Winter War.

Fallen Leaves (pictured; Aki Kaurismäki; 2023) Internationally acclaimed romantic tragicomedy of two lonely souls trying to build a relationship in Helsinki.

Bordertown (Miikko Oikkonen; 2016) 'Nordic noir' crime-drama series about a detective and his town by the Russian border.

Road North (Mika Kaurismäki; 2012) Comedy about an estranged father-and-son duo reuniting for a road trip across northern Finland.

🎧 LISTEN

Mastering Finland (2019) For expats in Finland by expats in Finland – a podcast exploring what it's like to live and work here.

Very Finnish Problems (Joel Willans; 2017) Podcast (plus book and popular Instagram account of the same name) delving into Finland's cultural quirks.

Mún (Wimmi; 2009) Kelottijärvi-born artist Wimme Saari explores the Sámi *'joik'* vocal tradition with hypnotic ambient beats.

Sibelius: Finlandia (Thomas Søndergard; 2018) Modern orchestra performance of the Jean Sibelius tone poem that has shaped national identity.

Bowl of *kesäkeitto*

THE FOOD SCENE

Finland's landscape is dominated by lakes and forests, which also influences the country's cuisine; prepare your palate for earthy flavours.

In recent years, Finnish chefs have turned to respecting and reinventing Finland's traditional gastronomy. And not just the Michelin-starred Helsinki establishments: you will find country house manors, restaurants and hotels all over the country offering the best of local produce – often in a picture-perfect setting, too.

Whether you are ordering seafood, meat or vegetarian dishes, it's all about simplicity and seasons here. Think locally fished perch, summery strawberries and autumnal mushrooms from the nearby forests, rich meats of moose or reindeer, with a hint of spruce tree and smoke lingering in the background, and you'll get the gist of Finnish cuisine.

Market halls in cities such as Helsinki, Tampere, Turku and Kuopio still offer a glimpse of the traditional Finnish dishes, from vendace (freshwater fish) in various forms to cinnamon buns or Karelian pies served with simple filter coffee. Still, nowadays there are also stalls serving gourmet versions of the old Finnish classics and other ethnic flavours from around the globe.

Finnish Food Traditions

Finnish home cooking has traditionally been a simple affair, varying from hearty meat stews and hefty casseroles in the winter to lightly fried pikeperch and delicate new potatoes in the summer. Many homeowners also grow berries and apples, and dedicate time in the autumn to make jams and juices for the winter months. Some also go hunting, with restricted licences for hunting moose and bear yearly, and the fines for poaching are hefty. People actively

Best Finnish Dishes

KARJALANPAISTI	LOHIKEITTO	KESÄKEITTO	PORONKÄRISTYS
Meat cubes stewed overnight with vegetables. Served with potatoes.	Salmon soup with a clear/creamy broth, served with dill.	Summer soup with seasonal vegetables, such as peas and cauliflower.	Sautéed reindeer served with potatoes and lingonberries or pickled cucumber.

forage too, and fill their freezers with frozen vitamin bombs, such as bilberries and sea buckthorn berries.

In fact, foraging isn't just a trend in Finland, but a skill often passed from one generation to the next. Visitors can also easily participate in this activity, as foraging courses are organised all over Finland. Another skill typically passed through the generations is bread making, with some families holding dear a heritage starter dough to make rye or white bread.

Ethical Eating

Helsinki is a haven for responsible eating, as the city offers plenty of choices for vegetarians and vegans – other bigger cities, such as Turku and Tampere, follow close behind. In more remote towns forward-thinking vegetarian and vegan establishments are popping up, but tasty veggie dishes might still turn out to be a rarity.

In rural areas, such as Saimaa Lakeland and Lapland, instead of vegan joints, you are likely to find restaurants taking pride in offering locally sourced organic food, varying from fish and meat to vegetables and berries, served in quaint settings.

Another way of tackling ethical eating is concentrating on food waste. Restaurants such as Nolla (meaning zero), with its zero-waste ethos, lead the way in Helsinki. You can also download the ResQ app and pick up a leftover restaurant meal at a reduced price. The app covers all of Finland, from Helsinki to Lapland's Ivalo, and the participating establishments vary from traditional bakeries to ethnic and fine-dining restaurants.

LOCAL FOOD FESTIVALS

Finland's summery market squares are a culinary delight where the fresh flavours of foraged mushrooms and berries and harvested strawberries mix with the treasures of the waters.

One of Finland's oldest public events is Helsinki Market Square's **Herring Market** (pictured; silakkamarkkinat.fi) held in early October and delighting locals and visitors since 1743. The event combines traditional atmosphere with modern foodie finds into a joyful ode to one small fish, the herring.

Another quintessentially Finnish food fair is the **Hillamarkkinat** (cloudberry market; hillamarkkinat.fi) in Ranua, Lapland's unofficial cloudberry capital. Held in August, this festival honours the 'gold of Lapland' in various forms.

In September, head to Åland's **autumn harvest celebrations** (skordefest.ax) to sample fresh produce directly from farmers or savour seasonal dishes offered by local restaurants.

Cloudberries

PAISTETUT MUIKUT
Small fish rolled in rye flour and fried in butter.

GRAAVILOHI
Thinly sliced cured salmon; can be served with rye bread.

LIHAPULLAT
Finnish meatballs served with mashed potatoes, brown sauce and lingonberries.

PANNUKAKKU
Thick pancake baked in the oven, served with jam and cream.

Specialities

Snacks

Lihapiirakka, lörtsy Deep-fried doughnut-like pie filled with minced meat and rice.
Omenalörtsy Same as above but with sweet apple jam filling.
Ruisleipä Rye bread.
Ahvenanmaan mustaleipä Sweetened and malty black bread from the Åland Islands.
Ohrapuuro Pearl barley porridge stewed overnight.
Kalakukko Traditionally vendace or European char and pork baked in a rye crust.
Karelian pasty Thin rye crust filled with rice porridge.
Munavoi Boiled eggs mixed with butter, served with Karelian pies.
Rönttönen Karelian pie made with rye or barley flour and filled with sweetened potato and berries.
Kaalikääryle Cooked cabbage leaves filled with minced meat and rice.
Viili Fermented milk, similar to yoghurt but sour, can be served with jam or sugar and cinnamon.

Favourite Sweet Treats

Leipäjuusto Squeaky baked cheese served hot/cold with cloudberry jam.

Korvapuusti

Mustikkakkukko Blueberry pie baked in rye crust.
Korvapuusti Cinnamon bun.
Vatrushka A bun-like Karelian pasty filled with quark and possibly raisins.
Lakkakakku Spongecake with cloudberries and cream, sometimes with a caramel topping.

Dare to Try

Mustamakkara Blood sausage served with lingonberry jam.
Salmiakki Salty and strong-flavoured liquorice.
Salmiakkisnapsi A vodka schnapps made of liquorice.
Mämmi Easter-time dessert made of rye flour and powdered malted rye, served with sugar and cream.

MEALS OF A LIFETIME

Laanilan Kievari (p230) Imaginative preparations of Lapland reindeer, elk and lake fish, plus veggie options, in a wooden cottage near Saariselkä.

Finnjävel Salonki and Sali (p72) Michelin-starred restaurant in Helsinki; Finnish traditional cuisine with a modern take.

Kalaliike S Wallin (p87) Sit on a bar stool in Turku Market Hall and order from Finland's second-oldest fish shop (1896).

Uhkua (p167) Showcases the best of Saimaa Lakeland hospitality in a charmingly rustic setting.

Kolin Ryynänen (p164) Experience a warm-hearted Karelian ambiance and *mustikkakukko* dessert in the gastro-pub near Koli National Park.

Sydvest (p177) Local and global ingredients combine with happy results in this tasteful, bistro-style restaurant in old Rauma.

THE YEAR IN FOOD

SPRING

Spring kicks off in Finland with a 1 May (or Vappu) party, when you will see people picnicking and sipping on *sima*, a termented lemony soda, and feasting on freshly baked doughnuts.

SUMMER

Finnish summer truly starts when strawberries appear in the markets in June. Also try freshly caught pikeperch with the summer season's delicately sweet new potatoes, served with butter and dill.

AUTUMN

Autumn marks the end of the foraging season, with people heading to forests to pick up the last of the chanterelles and berries, such as sea buckthorn, lingonberry and juniper berry.

WINTER

In December, visit Finnish Christmas Markets and sample the season's delicacies, such as *glögi*, the Finnish version of mulled wine, served with raisins and almonds and, if you like, a dash of vodka.

Plate of vendace

HOW TO... Eat Fried Vendace

Vendace (*Coregonus albula*), or *muikku*, is a prized catch for Finnish fishermen and cherished by Finns for generations. Found in nearly all large Finnish lakes and sea bays, this little fish and its roe are Finnish favourites. *Muikku* can be served salted, baked in a rye crust, in a pie or even as a pizza-topping, but enjoying them fried fresh off the pan is the most popular way.

Our Favourite Spots for Fried Vendace

The best vendace are fried and sold at summery market squares, such as Helsinki and Tampere Market Squares. In Helsinki Market Square, there are several stalls offering vendace in various forms. Choose your favourite, sit down and enjoy – just don't let the seagulls snatch your lunch.

You can also find stalls selling this delicacy in winter during events.

Muikku Ravintola Sampo in Kuopio has served vendace in different forms for over 90 years.

If bought from a supermarket, opt for the ones sold at the fish counter.

For a sustainable choice, make sure you buy vendace caught from Finnish lakes; exercise caution when it is bottom trawled from the Bothnian Bay.

Heads On or Off?

Some people eat vendace with the heads on, others off. You can choose your own preference. If you buy vendace from a shop they are normally gutted, or you can even get them as fillets.

Make at Home

To fry your vendace, mix rye flour (*ruisjauho*), breadcrumbs (*korppujauho*) and salt. Coat the fish in the mixture. Melt butter in a pan and fry the fish for about two minutes on each side. Serve with mashed potatoes. Another easy way to make a delicious vendace dish is to bake them in the oven. First, mix the rye flour, breadcrumbs and salt. Second, roll the gutted fish in melted butter and then coat it with the flour mixture. Bake for 12 minutes at 200°C on a baking sheet. Serve with lemon slices and the accompaniments of your choice.

What's the Best Way to Serve Vendace?

If any side dishes are offered with fried vendace, the most common one is mashed potatoes (*perunamuussi*).

Another traditional way to serve vendace is in *muikkukukko*, where it is baked inside a rye crust.

Vendace roe is delicious with blinis. As roe is collected in autumn, most vendace sold during this season is gutted and cleaned.

You can also sample some tasty smoked vendace.

Vendace is always served with a smile – in Finland, people say *muikku* instead of cheese when grinning for the camera. You'll often find this dish enjoyed at festive gatherings, adding to its joyful association.

Nuuksio National Park (p53)

THE OUTDOORS

Stretching for 1157km from south to north, Finland's landscape varies from the relatively flat lakesides of the south to the fells and waterfalls of north.

With three-quarters of Finland covered with forests, and the rest of the land holding some 188,000 lakes, almost the whole country is an outdoorsy backyard awaiting exploration, whether that be by foot, skis, bike or paddle. It can be as simple as popping to Nuuksio National Park from Helsinki for a day hike, or packing a tent for a multiday hike, with Everyone's Rights giving you the freedom to roam, forage and enjoy the land for free.

Hiking

Finland's old-growth, coniferous forests, clean air and network of lakes and rivers make a beautiful setting for hikes. In fact, walking in nature is part of the Finnish identity, and may even contribute to people's happiness levels, with Finland consistently ranking among the happiest nations on Earth. The best time for hiking is from May to October, although during summer months, mosquito repellant is a must. The spectacular show of autumn foliage begins in Lapland in early September and reaches southern Finland by the beginning of October. Finland's 41 national parks cover over a million hectares of land, and there is a national park or two near all major cities. Arctic wilderness with vast boglands and bare fells can be experienced in any part of Lapland, whereas further

Wildlife-watching

BEAR-WATCHING IN WILDERNESS
Stay overnight in one of the huts or cottages in the wilderness surrounding **Kuhmo** (p165) in eastern Finland.

BIRDWATCHING ON AN ISLAND
Kylmäpihjala (p180) island in Rauma's archipelago is home to 28 nesting bird species.

SEAL-SPOTTING
Look for endangered Saimaa ringed seals on an eco-boat trip around the **Saimaa archipelago** (p144).

FAMILY ADVENTURES

Hire a kayak or SUP from **Cafe Regatta** (p69) and explore Helsinki's seaside – in winter, take a hike on the ice and then enjoy hot chocolates and cinnamon buns after.

Head to a lighthouse on Oulu's popular summer spot, **Hailuoto island** (p196).

Stroll around Moomin central at **Muumimaailma** (p91). Moomins sleep in the wintertime, but the area is still accessible.

Say hello to Santa, and then ride a reindeer sled at the **Santa Claus Village** (p211).

Ranua Wildlife Park (p218) homes Arctic animals varying from brown bears and lynxes to Arctic foxes.

Chill out on 6km-long **Yyteri beach** (p178), with a host of activities for children, from horse riding to a water trampoline and climbing park.

---

south you will find serene lakes lined with enchanting pine, spruce and birch forests. An extensive network of wilderness huts makes multiday hikes easier. In summer, you can also enjoy a forest setting by spending a night in a tent.

Snow Activities

There's something mesmerising about a white, snow-covered landscape, which lasts approximately from late November to April in southern parts of Finland and October to May in Lapland. For adventurous skiers, Lapland's slopes, such as Ounasvaara near Rovaniemi, offer the rush of adrenalin, while cross-country tracks wind around rural and urban landscapes all over Finland. Many hotels and rental spots also offer snowshoes to tackle the terrain at a slower pace. Or you could have a once-in-a-lifetime experience, hopping onto a sled pulled by reindeer or huskies and racing through Lapland's Christmas-card scenery. Further south, Koli National Park's peaks offer Lapland-like winter activities as well as scenery with its snow-laden tree branches.

BEST SPOTS
For the best outdoor spots and routes, see the map on p38.

Water Sports

Finland's lakes, rivers and rapids offer multiple ways to explore the country from the water level, whether you're a beginner or a heavyweight paddler. Kayak, canoe and SUP rentals are easy to find across the country, from Helsinki's city centre to Lapland's wilderness. Or, if you want to take it easy, hop aboard a slow boat in Savonlinna to navigate the lakes and canals of the Finnish Lakeland. The lakes freeze over in winter (approximately December to April) and offer other unique activities to try: ice-hole fishing for the patient visitor and, for the more daring, ice-hole swimming, which can be experienced in all major cities as well as some hotels and cottage rentals across the country.

Husky-drawn sled

WILDLIFE PHOTOGRAPHY
In Rovaniemi, **Lapland Welcome** (p219) provides nature trips, including one focused on moose-spotting.

REINDEER FARMS
Visit a Sámi reindeer farm in **Inari** (p216), close to the northern tip of Lapland.

BEAR-WATCHING NEAR A SKI RESORT
Finland's most popular ski resort, **Ruka** (p199), also offers bear-spotting trips.

CLIFFSIDE BIRDWATCHING
Birdwatchers head to Olhavanvuori in **Repovesi National Park** (p150), where flocks of red-throated loons live by an imposing cliff.

ACTION AREAS

Where to find Finland's best outdoor activities.

Northern Light Hunting
1. Saariselkä (p229)
2. Rovaniemi (p208)
3. Inari (p224)
4. Ruka (p197)

National Parks
1. Urho Kekkonen National Park (p229)
2. Oulanka National Park (p197)
3. Hossa National Park (p200)
4. Bothnian Sea National Park (p214)
5. Nuuksio National Park (p53)

Snow Activities
1. Ruka skiing (p197)
2. Kemi sleigh rides (p217)
3. Ounasvaara cross-country skiing (p211)
4. Snowshoe safaris in Kuhmo (p166)
5. Ice-hole swimming in Helsinki (p59)

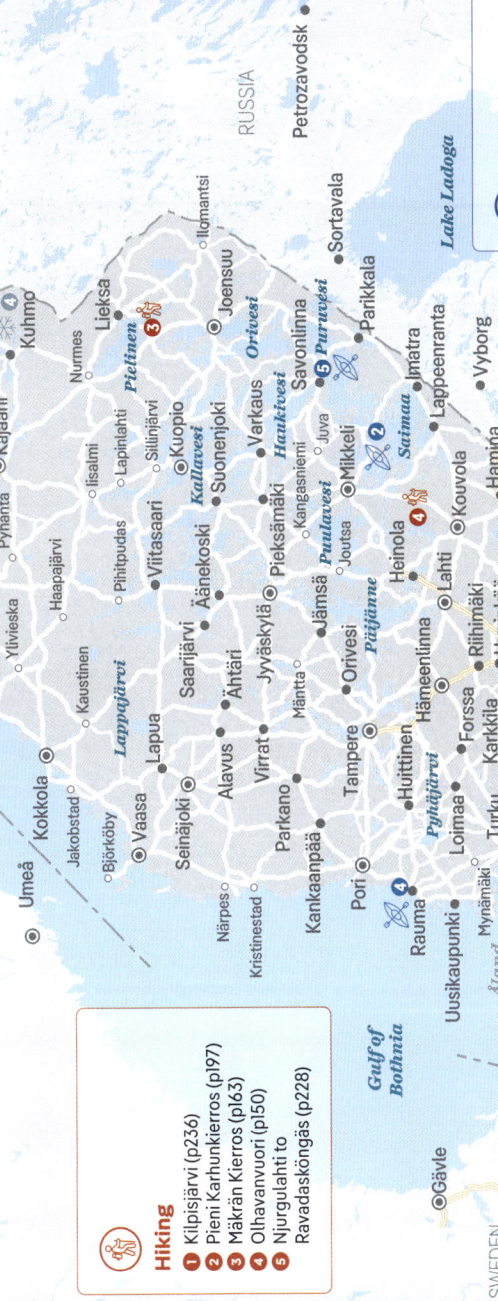

FINLAND
THE GUIDE

Chapters in this section are organised by hubs and their surrounding areas. We see the hub as your base in the destination, where you'll find unique experiences, local insights, insider tips and expert recommendations. It's also your gateway to the surrounding area, where you'll see what and how much you can do from there.

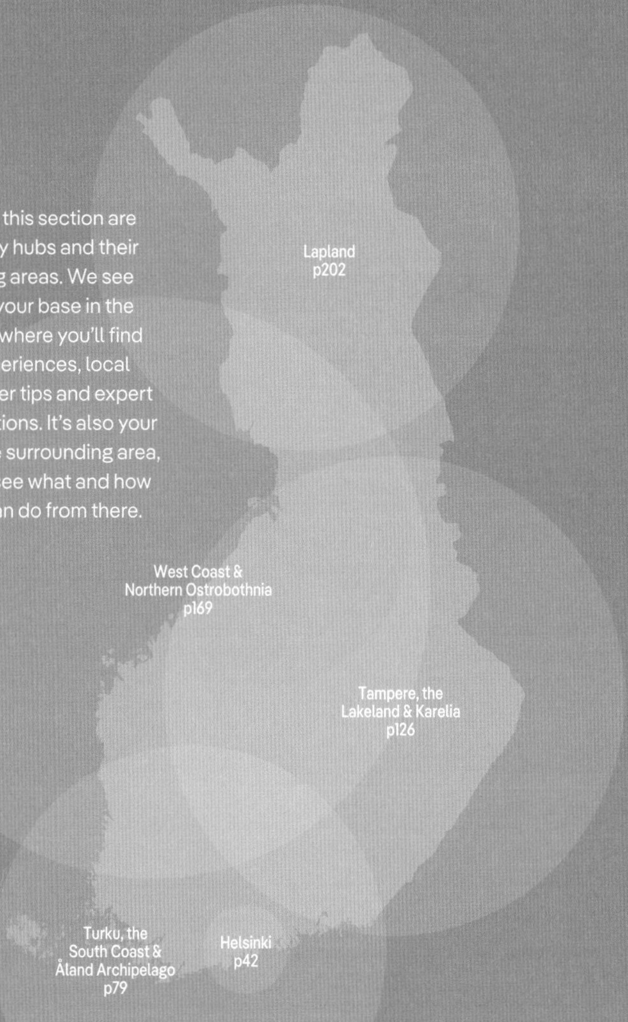

Lapland
p202

West Coast &
Northern Ostrobothnia
p169

Tampere, the
Lakeland & Karelia
p126

Turku, the
South Coast &
Åland Archipelago
p79

Helsinki
p42

Lapland (p202)
BLUEORANGE STUDIO/SHUTTERSTOCK ©

Helsinki

NORTHERN COOLNESS WITH A NEIGHBOURLY TWIST

The seaside capital is coolly becoming a northern hotspot for food and design, while also attracting visitors with its nature-driven lifestyle.

When the Prussian architect Carl Ludwig Engel set foot in Helsinki in 1816, the city held a mere 4000 inhabitants. Seven years earlier, Finland had been annexed to Russia after more than 600 years of Swedish rule, and Alexander I of Russia was keen to transfer Finland's capital from Turku to a place closer to home. He chose Helsinki, appointing Engel to upgrade its buildings. When the architect arrived, he didn't like what he saw, but he was on a mission: to create a worthy capital for the new Grand Duchy of Finland.

In the end, Engel reluctantly stayed in Helsinki for the rest of his life and completed about 30 buildings in the city. Some 50 years later, Helsinki's population had grown to 70,000 inhabitants, and the city began to fill with other types of buildings, such as the Helsinki Central railway station, designed by Eliel Saarinen, and the Stockmann department store, the largest such store in the Nordic countries, designed by Sigurd Frosterus. The city also saw the emergence of the Jugendstil, or art nouveau style, between Engel's neoclassical architecture and these early 20th-century creations.

But all this grand architecture is just a backdrop to everyday life in the seaside city, which is bordered by more than 130km of coastline. With seaside promenades, cycle lanes, cafes and beaches, the coast is very much a part of Helsinki's lifestyle, as well as the 300 islands scattered nearby, providing natural escapes from the city. Elsewhere, Helsinki's many parks, from the posh Esplanadi to small patches of greenery in every neighbourhood, provide calm respite.

During the last few decades, Helsinki's city scene has also changed drastically, and not just because of all the new architecture, from the award-winning Oodi library to the subterranean eye-catcher Amos Rex, but also in the city's atmosphere. There is now more diversity, bursts of joyous festivals, fine-dining restaurants respecting Finnish roots and bustling cafes. Maybe, if Engel could set foot in the Helsinki of today, he too would be happy here.

THE MAIN AREAS

CITY CENTRE, KRUUNUNHAKA & KATAJANOKKA
Art nouveau and artsy. **p48**

EIRA, ULLANLINNA & KAIVOPUISTO
Prestigious seaside setting. **p55**

PUNAVUORI, KAMPPI & HIETALAHTI
Bohemian vibes and boutique finds. **p61**

TÖÖLÖ, KALLIO & KAISANIEMI
Beaches, bays and bohemian charm. **p69**

For places to stay in Helsinki, see p76

THE GUIDE

HELSINKI

Left: Helsinki cityscape; Above: Helsinki Cathedral (p48)

Find Your Way

Helsinki has only about 500,000 residents, but geographically the city is quite vast to tackle on foot. Luckily, the public transport network, including bus, tram and the underground, is extensive and prompt. To help your exploration, we've highlighted the main areas and landmarks in this seaside city of parks and wide boulevards.

FROM THE AIRPORT

From the underground station at the airport, it's a half-hour ride to the centre of Helsinki. It takes about the same time by car. Allow a little more than 40 minutes for shuttle bus 600 to reach the city.

WALK

The best way to explore is on foot, as the city is almost completely flat. If you are up for urban hikes, wear comfortable shoes and tackle your city-centre sightseeing on foot, as there is plenty to see along the way.

Töölö, Kallio & Kaisaniemi p69

THE GUIDE — HELSINKI

Punavuori, Kamppi & Hietalahti p61

City Centre, Kruununhaka & Katajanokka p48

Eira, Ullanlinna & Kaivopuisto p55

0 – 1 km
0 – 0.5 miles

TRAM
Trams are a good option to ease the strain on your feet. Line numbers 2, 3, 6 and 7 whisk by many main sights – line 2 is particularly useful, passing the Old Market Hall and Market Square, Senate Square, Amos Rex art museum and Kamppi.

METRO
Helsinki's retro-style orange metros take passengers from one side of the city to the other in a matter of minutes. If you wish to explore areas outside the city centre, local trains leave from Helsinki Central station.

Map labels: KATAJANOKKA, Eteläsatama, Katajanokanluoto, Valkosaari, Tässä (Klippan), Pihlajasaari, Ruoholasaari, Puolimatkansaari, Kruunuvuorenselkä, Suomenlinna, Gulf of Finland, Harakka, Pohjoinen Uunisaari, Liuskasaari, Sirpalesaari, EIRA, ULLANLINNA, KAIVOPUISTO, Kaivopuisto, Tähtitorninvuoren puisto, Design Museum, PUNAVUORI, KAMPPI, KLUUVI, HIETALAHTI, JÄTKÄSAARI, MUNKKISAARI, RUOHOLAHTI, Atlas Sea Pool

Plan Your Days

Kick off the days with coffee before venturing out to explore Helsinki's sights, which range from flashy art museums to cosy cafes and seaside saunas.

Ateneum Art Museum (p51)

Day 1

Morning
● Start in Old Market Hall's **Story** (p51) restaurant before taking in Senate Square, anchored by **Helsinki Cathedral** (p48). Work up an appetite with a spree of shopping in the boutiques of **Torikorttelit** (p50) and stroll through **Esplanadi Park** (p50), where **Kappeli** (p50) is a flashy spot for lunch.

Afternoon
● Jump on a ferry to **Suomenlinna sea fortress** (p52) and explore the island's museums and fortifications. Have a cinnamon bun in **Cafe Silo** (p52) before heading back to the city.

Evening
● Round out the day in Punavuori's **Nolla** (p67), a zero-waste restaurant, followed by cocktails in **Bar Mate** (p68).

You'll Also Want to...
Embrace small neighbourhood finds, pop beyond Helsinki's edges, witness the Finns going crazy at a hockey game, and enjoy a cinematic experience in Kallio.

WATCH THE ICE HOCKEY
Starting in September and ending in March, the SM league (Finnish Elite League) provides thrills and chills in Helsingin Jäähalli. Helsinki's own teams are called HIFK, the league's most succesful team, and Jokerit.

LEARN SOMETHING NEW
Located in Helsinki's neighbouring city, Vantaa, Heureka science centre's immersive take on science and inventions is fun for the whole family. An exhibition on space educates through tasks set on a space station.

GO TO A CINEMA
Helsinki's most hedonistic cinema, Riviera, comes with a bar, restaurant and velvet seats – there's one in Kallio and another in Punavuori. Book dinner and have a movie date night Helsinki-style.

Day 2

Morning
- Head to popular breakfast spot, **Way Bakery** (p71). Then, take a ride on the wooden roller coaster at **Linnanmäki** (p74) amusement park before catching tram 3 or 9 to the **Ateneum Art Museum** (p51) and Museum of Contemporary Art **Kiasma** (p51). Have a late lunch at **Finnjävel Salonki and Sali** (p72).

Afternoon
- Take in more art by visiting **Taidehalli** (p74), located in the same building as Finnjävel and focusing on contemporary Finnish art, design and architecture. Then, quieten down in **Temppeliaukion Kirkko** (p73).

Evening
- Head back to Kallio to take the heat in **Kotiharjun Sauna** (p75), and then stop for dinner at nearby **Konepaja** (p74), with rooftop bar **Loi Loi** (p74).

Day 3

Morning
- Kick off the day with coffee and a croissant in Helsinki's oldest cafe, **Ekberg** (p66), before descending to the **Amos Rex** (p61) museum. Continue to **Oodi** (p54) library, then take a tram to lunch in **Hietalahden Kauppahalli** (p65).

Afternoon
- Stroll around **Punavuori** (p63), popping into its design boutiques and art galleries, and the vintage shops in **Iso Roobertinkatu** (p63). In the neighbouring Ullanlinna district, climb to **Observatory Hill Park** (p58) to take in the views towards Market Square and Helsinki Cathedral's turquoise dome.

Evening
- Join the locals for dinner in the **city centre** (p51), then sneak in for speakeasy-style cocktails at **Trillby & Chadwick** (p50).

COUNT SHEEP
Visit the Lammassaari (sheep island) nature reserve, with its duckboards making the island accessible to wheelchairs. In spring and autumn, thousands of migrating birds have a rest here. And how many sheep are here? None.

SEE STREET ART
The city centre's best street art is along Baana, a pedestrian and bicycle corridor running from the Museum of Contemporary Art Kiasma to Ruoholahti. The most famed work is by OsGemeos and the Helsinki-based EGS.

FOODIE CENTRAL
Clustered around the city's old slaughterhouse, Teurastamo in Kalasatama has eateries ranging from bakeries to smokeries and taquerias, as well as a distillery with a taproom. Jädelino's ice creams are a perfect desert.

VISIT AN ISLAND ZOO
Korkeasaaren eläintarha (Korkeasaari Zoo) is located on its own island, reached by a daily ferry from Kauppatori (Market Square) between June and August; otherwise, metro (1, 2) or bus (16) can get you close by.

City Centre, Kruununhaka & Katajanokka

ART NOUVEAU AND ARTSY

GETTING AROUND

Helsinki Central Railway Station is located in the city centre and has a metro stop, with tram lines 3, 5, 6, 7 and 9 stopping in front. Several buses depart from both sides of the station, and taxis wait near the side entrance.

City Centre, Kruununhaka and Katajanokka are all well served by public transportation, with trams and the metro being the most convenient options. In summer, you will also find city bikes and e-scooters on many street corners.

The area is easily explored on foot too.

☑ TOP TIP

Katajanokka is an island connected to the mainland by bridges, and includes some of Helsinki's major sights. But venture beyond, and you will find art nouveau quarters. Finish your walk on the island's northern harbour, with restaurants and cafes and a quay for icebreakers.

Looking at the magnificent buildings of Kruununhaka, it's hard to believe that the area was no more than a modest harbour and pastureland for the Crown's horses when the Swedish count Per Brahe the Younger decided to transfer Helsinki here from its original spot some 6km away in 1640. Now, Kruununhaka and its neighbours, the city centre (consisting of Kluuvi and Kaartinkaupunki) and Katajanokka, contain many of Helsinki's main sights and are easily explored on foot, with many cafes and restaurants along the way.

Most of the tourist activities here focus on Senate Square and its centrepiece, Helsinki Cathedral. Another hub is nearby Esplanadi park, lined with stylish cafes and restaurants as well as high-end shops, such as Marimekko's flagship store. The park leads towards the Market Square and the Old Market Hall and then to Katajanokka, with its residential buildings representing some world-class examples of art nouveau architecture.

Tsar's Tribute

Spot grand architecture

Looming above the pastel-coloured buildings of Helsinki's shoreline, **Helsinki Cathedral**, or Tuomiokirkko (*helsingin tuomiokirkko.fi; adult/child €8/free*), dominates the city's skyline. The cathedral was built from 1830 to 1852 in honour of Tsar Nicholas I of Russia, the Grand Duke of Finland. On the cathedral's roof, 12 statues of the Apostles keep an eye on people photographing the building. The cathedral was designed by CL Engel, but the statues were a later addition – after Engel's death, it was noticed that the church's proportions were not in perfect symmetry. Outside summer months (early June to end of August) the cathedral is free to visit, but in summer an entrance fee is collected from those over 19.

HELSINKI CITY CENTRE, KRUUNUNHAKA & KATAJANOKKA

HIGHLIGHTS
1. Allas Sea Pool
2. Ateneum
3. Helsinki Cathedral
4. Kiasma
5. Suomenlinna
6. Vanha Kauppahalli

SIGHTS
7. Esplanadi Park
8. Helsinki City Museum
9. Kauppatori
10. Rautatientori

ACTIVITIES, COURSES & TOURS
11. Helsinki University Library Kaisa
12. Kansalliskirjasto
13. Oodi

SLEEPING
14. Eurohostel
15. Grand Hansa
16. Hobo Hotel Helsinki
17. Hostel Suomenlinna
18. Hotel Fabian
19. Hotel Finn
20. Hotel Haven
21. Hotel Kämp
22. Hotel Katajanokka
23. Hotel Ul4
24. Katajanokka II
25. Pier 4
26. Radisson RED
27. Scandic Grand Central
28. Villa Silo

EATING
29. Café Aalto
30. Cafe Eliel
31. Café Engel
32. Cafe Silo
33. El Fant
• Erikssonin osteribaari (see 6)
34. Kolme Kruunua
35. Magu
36. Palace
• Story (see 6)
37. Strindberg

DRINKING & NIGHTLIFE
38. Kappeli
39. Trillby & Chadwick

SHOPPING
40. Torikorttelit

TRANSPORT
41. Helsinki Central Railway Station

ATENEUM'S ART EVENTS

Keep an eye on Ateneum's upcoming exhibitions, which tend to be an event in the Finnish art scene.

For example, in 2025 and 2026, Ateneum will host an exhibition celebrating women artists from the Nordics, Baltics and beyond, highlighting their struggles and triumphs in overcoming societal barriers to study art in 19th-century Germany.

Many of these trailblazing artists became role models for later women in art, such as Helene Schjerfbeck – many of her works fetch hundreds of thousands of euros in today's auction rooms.

Another highly anticipated exhibition will explore the connections between one of Finland's most prolific artists, Akseli Gallen-Kallela, and Vienna-born-and-bred Gustav Klimt. The exhibit brings not only paintings but also fashion and design to the forefront.

Esplanadi Park

Classy Cocktails

Slip into a speakeasy

Sneak down the cobblestoned Katariinankatu from Helsinki Cathedral, knock on a door between blackened windows and step inside **Trillby & Chadwick** (*sonofapunch.com*), a speakeasy with a 19th-century detective-fiction theme. The dimly lit interior features comfy sofas and armchairs, frilly lampshades and super-retro phones. The menu offers an intriguing backstory for each skilfully prepared cocktail.

Settle into the speakeasy after touring the surrounding alleys of **Torikorttelit** (*torikorttelit.fi*), which feature a cluster of small museums, souvenir shops, design and craft boutiques from sauna linen to jewellery, and cafes and restaurants.

Leafy Core of Finnishness

Stroll in a park

The leafy **Esplanadi Park**, lined with cafes and shops, is a breath of Central European sophistication in the middle of Helsinki. In fact, this is where Finland's cultural elite – writers, painters and composers – have gathered since the Finnish language and cultural identity, in opposition to Swedish and Russian ones, were being promoted in the late 19th and early 20th centuries. These figures, from composer Jean Sibelius to painter Akseli Gallen-Kallela, met in Esplanadi's glitzy **Kappeli** glass building, adorned with glittering chandeliers, eating and drinking till the small hours of the morning.

Kappeli means 'chapel' in Finnish, and the restaurant is truly a holy institution, beloved by locals and visitors. In summer, sit on the terrace and watch the world go by; at other times get cosy indoors and order the gourmet salmon soup.

A Pool with a View
Take a swim and a sauna
Open year-round, **Allas Sea Pool** (*allasseapool.fi; adult/child from €18/10, under two years free*) is an urban sauna and spa oasis located right beside Market Square. The spa features fresh and saltwater pools, as well as sauna and wellness facilities. The pools are open till 9pm or 10pm, which, especially in autumn and winter, offers memorable possibilities for moonlight swims. For less wellness and more wow, take in Helsinki's city lights from Allas Sea Pool's upper-floor bar after you've had a relaxing steam in the sauna.

Classic & Modern Masterpieces
Explore the art centrals
Opposite Helsinki Central railway station, **Ateneum art museum** (*ateneum.fi; adult/child €22/free*) forms a part of the Finnish National Gallery. The museum's art collection spans from 18th-century rococo to 20th-century art movements, and provides a crash course on Finnish art. Notable Finnish works include Eero Järnefelt's scenes from Koli National Park, Akseli Gallen-Kallela's paintings of Finland's national epic poem *Kalevala,* and Helene Schjerfbeck's striking portraits as well as masterpieces from the likes of Paul Cézanne and Edvard Munch. The recently renovated museum now has also a fabulous cafe with views of the iconic Helsinki Railway Station and the Finnish National Theatre. Nearby, the Museum of Contemporary Art **Kiasma** (*kiasma.fi; adult/child €22/free*) has a mix of foreign and Finnish exhibitions and runs tours in English every other Friday. Both museums are closed on Mondays.

Fine Finnish Foods
Taste the traditions
Adjoining the bustling Kauppatori (Market Square), **Vanha Kauppahalli** (Old Market Hall), built in 1889, features stall after stall selling traditional Finnish foods and international flavours (*vanhakauppahalli.fi*). The market hall retains its revered knowledge of modern food trends – in fact, it has been featured in listings of the world's best foodie spots. Try the traditional creamy salmon soup at **Story** restaurant (*storyrestaurants.fi*), or sit down at **Erikssonin osteribaari** (*kalatukkueriksson.fi*) for oysters hailed as the best in Helsinki. The market also has a selection of Finnish meats, such as moose, bear, reindeer, Karelian pies and fried vendace.

STORY OF SUOMENLINNA

Founded in 1748 by Sweden, Suomenlinna sea fortress, one of Europe's largest maritime fortresses, was originally named Sveaborg (Sweden's Fortress).

The fortress was designed by the architect Augustin Ehrensvärd to strengthen Sweden's defences against Russian expansion. While exploring the fortress visit Ehrensvärd's tomb at the Great Courtyard, next to his home museum.

In 1808, Suomenlinna fell to Russian forces, marking the start of over a century of Russian rule in Finland. After Finland gained independence in 1917, the fortress was renamed Suomenlinna, the 'Castle of Finland'.

It played military roles in both World Wars before being decommissioned. Today, Suomenlinna is one of Finland's most popular attractions, with almost a million visitors per year.

 EATING IN CITY CENTRE, KRUUNUNHAKA & KATAJANOKKA

| **Magu:** Vegan fine dining that won't blow your budget, especially the eight-course option. Try out the ecological wines, too. *4-10pm Wed-Sat* €€€ | **Kolme Kruunua:** Beloved classic serving homey dishes from meatballs to fried vendace. *4pm-1am Mon-Thu, to 1.30am Fri, noon-1.30am Sat, to 1am Sun* €€ | **Palace:** Finland's only two-Michelin-starred restaurant serves seasonal Nordic cuisine and has stellar balcony views. *6-11.30pm Wed-Sat* €€€ | **El Fant:** Natural wines, light lunches and smashing ice teas are served on a cobbled street near Senate Square. *from 11am, closed Mon.* € |

PHOTOGRAPHER'S SPOTS

Henri Kallio, a photographer based in Helsinki, shares his love for the city on his Instagram *@henrifromhelsinki*.

The National Library of Finland: One of my favourite libraries in Helsinki and in the world. Stunning architecture but also great for book lovers.

Luotsikatu Street: Pearl of Helsinki art nouveau in the heart of Katajanokka. Full of stunning details, so make sure to slow down and look up as well.

Halkolaituri Pier: Head here for those postcard-perfect views over Pohjoisranta and Kanavaranta, combining Helsinki seaside, old wooden boats and Uspenski Cathedral.

Helsinki Cathedral: My favourite spot for capturing this white beauty is from the hill of Uspenski Cathedral. Also a perfect spot for sunset views over the city.

Suomenlinna sea fortress

A Garrison Getaway
Explore a UNESCO Heritage site

Helsinki has more than 300 islands, and the main sight among them is **Suomenlinna sea fortress** (*suomenlinna.fi*), dating from the 1740s and Helsinki's only UNESCO World Heritage site.

On the island, be prepared to walk as Suomenlinna's fortifications and barracks host multiple little museums, from toy and military collections to **Suomenlinna-Museo** (*adult/child €9/4*), which showcases the fortress' history. Peek inside the WWII *Vesikko* submarine, and wander around the old walls and cannons. Luckily, there are also a dozen cafes and restaurants where you can rest your feet. If you fancy a tasty cinnamon bun, try **Cafe Silo** (*silo.fi*), located near the main entrance.

 COFFEE SHOPS IN THE CITY CENTRE: OUR PICKS

Café Engel: Fabulous spot for breakfast right opposite Helsinki Cathedral; also serves lunch and cakes. *8am-10.30pm Mon-Fri, from 9am Sat, from 10am Sun* €€

Strindberg: Located by the Esplanade park, this cafe has a buzzing summer terrace. *9am-9pm Mon & Tue, to 10pm Wed-Fri, 10am-10pm Sat, 11am-8pm Sun* €

Café Aalto: Head to the 2nd floor of bookstore Akateeminen Kirjakauppa to enjoy a coffee break. *9am-8pm Mon-Fri, to 7pm Sat, 11am-6pm Sun* €

Café Eliel: Grab a coffee at Helsinki Central Station, designed by the Finnish architect Eliel Saarinen. *7am-9pm Mon-Thu, to 10pm Fri & Sat, to 7pm Sun* €

Suomenlinna is accessible throughout the year: spring and summer draw in crowds with picnic baskets, whereas autumn foliage transforms Suomenlinna into a romantic getaway. Suomenlinna is at its most magical in winter, with the pink barracks covered with snow and the island surrounded by a frozen sea.

HSL (Helsinki Regional Transport Authority) ferries leave from **Kauppatori** (Market Square). Buy tickets (*zone AB, single adult/child €2.95/1.50*) at the platform, online (*hsl.fi*), or with the HSL app.

Metro to Modern Art
Grand art inside grand architecture
To visit Finland's biggest art museum, jump onto metro M1 or M2 at Helsinki central station and head towards Espoo, Helsinki's neighbouring city and part of Greater Helsinki. From the station at Tapiola – Espoo's urban centre, built in the 1950s and '60s – it's a 15-minute walk to the **Espoo Museum of Modern Art (EMMA)** (*emmamuseum.fi*). EMMA's contemporary art and design works are exhibited in a former printing house, a 1960s architectural masterpiece in concrete. Admission is pricey (*€20 for adults aged over 29*) but the exhibits are worth every cent. EMMA is free to visit every Friday from 3pm; closed on Mondays.

Nature's Call
Nature on the urban doorstep
Nuuksio National Park (*visitespoo.fi*) makes a peaceful day's outing from Helsinki, with landscapes varying from ponds and lakes with clear waters to age-old forests, cliffs and gorges. To get here, take bus 245 from Espoo to Suomen luontokeskus Haltia (Finnish Nature Centre Haltia, *haltia.com*), where you can get park maps. The bus ride takes about 20 minutes. Around Haltia, there are several loop trails with viewpoints and campfire spots, as well as a centre for downhill mountain biking. You can also get off the bus in Kattila and walk along trails to the nature centre. There are a few accommodation providers in the park should you wish to relax in nature overnight.

Step into History
Learn history through play
Free of charge and open daily, **Helsinki City Museum's** (*helsinginkaupunginmuseo.fi*) exhibits, such as the immersive experience of the work of Finland's first female photographer, Signe Brander, bring the city's history to life. Part of the museum, Children's Town tells the city's history through play – let your kids enjoy, and you can relax for an hour or two.

BEST VINTAGE SHOPS IN KATAJANOKKA & KRUUNUNHAKA

Play it again, Sam
Fabulous vintage clothing from the 1920s to the 1970s, from satin dresses to accessories and tailored Finnish suits from brands like Kaleva.

Vintage Finland
This Liisankatu shop neatly stocks all things American (think Levi's jeans, jerseys, baseball caps), and is known for its collection of collectible sneakers.

Almost New
Unisex clothes, trendy streetwear from hoodies to sneakers, and some flashier items are sold at Torikortteli.

Fargo Vintage and Design
Unique pieces of high-end Finnish design items from the likes of Alvar Aalto and modern Danish classics.

Bukowskis
One of Finland's most prestigious auction houses, originating from Sweden, dedicated to Scandinavian antiques.

A BOOKY JOURNEY ON FOOT

Discover Helsinki's libraries' striking facades and enchanting interiors on this city-centre walking tour.

START	END	LENGTH
Oodi library	National Library of Finland	1.4km; 1½ hours

Helsinki's central libraries epitomise the country's long dedication to learning. Start from the modern, award-winning ❶ **Oodi** library, which hides an airy space for books and games behind its curvy contours. There is a cafe and a terrace upstairs, with views towards the imposing Parliament House, which was built in the 1920s, as well as the glassy concert hall Musiikkitalo, with Finnish and international artists performing jazz, classical, folk and pop music.

After Oodi, walk past the adjoining ❷ **Helsinki Central railway station**, dating from 1919. The station, with grand granite statues guarding its entrance, is often named on lists of the world's most beautiful railway stations. The station is located by ❸ **Rautatientori**, where you can test your skating skills on an ice rink in winter.

Continue uphill on Kaivokatu street, which is lined with restaurants and cinemas. At the top of the street, check out the modern ❹ **Helsinki University Library Kaisa** with its striking staircases and windows, and then continue to the ❺ **Kansalliskirjasto**, the National Library of Finland, located by Senate Square. The oldest part of the building was designed by CL Engel in the 1840s. The library's sturdy wooden doors lead into a book shrine with vaulted, decorative ceilings, wooden banisters and Corinthian columns guarding the bookcases – take your time to enjoy the atmosphere.

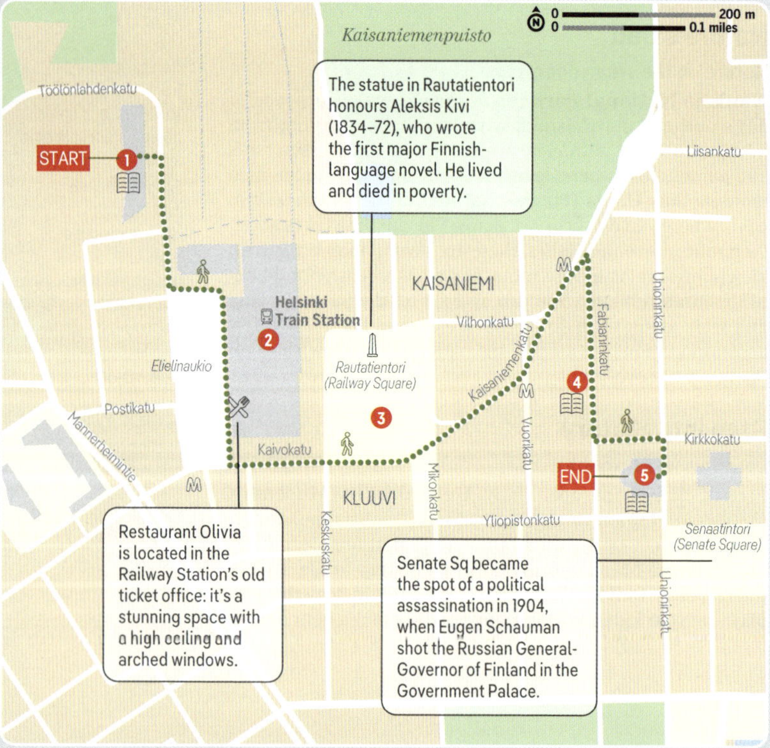

The statue in Rautatientori honours Aleksis Kivi (1834–72), who wrote the first major Finnish-language novel. He lived and died in poverty.

Restaurant Olivia is located in the Railway Station's old ticket office: it's a stunning space with a high ceiling and arched windows.

Senate Sq became the spot of a political assassination in 1904, when Eugen Schauman shot the Russian General-Governor of Finland in the Government Palace.

Eira, Ullanlinna & Kaivopuisto

PRESTIGIOUS SEASIDE SETTING

These neighbourhoods form part of Helsinki's most distinguished areas, with plenty of architectural treasures to discover. And yet, it is the seaside that is their greatest lure.

The shoreline here stretches from Kaivopuisto past Ullanlinna all the way to Eira and beyond. There are walking and cycling tracks lining the shore along this southern part of Helsinki's city centre. In warmer months, people gather to exercise or buy snacks and ice creams from the handful of seaside cafes and kiosks. Or you can pack a swimsuit and join others for sunbathing and a quick dip in the sea – an activity you can also try in the winter months when the seaside magically transforms, with snow covering the shores and the water freezing over.

Leaving the coast, you will find a bunch of little shops, restaurants and cafes varying from upscale bakeries to kiosks.

Picnics & Parties
Beloved park by the sea

Kaivopuisto is one of Helsinki's best-loved parks, lined by the Baltic Sea and some of the city's most grandiose buildings. The park became a bourgeois destination for leisurely strolls and spa treatments in the 19th century, but now Helsinki's inhabitants from every walk of life visit the park with their dogs, friends and picnic baskets, especially during Labour Day celebrations from 30 April to 1 May, when tens of thousands of people gather here.

Visit a War Hero
Step inside a presidential villa

Finland's revered president and war hero, CGE Mannerheim, who steered the nation out of WWII, lived in this Kaivopuisto **villa** from 1924 to his death in 1951. Most of the villa remains as it was when Mannerheim lived here. Anyone with a sweet

GETTING AROUND

Eira, Ullanlinna and Kaivopuisto are best explored on foot. The areas feature some of Helsinki's finest art nouveau architecture, and are dotted with pretty parks and lined by the seashore.

The second best option is the tram. In fact, tram number 3 running from Kaivopuisto through Eira is dubbed the 'tourist tram' of Helsinki as it traverses many of the city's most beautiful areas.

Helsinki's metro doesn't reach these parts, but that's not a bad thing as you want to keep your eyes on the pastel-coloured facades.

☑ TOP TIP

One of the best ways to feel the sea breeze on your skin is to rent a city bike. The yellow bikes are dotted around the city and work with the HSL app. Start from the Old Market Hall, and within 3km you'll have passed cafes, parks and beaches..

EIRA, ULLANLINNA & KAIVOPUISTO HELSINKI

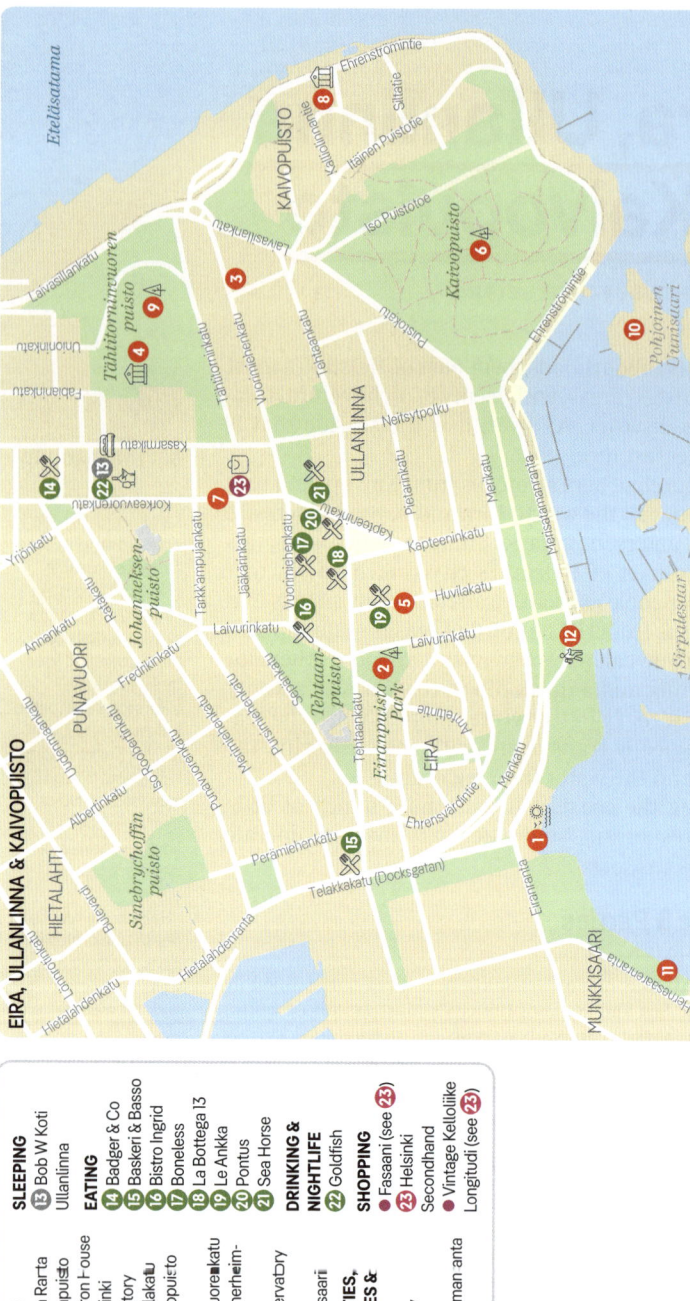

EIRA, ULLANLINNA & KAIVOPUISTO

SIGHTS
1. Eiran Ranta
2. Eiranpuisto
3. Flatiron House
4. Helsinki Observatory
5. Huvilakatu
6. Kaivopuisto
7. Korkeavuorenkatu
8. Mannerheim-museo
9. Observatory Hill Park
10. Uunisaari

ACTIVITIES, COURSES & TOURS
11. Löyly
12. Merisataman ranta

SLEEPING
13. Bob W Koti Ullanlinna

EATING
14. Badger & Co
15. Baskeri & Basso
16. Bistro Ingrid
17. Boneless
18. La Bottega 13
19. Le Ankka
20. Pontus
21. Sea Horse

DRINKING & NIGHTLIFE
22. Goldfish

SHOPPING
23. Fasaani (see 23)
23. Helsinki Secondhand
• Vintage Kelloliike Longitudi (see 23)

tooth will also appreciate the fact that the villa is owned by the Finnish chocolate manufacturer Fazer – before Mannerheim, Fazer's workers used to live here. Mannerheim-Museo is scheduled to reopen in the spring of 2025 after renovations.

A Slice of Paris
Vaunted vintage souvenirs

As these districts are some of Helsinki's most fashionable quarters, you can make astounding antique and vintage finds. Head to **Korkeavuorenkatu**, said to be the most Parisian street in Helsinki, and you'll find the colourful buildings – mostly in art nouveau and functionalist style – have dozens of cafes, restaurants and small boutiques and antique stores on their ground floors. In **Helsinki Secondhand** and **Fasaani**, you can buy vintage Finnish glassware or, if your budget – and luggage restrictions – allow, there's a range of exceptional furniture, too. Next door, in **Vintage Kelloliike Longitudi**, you'll find easy-to-carry vintage watches. When you're done browsing here, stroll around and make your own finds!

Calm Island Escape
Find tranquillity

The little island of **Uunisaari**, just offshore from Kaivopuisto, is a popular spot throughout the year. In summer, be your own captain and hop aboard a zero-emission, electric Callboat at Kaivopuisto's Merisatama (*callboats.com*). The boats run automatically, so no sailing experience is needed. In winter, the way to Uunisaari is no less memorable, with a pedestrian bridge stretching across the frozen sea from mid-November to mid-April. The small island has walking paths crisscrossing it, offering a quaint place for strolls.

The island has a beach, a restaurant and a cafe with two saunas (book at *uunisaari.fi/sauna*). Opening times vary according to season.

Seaside Stroll
Experience Helsinki as the locals do

When the sun finally emerges after the long, dark winter months around April, join the locals for a scenic stroll along **Merisatamanranta**, one of Helsinki's most charming seaside promenades. This picturesque stretch of road hugs the coastline, offering a perfect snapshot of life in Helsinki. The walkway is bordered by a park, which in turn is lined with

continued on p60

ICE SWIMMING

Often credited as a key factor in Finland being ranked the world's happiest nation year after year, winter swimming offers visitors a unique glimpse into the Finnish lifestyle. This invigorating practice involves dipping into icy waters, which is said to boost blood circulation, reduce stress and enhance mental wellbeing. The cold plunge is also believed to strengthen the immune system and improve metabolism, making it a refreshing health ritual. In Helsinki, there are around 20 private ice swimming clubs available for members – but visitors can participate in the fun too, in outdoor swimming spots such as Löyly and Allas Sea Pool, providing a perfect blend of wellness and adventure.

 BEST FOOD & DRINK IN ULLANLINNA: OUR PICKS

Badger & Co: Intimate space with a good range of beers and cocktails, as well as bar food. *3pm-midnight Sun & Mon, to 1am Tue-Thu, to 2am Fri & Sat* €

Goldfish: Old-fashioned library aesthetic meets modern bar, with a classic cocktail list. *4.30pm-midnight Tue-Thu, to 1am Fri & Sat* €€

La Bottega 13: Excellent wines, aperitifs and high-quality delicacies from the deli counter. Warm dishes are also available. *4-11pm Tue-Sat* €€

Pontus: Unfussy spot for pizza and wine – or something more exotic, such as Baltic herring *boquerones*. *4-11pm Mon-Sat, to 10pm Sun* €€

WALKING & CYCLING TOUR

A Seaside Tour

Seaside and city life mix charmingly in this walking and cycling tour around Helsinki's most prestigious neighbourhoods. Start by climbing onto a hill for smashing views of Helsinki Cathedral, then pick up a city bike and cruise along the shoreline, stopping at charming cafes for traditional Finnish food. Wrap up the experience by visiting Löyly to have a sauna and dip in the Baltic Sea. In winter, you can walk this tour.

❶ Observatory Hill Park
Start at **Observatory Hill Park**, a 30m hill with fabulous views towards the turquoise-domed Helsinki Cathedral. Pathways crisscross the hilltop park, and it's hard to imagine that the parking hall carved into the rock beneath also functions as an air-raid shelter.

❷ Observatory & Flatiron House
The most dominant building on the hill is the **observatory**, dating from 1834. When it was built, the observatory was ahead of its time. Today, the tower functions as an astronomy visitor centre, open from Thursdays to Saturdays (*adult/child €10/free*). Descend Tähtitorninvuori on its southern side and walk past Helsinki's **Flatiron House**, located on Vuorikatu 4.

The ride: Pick up a city bike *(hsl.fi/citybikes)* at Laivasillankatu near Olympiaterminaali. Cycle 2km along the seashore to the next bike drop-off point at Kapteeninpuistikko. Walk one minute to your lunch spot.

Observatory

❸ Sea Horse

Sea Horse has fed the hungry and the famous – from Finnish artists to writer Jean-Paul Sartre and poet Pablo Neruda – since 1934. The restaurant has made very few concessions to ever-changing food trends, apart from adding a couple of vegetarian options to the menu. Classics include fried Baltic herring and pepper steak. The food is tasty, but the prices can feel a bit salty.

The walk: It's a five-minute walk to the next stop, Eiranpuisto, so wander around and take your time to admire the architecture here.

❹ Eiranpuisto & Huvilakatu

Eira boasts some of Helsinki's most magnificent homes. To rest your eyes from the grandeur, visit **Eiranpuisto**, a park that feels somewhat hidden. On your way to Eiranpuisto, stop by at **Huvilakatu**. With its colourful art nouveau buildings, this is one of the most photographed streets in Helsinki. The street and its buildings were constructed between 1906 and 1910 and, apart from one change, it has kept its original looks.

The ride: Walk back to pick up your bike from Kapteeninpuistikko station. Continue cycling along the shore for 1km to Hernesaarenranta bike-drop, close to Löyly's sauna.

❺ Löyly

Löyly (meaning 'the steam' or 'the heat of sauna') is an urban sauna and restaurant complex located by the Baltic Sea (*loylyhelsinki.fi; two hours €25*). Book a sauna, take in some heat, plunge into the water from Löyly's platform, and make a dash back to the sauna. Afterward, enjoy some food and drinks in Löyly's restaurant. Löyly is open year-round – meaning smart possibilities for ice-hole swimming in the winter.

Eiran Ranta

FERRY TO SWEDEN

North of Kaivopuisto lies Olympiaterminaali, one of Helsinki's ferry terminals, originally built for the 1952 Olympic Games.

Today, it primarily serves the Tallink Silja Line, providing cruises between Helsinki and Stockholm. Taking an overnight cruise to the Swedish capital is a beloved tradition among Finns. The ships boast a range of amenities, including bars, discos, restaurants, tax-free shops and game arcades.

While the atmosphere can get festive and boisterous during the Christmas party season, summer brings families with children eager to enjoy their vacations.

For a more tranquil experience, consider booking a weekday crossing, where you can relax and soak in the beautiful Baltic Sea views with the islands of both Helsinki's and Stockholm's archipelagos dotting the shorelines.

continued from p57

stunning examples of art nouveau architecture. Scattered along the way, you'll find cafes and ice-cream kiosks – no wonder people gather here to walk their dogs, meet with friends and play a round of mini-golf. As you continue eastward, you'll come across the small but inviting beach of **Eiran Ranta**. Here, the sandy shore is ideal for sunbathing, while the smooth, sun-warmed cliffs surrounding it make excellent places to sit and enjoy your ice cream with a view of the shimmering Baltic Sea. Though Merisatamanranta is a slice of summer paradise, it's enjoyable to visit in the winter months, too. When temperatures drop and the sea freezes over, the area takes on an ethereal beauty.

EATING IN EIRA & ULLANLINNA: BEST RESTAURANTS

Bistro Ingrid: Intimate and cosy, Ingrid serves bistro classics – lunch is excellent value for money. *11am-11pm Tue-Fri, from 4pm Sat* €€

Boneless: A rare budget find, Boneless serves juicy chicken and various types of hamburgers, including vegetarian, in the heart of Ullanlinna. *hours vary* €

Baskeri & Basso: Bistro serving natural wines, with a sibling establishment, BasBas Kulma ('Corner'), next door, using a charcoal grill. *4pm-1am Tue-Fri* €€

Le Ankka: Michelin-starred dishes served on classic Finnish designer plates. *5pm-midnight Tue-Fri, from 2pm Sat, 3-8pm Sun* €€€

Punavuori, Kamppi & Hietalahti

BOHEMIAN VIBES AND BOUTIQUE FINDS

Shops from high-street brands to design and vintage finds, with art galleries, cafes and restaurants in between: this is Kamppi and Punavuori in a nutshell.

But there is more to these two districts than the glitzy shop fronts. Punavuori is Helsinki's old bohemian district, once housing the city's workers and threadbare students. This is also where, in Finland's Prohibition era from 1919 to 1932, secret bars were tucked away. Modern Punavuori has been somewhat hipsterfied, and is also the epicentre for Helsinki's Design District, though it's held onto its friendly neighbourhood vibes.

Kamppi has gone through a similar modernisation in recent decades, with world-class museums and a swanky shopping centre, but wander to the side streets and you'll discover edgy cafes, restaurants and galleries.

Hietalahti is a bit of a side note to its bustling neighbours, but its market square with regular flea markets draws in bargain hunters.

Functional Fancies

Shop in a glass palace

Lasipalatsi's ('Glass Palace') name might bring to mind grandiose architecture, but this is actually a sober, 1930s functionalist-style building with a glitzy twist.

Lasipalatsi's biggest draw is the **Amos Rex** museum, but don't ignore the building's little shops – you might leave with a bag full of Finnish fashion, from Karhu sneakers and Makia hoodies to all things Moomin. There are also cafes and restaurants. At night you can admire Lasipalatsi's retro neon signs.

Underground Art, Literally

Explore art below and above ground

Built beneath an old bus station, the Amos Rex museum witnessed queues when it first opened in 2018, and those queues persist on busier days (not on Tuesdays, when the museum is

GETTING AROUND

Punavuori, Kamppi and Hietalahti are great neighbourhoods to stroll around. Bulevardi has a good lane for cyclists.

Kamppi is one of Helsinki's main transport hubs, with many buses and trams stopping here. Underneath the Kamppi shopping centre, you'll find the bus station for regional buses and the budget-friendly Onnibus.

Trams 1, 3, 6, 7 and 9 traverse the at-times cobbled streets of the area, and city bikes and e-scooters are dotted around.

☑ TOP TIP

To step out of the city centre and check out Helsinki's modern side, head to the neighbouring Jätkäsaari ('bloke island') district. Here, you'll find new hotels and restaurants, as well as a terminal for ferries to Tallinn. Kamppi is just a few minutes away by tram.

PUNAVUORI, KAMPPI & HIETALAHTI

HIGHLIGHTS
1. Amos Rex
2. Design Museum

SIGHTS
3. Bulevardi
4. HAM
5. Iso Roobertinkatu
6. Johanneksenkirkko
7. Kampin Kappeli
8. Luonnontieteellinen Museo
9. Mikael Agricolan kirkko
10. Sinebrychoff Art Museum
11. Tavastia
12. Tennispalatsi
13. Vanha kirkkopuisto

EATING
14. Daddy Greens
15. Eerikin Pippuri
16. Ekberg
17. Georgian Kitchen
18. Goose Pastabar
19. Hietalahden Kauppahalli
20. Konstan Mölja
21. Latitude 25
22. Levain
23. Natura
24. Nolita
25. Ravintola Nolla
26. Restaurant MoMo
27. Salve
28. Yes Yes Yes

DRINKING & NIGHTLIFE
29. Ateljee Bar
30. Bar Llamas
31. Bar Mate
32. Bob's Laundry
33. Chihuahua Julep
34. Viinibaari Apotek

ENTERTAINMENT
35. Orion Theatre

SHOPPING
36. Fida Roba
37. Flea
38. Lasipalatsi
39. Relove Freda

Design Museum

closed). And no wonder – the contemporary art exhibitions here are from the top names of the art world, with works that are a perfect match for the somewhat eerie underground museum space (*amosrex.fi; adult/child €20/free, under 30 €5*).

Above ground, it's all fun and games though, with the museum's skylights, bulging from the ground, forming a utopian sight that adults and kids cannot stop exploring.

Vintage & Food
Stroll along Punavuori's artery

Iso Roobertinkatu runs through the heart of Punavuori from the leafy Sinebrychoff park to the tiny Kolmikulma park. 'Iso Roba' ('The Big Roba') is mainly a pedestrian street, lined with shops, bars and restaurants.

Vintage fashionistas, in particular, should take a stroll, as some of Helsinki's most fabulous vintage shops are here, with both flea markets and high-fashion finds guaranteed. Pop into **Fida Roba** (*fida.fi*) for bargains, **Relove Freda** (*relove.fi*) for high-street brands and a cup of coffee, and **Flea** (*fleasecondhand.com*) for design and luxury names.

Iso Roba has plenty of bars and restaurants in which to take a retail break, with options varying from **Natura's** (*restaurantnatura.com*) sustainably sourced ingredients to vegetarian dishes in **Yes Yes Yes** (*yesyesyes.fi*). Or sip on a cocktail and soak in the atmosphere in **Bar llamas**.

Dashing Designs
Explore the art of living

Located on the border of design-central Punavuori and neighbouring Kaartinkaupunki, the **Design Museum** (*designmuseum.fi; adult/child €20/free*) is for anyone intrigued by the Finns' take on creating bold everyday objects. The exhibits have varied from Ilmari Tapiovaara's woodwork and Eero Aarnio's

---

BEST BOUTIQUE SHOPPING

Nina Jatuli, owner and designer of Design District–based shop Jatuli, shares her tips on the area's best boutique finds.

Lokal
Gallery meets boutique, changing exhibitions and designer pieces by local artisans.

Papershop
Lovely boutique focusing on all things made of paper. A fabulous array of printed items for all paper-lovers. The Papershop is located on one of Punavuori's main shopping streets, Iso Roobertinkatu.

PIHKA collection
Produces elegant and minimalistic bags in Nordic style with carefully selected materials. Also arranges workshops so you can sign up and make your own bag!

Liike
A co-owned shop displaying several Finnish fashion designers' products. Liike is a collective shop, so you will be buying the pieces straight from some of the makers.

THE OLDEST BREWERY IN THE NORDICS

With a rich history spanning over 200 years, Sinebrychoff holds the title of the oldest brewery in the Nordic countries.

In the late 18th century, Peter Ivanovits Sinebrjukov left his hometown near Moscow in search of a better life in Kymi, Finland. He became a successful merchant and began brewing beer. His eldest son, Nikolai, eventually took over the business. Due to political changes, Nikolai relocated to Helsinki, where he obtained exclusive rights to brew beer.

On 13 October 1819 he purchased land in Hietalahti and established his brewery. Nowadays, this date is celebrated as the Day of Finnish Beer. Since 2000, Sinebrychoff has been part of the Danish Carlsberg group, but it still brews brands dear to the Finns, like KOFF.

chairs and lamps, to Lotta Nieminen's contemporary take on design. The museum is closed on Mondays from September to the end of May. For glassware aficionados, a trip to the Design Museum's satellite space in Arabianranta's **Iittala & Arabia Design Centre** *(iittala.com)* is a must. Take tram 6 from Central railway station to reach it.

Rock & Roll Way of Life
Listen to the sounds of music

The relatively small **Tavastia** *(tavastiaklubi.fi)* is one of the most coveted music venues in Finland. Opened in 1970, it is one of Europe's oldest rock clubs, and during its rowdy history, some of music's most influential names have performed here, from the Finnish HIM, Children of Bodom and Nightwish, to the Foo Fighters and Siouxsie and the Banshees. Tavastia occasionally givings the floor to upcoming bands, too. And whether the gig is big or small, the atmosphere is always magnificent.

Art by a Park
Old Masters and genteel living

For anyone into old European Masters and grand home inspections, a visit to the **Sinebrychoff Art Museum** *(sinebrychoffintaidemuseo.fi; adult/child €20/free)* is a must.

Around the turn of the 20th century, the brewery was run by Paul Sinebrychoff, and the museum was founded on the art collection of Sinebrychoff and his wife Fanny. Walk down the Bulevardi and step inside the refined city manor, which is where Paul and Fanny lived. The museum is part of the Finnish National Gallery and is closed on Mondays.

Be sure to take a stroll around the Sinebrychoff park behind the museum. In summer, this is a popular gathering place for the city's young and young at heart.

Market Square by the Water
Foodie and vintage finds

At the end of leafy Bulevardi, Hietalahti's seaside vista opens up. The area has a mixed history, with the proximity of the sea and harbour bringing in both fishermen and large industries needing water, such as the Sinebrychoff brewery turned art museum.

Today, the harbour hosts an assortment of pleasure boats, varying from little dinghies to boats with saunas and jacuzzis for private hire. Behind the small harbour looms an industrial harbour where both luxury yachts and sturdy icebreakers are built.

EATING & DRINKING IN EERIKINKATU: OUR PICKS

| **Eerikin Pippuri:** After catching a film in the Orion, pop over for a snack at this popular kebab and falafel spot. *10am-midnight Sun-Thu, to 5am Fri & Sat* € | **Viinibaari Apotek:** One of Helsinki's best wine bars. In summer, the corner-shop-bar's terrace is especially lively. *4pm-midnight Tue-Thu, 2pm-2am Fri* € | **Goose Pastabar:** Although the pasta is delicious and handmade, it's more about the friendly buzz in this restaurant. *3pm-midnight Wed-Sat* €€ | **Konstan Möljä:** This is one of Helsinki's most iconic spots to try traditional Finnish dishes. *11am-2.30pm Tue-Fri, plus 5-10pm Tue-Thu, 4-11pm Fri & Sat* €€ |

Hietalahden Kauppahalli, with flea market in foreground

Still, the heart of Hietalahti is solidly ashore. The Hietalahdentori (market square) buzzes during the summer months but remains open all year. Hietalahden kirpputori (flea market) is especially popular on summer weekends, when you can make fabulous fashion finds as well as stock up with retro knick-knacks and Finnish glassware.

Hietalahden Kauppahalli (*hietalahdenkauppahalli.fi*), or Market Hall, is a budget-friendly (by Helsinki's standards) spot for lunch. **Mama's Phở** is popular for Vietnamese food, while **Petiscaria** offers Portuguese feasts and **Super Bowl** whips up healthy dishes in bowls.

Animals of All Sizes

Become an explorer

With an African elephant greeting you in the lobby, families with kids will particularly enjoy visiting the **Finnish Museum of Natural History**, or Luonnontieteellinen museo (*helsinki.fi/en/luomus; adult/child €19/7*). The collection of some 13 million specimens varies from Africa's biggest animals to rocks and fungi. There are exhibits showcasing Finnish nature, as well as rooms dedicated to nature's diversity around the world. Visitors can also familiarise themselves with evolution and climate change.

Apart from all things furry and skeletal, pay attention to the flamboyant architecture. The baroque revival building was originally a Russian-speaking cadet school until the University of Helsinki established its Natural History Museum here in 1923.

Holy Moments in Punavuori

Take in the heights

Named after Bishop Mikael Agricola, the father of the Finnish literary language, his namesake **church** stands tall above the rooftops of Punavuori and Eira (*helsinginseurakunnat.fi, free*).

CANOPY KIOSKS

Helsinki's first canopy kiosks, designed by the city architect Gunnar Taucher in the 1920s, were the city's first functionalist buildings.

You can still marvel at some of these original round, concrete 'wire spool kiosks' in places like Esplanadi Park as you meander through the city.

The 1952 Olympic Games heralded the construction of more kiosks, this time with an angular design by Hilding Ekelund. Today, this type of canopy kiosk, or *lippakioski*, is the most prevalent.

In summer, the kiosks are cute little stops for refreshments, from ice creams to coffee and drinks. In Punavuori and Kamppi districts, you can spot these yellow kiosks near landmarks such as the restaurant Seahorse, the Design Museum and Hietalahdentori market square.

PUNAVUORI'S PAST & PRESENT

Punavuori's name is shrouded in seedy, bohemian flair. Named after cliffs with a reddish hue in the area, Punavuori (Red Mountain) is a seaside neighbourhood that was once inhabited by sailors living in their wooden huts.

By the late 19th century, working-class housing began attracting more residents to the area. During the early 20th century, Punavuori, or Rööperi in local slang, gained a bad reputation, primarily due to illegal alcohol smuggling during Finland's strict prohibition laws and various other criminal activities.

However, today, Punavuori has undergone gentrification and is favoured by both well-to-do residents and students alike. As Helsinki's most populated area, it offers abundant shopping options and a vibrant nightlife scene, perfect for bar-hopping and leisurely strolls.

Cafe Ekberg

As one of the most frequently used churches in Finland, it remains a central part of the community. Architect Lars Sonck designed the church, which was completed in the spring of 1935 and represents the neo-classic style. Its 103m tower became a southern Helsinki landmark, visible from the sea. However, during the war, the 30m spire was lowered inside the tower to prevent enemy pilots from using it as a navigation beacon.

Johanneksenkirkko is a 10-minute stroll away. The church was built on a site where bonfires were once lit, and it was named after John the Baptist (Johannes in Finnish), who is believed to have been born on Midsummer. Dating back to 1891, Johanneksenkirkko is more decorative than Mikael Agricola's Church, featuring fine wood carvings and beautiful altarpieces.

Get Swept Up in the Spirit of Subculture

Learn about Finnish punk

For many, Kamppi is synonymous with the shopping centre that shares its name, but the neighbourhood is also a vibrant hub for music venues, record stores and bars featuring live gigs. This might be one of the reasons why Kamppi also hosts the intriguing Punkmuseo (*punkmuseo.fi; adult/child €5/free*), a museum dedicated to 'all things Finnish punk' from the 1970s onward. The museum is curated by Finnish punk musicians and aficionados and showcases the spirit of the genre – freedom of creating and the can-do attitude – in its rotating exhibitions.

Cakes & Coffee

Stroll like a flâneur or flâneuse

With its Central European atmosphere, and running from Esplanadi park slightly downhill to Hietalahti, **Bulevardi** is lined with cafes, restaurants, art galleries, hotels and boutiques. The street draws a line between Kamppi and Punavuori districts. The best way to take in Bulevardi's atmosphere is to stroll without a hurry, and stop by cafe **Ekberg** (*ekberg.fi*).

This historic cafe, dating from 1852, is a place to see and be seen. Just before the cafe, there's also a charming little park, **Vanha kirkkopuisto** (Old Church Park), also known as Ruttopuisto (Plague Park) as during the plague in 1710 victims were buried nearby. The park itself used to be a cemetery till the early 19th century, but nothing remains of this history: now the park is a calm oasis beside Bulevardi's flutter. Sinebrychoff Art Museum is located towards the other end of Bulevardi, just before Hietalahti and its market square.

Serene Silence in the City
Keep calm
Beside the busy Kamppi shopping centre, the conical wooden structure that is **Kampin Kappeli** (*kampinkappeli.fi*), or the Kamppi Chapel, is an ecumenical place to promote a very Finnish virtue: silence. Everyone is welcome to enter and sit in silence, surrounded by some of the busiest parts of the city. Although eye-catching from the outside, the chapel is particularly beautiful inside with its curving wooden walls. Visit in winter season (September–May) for free; at other times adults pay €5.

Olympian Art
See art and movies
While in Kamppi, you will notice a white hall-like structure with an arched roof. This is **Tennispalatsi** (Tennis Palace), originally meant as a car maintenance hall for the 1940 Olympic Games (which were subsequently postponed until 1952 because of WWII), but which also included four tennis courts. The building by Helge Lundström took a long time to gain merit in people's minds, and was left to deteriorate after the 1960s. Finally, in the 1990s, the City of Helsinki started to investigate the possibility of transforming the space into a cultural centre, and it now hosts **HAM** (*Helsinki Art Museum; hamhelsinki.fi; adult/child €18/free*), an art gallery with changing exhibitions and a permanent space for Tove Jansson's work, as well as a cinema complex. Today, Tennispalatsi is also one of the prime examples of the functionalist style in Helsinki.

TORNI HOTEL

Opened in 1931, the iconic Torni Hotel in Helsinki was Finland's tallest building at 70m, with a striking tower.

With its art deco and functionalist style, the hotel quickly became a symbol of modern Helsinki – in fact, it was Finland's first fully electrified building. The hotel's beginnings were somewhat tumultuous: during WWII it served as a base for German forces, while during the Winter War foreign journalists were posted there. Post-war, it housed the Allied Control Commission.

Later, Torni evolved into a cultural hotspot, attracting artists, journalists and politicians, and it is still a treasured landmark in Helsinki.

EATING IN PUNAVUORI: OUR PICKS

Levain: Beloved bakery, cafe and restaurant with airy, industrial space close to Eira and the seaside – the *pastéis de nata* are a hit. *9am-5pm* €	**Restaurant MoMo:** Small restaurant on a street corner with the best dumplings in town – meat, chicken or vegan. *11am-5pm Wed-Fri, noon-4pm Sat* €	**Nolita:** The trio behind the zero-waste Nolla brings you this cosy bakery-restaurant. *11.30am-10pm Tue-Thu, to 11pm Fri, noon-11pm Sat* €€	**Daddy Greens:** A pizza bar with a strong emphasis on vegetarian and vegan ingredients – try the Bee Sting. *hours vary* €€
Georgian Kitchen: A warm-hearted feeling and Georgian flavours are guaranteed. *3-11pm Mon-Thu, to 1am Fri, noon-1am Sat, 1-10pm Sun* €€	**Salve:** Serves Finnish classics, and possibly one of the best Baltic herring dishes in the country. *11am-10.30pm Mon-Fri, from noon Fri & Sat* €€	**Ravintola Nolla:** Zero-waste, inventive fine dining with its own microbrewery. *5-11pm Tue-Thu, to midnight Fri & Sat* €€€	**Latitude 25:** Popular *omakase* restaurant that serves delicately seasoned sushis (booking advisable). *5-9.30 Wed & Thu, 4-11pm Fri & Sat* €€€

KAMPPI & PUNAVUORIS ART FINDS

Lincoln Kayiwa, designer, artist and art collector, shares tips for the best galleries in his neighbourhood. *@lincolnkayiwa*

Galerie Forsblom: Hosts and represents established artists. The impressive space is located in a historic building from 1911.

Galerie Anhava: Finnish contemporary art with a roster of emerging, mid-career and established artists.

Helsinki Contemporary: A wide range of artists with a growing global presence.

Zetterberg Gallery: Initially established out of enthusiasm for just one artist: Jani Leinonen. Today exhibits four to six dynamic shows yearly.

Galleria Halmetoja: Holds exhibitions at its own gallery space and collaborates on exhibitions at other locations. Artworks can be purchased in instalments.

Big-Screen Architecture
Watch a film

Rare is the opportunity to enjoy cinema classics in an art deco building, but it can be done in Kamppi's **Orion**, one of Helsinki's oldest cinemas, dating from 1928 (*cinemaorion.fi*). Tickets start from €12, and the programme consists of Finnish and acclaimed films from around the world – no modern Hollywood spectacles here, though. The cinema is located on Eerikinkatu, so after the film, it's easy to head for a drink or dinner nearby.

Orion cinema

DRINKING IN KAMPPI & PUNAVUORI: OUR PICKS

Bar Mate: Highball cocktails and tasty bar snacks make a perfect combination. *4-11pm Tue, to midnight Wed & Thu, to 2am Fri & Sat, 6pm-2am Sun*

Chihuahua Julep: Step inside this mobile phone-free zone with mismatching furniture and a fabulous cocktail menu. *7pm-1am Tue-Thu, from 6pm Fri-Sun*

Ateljee Bar: Torni Hotel's bar boasts the best views over Helsinki but they come with high price tags. *noon-midnight Mon-Thu, to 2am Fri, 8am-2am Sat, from 10am Sun*

Bob's Laundry: Hidden behind, neon-sign-adorned retro laundromat, Bob serves smashing drinks and snacks. *5pm-midnight Tue-Thu, to 2am Fri, 3pm-2am Sat*

Töölö, Kallio & Kaisaniemi

BEACHES, BAYS AND BOHEMIAN CHARM

Even though Töölö and Kallio have very different reputations, with Töölö dubbed a 'village in the city', homing many of the city's elderly, and Kallio famed for its bohemian atmosphere that draws in the city's creatives, the two districts share some similarities – friendly neighbourhood feelings and collections of corner-shop bars and cafes.

Töölö's vibe is calm, the streets are lined with prestigious, early-20-century buildings and nature is never far away. Kallio is another story, with the former working-class district now a trendy area filled with small bars and restaurants.

But you will find a bit of nature here, too, with Kaisaniemi Bay – separated from Töölö Bay only by train tracks – stretching across Kallio's southern borders. Here, packed into a small patch of land, a flourishing park and a botanic garden form a tranquil urban oasis, all hidden behind Helsinki Central railway station.

A Regatta Gala – of Cinnamon Buns
Take in the seaside setting

Cuteness – and cinnamon bun – overdose awaits at **Cafe Regatta** (*caferegatta.fi*), a seaside Töölö cafe. The red hut is unmistakable, and its freshly baked cinnamon buns are legendary. In summer, it buzzes with activities: people enjoying cold drinks and coffees on its terrace, and others renting the cafe's kayaks, canoes or SUPs to get another kind of viewpoint on the city.

In winter, there is an outdoor fire pit, giving warmth to people grilling sausages or sipping on hot chocolate around it.

A Seed That Survived a War
Step into a tropical breeze

Kaisaniemi's small patch of greenery is located just behind Helsinki Central railway station, next to Töölö. Here, hidden

GETTING AROUND

Töölö, Kallio and Kaisaniemi are made for walking. But if you wish to speed up, buses shuttle along the streets as well as tram numbers 1, 2, 4, 8 and 10. The metro doesn't stop in Töölö.

Kallio has some hills, but it's still a very walkable neighbourhood. Tram is also a good option, with lines 1, 3, 6, 7, 8 and 9. The metro also stops in Kallio.

Kaisaniemi is a leafy area for walking and cycling, with the Central Railway Station as a transport hub close by.

TOP TIP

HSL (*hsl.fi*) city bikes dot Helsinki from the beginning of April till the end of October. Download its app and set out cycling around Töölönlahti, a 4.9km-long bay located behind Helsinki Central railway station. Take a break at the summer cafe Sinisen Huvilan Kahvila, with views over the bay.

TÖÖLÖ, KALLIO & KAISANIEMI HELSINKI

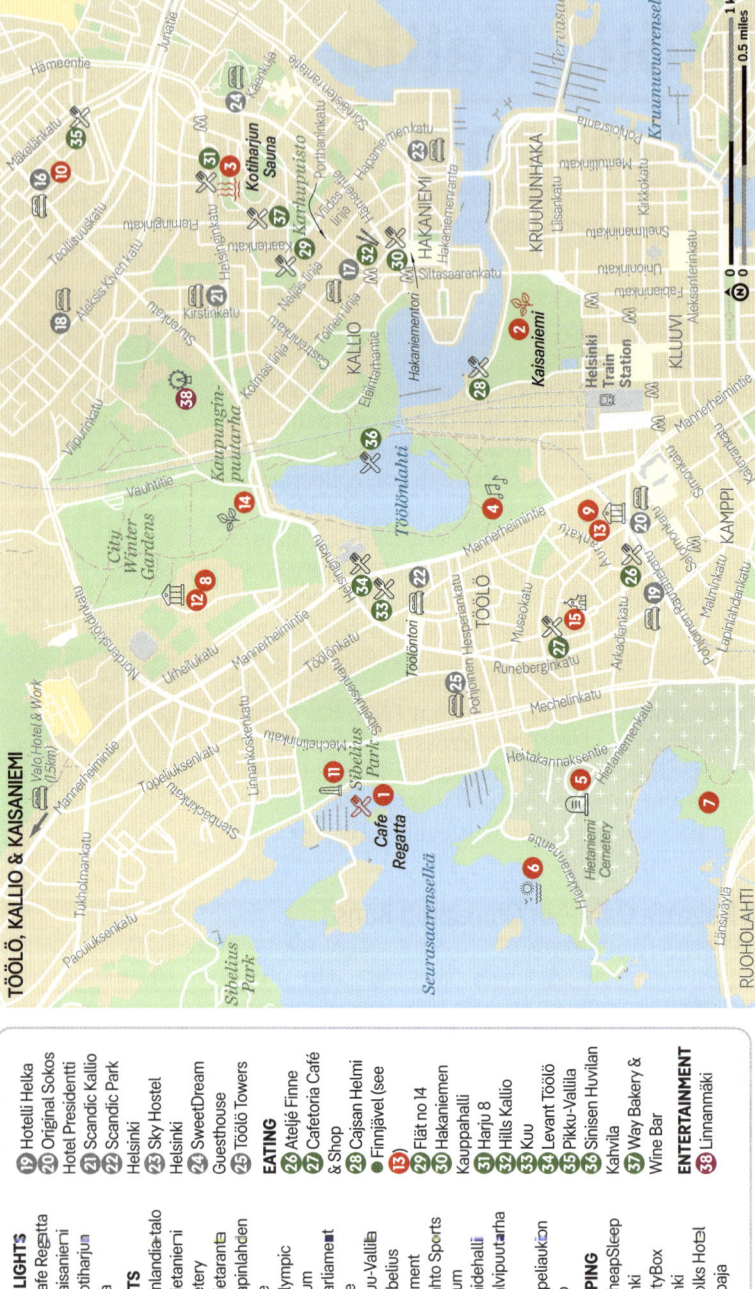

TÖÖLÖ, KALLIO & KAISANIEMI

HIGHLIGHTS
1. Cafe Regatta
2. Kaisaniemi
3. Kotiharjun Sauna

SIGHTS
4. Finlandia-talo
5. Hietaniemi Cemetery
6. Hietaranta
7. Lapinlahden Lähde
8. Olympic Stadium
9. Parliament House
10. Puu-Vallila
11. Sibelius Monument
12. Tahto Sports Museum
13. Taidehalli
14. Talvipuutarha
15. Temppeliaukion Kirkko

SLEEPING
16. CheapSleep Helsinki
17. CityBox Helsinki
18. Folks Hotel Konepaja
19. Hotelli Helka
20. Original Sokos Hotel Presidentti
21. Scandic Kallio
22. Scandic Park Helsinki
23. Sky Hostel Helsinki
24. SweetDream Guesthouse
25. Töölö Towers

EATING
26. Ateljé Finne
27. Cafetoria Café & Shop
28. Cajsan Helmi
  • Finnjävel (see 13)
29. Flåt no 14
30. Hakaniemen Kauppahalli
31. Harju 8
32. Hills Kallio
33. Kuu
34. Levant Töölö
35. Pikku-Vallila
36. Sinisen Huvilan Kahvila
37. Way Bakery & Wine Bar

ENTERTAINMENT
38. Linnanmäki

behind the trees, is one of the city's most visited attractions, the botanic garden (Kaisaniemen kasvitieteellinen puutarha) with its glasshouses protecting more than 800 species. Most magical of all is the Santa Cruz water lily (Victoria cruziana), the seeds of which survived the Continuation War (1941–44) bombings that destroyed most of the garden. There is also a lush Rainforest House with coffee bushes and a Palm House with delicate orchids. A visit makes an enchanting outing for the whole family throughout the year.

Explore Talvipuutarha
A Winter Garden oasis

Talvipuutarha (Winter Garden) is a serene oasis between Töölö Bay and the Olympic Stadium. Established in 1893, this historical greenhouse has over 200 plant species, including palm trees, succulents, and seasonal flowers like azaleas and chrysanthemums, which make it a warm and colourful escape during the cold winter months when the world outside is blanketed in snow. Visitors can wander through three main rooms: the Palm Room, the Cactus Room and the West Wing. The garden is open year-round (except on Fridays) and free to enter. With its tranquil atmosphere, koi ponds and benches to rest your feet, Talvipuutarha is a great pitstop between sightseeing. For a festive visit, pop over during Christmas and Easter, when seasonal flowers from poinsettias to tulips are in bloom.

Symphonius Sculpture
See the spirit of music

Rising atop a small cliff, and surrounded by the seaside Sibelius Park in Töölö, the metal tubes of the **Sibelius Monument** seem to form a symphony of their own. Made in 1967 by the Finnish sculptor Eila Hiltunen, who wanted to embody the spirit of Sibelius' music, the monument received controversial reviews but has since become a national landmark.

Stroll also to the nearby Ilmatar and sotka, an art deco–style statue by Aarre Aaltonen, depicting the birth of the world according to Finland's national epic, *Kalevala*.

A Landmark Stadium
Admire Helsinki's rooftops

Take an elevator to the top of its 72m-high tower to get a bird's-eye view over Helsinki, or admire the functionalist-style **Olympic Stadium** from ground level; either way, this is one of the city's

BAR IN A TRAM

Step aboard the red SpåraKoff, a bar housed in a vintage tram. Inaugurated in 1995, this charming tram bar is so loved that it stills rolls through the streets of Helsinki during the summer months and the Christmas season. The name 'SpåraKoff' derives from the Swedish word *spåra* (tram) and Koff, a reference to the renowned beer from Finland's oldest brewery, Schinebrykoff. Entry costs €12, granting you an hour-long tour that accommodates 24 guests. Onboard, you'll find a bar and a restroom. This 1959 tram clatters through Kallio, Töölö and other central neighbourhoods, offering plenty of time to enjoy a refreshing Finnish Lonkero gin drink or a cold Koff beer!

 EATING IN TÖÖLÖ AND KALLIO: BEST CAFES

Way Bakery & Wine Bar: Local favourite with fab brekkies, tasty pasta lunches and dinners and moreish wines. *8am-8pm Mon-Fri, from 9am Sat* €	Cafetoria Café & Shop: A Latin-Nordic cafe and roastery dedicated to bringing the best coffee aromas. *10am-6pm Mon-Fri, to 4pm Sat* €	Flät no 14: Build your own three-, five- or seven-piece breakfast menu – available from 9am to 4pm. *9am-5pm Sun & Tue, to 11pm Wed-Sat* €€	Sinisen Huvilan Kahvila: A summertime cafe located in an 1896 villa on the shores of Töölö Bay. *10am-10pm Apr-Sep* €

TÖÖLÖ BAY

Töölö Bay, a serene oasis in Helsinki, lies between the neighbourhoods of Töölö and Kallio.

A popular 2.2km walking and cycling path encircles the bay, offering scenic views and notable sights like the Botanical Gardens and Finlandia Hall. The area provides a peaceful retreat and a chance to experience Helsinki's natural beauty dotted with landmarks. In summer, hop on a city bike and cycle around it, stopping at Sinisen Huvilan Kahvila along the way for refreshments.

most famous landmarks. The tower is open daily (*stadion.fi; adult/child €6,50/4*) and you can also book tours of the stadium which include a visit to the sports museum **Tahto** and entrance to the tower (*tahto.com; adult/child €16/4, combination ticket for the tower and Tahto adult/child €20/14*). The stadium was originally intended to be the host venue for the 1940 Olympic Games, but the Games were postponed until 1952 due to the outbreak of WWII.

Big & Small Finlandia
Visit Alvar Aalto's magnum opus

The bright white **Finlandia-talo** (*Finlandia Hall; finlandiatalo.fi*) rising near the Töölönlahti shoreline is an

EATING IN TÖÖLÖ, KALLIO & KAISANIEMI: OUR PICKS

Harju 8: With a menu full of Finnish flavours this is one of Helsinki's best spots to have brunch, drink and enjoy the atmosphere. *11am-10pm* €

Cajsan Helmi: Set in an 1820s building, this is a great pit stop for a sandwich or a savoury pie. *11am-7pm Tue-Sat, to 6pm Sun* €

Hills Kallio: Known for its tasty dumplings, Hills also serves smashing cocktails, with ingredients varying from Pimm's to Mezcal. *from 6.30pm* €

Levant Töölö: Middle-Eastern street-food classics from hummus and kebbeh to tabbouleh and hearty soups are made with love. *hours vary* €

Hakaniemen Kauppahalli: Light and spacey, this is Helsinki's trendiest market hall, with dining options on two floors. *hours vary, closed Sun* €€

Ateljé Finne: Located in Gunnar Finne's studio, with a dining experience based around Finnish ingredients. *5-11pm Mon-Thu, from 4pm Fri & Sat* €€

Kuu: This nostalgic restaurant dating from 1966 is a Töölö neighbourhood favourite. *5-11pm Mon-Fri, from 2pm Sat, 4-11pm Sun* €€

Finnjävel Salonki and Sali: Traditional Finnish ingredients at this Michelin-starred restaurant located in Taidehalli. *5-11.30pm Tue-Sat* €€€

Finlandia-talo

unmistakable sight. When Alvar Aalto was commissioned by the City of Helsinki to create new plans for the city centre in 1959, the architect wanted to highlight Finland's independence, and designed a striking concert and congress hall almost opposite the Parliament House. The aim was to create a cultural zone matching CL Engel's Senate Square. Unfortunately, only Finlandia Hall ever materialised from these plans – the building was opened in 1971. Every detail has been carefully planned – with the architect Elissa Aalto, Alvar Aalto's second wife, and interior designer Pirkko Söderman leaving their mark in the interiors. Book a ticket to one of the concerts held here or just admire the architecture and design – don't forget to also visit the Pikku-Finlandia, 'Little-Finlandia', next door, with a cafe and a wine bar as well as architectural significance in its own right.

A Rock-Solid Sight

A church carved in rock

The circular **Temppeliaukion Kirkko** (Temppeliaukion Church) is the antithesis of what people normally expect from church architecture: this church doesn't have spires reaching to the skies; instead, it is carved inside a rock. And it pays to think outside the box because this church, also known as the Rock Church, has been one of Helsinki's favourite sights since 1969. The construction was postponed during WWII, but finally, in the 1960s, the project kicked off again, with new designs from the architect brothers Timo and Tuomo Suomalainen. The interior is carved directly into the rock and the

TÖÖLÖ'S MANY FACADES

Töölö's history began in the 19th century as a Helsinki suburb with charming villas, but its character started shifting in the early 20th century. Etu-Töölö (closer to the city centre) was developed between 1910 and 1930, while Taka-Töölö (further from the city centre) was built between 1920 and 1940.

Strolling through these areas reveals Finnish late Jugendstil, classicism, art deco and functionalism. Etu-Töölö hosts notable sites like **Eduskuntatalo** (Parliament House), **Taidehalli** and **Hietaniemi Cemetery**, where many prominent Finns from writers to presidents are buried.

In Taka-Töölö, you can visit the **Sibelius Monument** (p71) in a park near a seaside promenade. Continue north, and you'll end up in **Seurasaari**: an island and an open-air museum.

>
> **CHURCHES OF DIFFERENCE**
> To find another of Helsinki's unusual churches, be sure to visit the **Kamppi Kappeli of Silence** (p67).

dome is supported by a skylight, providing plenty of natural light to the space. There are also no bells, though a recording of bells is played on loudspeakers.

The church is open daily to visitors (*temppeliaukionkirkko.fi, adult/child €8/free*), except when a service is being held – check the church website for service times before visiting. There are also a handful of nice bakeries and cafes nearby in which to soak in Töölö's quaint neighbourhood feel.

For Budding Picassos
A pink hall to house art

Just around the corner from Temppeliaukion Church is **Taidehalli** (*Kunsthalle Helsinki; taidehalli.fi, adult/child €20/11*), unmistakable due to its pink exterior and photogenic lines.

Taidehalli hosts changing exhibitions, mainly of contemporary Finnish art, design and architecture, from the likes of Aino and Alvar Aalto and Paul Osipow. The building itself is a prime example of the 1920s Nordic classicism.

If you are a budding Picasso, bring your pen, as Taidehalli organises life-drawing Croquis Nights every Tuesday, with limited attendance (*€10*). The museum is closed on Mondays.

Cosy Quarters & Industrial Corners
Venture to Vallila

Step north of Kallio to Vallila, an old working-class neighbourhood on the rise. For decades, Vallila's big draw was its **Puu-Vallila** district. Here, colourful wooden villas line quiet streets and it's hard to believe you're still in Helsinki. The best spot to rest is **Pikku-Vallila** (*pikkuvallila.fi*), a quirky corner restaurant. But apart from its cosy quietness, Vallila has recently had an upgrade to its rougher, and a touch rowdier, areas too. A cluster of bars and restaurants, as well as a hotel, are located in red-brick buildings known as **Konepaja**, the workshops for the Finnish railroad company VR's train carriages and also the name of the area. Konepaja is quickly becoming a favourite Helsinki hangout. There are also some of the city's newest rooftop bars, **Loi Loi** (*loiloirooftop.com*) and **Alexis** (*alexiskatollaan.fi*) – the latter is part of **Folks Hotel**, which combines a fab location with reasonable prices, and a well-needed hotel addition in these parts of Helsinki.

Fun for the Family
Take a ride

Perched on top of a cliff adjoining Kallio, **Linnanmäki** (*linnanmäki.fi, entry to all rides €51*) has been Helsinki's centre of fun since the 1950s, and is now Finland's oldest and most popular amusement park. The seemingly rickety wooden roller coaster has provided sturdy rides for the daring since 1951, when it was Europe's tallest roller coaster. There are 42 other

---

OLYMPIC DRINK

In 1952, Helsinki was set to host the long-awaited Olympic Games. However, there was a problem: the city, emerging from WWII, lacked bars and experienced bartenders to cater to the thirsty visitors' needs. A ready-made cocktail drink was needed. Enter lonkero, a combination of gin and grapefruit soda – a uniquely sour and lightly carbonated cocktail manufactured by the Hartwall brewery. Lonkero quickly gained popularity, becoming a staple in Finnish culture and social settings. Over the years, various flavours, from cranberry and lemon to mango, have emerged, but the classic gin and grapefruit combination remains beloved. Today, lonkero is a symbol of Finnish summer. You can sip one in most bars or buy it at any supermarket.

Linnanmäki

WHY I LOVE TÖÖLÖ

Paula Hotti, writer

I might be biased in my love of Töölö, as this was the Helsinki neighbourhood I called home when I first moved here as a student. Even though Töölö is well connected to the university with buses and trams, I would usually walk, especially in spring, when I could witness the elderly shop owners brushing the sidewalks and well-to-do ladies walking their little dogs. Maybe time has added some gloss to these village-like images of the Töölö of my youth, but it can't be just my fancy because the neighbourhood is generally known as a village inside a city.

And this is why I still love Töölö as a recent returnee: for its warm neighbourly feel, but with the conveniences of a capital city.

rides in Linnanmäki as well as views over Helsinki from the park's hilltop location. Note also the colourful carousel dating from the end of the 19th century.

Outdoors in Every Season

Bask on a beach

South of Sibelius park, Hietaniemi peninsula is home to the popular summertime beach of **Hietaranta**, with beach volleyball courts and a cafe. In fact, the whole west side of Töölö makes a fabulous place for seaside strolls, cycling trips or kayaking tours. There are also a few historic sites, such as the tranquil **Hietaniemi Cemetery** (p73) and **Lapinlahti**'s former mental institution, now a creative hub with cafes, bakeries, art and events (*lapinlahdenlahde.fi*). There is also a Mental Museum sharing insight into the institution's history (*free*). In winter, the sea is frozen and the peninsula is a popular place for walks and taking in the natural beauty.

Steamy Traditions

Take the heat

Dating from 1928, **Kotiharjun Sauna** (*kotiharjunsauna.fi; €16*) is Helsinki's oldest public sauna, with a wood-burning stove providing gentle steam. The sauna is located in Kallio and has an endearing feel to it. Men and women bathe separately, but you can also rent a private sauna at a reasonable price. Towels, seat covers (*pefletti*) and anything else you might need for the sauna can be rented or bought on the spot. To top up the experience, the sauna also sells 'sauna *vihtas*', or bath brooms (*€7*). Whack yourself with the *vihta* a few times and you will soon understand the point of it, with the practice not only cleaning your skin but also speeding up your blood flow and metabolism.

Places We Love to Stay

€ Budget €€ Midrange €€€ Top End

City Centre, Kruununhaka & Katajanokka MAP p49

Hostel Suomenlinna € Mixed and female dorms, as well as double and family rooms, on the World Heritage fortress island of Suomenlinna.

Eurohostel € With morning and evening sauna, great location on Katajanokka and bikes available for rent, this hostel is a bargain.

Hobo Hotel Helsinki €€ Great value for money; Hobo's restaurant and urban retro vibes keep you happy bang in the city centre.

Hotel Finn €€ No-frills rooms right off Helsinki's main street, Mannerheimintie, and near the Stockman department store.

Hotel Fabian €€ A fabulous part of the Helsinki-based Kämp collection hotels, with a great lobby bar and accessibility.

Grand Hansa €€ NH Collection's luxury hotel was renovated in some of the city centre's grandest buildings and comes with Finnish designer pieces and one of Helsinki's most hyped rooftop bars, Kupoli.

Noli Katajanokka II €€ In this red-brick building with simply yet stylishly furnished apartments with kitchens, you'll feel like a resident of urban Helsinki.

Radisson RED €€ Nestled within the greenery of Kaisaniemi Park, yet just steps from the Central Railway Station, the rooms here come with big windows that invite the city in.

Hotel Katajanokka €€ Set in a refurbished 1888-built prison, with some original features still on display, the rooms stretch over two to three former cells, making them spacious and stylish.

Pier 4 €€€ Scandinavian seaside chic is highlighted with wooden architecture and scenic windows – the sauna, restaurant and rooftop bar are a bonus in this Solo Sokos Hotel.

Hotel Haven €€€ Five-star hotel with one of the city's best breakfast views over Old Market Hall and Market Square.

Villa Silo €€€ Stay in the charming apartment at the UNESCO-heritage Suomenlinna island, next door to the Café Silo.

Scandic Grand Central €€€ 1930s railway romance in the Eliel Saarinen–designed building, which also hosts Helsinki Central Station.

Hotel Kämp €€€ Finland's grand hotel dates from 1887 and is located by Esplanade park – order an afternoon tea and watch the world stroll by.

Hotel U14 €€€ Family-owned boutique hotel near the Esplanade and Market Sq with a sauna and fitness centre – slow breakfast is served till 2pm.

Eira, Ullanlinna & Kaivopuisto MAP p55

Bob W Koti Ullanlinna €€ This eco-conscious aparthotel is in a prestigious Ullanlinna building, near the Design Museum. Customer service is swiftly reachable by WhatsApp.

Punavuori & Kamppi MAP p61

Yard Hostel € With dormitories and private rooms of different sizes and a central location in Kamppi, this is a good base for exploration.

Hostel Diana Park € Fabulously located near Bulevardi, this guesthouse-like hostel offers dorm beds and one apartment as well as great communal areas.

Forenom Kamppi € The Finnish aparthotel chain's budget-friendly flats won't have flashy gimmicks but offer an excellent-value base to explore the city.

GLO Hotel Art €€ Located in a castle-like 1908 stone building, with modern and stylish rooms and beautiful original features elsewhere.

Klaus K €€ On a prime spot along the Bulevardi, with a rooftop terrace open in summer and tasty breakfast with Finnish flavours all year round.

Hotel Anna €€ This calm, simple, Central-European–styled hotel is an excellent choice for families and has a sauna for its guests.

Hotel Finn €€ Very centrally located near the Railway Station, rooms have moody wallpaper and breakfast can be enjoyed in one of the many nearby cafes.

Omenahotelli Lönnrotinkatu €€ Furnished with bright red and white, the budget-friendly rooms include a kettle and a microwave.

Radisson Blu Aleksanteri €€ Stylish rooms have an old-world feel, some with dark red wallpaper, others in light colours; great-value find near Bulevardi.

Hotel Indigo €€ Excellent-value ecological hotel in Bulevardi, with rooms designed by Finnish artists and free bikes for the guests to use.

Hotel Mestari €€€ Close to Kamppi shopping centre, the hotel feels calm with dim lighting and dark-panelled rooms; the downstairs restaurant is a fab spot for a nightcap, too.

Hotel Lilla Roberts €€€ Design District's fabulous base with style varying from art nouveau and art deco to mid-century – try the cocktails in the bar.

Lapland Hotels Bulevardi €€€ Lappish vibes in central Helsinki are the draw here as well as over 100 rooms with a sauna.

Sokos Hotel Torni €€€ An iconic landmark and once the tallest building in Helsinki with an art deco feel and a rooftop bar.

Töölö, Kallio & Kaisaniemi   MAP p70

CityBox Helsinki € Budget-friendly and stylish Scandi-design rooms with a laundromat in the building and a great location in Kallio, surrounded by restaurants.

SweetDream Guesthouse € Hostel with female and mixed dorms near Kallio's trendy quarters and with a bookable sauna.

CheapSleep Helsinki € Clean hostel with rooms varying from 26-bed dorms to twin and double rooms in Vallila, next to Kallio.

Sky Hostel Helsinki € All rooms are single or double, with views to the sea or the city – walking distance from Kallio and Hakaniemi market square and its public transport connections.

Hotelli Helka €€ Welcoming staff and relaxed atmosphere mixed with rooms decorated in Finnish design – with a small souvenir nook and homey bar in the lobby.

Scandic Park Helsinki €€ Near Töölö's Sibelius monument and Opera House, the hotel comes with a top-floor sauna and a swimming pool.

Folks Hotel Konepaja €€ Located in Vallila, this trendy hotel is the best base for exploring the bohemian neighbourhoods surrounding it.

Scandic Kallio €€ A solid base near Linnanmäki amusement park with friendly staff and a vast and varied breakfast buffet.

Töölö Towers €€ Simply furnished apartments, from twin studios to penthouses, surrounded by Töölö's sights.

Valo Hotel & Work €€ A bit north of Töölö, Valo has comfortable and compact rooms as well as a swimming pool and a sauna with views.

Original Sokos Hotel Presidentti €€€ A prime location close to Kamppi with rooms designed by the Finnish designer Ivana Helsinki.w

Hotel Katajanokka

Above: Porvoo, Tuomiokirkko in background (p113); Right: Kökar archipelago (p102)

> For places to stay in Turku, the South Coast & Åland Archipelago, see p125

Turku, the South Coast & Åland Archipelago

ENDLESS ISLANDS, HISTORIC TOWNS AND COASTAL ALLURE

Sweeping beaches and merry ferry adventures: seaside living is easy across tiny villages, yet a rugged history of seafaring and battle remains.

The majority of Finland's nearly 180,000 islands spill off the country's southern coast, forming the fragmented borderland that the Swedish and Russian empires fought over for centuries. While only about 550 of these islands have a permanent population – with places like Tammio, off Kotka, counting only one resident – lonely fortresses and watchtowers testify to the strategic importance of this region. Some of the largest naval battles in the Baltic Sea happened south of Finland's mainland, although you wouldn't know it from the relaxed atmosphere of the historic towns dotting the coast. Anchoring the country's southwest is Finland's former capital, Turku, a striking seafaring city with cutting-edge galleries, museums and restaurants. Turku is Finland's gateway to the glorious Åland archipelago, an interesting geopolitical anomaly that has more islands than inhabitants; though technically part of Finland, it is politically autonomous and Swedish-speaking. Åland is the sunniest spot in northern Europe, and its sweeping white-sand beaches and flat, scenic cycling routes attract crowds of holidaymakers during summer. Yet outside the capital, Mariehamn, a sleepy haze hangs over the islands' tiny villages; finding your own remote beach among the 6500 skerries (rocky islets) is surprisingly easy. East of the capital is Porvoo, Finland's second-oldest town and one of the most picturesque, followed by historic towns that developed in the country's early industrial days, manors of noble families established on the edge of the Swedish empire, and traces of WWII still marking the forests that stretch across the border.

HEIKKI WICHMANN/SHUTTERSTOCK ©

THE MAIN AREAS

TURKU
Modern harbour city. **p84**

MARIEHAMN
Island escape. **p94**

HANKO
Historic seaside retreat. **p103**

PORVOO
Quaint medieval town. **p113**

79

Find Your Way

It's possible to see much of the region by public transport, but having your own vehicle is easiest. Trains are useful to reach larger towns, such as Turku and Hanko, otherwise bus routes are more frequent.

Turku, p84
Finland's oldest city is also a contemporary juggernaut. Explore a cityscape delightfully blending old and new, from medieval masonry to experimental art.

Mariehamn, p94
Surrounded by peaceful forests, Mariehamn is Åland's capital and one of northern Europe's sunniest spots. Humming local life mixed with atmospheric seclusion will surely fill your cup.

Hanko, p103
Seaside Nordic life at its prime. Discover war history and empire-style architecture in a charming port town full of friendly folk and fascinating stories.

CAR
Rent a vehicle at Helsinki Airport and explore all the way to Åland with ease. On the islands, car rentals are limited and more expensive. Expect to shell out for parking in centres such as Turku and Mariehamn.

BUS
Buses run east and west from Helsinki, stopping in all towns and villages along the southern coast. The Turku archipelago is well served by buses from Turku, as is all of Fasta Åland from Mariehamn.

FERRY
Jump on a ferry to get from Turku to Åland, or to Sweden – joining the Finnish holidayers indulging in a bit of karaoke on board. Island-hopping routes around Åland connect remote shores with the mainland.

Porvoo, p113
Porvoo's Old Town is a must-see – and only 52km from Helsinki. Wine, dine and wander around historic wooden houses and cobblestone streets.

Plan Your Time

Leave time to linger along the southern seaside. Discover the deserted beaches and harbours around fortresses and other sights. Chock-full artisan and antique shops also demand unhurried exploration.

Strömfors Iron Works (p119)

If You Only Do One Thing

● Head straight for **Turku** (p84) to see its famed cathedral, originally built in the late 13th century and still standing as one of Finland's most important religious landmarks; then peruse downtown's antique shops and art galleries. For lunch, slurp soup at the **Kauppahalli** (p87), then stroll (or e-scooter) the 3km harbour stretch to Turku's main highlight, its **Turun Linna** (p85).

● Head back, cross the river with the **Föri** (p84), and slip into the **Aboa Vetus & Ars Nova** (p84) museum for a couple of hours of ruin-spotting.

● Watch the sun go down with craft beers and Finnish fare on a riverside terrace (p90) – and if you've still got energy, carry on for more drinks at a live-music pub or karaoke bar (p88).

Seasonal Highlights

Summer is the south's favourite season, when festivals and harbour hoopla abound. From October to April, main attractions – beaches, castles – close, but can still be strolled around in alfresco solitude.

MARCH

Hot bebop and smoking sax hits Turku at several venues during its annual **jazz festival**.

JUNE

Turku's lively **Medieval Market** features historic reenactments and frilly costumes against the backdrops of the Cathedral and Old Square.

JULY

Join in the **Hanko Regatta**'s carnival atmosphere – and discover Finnish metal at the thousands-strong rock fest, **Ruisrock**, in Turku.

Three Days to Travel Around

● Take a stroll around Porvoo's **old town** (p113) to admire the historic architecture that lines the cobbled streets branching out from the **Tuomiokirkko** (p113). Stock up on handmade sweets for a road trip to the little-visited southeastern part of the country.

● Follow the coastline to reach picturesque Loviisa and break your journey with stops at the fascinating **Strömfors Ironworks** (p119), a 19th-century industrial village turned into a space hosting artisan workshops and crafts stores.

● Talking about craft – pick up some organic beer at **Malmgård Manor** (p118) before continuing onward to **Kotka** (p119), where you can learn about the Baltic Sea's largest naval battle at the **Merikeskus Vellamo** (p119) before setting out to explore the remote archipelago stretching toward the Russian border.

If You Have More Time

● How low can you go? From the capital, head west to **Hanko** (p103) to enjoy seaside relaxation – a spa afternoon or a quick wade at the town's sandy beaches. Enjoy a cosy pub evening rubbing shoulders with locals, and don't miss the wartime relics at **Rintama Museo** (p107).

● Make a stop in the artisan village of **Fiskars** (p112) before continuing to Turku's harbour to catch the six-hour ferry to **Mariehamn** (p94). Escape into lush forests and fruit orchards, discovering historic ruins and hidden harbours, between impeccable surf 'n' turf meals.

● Should nature call for getting even further off the grid, skip off to Åland's southernmost islands, such as **Föglö** (p102) and **Kökar** (p102), where untouched crags and countryside fulfil playful pirate fantasies.

AUGUST
East of Porvoo, the week-long **Hamina Tattoo** sees marching bands perform in a military music festival every even-numbered year.

SEPTEMBER
Feast on Åland's bounty during the **Skördefesten** (**Harvest Festival**) with open farms and special restaurant menus.

NOVEMBER
Gorgeous Åland restaurants, such as **Smakbyn**, hold Christmas buffets from late November, with fish delicacies, meatballs and more.

DECEMBER
Traditional Christmas markets light up the holidays. Porvoo's **Town Hall Square** is a Finnish favourite.

Turku

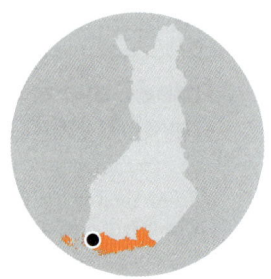

MEDIEVAL ARCHITECTURE | GATEWAY TO THE ARCHIPELAGO | CULTURE HUB

Turku (Åbo in Swedish) is Finland's second city – or first, by some accounts, as it was the capital until 1812. The majestic Turun Linna (Turku Castle) and the ancient Gothic wonder Turun Tuomiokirkko (Turku Cathedral) – both dating from the 13th century, when the city was founded – are testaments to the city's storied past. Contemporary Turku is even more enticing, challenging Helsinki's cultural preeminence with cutting-edge art galleries, summer music festivals, and innovative restaurants. The University of Turku, the first in the country, traces its roots back to 1640, when it was established by the Swedish king as the Royal Academy of Turku, and it still draws young minds to the city. University students keep cafes and clubs buzzing, while designer boutiques and secondhand shops offer limitless scope for browsing beauty and buried treasure. Through the age-old network of atmospheric streets and squares, the Aurajoki (Aura River) meanders picturesquely out to sea. For nature lovers, Turku is the gateway to the glorious Turku archipelago.

GETTING AROUND

Downtown Turku is easily explored on foot. Bikes and ride-sharing scooters are also popular in the summer. Airport service is limited; usually it's cheaper to reach Turku from Helsinki by car or train, or Stockholm by ferry. Multiple ferries depart daily from the city's harbour to Åland, taking approximately six hours to reach Mariehamn.

Masterpieces Old & New
Avant-garde art meets archeology

The riverside **Aboa Vetus & Ars Nova** (Old Turku) museum (*avan.fi; adult/child €16/11*) draws visitors underground to Turku's medieval streets with imposing stone ruins. Some 37,000 artefacts, from ceramics to buried gold, have been unearthed from the site below (digs still continue) and are now exhibited between 14th- and 15th-century cellars, church foundations, and building walls buried following the great fire of 1827. Stop by the Old Turku model to get an idea of what this city quarter may have looked like before its destruction. Above ground level find the contemporary art exhibition of the Aboa Vetus Ars Nova Foundation, covering a century of experimental Finnish work and including regular temporary shows.

☑ TOP TIP

You'll get a kick out of hopping on the **Föri** – all day, the free mini-ferry conveniently shuttles walkers and bikers across the Aura in two minutes flat. Chugging since 1904, the orange commuter is Finland's oldest daily transport. Find it a few blocks southwest of the Martinsilta.

HIGHLIGHTS
1 Aboa Vetus & Ars Nova
2 Luostarinmäen Käsityöläismuseo
3 Turku Cathedral
4 Turun Linna

SIGHTS
5 B-Galleria
6 Dynamo
7 Posankka
8 Qwensel House & Pharmacy Museum
9 Sibelius Museum

ACTIVITIES, COURSES & TOURS
10 MS Aurella
11 MS Rudolfina

SLEEPING
12 Bridgettine Sisters' Guesthouse
13 Hotel Kakola
14 Laivahostel Borea
15 Park Hotel

EATING
16 Blanko
17 Kakolanruusu
18 Kauppahalli
19 Smör
20 Tiirikkala

DRINKING & NIGHTLIFE
21 Bar Ö
22 Bar4
23 CaféArt
24 Cosmic Comic Café
25 Kakola Brewing Company
26 Panimoravintola Koulu
27 Surf Shack
28 Teerenpeli
29 Tintå
30 Uusi Apteekki
31 Walo

TRANSPORT
32 Föri Ferry

Feudal Fortress

Finland's largest castle

Founded in 1280 as a Swedish military outpost at the mouth of the Aurajoki, the gargantuan **Turun Linna** (*turku.fi/en/turku-castle; adult/child €14/6*) is easily Finland's biggest castle. It's free for visitors to roam the annexes of its stony outdoor courtyard, but admission to the museum inside is worthwhile too. The labyrinthine layout features dungeons, banquet halls and the castle's impressive Old Bailey, exhibiting

ONCE UPON A CAPITAL

Åbo (Turku's original Swedish name), once Sweden's second-largest town, comes from a settlement *(bo)* on a river *(å)*. When the Russians took over, the city, still deeply connected to Sweden, lost its capital status to Helsinki and became a commerce hub. The name Turku is an archaic Russian word for 'marketplace'.

Today, the Aurajoki, lined with terrace restaurants and cultural sights, is Turku's hub for local life. These riverbanks, though, have been inhabited over millennia.

Archaeological finds date back to the Stone Age, but Turku was founded with a Catholic settlement in 1229. In the 14th century, a new church and the Turku Castle saw the city consecrated as an administrative and spiritual base.

objects and artefacts once belonging to the ruling elite. The structure grew and was embellished with many Renaissance touches after King Gustav Vasa took over the throne in 1523. Swedish count Per Brahe ruled Finland from the castle in the 17th century, while Sweden's deposed King Eric XIV was imprisoned in its round tower in the late 16th century. The castle was seriously damaged by the Soviet bombing campaign in 1941 and brought back to its former glory only after the war. Today, most Finns recognise the castle's distinctive architecture as the logo for Turun Sinappi (Turku Mustard).

Fixture of Faith

Catch an organ concert in Finland's most important religious building

Consecrated in 1300, **Turku Cathedral** was rebuilt many times after damaging fires, but still looks majestic. Besides the impressive Gothic interior and the 1836 altarpiece depicting the *Transfiguration of Jesus* created by Swedish artist Fredric Westin, the cathedral houses a small museum *(adult/child €2/1)* filled with religious artefacts and ritualistic tools dating back to the 15th and 16th century. Tune into Finland's YLE1 Radio

EATING IN TURKU: OUR PICKS

Smör: Organic, locally sourced dishes lit by flickering candles in a vaulted cellar. *5-11pm Wed & Thu, to midnight Fri; 4pm-midnight Sat* €€€

Tiirikkala: Cool brunch restaurant and cocktail bar; jazz and blues live-music programme. *9.30am-9pm Tue-Thu, to 11pm Fri & Sat, 11am-4pm Sun* €€

Blanko: Hip venue with great lunch specials and the best Sunday brunch in town. *11am-11pm Mon-Thu, to 3am Fri, noon-3am Sat, 1-9pm Sun* €€

Kakolanruusu: Seasonal modern fare and open-fire cooking. *4-11pm Tue-Thu, noon-2.30pm & 4pm-midnight Fri, 1pm-midnight Sat* €€€

Kauppahalli

at noon to hear the church's distinctive hourly bell – it's a patriotic reminder of the Continuation War, when Finns prayed together for victory. If you are in Finland in the summer, try to catch one of the Turku International Organ Concerts – every Tuesday at 8pm in June, July and August the Turku Cathedral hosts free-access organ concerts performed by musicians from different corners of the globe.

Finnish Food Tour

Eat your heart out

Turku's fabulous **Kauppahalli** (*Market Hall; kauppahalli.fi*) is easily its cosiest, most atmospheric lunch spot. The historic covered market, built in 1896, is where locals of all ages gather for bites and coffee-break chatter across rich wood counters and tables. Vendors sell local delicacies, including artisan cheeses, meats, seafood and baked goods, but there's also multicultural cuisine and a vegan kitchen too. Operating since 1887, the **Kalaliike S Wallin** fish counter serves the perfect hearty salmon soup – with cream or without. Meanwhile, cafes such as **Sininen Juna Aschan**, set in an old railway carriage, and **Piece of Cake** dole out sky-high desserts and seriously good espresso. Closed Sunday.

HEADBANGING AT RUISROCK

Finland's summer rock festival, Ruisrock, is a 100,000-person-strong, once-in-a-lifetime affair. Gigantic stages and pyrotechnics galore take over Turku's Ruissalo Island for a single weekend every year. Essentially Finland's Woodstock, it's the oldest Finnish rock festival and the second oldest in Europe, held since 1970.

Many a rock god has gone head-to-head with the Ruisrock masses, including Bowie, Bob Dylan, Ozzy Osbourne, Oasis and The Clash. What's fascinating is also taking in Finland's famous metal bands on home turf – and especially, their fandom crowd-surfing and moshing up a sweat.

Don't expect a sea of black band T-shirts, though. The festival gear here is colourful and vibrant, plus meadows and beach stages provide uplifting scenery. Swimming, camping and activities such as yoga are all part of rocking out here.

 DRINKING IN TURKU: BEST CRAFT BEER

Kakola Brewing Company: Craft beers, served atop Kakolanmäki, ideal for long summer nights. *4-10pm Wed & Thu, to 11pm Fri, noon-6pm Sat*

Cosmic Comic Café: Manga-lovers' dream pub. Comic paper walls, huge collection and craft beer. *4-10pm Tue, to midnight Wed & Thu, to 2am Fri & Sat*

Panimoravintola Koulu: Former school turned elegant brewpub. *11am-midnight Mon-Thu, to 2am Fri, noon-2am Sat, noon-midnight Sun*

Teerenpeli: The welcoming bar of the Teerenpeli Distillery warms you up with Finnish whisky or cools you down with a local craft beer. *3-11pm*

Art Chapel
Inside the light-flooded contemporary wood architecture

Across the river on Hirvensalo island is the **Taidekappeli** (*St Henry's Ecumenical Art Chapel; taidekappeli.fi; adult €5*), a piece of award-winning architecture designed by Matti Sanaksenaho and built in 2005. Shaped like a fish and surrounded by pine trees, the chapel covers a medieval wooden granary named after Finland's first bishop. Its timber interior looks more like a Burning Man installation than a worship place, curving into a hypnotic Reuleaux triangle framing the altar in light. From outside, gaze at the strange, spectacular copper-clad structure bathed in sun on its rocky perch. Getting there with public transport takes a little over half hour – take bus 50, 51 or 54 from Market Sq.

GRAND COVERED MARKETS
Turku's market hall is Finland's second oldest, built in 1896, three years after **Helsinki's Vanha Kauppahalli** (p51). Both were designed by architect Gustaf Nyström.

Pharmaceutical Heritage
Step into a 170-year-old apothecary

Among the prominent figures that lived in **Qwensel House**, first designed for the city's aristocracy by Finland's Governor Count Per Brahe, is Josef Gustav Pipping, Finland's first professor of surgery at the University of Turku. In a historical coincidence, the residence has kept its affiliation to medicine long after Pipping's passing. Part of the building is a home-museum showcasing the lifestyle of the capital's elite, while three rooms now host the **Pharmacy Museum** (*turku.fi/en/pharmacymuseum; adult/child €7/5*) exhibiting the preserved interiors of an Oulu pharmacy dating back to 1850, acquired by the Turku Association of Pharmacists.

One Big Puck
A puzzling piece of postmodern public art

Confusion is justified when standing under Alvar Gullichsen's **Posankka**, the bright pink, 4m-tall sculpture standing steps away from the University of Turku campus. If you find yourself wondering whether this piece of fibreglass public art is a pig or a duck, well, it's both. The name blends the Finnish words for pig *(possu)* and duck *(ankka)* – in short, a Puck. Gullichsen created the sculpture as an ironic critique of genetic technology and while it initially divided the city, it has now become one of Turku's loved icons.

Cool Cruises
Along the Aura and onto the archipelago

Archipelago and river cruises are popular in the summer, with most boats departing from the quay at Martinsilta. Cruises, while tending to be a little touristy, are an effortless way to see the city and the islands from water level. **M/S Rudolfina** (*rudolfina.fi; from €37*) provides lunch and dinner harbour cruises overlooking Turku Castle, Pikisaar Island and Ruissalo

KILLER KARAOKE

A little-known fact about Finland? Karaoke is a favourite pastime. A few mics, a machine and a screen are typical staples of pub culture. Don't be surprised if you witness a typically shy Finn transform into a full-blown rock star the moment the mic is in hand. Finns, a normally reserved folk, perform with a stage presence that would impress reality show judges – and pub-goers young and old alike adore it. Cheering for all and tipping the karaoke host is good etiquette. Many pubs around the city organise weekly karaoke nights, but **Karaoke CocoLoco** and **Karaokebar Pelimies** are two of Turku's best bars for all-night croon sessions.

Taidekappeli

Island, while evening cruises show off Naantali Harbour and the Kultaranta (president's summer residence). If you are short on time, the **M/S Aurella** (*river-cruises.fi; from €9*) takes you along the Aura River with its 1½-hour-long guided tours from the Pharmacy Museum to the Ruissalo Shipyard.

Sweet Prison Dreams

Sleep, eat or drink in the former Kakola detention centre

Given it's location on top of the second tallest hill in Turku, the former Kakola prison functioned as an effective reminder for all Turku residents of what committing a crime would entail. At its peak in the 1930s, Kakola detained over 1300 people. The prison was moved to a new location in 2007, and in 2020 it reopened as a one-of-a-kind heritage **hotel** (p125), which has maintained many of the building's original features. The latest addition is the **Kakola Brewing Company** (p87), opened in 2022 – visit the taproom for a drink in a bar behind bars. A recently built, free funicular runs from Linnankatu 55b up to Kakolanmäki Hill.

Crafts From the Past

Artisanship over the ages

Handiwork is a centuries-old tradition in Turku. Don't miss rambling around **Luostarinmäen Käsityöläismuseo** (*turku.fi/luostarinmaki; adult/child €10/4*), a national treasure weaving together the past and present of local craftwork since 1940. This

BEST ANTIQUE SHOPS IN TURKU

The centre of Turku is dotted with many antique stores, selling preloved furniture and homeware from all eras.

Osto- ja Myyntiliike KJ Simolin: Treasure shop with vases and ceramic tchotchkes – fight through the crowded doorway.

Osto- ja Myyntiliike Kalustepalvelu: Squeeze between tiny aisles piled with grand wooden furniture and statement lamps.

Antiikkiliike Wanha Elias: All shapes and sizes of miscellaneous bric-a-brac collected from estates.

Art+Design: Turku's most colourful antiques shop. Deals in 20th-century antiques, clothing and accessories.

🍸 NIGHTLIFE IN TURKU: OUR PICKS

Surf Shack: Laid-back SoCal vibes meet Scandinavian finesse - DJs, cocktails and vegan soft serve. *4pm-midnight, to 2am Fri & Sat*

Bar Ö: Bar with cosy living-room vibes, DJs and live bands. *4pm-2am Mon-Thu, to 4.30am Fri & Sat*

Dynamo: Local DJs vie with national bands at this central venue. Great outdoor terrace. *10pm-5am Thu-Sat*

Bar4: Popular, chic cocktail bar that proudly mixes unique drinks at a fair price. *6pm-2am Mon-Wed, from 4pm Thu, 4pm-3am Fri, 4pm-4am Sat, 10pm-2am Sun*

Sibelius Museum

MEDIEVAL MARKET

Turku's history isn't found in museums alone. Every year at the end of June the city pays homage to its medieval roots by hosting its much-awaited **Medieval Market**, a family-friendly event running for four days in Vanha Suurtori, the old market square found steps away from the cathedral. Dozens of craft stalls and food trucks surrounded by participants in medieval costumes populate Porthaninpuisto Park and its surroundings, with live theatrical performances inspired by ancient musical and scientific traditions drawing thousands of visitors to the green corner of the city. Check out the programme at *keskiajanturku.fi*.

open-air handicrafts museum comprises stocky 19th-century wooden workshops and houses, situated along tiny lanes and grassy yards. In the workshops, there are 30 artisans (among them a silversmith, a watchmaker, a baker, a potter, a shoemaker and a printer) plying their trades in period costume. All the buildings are, surprisingly, in their original locations – spared by the Great Fire of 1827, which destroyed much of Turku.

Artist-run Art Space

Get into the local creative scene at B-Galleria

The artist-run, nonprofit **B-Galleria** (*bgalleria.net*) showcases young up-and-coming international artists working with a variety of mediums, from painting to photography and performance art events. Remove your shoes at the door and get up close to experimental installations or support the network of artists by purchasing some of the cards, pins and illustrations on display.

Concrete House of Classical Music

Jean Sibelius's legacy in Finland's oldest music museum

A fine piece of Brutalist architecture from the 1960s houses Finland's first music museum, dedicated to national composer Jean Sibelius. Exhibited in the concrete frame of the **Sibelius Museum** (*sibeliusmuseum.fi; adult/child €7/5*) are some of the 2000-plus instruments illustrating the history of Finnish classical music.

 DRINKING IN TURKU: COFFEE, WINE OR COCKTAILS

CaféArt: Riverside cafe, serving a great selection of homemade cakes in a historic building. *10am-7pm Mon-Fri, to 6pm Sat, 11am-5pm Sun*

Tintå: Riverside wine bar with a cosy exposed-brick interior and terrace. *11am-midnight Mon-Fri, noon-midnight Sat, noon-9pm Sun*

Uusi Apteekki: Rest your pint on dispensing drawers turned tables in a former pharmacy. *2pm-midnight, to 2am Fri & Sat*

Walo: Turku's first rooftop bar overlooks the city from its privileged position near Market Sq. *noon-midnight Sun-Tue, to 2am Wed & Thu, to 3am Fri & Sat*

Beyond Turku

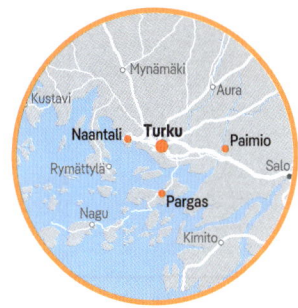

Dance with Moomins, relax in saunas or savour forest solitude just a ferry ride away from Turku.

Turku is a stepping stone to sea-salt retreats and wild islands elsewhere along the coast, to Åland, Sweden and beyond. For example, an awesome 20,000 islands and skerries (rocky islets) make up the Turku Archipelago, one of Finland's most spectacular natural attractions – just a hop, a skip and a ferry ride or two away. These shores offer no big-ticket sights, just quiet settlements, abundant birdlife and ever-changing views of sea and land.

The most effortless summer day-trip from Turku is the charming spa town Naantali (Swedish: Nådendal), only 15km east. From June to August, Moominworld (Muumimaailma) keeps Naantali very busy. Out of season, it's a misty ghost town – although locals work hard behind the scenes running Finland's third-busiest port.

Places
Naantali p91
Pargas p92
Paimio p93

Naantali

TIME FROM TURKU: 45MIN

Meet the Moomins

Beloved throughout Finland and beyond, the Moomins are a famous eccentric family of nature-loving, white-snouted, hippo-like trolls. Grab squishy hugs from them at **Muumimaailma** (*Moominworld; muumimaailma.fi; from €39*). The no-rides amusement park, a 15km-drive from Turku, delights kids with hands-on activities across interactive playrooms.

Bump into costumed characters rambling through the Moominhouse and the Groke's Cave, and stir up an invention in Snork's Workshop. Other Muumimaailma highlights include a swimming beach and Emma's Theatre.

The two-day ticket is also good for **Väski Adventure Island**. At Väski, older adventure-seekers will get their thrills on an island that features rock climbing, gold panning, zip lining and rope obstacle courses. Free shuttle boats depart every 30 minutes from Naantali near the bridge to Muumimaailma.

A dandy old town

Naantali's photogenic Old Town, easily reached by bus or a 15km drive from Turku, is a picturesque mix of harbour views and cobblestone streets. Centuries-old wooden houses

GETTING AROUND

SS *Ukkopekka* sails between Turku and Naantali in summer, arriving at the passenger quay on the south side of the harbour. Frequent, free public ferries connect the Turku Archipelago. Meanwhile, the MS *Eivor* shuttles to the archipelago's more obscure islands. In summer the mini-train Minijuna Aikataulu does a handy circuit between Naantali Spa and the harbour.

THE STORY BEHIND THE MOOMINS STORY

Characters Moominpappa, Moominmamma and their timid child Moomintroll are based closely on creator Tove Jansson's bohemian upbringing with her artist parents. Others include the eternal wanderer Snufkin; the eerie Hattifatteners, who grow from seeds and are drawn to electrical storms; and the icy Groke, who leaves a frozen trail wherever she drifts.

Jansson, once a satirist lampooning Hitler and Stalin, first published the wholesome Moomin drawings in her political cartoons. She wrote the first of her nine children's books, *The Moomins and the Great Flood*, during WWII, followed by several cartoon books. Her comic strips debuted in the *London Evening News* in 1954, before being syndicated worldwide.

Adaptations include a popular Japanese cartoon series, film and album.

are now home to handicraft shops, art galleries, antiques shops and cafes. At Naantali's **museum** (*adult €3*), trace the town's history from its convent roots. Housed in three wooden Old Town buildings dating from the 18th century, artefacts and exhibits cast light on disappearing trades such as needle making and goldsmithing.

Ancient gems unearthed

Discover Naantali's origins as a monastic town with a visit to **Naantalin Kirkko** (Naantali Convent Church). Medieval Naantali, a 20-minute drive from Turku by car or 30 minutes by bus, grew up around the Catholic Convent of the Order of St Birgitta, which was dissolved after the 1527 Reformation. Towering above the harbour, the massive 1462 church is all that remains. Archaeological digs have unearthed some 2000 pieces of jewellery, coins and relics now in the Naantali Museum. At 8pm on summer evenings, hear a trumpeter play vespers (evensong) from the belfry. There are also regular organ concerts.

Pargas

TIME FROM TURKU: **35MIN**

Nature-lovers' pilgrimage

A popular way to experience the Turku archipelago is to cycle (or drive) the **Archipelago Trail**, a 230km circular route that starts and ends in Turku. Twelve bridges and nine ferries connect tiny, diverse islands, each with their own laid-back flair. From mid-May to August, the entire route can be completed from Turku. The further you travel, the more forward planning is required, as ferries run less frequently between the outer islands. Completing the whole loop on a bike can take between three days and a week, depending on how often you choose to stop. The route is typically tackled clockwise – from Turku go in the direction of Parainen (Pargas in Swedish), the largest municipality in the archipelago, and Nauvo (Nagu in Swedish), then continue past rural Korpo where you'll start returning toward the mainland. In case you are not ready to commit to the full itinerary, you can also opt for the **Small Archipelago Trail**, a shorter route running for 120km. Links to updated GPX tracks can be downloaded via v*isitparainen.fi*, while ferry timetables are available at *finferries.fi*.

EATING IN NAANTALI: OUR PICKS

Peculiar Café: Stop by for a slice of pie in this cute house adorned with Moomins memorabilia. *10am-7pm* €

Tavastin Kilta: Naantali's best restaurant has a sun-drenched terrace and superb seafood. *noon-10pm* €€

Merisali: In a restored spa pavilion, savour buffets, a pier-side terrace and live music. *4-10pm Wed & Thu, to 2am Fri, noon-2am Sat, noon-5pm Sun* €€

Trappi: Old-school restaurant serving Finnish comfort food and pizza. *11am-6pm Mon & Tue, to 10pm Wed & Thu, to 11pm Fri, noon-11pm Sat, noon-6pm Sun* €€

Paimio

TIME FROM TURKU: **30MIN**

Modernist wellbeing

Alvar and Aino Aalto first presented the project for the **Paimio Sanatorium** (*paimiosanatorium.com*) in the late 1920s after winning a competition for the design of a tuberculosis hospital in the woods of southwestern Finland. Considered a monument of early modernist architecture, the sanatorium was developed as a space that would contribute to the healing process of the patients, through exposure to sunlight, airy open spaces and a direct connection to the surrounding nature. The Aaltos designed not just the buildings, but every detail of the interior including the famous 'Paimio' armchairs still produced and sold by Artek. The Paimio Sanatorium was converted into a general hospital in the 1960s and ceased operations in 2014. Guided group tours of the structure are held daily (excluding Monday, from €20) between May and September.

Paimio Sanatorium

ISLAND-HOPPING

The five largest inhabited islands of the Turku Archipelago make up the municipality of Pargas and, like most of the southern coast, are primarily Swedish-speaking.

Parainen (Swedish: Pargas) The de facto 'capital' of the archipelago. A worthwhile quick stop for its interesting sights.

Nauvo (Swedish: Nagu) Shoreside harbour huts sell designer sailor-wear and smoked salmon; walking trails reveal birdlife.

Korppoo (Swedish: Korpo) The last of the 'inner islands'. Pristine forests, hidden beaches and welcoming island culture.

Houtskari (Swedish: Houtskär) Short on sights, yet delightfully tranquil. Islanders are hardy fishers, sailors and nature-lovers.

Iniö A tiny population and mighty sea landscapes. Of 1000 islets and skerries, only 10 are liveable. Its stone church is sweetly rewarding.

Mariehamn

MARITIME HISTORY | ÅLAND'S POLITICAL HEART | RELAXED SUMMER TOWN

GETTING AROUND

As soon as you step out of the ferry you'll notice the sign welcoming you to autonomous and demilitarised Åland. It will take you 15 to 20 minutes to walk from the harbour to the city centre – it's a pleasant stroll through the tree-lined Storagatan running next to Sankt Göran's Kyrka. Most services are found in the area between Ålandsvägen and Torggatan. Mariehamn is great to cycle around as well, you can rent a bike from €14 a day at Ro No Rent, right at the harbour.

☑ TOP TIP

Mariehamn contains the bulk of Åland's lodgings. Business and tourist hotels, as well as campgrounds and guesthouses, cover a wide range of prices and styles. Booking ahead is recommended, especially for weekends.

The core of Åland is made up of a dozen or so larger islands connected by bridges. Known as Fasta Åland (Ahvenanmaa in Finnish), the region's main island comprises 70% of the archipelago's land area – including its only town, Mariehamn. Named by Alexander II after Empress Maria, Mariehamn is the political core of this demilitarised Swedish-speaking autonomous region within Finland established in 1920. Home of the Åland Parliament, Mariehamn is the busiest spot in Åland – though still very laid-back. The harbour – Mariehamn's *hamn* – links the city to Turku, Stockholm and Tallinn, and from there, a short walk through its broad Storagatan esplanade lined with linden trees – whose leaves are displayed on the city's coat of arms – leads to the city's heart. The pedestrian-friendly centre plays host to a handful of shops, pubs and restaurants, while its historic quays and marinas pay tribute to the town's long-standing relationship with the sea, still the main driver of the local economy.

Maritime Heritage
History of life above water

At the state-of-the-art **Sjöfartsmuseum** (*Åland Maritime Museum; sjofartsmuseum.ax; adult/child €16.50/11.50*), peruse preserved boats exploring Åland's marine heritage. Ships in bottles, sea chests and accoutrements abound – as well as the centrepiece, a reproduced ship complete with mast, saloon, galley and cabins. Anchored outside is another star specimen, the **Museumship Pommern**. The beautifully preserved four-masted merchant barque was built in 1903 in Glasgow.

Autonomy in Context
Åland throughout the ages

How was a Finnish, Swedish-speaking, autonomous, demilitarised, neutral region born? To gain a better understanding

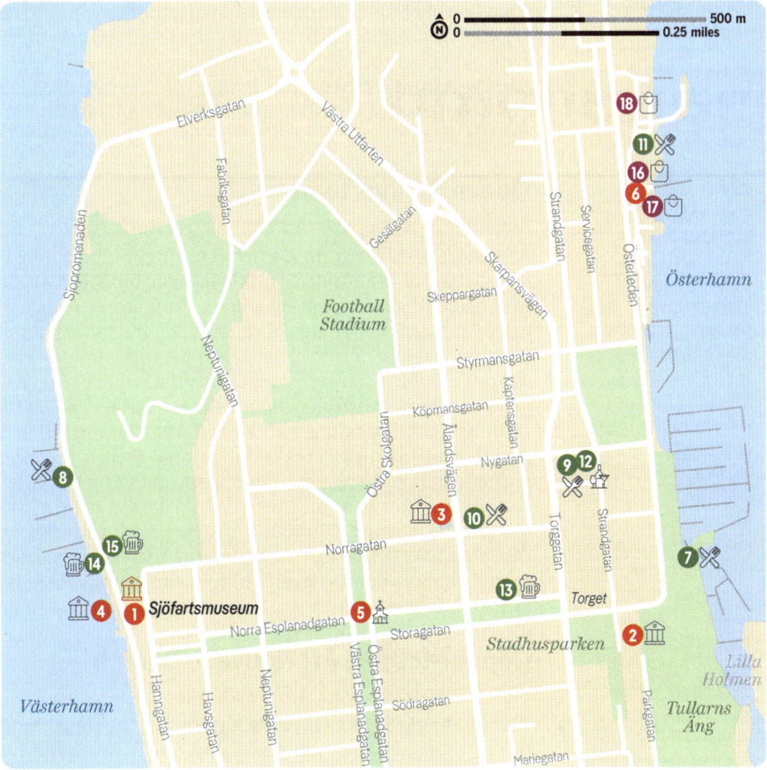

TOP SIGHTS
1 Sjöfartsmuseum

SIGHTS
2 Ålands Kulturhistoriska & Konstmuseum
3 Mariehamnsmuseet
4 Museumship Pommern
5 Sankt Göran's Kyrka
6 Sjökvarteret

EATING
7 Ångbåts Bryggan
8 ÅSS Paviljongen

9 Indigo
10 Kvarter 5
11 Pub Niska

DRINKING & NIGHTLIFE
12 Dino's Bar & Grill
13 Park Ålandia Pub
14 Pub Albin
15 Pub Bastun

SHOPPING
16 Guldviva
17 Salt
18 Zyged Art

DRINKING IN MARIEHAMN: BEST PUBS

Pub Albin: Steps away from the marina north of the Pommern ship, this cosy pub serves good pizzas and a wide selection of beers. *11am-9pm*

Park Ålandia Pub: Mariehamn's favourite living-room bar. Local Stallhagen brews on tap. *2pm-midnight Sun-Tue, to 2am Wed-Sat*

Pub Bastun: Cult-status live-music venue in a former sauna. Hosting Nordic underground bands since the 1970s. *8pm-2am Tue-Sat*

Dino's Bar & Grill: Busy local favourite, running karaoke and live-music nights regularly. *10.30am-midnight Mon-Thu, to 4am Fri, noon-4am Sat, noon-midnight Sun*

MARIEHAMN'S FESTIVALS

Midsommar: Maypoles pop up all over the archipelago during Midsummer, one of the most celebrated events in Åland (and all of the Nordics). In Mariehamn locals gather in Engelska Parken to pull up the temporary monument.

Åland Sea Jazz: Each year in mid-August musicians from all over the Nordic countries play in an intimate atmosphere in Mariehamn. *alandseajazz.fi*

Rockoff: Swedish and Finnish rock bands join forces in July at Åland's biggest music festival. *rockoff.nu*

Vera Film Festival: Screening films from both Åland and international filmmakers, the Vera Film Festival celebrates Nordic cinematography in March. *verafilmfestival.ax*

of the roots of this geopolitical oddity, pay a visit to the **Ålands Kulturhistoriska & Konstmuseum** (*kulturhistoriska.ax, adult €8*), which traces the evolution of the archipelago over millennia through a permanent exhibition that will take you from the first human settlements during the Stone Age to the Middle Ages and its Christian influence to the era of self-government in the 20th century. In the same building you'll also find the **Åland Art Museum**, exhibiting the work of changing Ålandic artists, with a special focus on contemporary productions.

Quaint Sjökvarteret
Stroll through Mariehamn's charming historic quay

At a short distance from Mariehamn's light blue public library, find the atmospheric maritime quarter **Sjökvarteret**, lined with traditional schooners, craft stores and boats under construction. Many of the wooden huts found along the quay have been converted into artisans' studios – take a stroll in Sjökvarteret to find **Guldviva**, which specialises in brooches, cufflinks and necklaces influenced by the islands' flora and fauna, and **Zyged Art**, the workshop of Swedish silversmith Per-Åke Johansson. **Salt** is an excellent craft shop displaying local work, including textiles, ceramics, silverware and jewellery. The red-brown timber shed also stocks Finnish delicacies, such as sea-buckthorn jam. At the pier's end is the tiny reconstructed seafarers' chapel and, if you get hungry, you can take a break at **Pub Niska**.

Copper-topped Art Nouveau Church
Visit Mariehamn's Sankt Göran's Kyrka

The red-brick **Sankt Göran's Kyrka** may be much more recent than the other churches that dot Fasta Åland but it's nonetheless worth a visit. Local architect Lars Sonck designed Mariehamn's main church in 1927, taking inspiration from the art nouveau style in vogue at the time. Bruno Tuukkanen was responsible for the interior's decorations, from the beautiful stained-glass windows to the mosaic altarpiece.

EATING IN MARIEHAMN: OUR PICKS

Kvarter 5: Nordic cuisine with a sophisticated twist. Local ingredients, such as reindeer; everything made from scratch. *2-10pm Mon-Sat* €€€

Indigo: Contemporary menu in historic building with courtyard. Specials include Åland beef. *11am-midnight, to 4am Fri, noon-4am Sun* €€

ÅSS Paviljongen: Marina views and lovely local seafare – cod, perch, smoked shrimp and more. *11am-4pm & 5-10pm Mon-Fri, noon-10pm Sat & Sun* €€€

Ångbåts Bryggan: Semi-swanky harbourside place where the grill gets a workout. Live music and gorgeous sea views. *5-11pm* €€€

Sjökvarteret

Mini Mariehamn
Åland's capital in 1920

For a bird's-eye view on Marienhamn's evolution over the past century visit **Mariehamnsmuseet** (*mariehamnsmuseet.hembygd.fi*), the local history museum containing a miniature model of Mariehamn as it appeared in 1920, the year in which the Autonomy Act of Åland was signed. Built by a group of local pensioners in the late 1980s, the scale model displayed in protective glass cases showcases loyal representations of wooden houses, farms, parks and architectural elements as they looked when Åland was officially recognised as an autonomous region. Entrance is free, but the museum is only open between mid-June and mid-August.

ÅLANDIC TREAT

In celebration of Åland's 100-year anniversary in 2022, residents voted Ålandspannkaka (Åland pancake) the islands' dish of the century. Oven-baked, yet served either hot or cold, this isn't a pancake as you might imagine. It's a spongy treat, served like a pie slice, made with semolina and a hint of cardamom. Standard toppings include stewed prunes or raspberry jam and whipped cream (called *snömos* or 'snow mash' in Åland). It's available either as a dessert or as a sweet afternoon snack at most Åland cafes and restaurants. On Åland's Autonomy Day (9 June), pancakes are also festively served in Mariehamn's main square.

Beyond Mariehamn

While Fasta Åland is home to 90% of Åland's population, the archipelago includes over 6500 islands scattered between Finland and Sweden.

Places
Sund p98
Jomala p100
Finström p100
Kumlinge p101
Lappo p102

The vast majority of Åland's islands are tiny, uninhabited slices of land that could hardly be more remote – only about 60 of them host permanent residents, leaving the rest untouched and unexplored. Historical and cultural sights – from ruins marking the Russian Empire's final frontier to medieval churches built by early Christian settlers – are mostly found in easily cyclable Fasta Åland. However, if you are craving an outdoor adventure beyond the main island, you can hop on a ferry and reach one of the many smaller islands dotting the seas. The thousands of islets in the outer archipelago fall into two geographic groups, served by two different ferry lines. The northern archipelago includes Kumlinge, Lappo, Brändö, and Jurmo, while the southern archipelago includes Föglö, Sottunga, and Kökar.

GETTING AROUND

The best way to explore beyond Mariehamn is by car. Given the low availability of vehicles, the prices tend to be higher than on the mainland. Bike rentals are available at Ro No Rent in Mariehamn (from €14/day) and at Godby's Idrottscenter (from €10/day). There is a good network of cycling paths in Åland and car traffic is generally not overwhelming. Brändö, Torsholma, Åva and Jurmo are connected by bridges and free ferries to Fasta Åland.

Sund
TIME FROM MARIEHAMN: **30MINS**

The archipelago's stronghold

Founded in the late 14th century, **Kastelholm Slott** (*museum.ax; adult/child €8/5*) is Åland's only medieval castle, still standing 2km south of Sund's stone church, another fascinating remnant of the archipelago's distant past. On a picturesque hill surrounded by water, Kastelholm was converted from defensive structure to opulent fishing lodge by Swedish King Gustav Vasa, who commissioned the expansion of the property in the 1550s. Open for visits between May and September, the castle houses a permanent archaeological exhibition tracing the origins of the area. Included in the ticket is the entrance to the nearby **Fängelsemuseet Vita Björn**, a prison dating back to 1784 which functioned as Åland's main detention centre for nearly 200 years. For excellent photo opportunities, get on the other side of Kökshavet, the river stretching below Kastelholm, as the sun is setting.

Ålandic flavours

Get a crash course in Åland's special produce at **Smakbyn** (*smakbyn.ax*), a 'taste village' created by star chef and TV personality Michael Björklund with a farm shop, cookery courses, a bakery and an airy open-kitchen restaurant, where cooks work magic with seasonal organic produce and serve Åland

Bomarsund Fortress

staples, such as homemade *svartbröd* (the local dark bread that takes four days to make). The menu is always different but usually features delicious local perch fillets and the beloved open-faced steak sandwiches.

Island gin with a side of architecture

South of the Kastelholm, the **Jan Karlsgårdens** open-air museum houses an impressive collection of traditional 18th- and 19th-century Ålandic countryside buildings and towering windmills. The park housed the headquarters of Åland's only distillery, an extension of nearby Smakbyn aptly named Åland Distillery. Take a seat in the restaurant for a taste of the archipelago's first gin, distilled on site with local sea buckthorn berries.

Russian fort ruins

Built by the Russian Empire starting in 1832 following the 1809 Treaty of Fredrikshamn, which ceded the Åland Islands from Sweden to Russia, the **Bomarsund Fortress** (*museum.ax*) was part of the Tsar's efforts to strengthen the strategic military positions at the western edges of the Empire. The fortress's completion was interrupted by the Crimean War. In 1854, it was attacked and subsequently destroyed by a combined attack from the British and French armies. Today, the ruins of Bomarsund serve as a significant historical monument, stretching for 2km overlooking the sea. In the Huvudfästet (main fort), only three of the defensive towers were completed. Today, they are an impressive sight, particularly Brännklint tower, its walls scarred by cannon and rifle fire. The overgrown foundations of the garrison town Nya Skarpans, as well as the Notvikstornet viewpoint, with its seaward-facing canons and sniper perches, are also atmospheric.

The Bomarsund Visitor Centre, opened in 2022, provides information on the history and the design of the fortress – from here a hiking path runs across the bridge to the island of Prästö, which became Bomarsund's island of the dead, with a military

WARTIME BASTIONS

More than 100 Bronze and Iron Age *fornminne* (burial sites) have been discovered across the Åland archipelago, attesting to over 6000 years of human habitation. Though all are clearly signposted, most are in fairly nondescript fields.

The discovery of fortress ruins confirms that the archipelago was an important harbour and trading centre protected by the Vikings via maritime warfare.

During the Great Northern War of 1700–21 (dubbed the 'Great Wrath'), most Ålanders fled to Sweden. Further Russian incursions took place in the 1740s and 1809, with the Invasion of Åland, a 1918 WWI campaign, as the final act of militarisation ever here. Despite its many fortresses, the Åland archipelago has been peaceful, politically neutral and demilitarised ever since.

THE APPLE OF FINLAND'S EYE

A mild climate, lots of sunshine and long autumns mean apple orchards thrive here. About 270 hectares are cultivated by 40-plus Ålandic apple producers, and the majority of apples (and also pears) in Finnish supermarkets are grown on the islands.

Apple season usually starts at the end of May, and by mid-August producers pick the early bloomers, with harvest typically lasting until October. From August to January, apple juice is a beloved local nectar. Grannas Äppel presses a variety of apples, from Lobo to Amarosa, into delicious, preservative-free juice.

At the Öfvergårds farm you can buy delicious souvenirs, such as pickled apple shoots and apple mulled wine.

Stallhagen Brewery

hospital and separate Greek Orthodox, Jewish, Muslim and Christian graveyards for prisoners of war.

Early Christian monument

Constructed in the mid-13th century near the Kyrksundet Strait, Sund's **Sankt Johannes Kyrka**, the largest medieval church in the Åland Islands, is worth a stop to admire the high vaulted interiors, elegant stone columns and large windows hiding below thick granite walls. Wooden sculptures such as the 5m-tall Triumphal Crucifix and Mary in Mourning date back to the church's early days. Don't miss the striking west tower, the largest in Åland, and the churchyard with its distinctive octagonal shape.

Jomala

TIME FROM MARIEHAMN: **15MINS**

Ancient stone temple

The stone church of Jomala, **Sankt Olof Kyrka**, is believed to have been erected in the second half of the 13th century and is considered one of the oldest still-functioning stone churches on the archipelago, and one of the oldest in Finland.

Finström

TIME FROM MARIEHAMN: **20MINS**

Nerdy nostalgia

Don't miss traipsing around the **Ålands Fotografiska Museum's** (*cameramuseum.com; adult €8*) gigantic collection of audiovisual equipment from the ages – perhaps the world's

EATING & DRINKING IN ÅLAND: OUR PICKS

Kallas SkärGård: In Vårdö, seasonally changing menu spiked with produce from the next-door farm. *noon-7pm Tue-Fri, from 1pm Sat* €€€

Lolo's Seaside Café & Restaurant: Sumptuous burgers come with a side of beautiful views over the sea and the islands surrounding Snäckö. *11am-8pm* €€

Soltuna Restaurang: Åland's highest restaurant in Geta – impeccable views but also tasty food and friendly service. *noon-7pm Sat & Sun* €€

Stallhagen Brewery: Åland's best-known brewery – stop for a meal and try a few of the brews. *10.30am-9pm Mon-Thu, to 10pm Fri, noon-10pm Sat, noon-8pm Sun* €€

most comprehensive collection of camera gear. This delightful museum, spread across the rooms and halls of a former school, is an unexpected Åland discovery. Peruse cabinets packed with over 16,000 pieces of AV paraphernalia, capturing the camera's history from the 1830s to today. What makes the collection so unique is it comprises not just vintage shutters, but video- and sound-recording equipment rounded up from around the world – vinyl players, TV and darkroom technology, eight-tracks, Walkmans and much more collected over decades by husband-and-wife team Olle and Benita Strömberg. Open June to August.

Island microbrewing

Craft beer in Åland captures the remote essence of the archipelago, from swishy lagers reminiscent of forest greens and sea breeze to brews inspired by Viking traditions. Beer-lovers will feel right at ease at Åland's illustrious **Stallhagen Brewery** (*stallhagen.com*) in Finström. It's perhaps the prettiest gastropub you will ever lay eyes on, a fabulous brewery overlooking an idyllic lake and horse paddocks. Sample unique, well-priced beer flights and rib-sticking food while musical jam sessions strike up on the terrace. Beers range from basic (pale ale or Baltic porter) to berry (blueberry ale or raspberry stout).

Medieval place of worship

Believed to have functioned as Åland's main religious centre in the Middle Ages, **Sankt Mikael Kyrka** is one of Finland's most precious examples of medieval architecture. While its core dates back to the 12th century, major renovations took place in the 15th century, with the addition of the bell tower in 1467 giving the church its current shape. Sankt Mikael Kyrka is open for visitors from the start of May to the end of September – add it to your itinerary to get a glimpse of the archipelago's historical and religious heritage, and to admire the wall decorations created in the 1450s and a mysterious wooden sculpture dated 1185.

Kumlinge

TIME FROM MARIEHAMN: **2½HR**

Take the Kumlinge 'eight'

Kumlinge, a 2½-hour drive (including ferry transport) from Fasta Åland, is one of Åland archipelago's least-frequented islands, with some of the most gorgeous walking trails. Get a load of commanding sea and forest panoramas on the so-called **Kumlinge åttan** ('eight'): an infinity-loop-shaped route through the island's heart. The 12.5km trail covers all the main

ÅLAND'S UNIQUE HISTORY

Åland is an autonomous state with its own parliament, flag, stamps and web suffix: 'dot ax'. Locals speak Swedish, not Finnish, and the islands' 'special relationship' with the EU means it is demilitarised, can sell duty-free and make its own gambling laws.

Swedish-owned during the Middle Ages, the islands were ceded to Russia with Finland in 1809. Åland became Russia's westernmost outpost until the empire's defeat in 1856.

Residents called for secession from Finland and to return to Sweden. In 1921 a League of Nations convention crafted unique cultural and linguistic rights, and neutral political status here. Locals may tell you they feel neither Swedish nor Finnish. Despite this, the islands are a popular holiday destination for Swedes and Finns alike.

EATING IN ÅLAND: BEST SEAFOOD

Restaurant Seagram: Famed seafood buffet – a smorgasbord of grilled and smoked fish. *11am-8pm Tue-Fri, from 1pm Sat, from 2pm Sun* €€€

Restaurang Galeasen: Classic island fare, such as grilled whitefish and fried perch, overlooking Lappo's Guest Harbour. *8am-10pm* €€

Glada Laxen: On Bärö, slurp on lobster claws in an old coastguard station set by the marina. *2-9pm* €€€

Bodegan: Pier-side restaurant in Eckerö with delectable Nordic grills, from salmon to tenderloin. *5-9pm Mon-Fri, noon-10pm Sat, noon-7pm Sun* €€

BEST ARCHIPELAGO ISLANDS TO VISIT

Brändö: Northernmost municipality of Åland Archipelago, known for its approximately 1180 islands outnumbering approximately 500 inhabitants.

Föglö: With more than 500 residents, the largest outer-island municipality with more civil servants than farmers.

Kökar: Dangling off the archipelago's southern end, a rocky island with a lovely desolate air.

Kumlinge: Kumlinge is little-visited but much beloved for its peaceful forests and low-traffic walking trails.

Vårdö: So-called 'guardian island'; on its highest mountain, ancient bonfires once warned other islands of danger.

Kumlinge (p101)

historical sights with ample signposts and calming solitude – climb rocks, gaze out to sea and spot wildlife, probably without ever meeting any other visitors (let alone any of the island's 300 or so residents). Most trekkers start the trail at the quaint, medieval **Sankta Anna Kyrka**, which leads through town up to the **Kumlinge Apotek**, an old-fashioned, richly interiored pharmacy that's still in business today. Meanwhile, at **Hotel Svala**, you can see a former 'cottage hospital' turned cute boutique hotel. Look out for the village's maypole, which locals festoon with bright flowers during Midsummer celebrations. Along the way, pass by bucolic homes and, as you get deeper into green woodland, keep your eyes peeled for wildlife. Cranes, roe deer, fox and elk all make their home here. Reaching the jagged coastline, it's easy to see why Kumlinge has been historically called 'the rocky passage'. Take the chance to climb rocks and enjoy a picnic on the sea bay.

Lappo

TIME FROM MARIEHAMN: **4HR**

Preserving maritime history

At the **Archipelago Museum** in Lappo (*lappo.net/ skargardsmuseet; adult €4*), in the northeastern part of the archipelago, marvel at a collection of historic wooden sea craft of all sizes and functions. Ten boats, including the only preserved Storbåt boat in Åland, are exhibited here between mid-June and mid-August next to photographs paying tribute to the archipelago's fishing culture.

EATING IN ÅLAND: HOMELY CAFES

Stickstugan Hantverk & Cafe: This homely, rustic cottage in Järsö is worth the drive for its delicious cakes. *11am-4pm Fri-Sun* €

Amalia's Limonadfabrik: In Lemland, taste the rainbow of delicious organic spoils infused into sparkling sodas. *10am-4pm* €€

Furulundsgården: This garden cafe serves both local and international dishes, from freshly caught fish to Thai food. *11am-7pm Wed-Sat, from 1pm Sun* €€

Johannas Hembakta: Small, artisanal bakery in Godby; stop for a coffee break paired with a fresh cinnamon bun. *9am-7pm Mon-Sat, from noon Sun* €

Hanko

SPA TOWN | 19TH-CENTURY ARCHITECTURE | SANDY BEACHES

Hanko (Hangö in Swedish) has been defined by its geographical position at the southernmost tip of mainland Finland. Long before its official founding in 1874, the town was a strategic outpost overlooking the Baltic Sea, where major naval battles between the Russian and Swedish empires took place. In the 19th century, Hanko – one of Finland's sunniest spots – developed as a spa town, drawing the Russian aristocracy to its long, sandy beaches. Many of the villas and buildings built during this golden era, including Hanko's iconic Casino, still stand despite the drastic changes the town underwent during WWII.

During the final stages of the Winter War in 1940, a peace treaty between Finland and the Soviet Union included the ceding of Hanko to the USSR, which used it as a naval base for nearly two years. Hanko's population was evacuated and a Soviet garrison of 30,000 occupied the town until the end of 1941. While some traces of the turbulent past are still visible, contemporary Hanko is a relaxing resort town that comes to life in the summer. With over 30km of beaches, swimming and sunbathing are two of the town's chief attractions.

Views from Water Level
Admire the archipelago from Hanko's water tower

Peeking over the skyline with its 48m of height, Hanko's earthy red, modernist **Water Tower** is the town's icon and prime lookout spot. You'll notice it as soon as you get off the train. Built in 1943, the current structure replaced the first Finnish water tower, erected in 1910 and destroyed by the Soviet Army at the end of the Winter War, in 1941. Some of the bricks of the original water tower were used during the reconstruction period for the pavements in the area. During summer months, you can take the lift to the observation deck at the top (*adult €5*), where you'll find a collection of

GETTING AROUND

Few trains run directly from Helsinki to Hanko – most often you will have to switch in Karis. Buses also run several times daily. The centre of Hanko is easily reached from the railway station on foot, although some of the town's beaches may be a bit too far to walk to. Rent an orange Jopo bike from SunFun *(sunfun.fi, starting from €14)* at the STI petrol station to explore beyond the town's core.

☑ TOP TIP

Hanko's accommodation is limited, so booking ahead is essential – the **Tourist Office** provides a list of private accommodation. Home shares via online platforms may even be preferred to downtown accommodation. B&Bs in Hanko's Russian Empire–era villas often do not have en-suite bathrooms (back in the day, everyone washed at the spa!).

photographs showing you what the water tower looked like before the war and unchallenged views over the archipelago.

Energising Baths
Take the plunge

In the 19th century, Hanko was a popular spa town for Russian nobility. Today, the **Regatta Spa** (*regattaspahotel.fi*) is the best-known throwback to this period. The gorgeously modern facility features a massive glass-enclosed pool for soaking while enjoying 270-degree views of the sea and the sky. There's a full spa menu, including facials, massages and beauty treatments.

Worth the Gamble
Dine in Hanko's Old Casino

Perhaps Hanko's most iconic historic building, the symmetrical **Casino** (*hangoncasino.fi*) facing the Plagen beach takes you back to the town's golden age when relaxing spa sessions were accompanied by big bets around the roulette able. Designed in 1879 by architect Ferdinand von Christierson, the Casino acquired its current art nouveau features in the 1910s, and while it stopped functioning as a gambling hotspot during the Soviet takeover of the port town, it has managed to maintain its role as a space for entertainment. Today, the Casino houses a large restaurant known for its generous Sunday brunch and its vast selection of wines. In the summer, live-music events and performances are regularly held in the evenings, and a popup showroom of Finnish clothing brand Niinmun occupies a corner of the building.

The House of Four Winds
Coffee break in Marshal Mannerheim's cafe

Set on the rocky tip of Lilla Tallholmen, 2km from the city centre, the isolated **Neljän Tuulen Tupa** (House of Four Winds) gets its name from its exposed location – surrounded by water on three sides, you'll enjoy your coffee with a beautiful view over the Gulf of Finland's horizon stretching all around you. Yet, this is not just another picturesque cafe dotting the Finnish coast. Dating back to 1900, Neljän made it into Finnish history books when it was purchased and managed by one of the country's most prominent figures of the 20th century, Marshal Mannerheim. After a long career serving the Tsar in the Russian Imperial Army, Mannerheim returned to

DREAMS OF A BETTER FUTURE

As Finland's southernmost town Hanko has long been recognised for its strategic importance. Even before its official establishment in 1874, Hanko served as a vital anchorage for ships navigating the Baltic Sea. Yet, this location was not only crucial for maritime trade but also played a significant role in Finnish emigration.

Between 1880 and 1930, 400,000 Finns left behind their homeland in search of a better future abroad – a significant number considering that in 1900 the population of Finland was around 2.6 million.

Approximately 250,000 Finns embarked on life-changing journeys from Hanko's docks, seeking new opportunities in the US, Canada and Australia. A monument depicting three cranes flying out toward the Baltic sea now stands in Merikatu, commemorating the people who left Finland.

EATING IN HANKO: OUR PICKS

Huge portions!

Origo: Local, organic ingredients and a seasonal gourmet menu. *4-10pm Mon-Fri, from noon Sat, 3-9pm Sun* €€

Hangon Portti: A two-minute ferry journey from the East Harbour pier for meatballs and burgers. *4-10pm Mon-Thu, from noon Fri & Sat 2-9pm Sun* €€

På Kroken: The yacht-shaped buffet teems with options. The adjoining cafe serves cheaper dishes. *9am-8pm Mon-Thu, to 10pm Fri & Sat, 9am-6pm Sun* €€

Bryggan: Seafood-based dishes and burgers (veg options available) served on the terrace surrounded by water, right by the marina. *noon-9.30pm summer* €

UNDER SOVIET CONTROL

Triggered by the Soviet Union's demands for territorial concessions, Finland and the USSR fought the Winter War from November 1939 to March 1940. The Soviet Union gained the upper hand in the conflict and at the end of the Winter War, the Moscow Peace Treaty of 1940 required the ceding of Hanko as a naval base. The town's inhabitants evacuated as the Russians moved in with a garrison of 30,000 and fortified the town, seen as a strategic base to control the Gulf of Finland. Hanko was isolated from the Russian frontlines and eventually abandoned in December 1941. Citizens returned to see their damaged town the following spring. Learn more about Hanko's recent history at the Rintama Museo.

Finland following the Empire's collapse as a result of the October Revolution, and led the Whites to victory in the Finnish Civil War. In 1919 he took a break from political life and moved to Hanko, acquiring Villa Stormhälla opposite Café Neljän on Stora Tallholmarna. In 1927 he purchased the cafe as well, which he personally ran until 1933.

Lunch with Sibelius

Eat in the home of a local pianist

Combining her historical expertise with her musical talent, certified guide Leena Immonen will help you understand Hanko's cultural background while introducing you to the art of Finland's most beloved composer, Jean Sibelius. In addition to walking and cycling tours around the town, Leena also hosts lunches in her own home, accompanying local cuisine with private classical music concerts played on her grand piano. Book ahead via email at leena.immonen@saaritours.fi.

 DRINKING IN HANKO: BEST PUBS & BARS

Pub Grönan: Lively pub in a former military warehouse where revellers bop to live bands and DJs. *10am-1am*

Wallis: Hanko's favourite karaoke bar. Sip a drink on the waterfront terrace and sing with locals. *10pm-4.30am Wed-Sat*

Nöjen Vin & Öl: Rub shoulders with the afternoon crowd of locals warming up by the fire. *5pm-midnight Wed & Thu, to 1am Fri & Sat*

HSF Marine Café: HSF serves lunch and evening drinks on its sunny terrace, with regular live-music gigs. *8am-11pm Sun-Tue, to 2am Wed, Thu & Sat, 9am-2am Fri*

Monument of Liberty

On Finnish Frontlines
Remembering Hanko's history

Hanko's shores have been the backdrop for bloody battles, due to the port's beneficial strategic location. This important history of fights for freedom, and finally liberation, can be discovered at its museums and monuments. Step onto one of the Winter War's worst battlefronts outside the **Rintama Museo** (*Front Museum; rintamamuseo.fi; adult €10*) and see original trenches, bunkers and artillery guns left behind. Indoors, the permanent exhibition 'Hanko in Foreign Hands' tells the whole story. Afterwards, it's worth driving 5km further east to Skogby, where there are still earth-covered bunkers in the forests near the road. Back in town, where the Bulevardi (boulevard) meets the beach is the **Monument of Liberty**. The statue depicts two lions, Hanko's present-day protectors named Conrad and Aurora, who commemorate the landing of liberating German forces in 1918. The monument was taken down after WWII but re-erected in 1960 with new text simply stating 'For our liberty'.

Brewed by the Sea
Maritime craft beer

Kick back and relax at a brewpub inspired by the Scandinavian aesthetic and the seaside. In a restored red-and-white warehouse, the **Hanko Brewing Company** is one of the village's best places to stare out to sea. Light lagers and ales are perfect for long laid-back summer afternoons on the harbour-front terrace. Posters and bags with cool graphic designs inspired by Hanko's maritime history make for great souvenirs.

REGATTA EXTRAVAGANZA

Every July, Hanko's Regatta transforms these quiet shores into some of Finland's busiest. For several days up to the event, the town and its harbour become overrun with impressive yachts and thousands of spectators. More than 200 boats compete, and a high-spirited party atmosphere includes live bands and big terrace parties. Hanko at its liveliest is mighty intoxicating, but locals will probably tell you they are just as happy every year when the madness is over. If you plan to attend the regatta, reserve accommodation and restaurants several months in advance. Consider staying outside of Hanko – for example in Raseborg – to get some distance from the event.

Finland's Tallest Beacon
Follow the light

On a clear Hanko evening, you may be able to see **Bengtskär Lighthouse** casting light across the waves – and there's certainly nothing quite like climbing inside of it. Towering 52m above the waves 25km offshore from Hanko, the Nordic countries' tallest lighthouse was built in 1906 to protect ships from the perilous archipelago waters. It was damaged extensively during the Continuation War by the departing Red Army but has been refurbished. The Summersea ferry runs from Hanko's Eastern Harbour to Bengtskär between June and August (*adult/child €70/34*), allowing you to spend a few hours exploring this remote rocky island at the mouth of the Gulf of Finland. It is also possible to book one of the few rooms available at the lighthouse and spend the night in this isolated location – just check the weather as the ferry may not come to pick you up if it's too windy.

Age-old Graffiti Tags
Archipelago etchings

Visit **Hauensuoli**, or Pike's Gut, a narrow strait between Tullisaari and Kobben, to see how sailors from countries around the Baltic Sea once waited out storms. At the protected natural harbour, sailors killed time by carving their initials or tales of bravery into the rocks, earning the area the nickname 'Guestbook of the Archipelago'. Some 600 carvings dating back to the 17th century remain.

Hanko's Best Beaches
Make the most of the sunny southern coast

As one of the sunniest spots in Finland, Hanko's beaches are the main draw for summer visitors. While popular, the sandy shore dotted with colourful changing cabins manages to maintain a relaxed atmosphere year round, especially in the more secluded swimming spots found along the 130km of coastline. Besides the central **Plagen** and **Bellevue** beaches, ideal for kids thanks to their shallow waters, you can head to **Tulliniemi** beach, where golden dunes slope into the water. On the northern side of the peninsula, find the long **Silversand Beach** and the **Hangonkylä Beach**, with an accessible wooden platform guiding you directly into the water.

A NEW MUSEUM FOR HANKO'S HISTORY

Long functioning as the main exhibition space to learn about the past 150 years of Hanko's history, the **Museum of Hanko** is currently being revamped inside its new location in Pitkäkatu 17. Now housed inside the former factory building of the Manner Mechanical Workshop, the archive of thousands of pieces of art, photography and artefacts produced and donated by local residents form the core of the town's collective memory since 1870. An inaugural show was held in the new space in mid-2024, and while the museum is open for visitors, the complete exhibition will only be ready in late 2025. Keep an eye on *hangonmuseo.fi* for updates.

EATING IN HANKO: COFFEE & BUNS

Alan's Café: Enjoy house-baked treats, such as cinnamon buns, in an old wooden villa or its courtyard. *10am-4pm Mon-Sat, 12-3pm Sun* €

Cafe Bageri Lillan: Locally loved bakery – stop by for sandwiches, freshly made cakes and cloud-like buns. *8.45am-3pm Mon-Fri, 9am-2pm Sat* €

Beach Bar Plagen: Hanko comes to life during summer as does its best-known beach bar, serving cooling drinks on the town's central beach. *11am-6pm* €€

Stranden: Serves a great lunch plus coffee and refreshing drinks on its outdoor terrace. *8am-10pm Mon, to 11pm Tue-Sat, 9am-9pm Sun* €€

AN ARCHITECTURE WALK IN HANKO

Through the heart of Hanko, embark on an architectural walk through the villas and the art nouveau buildings that have become symbols of this resort town.

START	END	LENGTH
Hotel Regatta	Yacht Club	4.2km; 2½ hours

Start from the ❶ **Hotel Regatta**, designed by famous Ålandish architect Lars Sonck, responsible for some of Finland's most important National Romanticist buildings. Heading away from the shore, the ❷ **Lignell Building**, once a Jugendstil (art nouveau) landmark, was so badly damaged in WWII its facade was fully replastered. Until the 1990s, it served as a coastal artillery. Walk around the block to ❸ **Hanko's Church** and the ❹ **Water Tower** (p103) before continuing to ❺ **Appelgrenintie**, the villa strip. Take in the grand 19th-century properties according to their names: Villa Elisabeth (No 5), Villa Maija (No 7) and Villa Frenckell (No 8), in their varying stages of upkeep. Continue to the ❻ **Casino** (p105), a gorgeous Jugendstil restaurant and a last memory of Hanko's spa days. Don't miss going inside to gaze at the drippy chandeliers and rich wood furniture. The restaurant only operates seasonally, but these days there are also antique and designer vintage pop-ups. From the Casino, take a stroll on the 1.5km 'Love Path' that runs on the ❼ **Puistovuoret Cape** – this trail was built for guests of Hanko's spa as a therapeutic dive into nature. Spot the WWII remnants on the rocky peninsula, then loop back to the town's centre and reward yourself with a drink at the functionalist ❽ **Yacht Club**, designed by Bertel Liljeqvist in 1938.

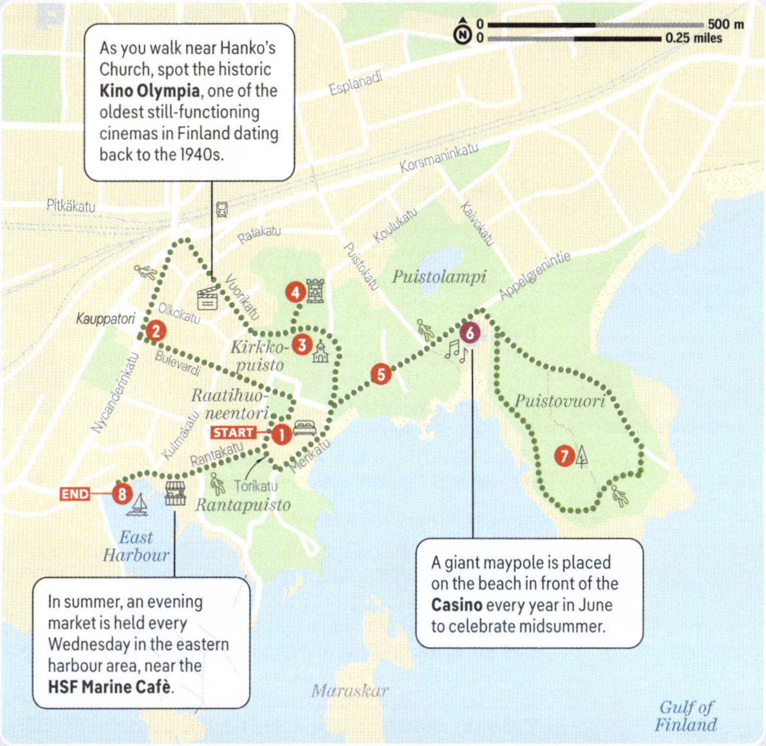

As you walk near Hanko's Church, spot the historic **Kino Olympia**, one of the oldest still-functioning cinemas in Finland dating back to the 1940s.

A giant maypole is placed on the beach in front of the **Casino** every year in June to celebrate midsummer.

In summer, an evening market is held every Wednesday in the eastern harbour area, near the **HSF Marine Cafè**.

Beyond Hanko

Cruise along the coast and discover a string of tiny villages and their treasures, from medieval buildings to modern artisanship.

Places
Raseborg p110
Fiskars p112

GETTING AROUND

A railway connects Hanko with Ekenäs and Karis. From Karis, trains depart frequently to both Turku and Helsinki. The villages of Snappertuna, where the Raseborg Castle is found, and Fiskars are not as well connected by public transport – you'll need your own vehicle to get there. Once you arrive, all towns in the area are easily explored on foot.

Built in the 1370s, the Castle of Raseborg represented the Swedish king's effort to counterbalance the growing commercial power of Tallinn, the Hanseatic League city on the opposite side of the Gulf of Finland. The move was hardly a success, but the fortification gave way to the construction of many historic towns dotting the fragmented coast between Turku and Helsinki. In 2009, three such villages – Ekenäs, Karis and Pohja – merged under the official name of Raseborg, though all names are still used. Ekenäs (Tammisaari in Finnish), one of the oldest towns in this part of Finland, still maintains its Swedish imprint, both in language and toponymy. Spend a couple of days here enjoying its picturesque Gamla Stan (Old Town), then set off to cruise the Ekenäs Archipelago National Park by boat. Save some time for a visit to the factory village turned Finnish creative hub of Fiskars, where artisans of all sorts keep alive the Finnish design tradition.

Raseborg

TIME FROM HANKO: **30MIN**

Holding court in Raseborg

Step back 500 years to explore what remains of one of Finland's most impressive medieval castles. Looming on a high rock overlooking a grassy sward, the late-14th-century **Raseborg Castle**, a 35km drive from Hanko, was strategically crucial in the 15th century, when it protected the trading town of Tuna, and exiled king of Sweden Karl Knutsson Bonde held his court here. The castle was abandoned in 1558 and lay deserted for more than 300 years. You can explore the ruins on your own or join one of the guided tours regularly organised during summer months (*book via raaseporinlinna.fi; adult/child €12/5*).

An artist's home by Alvar Aalto

The eclectic villa designed by Alvar Aalto for author and art historian Göran Schildt in 1969 is a great yet little-known example of Finnish modernism. The name *'skeppet'* – meaning 'boat' – refers to the shape of this residential building vaguely echoing a ship docking on Ekenäs' coast, a one-of-a-kind home created by Finland's visionary contemporary architect to convince his friend Göran to spend more time in the country. The Christine and Göran Schildt Foundation opened the building

Chappe Museum

to the public for the first time in 2020. Book a guided tour of **Villa Skeppet** (*villaskeppet.fi; adult €22*) to learn about the concept for this inspiring two-storey residence adorned with original Artek furnishing and prototypes, plus original artworks by Aalto and Roberto Sambonet.

Avant-Garde art in contemporary nordic architecture

Locals are divided on the minimalist dark-wood structure rising above Ekenäs' colourful houses that contains the **Chappe Museum** (*chappe.fi; adult €12 includes entrance to Raseborg Museum*), a forward-looking art gallery open since 2023 in the heart of town. The construction of such an innovative art house in Ekenäs was made possible by the Albert de la Chapelle Foundation, named after Finland's first professor of medical genetics who turned into an art collector at the end of his career. Besides the fascinating story of the founder, inside you'll find the work of local contemporary artists exhibited in the airy, light-flooded wooden halls of this fantastic example of modern Nordic architecture.

Second-hand everything

Right off Ekenäs' main artery, Kungsgatan, find the six red wooden buildings housing the **Betesda Second-Hand Shops**. From trinkets to clothing, furniture, paintings and two houses full of books, this historic corner of Gamla Stan (Old Town) is the place to find preloved objects donated by the local community to the charity running the open stores surrounding the garden.

Cruise the Ekenäs Archipelago National Park

Spilling off Finland's southern tip, the pristine **Ekenäs Archipelago National Park** marks the Gulf of Finland with 1300 mostly uninhabited islands shyly emerging from the Baltic waters. Rocky shores and serene waters characterise this protected nature reserve forming a sanctuary for over 60 species of birds. Given that over 90% of the national park is made of

SWEDISH IN DECLINE

When the municipality of Raseborg (Raasepori in Finnish) was created in 2009, uniting the towns of Ekenäs (Tammisaari), Karis (Karjaa) and Pojo (Pohja), it became the largest with a majority of Swedish speakers in mainland Finland.

Ekenäs, where Swedish is the first language of over 80% of the population, was founded in 1546 by King Gustav Vasa as a trading port to rival Tallinn in Estonia and its ties to Swedish heritage are still strong.

Yet, this is an exception. While the language is taught at schools throughout Finland, the percentage of Swedish-speakers in the country has declined by half over the last century, leaving only 300,000 Swedish-speaking Finns today (under 6% of the population).

Fiskars

ICONIC FINNISH BRANDS

Fiskars isn't the only Finnish brand that has become one of the country's design icons. Besides the orange scissors, other globally recognised symbols of Finnish style are Marimekko, the fashion and homeware brand celebrated for its bold patterns and colourful designs, and Iittala, a brand cherished for its timeless glassware and home decor.

Artek, the furniture brand of Alvar Aalto, continues to produce its renowned stools, just like Arabia produces fine ceramics as it has been doing for a century and a half.

Lesser known outside the country borders are also Jopo, the Hanko-based bicycle brand that has been producing its colourful city bikes since the 1960s.

water, the best way of exploring its scenery is by joining one of the summer cruises departing from Ekenäs' Norra Strandgatan on Wednesday and Friday between late June and early August *(€30 per person, book ahead by calling +358400436915)*. This journey will take you from Ekenäs to Jussarö on the M/S *Myggen* through the dreamy landscape of the archipelago. Alternatively, you can also reach Jussarö on the M/S *Salmetar* from Skogby, located 12km from Ekenäs, running Thursdays to Sundays from 8 June to 25 August *(€40 round-trip, no booking required)*. Beyond Jussarö, the archipelago offers other stunning destinations like Rödjan and Älgö, which can only be reached via private guided tours or boat taxis.

Fiskars

TIME FROM HANKO: 1HR

Reinventing old crafts

The former industrial town of **Fiskars** (*fiskarsvillage.fi*) has lent its name to one of Finland's most iconic design brands, best known for the orange-handled scissors seen in every Finnish home. It wasn't always cutting tools that were made here – the ironworks started as a horse plough production plant in 1649 and grew to become one of Finland's largest household item brands after 1822 when industrialist Johan Jacob Julin bought the factory. The **Fiskars Museum** *(adult €6)* gives you an overview of the Fiskars' history, although it's the thriving community of creatives that make the town worth visiting. From pottery workshops such as **Aarrekammari** and **Onoma** to handmade jewellery studios such as Timo Mustajärvi's **JALO** and **Sassi**, you are guaranteed to find a one-of-a-kind souvenir when stepping in and out of the ironworks' former buildings.

EATING IN RASEBORG: OUR PICKS

Café Gamla Stan: Enjoy fresh juice and pie in a shady apple orchard or at the cafe's cosy cottage. *11am-7pm* €

Restaurant GH Fyren: Pierside restaurant with an alluring terrace and sea views. *11am-6pm Mon, to 10pm Tue-Fri, noon-10pm Sat, noon-6pm Sun* €€

YLP!: The first zero-waste pizzeria in Finland and Scandinavia, using only ingredients from local producers. *4-9pm Tue-Sat* €€

EKTA Bryggeri: Founded in 2016, the EKTA Brewery runs its gastropub in the heart of Ekenäs' old town. *noon-10pm Tue-Thu, to midnight Fri & Sat* €€

Porvoo

HISTORIC ARCHITECTURE | RIVERSIDE STROLLS | PICTURESQUE OLD TOWN

During summer weekends, Porvoo's streets buzz with day-trippers from the capital enjoying the long days in one of Finland's oldest towns. Founded in 1380, Porvoo (Swedish: Borgå) developed as a crucial trading centre linking the Gulf of Finland with inland regions, thanks to its strategic position on the banks of the Porvoonjoki. In 1760, a major fire destroyed much of the medieval architecture that formed Porvoo's core. Luckily, authorities decided to preserve the existing foundation, maintaining the Old Town's original structure during reconstruction. The charming row of red riverside warehouses is a reminder of Porvoo's medieval mercantile heritage. Yet, Finland's collective memory values Porvoo for an event that would alter the country's history forever – in 1809, the Finnish Diet met in Porvoo's Cathedral to swear allegiance to Russian Tsar Alexander I, who granted Finland autonomy as a Grand Duchy, a significant step toward eventual independence.

A Cathedral for Finland's History Books
Discover Tuomiokirkko's convoluted past

Porvoo's stone-and-timber **Tuomiokirkko** (cathedral) dominates Porvoo's skyline from its hilltop setting above the Old Town. The church is a personification of *sisu* (the Finnish tradition of keeping tough). The church has been damaged by fire numerous times since the 16th century, most recently in 2006, although much of the art found inside, including the 18th-century Baroque pulpit, was saved and restored. The cathedral is an important stop for Finnish pilgrims; this is where Tsar Alexander I, whose statue is found inside the church right of the altar, convened the first Diet of Finland in 1809, giving Finland religious freedom.

GETTING AROUND

Multiple Onnibus buses depart every hour from Helsinki's Kamppi Sq to Porvoo, taking just under an hour to connect the two cities *(onnibus.com; €8-12 one way)*. Many buses continue onward to Kotka. From the station at Lundinkatu, Porvoo's Old Town is a short walk away. The Old City is compact – you can walk from one end to the other in less than half an hour. If you are driving, you can park for free near Porvoo's old railway station. From there, it's a five-minute walk to the old city.

☑ TOP TIP

It's possible (and pleasant) to arrive in Porvoo on a cruise from Helsinki. The noble old steamship *JL Runeberg* makes an excellent day trip, with various lunch options available. It's 3½ hours each way, so you may prefer to return by bus. Book via *msjlruneberg.fi*.

PORVOO

HIGHLIGHTS
1. Tuomiokirkko

SIGHTS
2. Chapter House
3. Devil's Stairs
4. Gallery Vanha Kappalaisentalo
5. Iso Linnamäki
- Castle Hill
6. Market Square
7. Näsi Glacial Erratic
8. Porvoon Museo
9. Porvoo Castle
10. Runebergin Koti
11. Simolin House
12. Taidetehdas

SLEEPING
13. Hotel Runo
14. Hotelli Onni
15. Hotelli Pariisin Ville

EATING
16. Café Cabriole
17. Fryysarinranta
18. Glückauf
19. Patisserie Teemu Aura
20. Porvoon Paahtimo
- SicaPelle (see 14)
21. zum Beispiel

SHOPPING
22. Brunberg

Porvoo's Past Through Art & Architecture
Learn about the town's origins and evolution at Porvoo's museum

Split between two buildings in the Old Town's main square, the **Porvoon Museo** (*porvoonmuseo.fi; adult €12*) chronicles the city's history through art, architecture and artefacts from centuries past. The core collection is housed behind the pink facade of the former Town Hall, spanning three floors. On the ground floor, a small room is dedicated to Finland's early history, with poetic captions guiding visitors from the retreat of the glaciers at the end of the Ice Age to the Swedish period, featuring taxidermied seals, foxes and birds.

To the left of the ticket counter is a collection showcasing two of Porvoo's renowned artists: glassware designer Saara Hopea-Untracht and Romantic painter Johan Knutson. Ascend the wooden stairs to discover the new exhibition dedicated to national painter Albert Edelfelt (1854–1905), established in 2024 to celebrate the artist's 140th birth anniversary. Edelfelt, one of Finland's most beloved 19th-century painters, spent many summers in Porvoo, creating over 200 landscapes and portraits, though only a dozen or so are on display. Particularly intriguing is the hall dedicated to paper silhouettes, the 'poor man's art' popular before photography, made by cutting out facial silhouettes drawn from a person's shadow.

Adjacent to the former Town Hall is **Holm House**, an extension of the Porvoo museum that showcases the residence of a successful 18th-century merchant. The building once belonged to industrialist Johan Holm, who had it constructed following the great fire of Porvoo in 1760. The rococo furniture inside has been collected by the museum from various owners throughout Eastern Uusimaa.

A Showroom for Avant-Garde Art
Step into the Holm House former stables to see a free show

Set in the green courtyard of Holm House in an 18th-century small wooden structure once used as the stables for the Holm family's animals, the free-to-visit **Gallery Vanha Kappalaisentalo** adds to Porvoo's art scene by showcasing contemporary installations, paintings and sculptures produced by up-and-coming artists. The gallery participates in the Porvoo Triennale (*porvoontriennaali.fi*), the visual arts festival held around various locations in the city every three years.

FINLAND'S NATIONAL ARTIST...

As you stroll through Porvoo notice the reproductions of landscape paintings created by Albert Edelfelt dotting parks and streets. Inspired by the Impressionist movement, Edelfelt worked in France before receiving honorary membership in St Petersburg's Russian Academy, where he was commissioned to paint portraits of the royal family. Yet, as Nicholas II attempted to Russify the Grand Duchy of Finland, Edelfeld joined the independence movement, becoming one of the most important promoters of Finnish culture worldwide. Between his trips to Paris and Saint Petersburg, Edelfelt worked in a villa in Haiko, 7km south of Porvoo, now converted into the Albert Edelfelt Studio Museum (*adult €10*).

EATING IN PORVOO: OUR PICKS

zum Beispiel: Spacious, light-filled cafe serving up modern international fare, from salads to pastas. *10am-9pm Mon-Sat* €€

Porvoon Paahtimo: Take a seat inside or on the boat docked outside to enjoy specialty coffee and pub food. *10am-midnight Sun-Thu, 9am-2am Fri & Sat* €

Glückauf: Pizzas and burgers served on the deck of a historic ship docked at Porvoo's promenade. *noon-9pm Sun-Tue & Thu, to 11pm Wed, Fri & Sat* €

Patisserie Teemu Aura: Home-made cakes and great coffee are served around the wrought-iron spiral staircase in this Old Town bakery. *10am-6pm* €€

...AND FINLAND'S NATIONAL POET

Albert Edelfelt isn't the only Porvoo-born artist who left a mark on Finland's history. Poet Johan Ludvig Runeberg is one of the most revered figures in Finnish national culture, often regarded as Finland's national poet because of his influence on national identity in the mid-19th century, when Finland's struggle for greater autonomy under Russian rule reached its peak. Although Runeberg wrote in Swedish, his patriotic verses were seen as representing a distinct Finnish character. Runeberg's Home Museum in Porvoo can be visited year-round (*adult €8*), but on 5 February you can join the celebrations for Runeberg Day by eating a Runeberg cake, invented by Runeberg's wife Fredrika and flavoured with almonds, rum and raspberry jam.

Iso Linnamäki Castle Hill

Porvoo's Lost Castle
Hike in the forests of Iso Linnamäki

The explanatory signs describing **Iso Linnamäki Castle Hill** present the site as 'one of Finland's best-preserved castle hills'. Truth is, there is no castle to be seen here. A series of wooden walkways extend within the forest that covers the hill, crossing the double moats that used to surround a mysterious, ancient wooden fortress. The wooden structure that stood on this privileged spot 350m from Porvoo's Old City was probably built by the Swedes in the late 13th century, as they advanced toward Karelia. The German administration that followed expanded and modernised the castle, but when the Swedes took back power they decided to destroy the structure to cancel every trace of the Germanic era. While you'll need some imagination to picture the historical context, Porvoo's Castle Hill still makes for a pleasant walk among the woods, with trails crisscrossing the thickly forested grounds opening to beautiful city views.

EATING IN PORVOO: OUR PICKS

Bosgård: Head to this farm restaurant for organic Charolais steaks and burgers. *11am-5pm Wed & Thu, to 6pm Fri & Sat, 11am-4pm Sun* €€€

Fryysarinranta: Local delicacies, including Porvoo snails, in one of Old Town's red wooden warehouses. *11.30am-11pm* €€

SicaPelle Wininq & Dining: Modern seasonal tasting menus with a fusion twist – for example, dashi scallops. *5pm-midnight Wed-Fri, from 2pm Sat* €€€

Café Cabriole: Gratifying lunch buffet and cakes galore in impressive art nouveau digs. *8.30am-6pm Mon-Fri, to 5pm Sat* €€

A WALK AROUND PORVOO

Explore the buildings that have made Porvoo's (and Finland's) history with a stroll through the town's ancient heart.

START	END	LENGTH
Simolin House	Porvoo Art Factory	3.3km; 2 hours

Start outside ❶ **Simolin House,** the yellow building housing Finland's oldest still-active department store, operating since 1854. Walk past the former residence of Vice Mayor JE Solitander, who hosted both Swedish King Gustav III and Russian Tsar Alexander I and thus nicknamed ❷ **Porvoo's Castle.** Reach ❸ **Porvoo's Old Town Hall** and step into the Porvoo museum. Cross the bridge on Mannerheiminkatu St and take a stroll along the river for an optimal view of Porvoo's red wooden houses, then get back to the city centre via the Old Bridge to reach the ❹ **Porvoo Cathedral** (p113) and the ❺ **Chapter House.** Keep walking north to the infamous ❻ **Devil's Stairs** (Ja Pirunportaat), a rock formation resembling a set of stairs that gets so slippery in winter you'll need to hold on to the handrail to get to the other side. Return to Vuorikatu St – the place where the Great Fire of Porvoo started in 1760, destroying over 200 historic houses – and walk to the newer part of town. Past the ❼ **Market Square** you'll find a number of Empire-era buildings on Lokiokatu St. Pay a visit to the ❽ **house-museum** dedicated to national poet JL Runeberg and conclude your tour with a show at ❾ **Porvoo's Art Factory** (Taidetehdas), on the other side of the river.

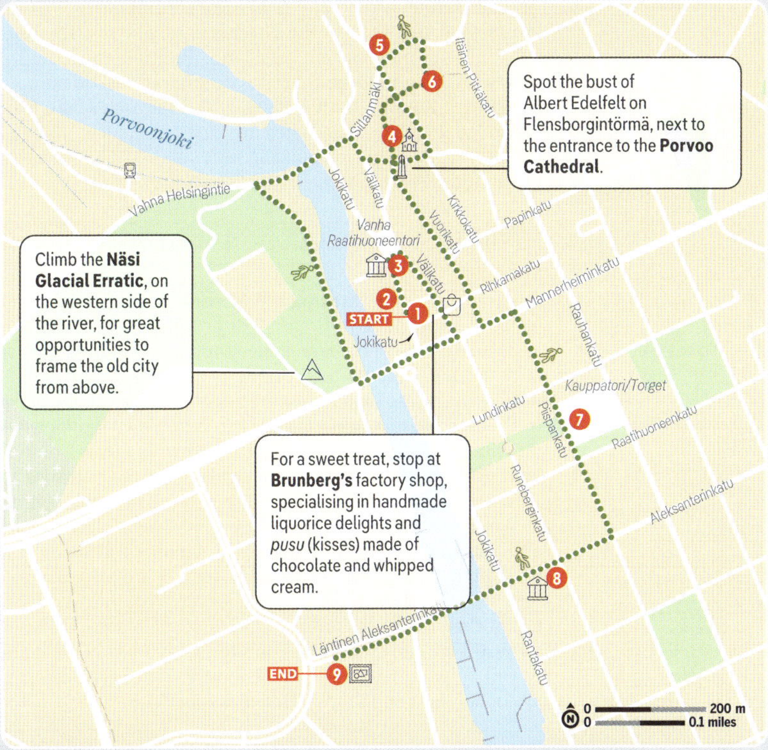

Spot the bust of Albert Edelfelt on Flensborgintörmä, next to the entrance to the **Porvoo Cathedral**.

Climb the **Näsi Glacial Erratic**, on the western side of the river, for great opportunities to frame the old city from above.

For a sweet treat, stop at **Brunberg's** factory shop, specialising in handmade liquorice delights and *pusu* (kisses) made of chocolate and whipped cream.

Beyond Porvoo

Discover quiet yet charming villages leading eastwards to Russia. Historic seafaring routes, lost fortresses and barely inhabited island are revealed on cruises in the archipelago of the eastern Gulf of Finland.

Places
Loviisa p118
Kotka p119
Hamina p121
Virolahti p122
Kouvola p122

Porvoo is a gateway to Finland's historic east. Today, the islands of the eastern Gulf of Finland emerge from the Baltic waters as calming nature retreats, far removed from the major tourist routes. Yet, in the past, this region was the site of some of the biggest clashes between the Swedish and Russian empires, which attempted to push their frontiers ever further conflict after conflict. Being a continuously shifting borderland has shaped the character of centres like Kotka, Finland's only city on an island, Hamina and Loviisa, where Swedish industrial heritage and aristocratic manors blend with Russian-built fortresses and the Tsar's own fishing lodge. Between these sites are vast forests few take the time to explore and some of the best small-scale breweries you'll find in Finland.

GETTING AROUND

Driving your own car is the easiest way of exploring beyond Porvoo. Trains run from Helsinki to Kouvola and then down to Kotka, although it's faster to reach the town by bus from both the capital and Porvoo. Going beyond urban centres with public transport can be difficult as local buses are few and far between. It's easier to just pick up a car in Helsinki if you are planning to visit rural areas. Ferries travelling to the archipelago's islands run between June and August.

Loviisa

TIME FROM PORVOO: **30MIN**

The count's beer

Book a tour of the **Malmgård Manor** (*malmgard.fi*) and friendly Count Henrik Creutz will personally show you the residence of one of the last noble families in Finland. One of only three Finnish counts, Creutz is a 13th-generation resident of the estate founded on the edge of the Swedish empire in the 17th century and expanded to become an opulent Renaissance palace in the 19th century. Showing traces of Finland's development as a nation – look up at the entrance to see 'tervetuola' and 'välkommen' written below the ceiling to welcome both Finnish- and Swedish-speaking guests – and a large collection of portraits of members of the dynasty, Malmgård is a piece of living history. It is also one of the first organic farms in Finland. Besides his locally loved oats, Count Creutz uses his grains to produce the Malmgård beer, an award-winning brew made on site. Group tours of the manor run between May and October, but the brewery and shop are open year-round for tasting sessions.

Merikeskus Vellamo

From industrial community to craft centre

Located in Ruotsinpyhtää, near Loviisa, **Strömfors Ironworks** is one of Finland's best-preserved ironworks communities. Originally founded in 1695, it has been reshaped by its owners over the centuries and now features an impressive showcase of Nordic industrial architecture. The buildings once functioning as a sawmill, a brewery, a tavern and a brick factory have been transformed into art galleries and craft stores – step into the Museum of the Lower Forge to put the ironworks into their historical context through the exhibition surrounding two 18th-century ovens. Continue to the village's focal point, the 19th-century **Ruotsinpyhtää church**, which houses the impressive Resurrection altarpiece created by Finnish modernist painter Helene Schjerfbeck (1862–1946).

Kotka

TIME FROM PORVOO: **50MIN**

Maritime heritage

The tanker-sized, wave-shaped **Merikeskus Vellamo** (*Maritime Centre; merikeskusvellamo.fi; adult €15*) hosts one of Finland's most impressive collections of icebreakers and shipwrecks. Starting from the retelling of the largest naval battle in the Baltic Sea, which saw the Swedish and Russian empires clash off the coast of Kotka in early July 1790, the museum recounts Finland's seafaring life and the events that have shaped the country's political history. In summer, the permanent exhibition extends to the vessels *Tarmo*, *Kemi* and *Telkkä*, docked at the quay of the Maritime Centre. The *Tarmo*, the world's third-oldest icebreaker (1907), ploughed Finnish waters until it was retired in 1970. In 2023, the maritime quarter's architecture was enhanced by the Event Centre Satama, Kotka's new entertainment hub designed by ALA, the same firm that created Helsinki's famous Oodi Library.

NATIONAL PARKS & NATURE RESERVES

Fancy a walk in the forest? Southeastern Finland is not just islands, farmland and rugged coastlines. Here are some of the best parks you can find in the region.

Rapovesi National Park: North of Kouvola, Rapovesi is the largest protected area in this part of Finland, with trails and bridges stretching through forests and across lakes, with beautiful views and no crowds.

Valkmusa National Park: Northwest of Kotka, the 17 sq km Valkmusa National Park features a network of boardwalks that cross bogs and swamplands typical of this corner of the country.

Siikakoski Rapids Park and Arboretum: A short distance from Kotka's city centre, Siikakoski is a small park extending around the rapids formed by the Kymi River.

MONUMENTAL FLAG

You'll spot it as soon as you enter Hamina territory – the mega-flag flying above the town's skyline. The world's largest Finnish flag was placed on a 100m-high pole (the tallest in Europe) in Hamina in 2018 to celebrate the 100th anniversary of Finland's independence.

The record-breaking monument wasn't completed easily – the raising of the flag, which weighs 55kg and measures over 16m in length, had to be delayed multiple times due to safety concerns.

Despite the obstacles, the celebration was eventually held in December 2018 and the flag has been flying over Hamina's skies ever since.

Varissaari island

Patches of green in the industrial city

Self-appointed Finland's park capital, Kotka wasn't always as green as it appears today. The industrial town transformed in the early 1980s, when landscape architect Heikki Laaksose was appointed city gardener – the youngest person to take on the role in Finland – and began developing a plan to embed as much nature as possible in the urban fabric. Of the seven parks that now dot Kotka's city centre, the largest is **Isopuisto**, surrounding the 18th-century Orthodox **Church of St Nicholas**. The most diverse, however, is the **Sapokka Water Park**, an oasis near the homonymous marina featuring many plant species and a 20m waterfall.

Lunch on an island fort

It's a short ferry ride from Kotka's Sapokka marina to **Varissaari**, the tiny island once known as Fort Elizabeth. Named after Peter the Great's daughter Yelisaveta Petrovna, this defensive structure was part of the larger Ruotsinsalmi Sea Fortress constructed in the late 18th century to counter the Swedish bases in Loviisa. Much of Ruotsinsalmi was destroyed during the Crimean War, but remains still stand in Varissaari. Seeking the traces of clashing empires is not the only reason to get here, however. The island hosts a sauna and the **Vaakku Restaurant**, built within the reconstructed fortress walls and run by energetic Niina Utter, who organises regular live-music sessions amid the cannons during the summer. In 2024 an extension of the Merikeskus Vellamo was also placed on the island – step into the museum hall to find sections of a wooden warship dating back to the Ruotsinsalmi era recovered from the seabed in the 1930s. The wooden M/S *Klippan*, built in 1971, departs from Kotka every hour between 10am and 9pm and takes approximately 10 minutes to reach the island.

The tsar's fishing lodge

Situated 5km north of Kotka amid the salmon-rich Kymijoki's rapids, the rustic wooden **Langinkoski Imperial Fishing Lodge** (*kansallismuseo.fi; adult €10*) was built in 1889 for the Tsar of Russia Alexander III. As one of the tsar's favourite fishing spots, Langinkoski became a frequent stop during the imperial cruises between 1888 and 1894. Containing the original furniture used by the emperor and his wife during their Finnish summer holiday, this house museum is a window into the habits and tastes of the autocrat who, while admiring the nature of southern Finland, worked to Russify the Grand Duchy, rescinding many of the more liberal policies his father, Alexander II, had introduced. The largest hall is the Drawing Room, the space where the tsar would meet his guests and share a cup of tea poured from the original samovar exhibited at the entrance. Next to it is the Empress Room where Maria Feodorovna would retire to rest and study, and the Emperor's Room is on the opposite side, right of the entrance. You'll notice that there are no beds – the royal couple always slept on their cruise ship and used the lodge only as a place to eat and gather guests after salmon fishing sessions. Walk downstream and discover the tsar's memorial fishing stone, as well as the area's gorgeous riverside forest setting, now a 28-hectare nature reserve with walking trails.

Hamina

TIME FROM PORVOO: 1HR

One-man land

Tammio, located about 25km southeast of Hamina, is a remote village island in the Gulf of Finland, sitting just a few nautical miles west of the Russian border. Colonised in the 16th century, Tammio's population peaked in the late 19th and early 20th centuries, when about 200 residents lived in 47 houses. Fishing, particularly for Baltic herring, was the primary livelihood, supplemented by shipping and seal hunting. The island's prosperity waned by the 1960s as young people left for the mainland. Today, Tammio only counts one permanent resident, with descendants of the original villagers returning to their cottages in summer. The Vikla Ferry, run by MeriSet (*meriset.fi; adult €35 return*), travels through the archipelago from Kotka's Sapokka Harbour to Tammio during the summer, taking under two hours to reach the island. Besides the picturesque red wooden houses dotting the coast, there is a museum exhibiting belongings of former residents and a local cultural centre (built with the logs of a Russian sauna imported from a nearby island), and what is likely to

THE BIGGEST NAVAL BATTLE IN THE BALTIC SEA

The Battle of Svensksund is remembered as the largest naval battle to ever take place in the Baltic Sea between the Swedish and Russian empires. The clash took place on 9 and 10 July 1790, off the coast of Kotka. Driven by Swedish King Gustav III's ambitions to reclaim territories lost to Russia in previous wars, the battle involved nearly 550 ships, plus smaller support vessels. Over 30,000 men participated in the conflict, with Russia suffering the majority of losses, believed to be between 9000 and 12,000. Of the dozens of ships lost during the battle, many are still lying on Kotka's seabed, too fragile to be recovered.

 EATING IN KOTKA & HAMINA: OUR PICKS

Alku: Hamina's best restaurant prides itself on preparing every dish with ingredients from local farms. *4-10pm Thu, to 11pm Fri, 2-11pm Sat* €€

Bistro V: Internationally inspired dishes served in a modern, inviting space behind the brick walls of a central Kotka historic buildings. *6.30-11pm* €€

Vausti: Housed inside the elegant Kotka Concert Hall, Vausti offers multi-course tasting menus of seasonal Finnish specialties. *3-10pm Wed-Sat* €€€

Rampsi Kitchen & Lounge: This outdoor terrace is a great lunch spot serving big salads and salmon. *11.30am-8pm Tue-Thu, to 9.30pm Fri & Sat* €

A PHONE-FREE ISLAND

In 2023, Kotka declared Ulko-Tammio (not to be confused with Tammio) a 'phone-free' island. The media campaign went viral and Ulko-Tammio gained a reputation as the ultimate destination for digital detoxing. Meriset (*meriset.fi*) runs a few cruises every summer to this remote, uninhabited island near the Russian border, allowing a few hours to hike the trails running along its coastline. To be clear: as no one lives on Ulko-Tammio, no one will check whether you have a phone or not (it might actually come in handy in case of emergency). Disconnecting while in nature – or anywhere – is a matter of personal choice, meaning that any island can be phone-free if you want it to be.

be the smallest public library in Finland (in Europe?), measuring no more than 2 sq m. A walking path runs around the island, and can be covered in less than one hour.

Musical discovery

Hamina, located just 40km from the Russian border (95km east from Porvoo), has long been a military town. Today, it is one of the best places in the world to discover military music at its semiannual **Hamina Tattoo**.

The week-long festival sees professional soldiers, otherwise known as field musicians, performing ceremonial tunes. The event is organised by the Finnish Defence Forces, yet rock and jazz shows, as well as visiting bands (from Scottish bagpipes to Caribbean steel-pan performers) provide diverse flair.

The main highlight is a parade through Hamina's picturesque town square. Concerts are held in Kesäpuisto Park and on 'Tattoo St' (Fredrikinkatu), and at the especially evocative ruins of the 18th-century fortress Hamina Bastion.

Virolahti

TIME FROM PORVOO: **1HR 20MIN**

The final frontier

Virolahti, the last town on the road to the currently shut border with Russia, is home to the isolated **Bunker Museum** (*salpakeskus.fi; adult/child €7/4*), an open-air collection of military infrastructure that keeps alive the memory of WWII frontlines. At the southern end of the Salpa Line, the system of trenches and defensive structures stretching for 1200km along the border formed the largest construction project in the history of independent Finland; the museum maintains the bunkers that were built starting from 1940. Follow the trails that branch out in the forest from the museum's headquarters and step into the concrete domes camouflaged under the vegetation. The military itinerary continues 13km north of Virolahti, in the town of Miehikkälä, where the **Salpa Line Museum** exhibits a T-34 tank. It is possible to hike from one museum to the other by following the 50km Salpa Route, the trail north from Virolahti along the Salpa Line.

A sip of award-winning Kaski

One of the best beers in Finland is produced in the country's southeastern corner, in the picturesque countryside of Virolahti, 20km from the Russian border. From wintery smoked dark ales to crisp summer lagers, all the beers of the **Takatalo & Tompuri** farm brewery (*takatalotompuri.com*) are made with oats and barley grown on-site. Tasting sessions and tours are available on request, but you can pick up any bottle at the store or pair the brews with a meal at the seasonal Navetta restaurant on the farm.

Kouvola

TIME FROM PORVOO: **1½HR**

Industrial heritage

Located approximately 30km from Kouvola, the UNESCO-listed **Verla Groundwood and Board Mill** takes you back to the 19th century, when small-scale industrial settlements began

Verla Groundwood and Board Mill

flourishing across northern Europe. The well-preserved groundwood mill, established in 1872, forms the core of this village turned into Finland's first mill museum in 1972, eight years after the plants ceased to operate. About 50 buildings dot the 10-hectare expanse, which you can tour for free following the various trails connecting the mosaic of this industrial architecture. The History Trail takes you through the red brick buildings where hundreds of workers spent most of their days until the 1960s, and by the owner's residence, designed by architect Eduard Dippell, and the dam protecting the site against floods. You can also add a dive into Verla's lush landscape by following the 2km Forest Trail stretching north of the Kymi River, or enter the museum of the groundwood and board mill where you'll find the original machinery (*guided tours €15, book ahead via verla.fi for languages other than Finnish*).

Century-old trees

Local and imported tree species have been growing in Finland's oldest arboretum since 1902, when Elimäki park was set up to test the possibility of cultivating international conifers in southern Finland. About 300 types of trees coexist in the area, together with rhododendrons, azaleas and other plants that attract a vast array of birds. But scientific research is not the only purpose of **Arboretum Mustila** (*mustila.fi; adult €10*) – over time, the park has acquired an artistic edge by hosting dozens of amateur wooden sculptures of animals and fantastic creatures now dotting the landscape. The best time to take a stroll through the zen-like paths that cut through the arboretum is between May and June, when rhododendrons bloom showing their true colours.

ARKTIKA DAYS

Each year in May and early June, millions of waterfowl and hundreds of thousands of geese travel through the Gulf of Finland, heading to their nesting grounds on the Arctic tundra. These birds, having spent the winter on the North Sea, make their journey back to the Arctic shores of Siberia, crossing the Gulf of Finland along the way. Virolahti is one of the best places to experience this wonder of nature. During this time of the year the town organises its Arktika Days, a series of events led by bird experts that help visitors see the migration. Check the full program on *visitvirolahti.fi*.

GOING AROUND IN CIRCLES IN HAMINA

Known as Fredrikshamn at its foundation in 1723, Hamina is one of the rare Finnish towns built following a circular plan. Tour on foot to discover its heritage.

START	END	LENGTH
Town Hall	Market Square	1.6km; 1hr

The border town of Hamina, enclosed within its star-shaped fortress, came to be when Vyborg was lost by the Swedish Empire and developed as an important military training centre during the Russian era in the 19th century. From the neo-classical ❶ **Town Hall** marking the heart of Hamina, walk east to find the ❷ **Town Museum**. Opposite the museum is the ❸ **Orthodox Church of Sts Peter & Paul** and a little further up the road is the ❹ **Reserve Officer School** (Reserviupseerikoulu), former Hamina Cadet School. The imposing building designed by famed architect Carl Ludvig Engel has hosted many prominent figures, including a young Gustaf Mannerheim, who entered the college in 1882 before moving to St Petersburg to serve in the Imperial Army. If you are interested in the military history of Hamina, continue on Kadettikoulunkato to the Reserve Officer Museum, otherwise turn left to reach the ❺ **Central Bastion** (Hamina Bastioni), the best-preserved portion of the fortress, now stage for the Hamina Tattoo Festival. At a short distance is the former ❻ **Mayor's House**, dating back to 1886, and another work by CL Engel, the light blue ❼ **Hamina Church**. From there walk south to the ❽ **Market Square** to spot the old Flag Tower, originally built to house the commander of the fortress.

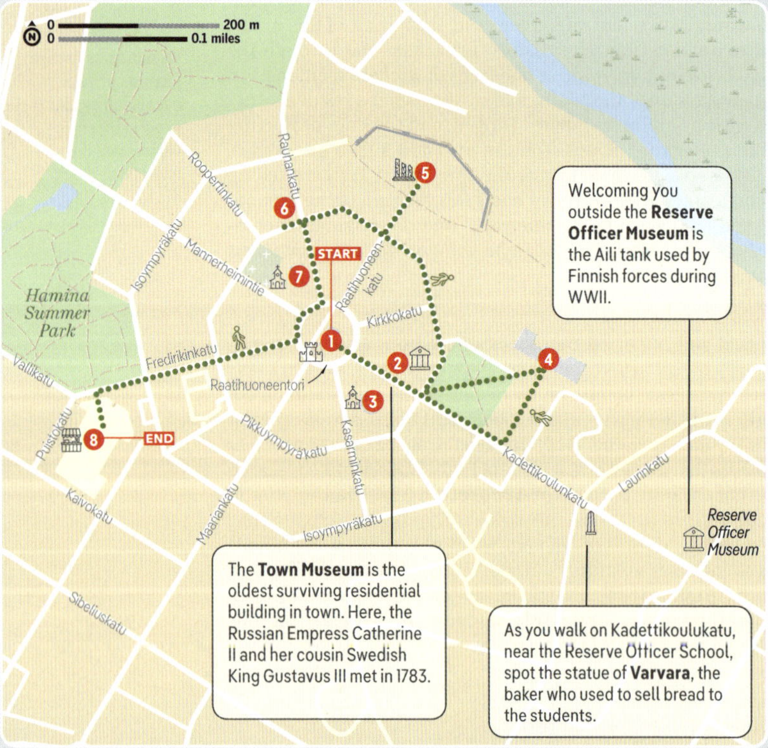

Welcoming you outside the **Reserve Officer Museum** is the Aili tank used by Finnish forces during WWII.

The **Town Museum** is the oldest surviving residential building in town. Here, the Russian Empress Catherine II and her cousin Swedish King Gustavus III met in 1783.

As you walk on Kadettikoulukatu, near the Reserve Officer School, spot the statue of **Varvara**, the baker who used to sell bread to the students.

# Places We Love to Stay

€ Budget €€ Midrange €€€ Top End

Turku
MAP p84

Bridgettine Sisters' Guesthouse € Run by nuns, this Catholic convent's guest wing is a haven with austere, spotless rooms.

Laivahostel Borea € The SS *Bore*, a passenger ship turned hostel, docks outside the Forum Marinum museum.

Ruissalo Camping € On Ruissalo Island, this campground has grassy sites, great cabins, saunas and Turku's closest beaches.

Park Hotel €€ Art nouveau building overlooking a hilly park. Characterful rooms, classical music and a lobby parrot.

Hotel Kakola €€€ Former prison transformed with plush, warm Scandinavian design – including a 'jailhouse chic' cell room.

Åland

Sandösund Camping € Idyllic campground with stylish townhouse rooms and well-kept beachside log cabins plus a 'floating sauna'.

Brändö Stugby € Splendidly located campground; cabins with kitchens and campsites. Hire a rowing boat to explore the seascape.

Hasslebo Gästhem € Outside Kumlinge village, eco-sensible campground with bio-toilets, solar power and organic breakfasts.

Hotell Cikada €€ Modern hotel in the heart of Mariehamn, easy to reach from the harbour on foot and close to all the town's sights.

Strandnäs Hotell €€ Just outside Mariehamn town's centre, with quiet, sun-flooded rooms and a generous breakfast served every morning.

Susannes B&B €€ Homely feels in Hammarland. Charming rooms in a 19th-century house.

Kvarnbo Gästhem €€ Gorgeously decorated historic guesthouse with idyllic countryside in Saltvik.

Pellas Gästhem €€ A former Brändö schoolhouse, delighting guests with activities ranging from picnicking to fishing.

Gästhem Enigheten €€ Creaky-floored rooms in Föglö with old stoves and period furniture.

Hanko
MAP p103

Villa Aurora €€ Lovingly restored villa with cute rooms and lovely common areas plus a knowledgeable tour-guide owner.

Hotel Bulevard €€ Converted from a police station (with some rooms in former cells); no-frills, budget-friendly stay downtown.

Villa Maija €€€ Flawlessly restored rooms in a 19th-century villa packed with character; some with wonderful sea views.

Raseborg

Hotel Sea Front €€ A tranquil, family-operated retreat in Ekenäs, Hotel Sea Front offers a pleasant seaside escape, perfect for unwinding near the water.

Motel Marine €€ Located in the heart of Ekenäs, Motel Marine provides budget-friendly accommodation with easy access to city attractions.

Billnäs Ironworks Hotel €€€ Experience a seamless fusion of history and modern comfort at Billnäs Ironworks Hotel, housed in the former ironworks headquarters, offering quality accommodation in a rich, historical setting.

Fiskars

Torby €€ Housed inside the former cutlery mill of the Fiskars Ironworks, the 24-room Torby adds a contemporary touch to the historic town, with designer influences very much in line with the creative atmosphere of the village.

Porvoo
MAP p113

Hotel Runo €€€ Modern boutique hotel in an art nouveau building, with art exhibits and an attic spa.

Hotelli Onni €€€ Opposite the cathedral, this gold-coloured wooden building is perfectly placed. Each room is unique.

Hotelli Pariisin Ville €€€ Plush place combining modern luxury with heritage atmosphere. Some rooms have mini saunas and courtyard views.

Loviisa

Strömfors Bed & Bistro €€ The large rooms in the refurbished upper floors of this 1892 wooden mansion offer a homely atmosphere in the heart of the village.

Kouvola

Verla Bostad Cottages €€ If you want to spend the night in Verla's UNESCO area, you can book one of the charming little cottages by the river that used to house mill workers in the 19th and 20th centuries.

Tampere, the Lakeland & Karelia

URBAN DISCOVERIES AND NATURE EXPERIENCES

Fairy-tale forests, glittering lakes and creative cities define Finland's central region.

Karelia's hearty feasts and riveting wildlife, Saimaa Lakeland's serene labyrinths of lakes and islets, Tampere's buzzing city life and Alvar Aalto's world-class architecture in Jyväskylä are just some of the highlights to be discovered in this central area. The region stretches from Karelia on Finland's eastern border to the country's third-largest city, Tampere, with the Lakeland and its thriving culinary scene in between.

Today, the scenes around Saimaa's waterways, where, until the end of the 20th century, Finland's 'green gold' - logged trees – used to float with the romanticised log drivers on top, are dominated by summer cottages and little boats moored beside lakeside hotels and city docks.

Tampere's edgy city scene has industrial roots, too. Located by the city-centre rapids of Tammerkoski, the Finlayson cotton mill and linen factory drew the working classes into the city in the 19th century, creating wooden house districts to home them. Now, these quaint neighbourhoods host museums, cafes and plentiful scenes of the cosy Finnish lifestyle.

In the eastern region of Karelia, the sparsely populated land feels like a true wilderness, even though during WWII more than 400,000 Russian Karelians crossed the border here into Finland, accompanied by a hearty culinary culture. Little by little, their tasty meals spread all over Finland, and now delicacies such as Karelian pies and stews are enjoyed everywhere.

THE MAIN AREAS

TAMPERE
City life with industrial undertones. **p138**

SAIMAA LAKELAND
Lakes, seals and scenic roads. **p141**

JYVÄSKYLÄ
Alvar Aalto's architecture. **p156**

HÄMEENLINNA
Castle and nature reserve. **p161**

KOLI NATIONAL PARK
Nature trails and Karelian feasts. **p165**

For places to stay in Tampere, the Lakeland & Karelia, see p167

THE GUIDE

TAMPERE, THE LAKELAND & KARELIA

Left: Tammerkoski channel (p132), Tampere; Above: Lake Saimaa (p141)

Find Your Way

Finland has over 100,000 lakes, and most of them are located in the Lakeland and its surroundings. Bigger cities are connected with trains and buses whereas remoter parts are best accessed by a car – or bicycle.

Jyväskylä, p156
Alvar Aalto's architecture dotted around the city, the energetic university life and lakeside setting make Jyväskylä a prime example of a Finnish city.

Tampere, p138
Known as Finland's sauna capital, Tampere's mix of industrial heritage and cosy wooden-house neighbourhoods topped up with world-class museums doesn't leave anyone cold.

Hämeenlinna, p161
A medieval castle, a nature reserve with a granite observation tower and charming house museums make Hämeenlinna a perfect pit stop between Helsinki and Tampere.

Koli National Park, p165

With its bare hilltops rising on the shores of Pielinen, which is dotted with forest-covered islets, Koli National Park is like a miniature Lapland.

Saimaa Lakeland, p141

It's all about nature here, with Saimaa's shimmering lakes and small islands making a picturesque setting for cottage life, cycling tours, hikes and water sports.

CAR

Hitting the road by car is the best way to explore the area, especially if you wish to experience the wildlife and nature trails in the more remote foodie spots of Karelia and Lakeland.

BUS

If you don't have a car, bus is the next best bet to reach remote places such as Koli and Kuhmo. Matkahuolto operates throughout Finland and various local bus services operate regionally. Red, two-storey Onnibussi is a low-fare option for shuttling between cities.

TRAIN

The region's main cities, Tampere, Jyväskylä and Savonlinna, are easy to reach from Helsinki by train. Trains to Tampere take just under two hours, with almost 50 departures per day. Trains depart for Jyväskylä almost every hour and take around 3½ hours. Trains to Savonlinna take more than four hours, with about five daily departures.

Plan Your Time

City life, soothing lakes and vast wilderness intermingle in the area around Tampere, the Lakeland and Karelia. Sample the distinctive cuisines, take a plunge in the refreshing lake waters and spot some wildlife.

Tammerkoski channel (p132)

If You Do Only One Thing

● Head straight to **Tampere** (p138) and its central Tammerkoski channel, where the former **Finlayson** (p132) linen factory stands by the rapids. The red-brick building is now a creative hub with museums, galleries, restaurants and cinemas.

● Next, pop over to the world's only **Moomin Museum** (p134) to explore the world of Tove Jansson and her famous characters, the Moomins. Then, walk along Tampere's main shopping street Hämeenkatu to the other side of the city, **Pyynikki** (p137) neighbourhood and its viewing tower. Rest your legs and enjoy freshly fried doughnuts and coffee in the tower's cafe.

● Finish the day by taking the heat in Finland's oldest public sauna, **Rajaportin sauna** (p137), a convivial space open for bathing since 1906.

Seasonal Highlights

Cold winter offers plenty of opportunities for snow sports. Summer is ideal for exploring the lakeside cities, while autumn is a perfect time for mosquito-free hikes.

JANUARY

Marvel at **Koli's tykkylumi**: the snow-laden branches of the fir trees create an otherworldly sight. Enjoy a sauna in **Tampere** followed by a dip into a frozen lake.

FEBRUARY

Enjoy cream-filled buns and sledge rides on **Shrove Tuesday**, or hot drinks and *korvapuusti* (cinnamon buns) on any day. **Valentine's Day** in Finland is a celebration of friendships.

MAY

1 May fills the city parks with **Vappu** (May Day) picnics. May is also the best time to try and spot one of the world's most endangered seals, the **Saimaa ringed seal.**

Three Days to Travel Around

- After a day in **Tampere** (p138), dive deep into the Lakeland, heading towards Mikkeli and its quaint manor houses with restaurants and shops. Along the way, stop to admire Alvar Aalto architecture in **Jyväskylä** (p152).

- From Mikkeli, continue on the A62, to stay overnight at **Sahanlahti** (p148). Enjoy the beautiful Saimaa Lakeland setting, delicious local food and learn about Sahanlahti's history as a sawmill community.

- Then continue to **Savonlinna** (p141) to visit its medieval castle, famed as a dramatic setting for the fabulous Opera Festival in July. Drive on to nearby **Punkaharju** (p148) to see the scenic ridge winding across the lake. This is one of Finland's most iconic landscapes, making it a perfect end for a tour in the area.

If You Have More Time

- Start in Helsinki and head east towards Koli National Park, with a stop en route at **Lappeenranta** (p145) to explore its hilltop fortress housing little museums and cute cafes. Continue deeper into the Saimaa Lakeland region and spend a night in Puumala's **Sahanlahti** (p148), located on Saimaa's shores. Continue to **Koli National Park** (p163) to explore nature trails and Finland's archetypal national landscape with barren clifftops and lakeside scenes.

- Then, drive further north for the chance to spot wildlife **in Kuhmo** (p165) – sightings of bears, wolves and wolverines are possible. From Kuhmo, start driving back towards Helsinki, stopping at **Jyväskylä** (p152) to explore Alvar Aalto's architecture, and **Tampere's thriving city life** (p138), with the Moomin Museum, public saunas and busy nightlife, along the way.

JUNE
Temperatures rise above 20°C and **markets** fill with berries and vegetables. Kuopio is famous for its summery market life. Mid-summer is celebrated with bonfires in cities and countryside.

JULY
Spend a night in one of Kuhmo's **wildlife huts** as the sun stays below the horizon only a couple of hours a night. Savonlinna hosts the annual **Opera Festival**.

OCTOBER
Autumn foliage reaches central Finland. Beautiful, and mosquito-free, time for **hikes** in the many national parks, such as Repovesi and Helvetinjärvi.

DECEMBER
The **Christmas Market** in Tampere opens. Vendors arrive from all over Finland to sell Yuletide foods, drinks and crafts. Jyväskylä's Church Park is decorated with **Christmas lights**.

Tampere

MOOMIN MUSEUM | SAUNA DESTINATION | CUTTING-EDGE CULTURE

If the world's only Moomin Museum isn't reason enough to visit Tampere, there's plenty more to explore, from the red-bricked, city-centre Finlayson museum and restaurant hub lining the powerful rapids of Tammerkoski, to the pretty wooden-house neighbourhood with a historic public sauna – it's the perfect warm welcome to the city.

Tampere's wooden houses and red-brick facades hide an industrial past set in motion in 1820 when the Scot James Finlayson established a linen factory here. By the beginning of the 20th century, one-third of Tampere's inhabitants were factory workers. This set the tone for the working-class city's later development as a central stage in Finland's Civil War, when the bourgeois 'whites' fought against the working-class 'reds'.

Today, Tampere is the self-proclaimed sauna capital of the world, and the city's industrial heritage mixed with its creative energy provides many layers to explore.

Historic Hub by the Rapids
The white-water core of Tampere

The rapids of the Tammerkoski channel create a powerful backdrop to the city's main shopping street, Hämeenkatu. Visiting the industrial red-brick buildings lining the rapids, you will quickly get the gist of Tampere's past and present.

Start from **Vapriikki** (*vapriikki.fi; adult/child €15/7*), a cluster of museums located in an old factory that once manufactured turbines and locomotives. The building is a marvellous sight, and inside there are more than a dozen small museums. Kids will love the retro vibes of the **Finnish Museum of Games**, whereas visiting the **Finnish Hockey Hall of Fame** helps to make sense of Finland's wintry obsession.

Next, head to the **Finlayson Centre** (*finlaysoninalue.fi*) on the other side of the rapids. There are restaurants, cinemas and shops in the area, and guided tours to the rooftop of the

---

GETTING AROUND

Tampere is easily explored on foot, with the help of public transport if needed. You can also rent a city bike or e-scooter via apps (Tampereen kaupunkipyörät for bikes, Voi or Tier for e-scooters).

Most hotels in Tampere have parking facilities. There is also street-side parking around the city. Payment requires a credit card or an app.

Trains to Tampere depart from Helsinki's Central Railway Station every 30 minutes, running from around 4am to 11pm. Buses also run regularly. The journey takes from 1½ hours to 2¾ hours.

☑ TOP TIP

Tampere is renowned for a gloried rock scene, known as 'Manserock', and hosts several notable festivals. Tuhdimmat Tähdit, a new two-day metal festival, is in early July. Also in July, Tammerfest attracts tens of thousands.

THE GUIDE

TAMPERE, THE LAKELAND & KARELIA TAMPERE

HIGHLIGHTS
1. Särkänniemi
2. Vapriikki

SIGHTS
3. Amurin Työläismuseokortteli
4. Finlayson Centre
5. Muumimuseo
6. Pyynikin Näkötorni (see 6)
6. Pyynikki Hill
7. Sara Hildénin Taidemuseo
8. Tampere Art Museum

SLEEPING
9. Dream Hostel
10. Solo Sokos Hotel Torni
11. Unity Tampere

EATING
12. 4 Vuodenaikaa
13. Bistro C
14. Gastropub Tuulensuu
15. Kaffila
16. Kahvila Runo
17. Kajo
18. Muusa
19. Panimoravintola Plevna
  • Pyynikin Munkkikahvila (see 6)

DRINKING & NIGHTLIFE
20. G Livelab
21. Konttori
22. Pyynikin Brewhouse
23. Ruby & Fellas
24. Telakka

SHOPPING
25. Tallipiha

133

Särkänniemi

SAUNA CAPITAL

Included on UNESCO's List of the Intangible Cultural Heritage of Humanity in 2020, the sauna has been integral to Finnish identity for centuries. One cherished tradition is the public sauna, which was particularly popular around the turn of the 20th century. However, since the 1950s and especially the 1970s, the rise of private saunas led to a decline in public ones. Today, Finland's oldest sauna, **Rajaportin** (p137), is located in Tampere. Another beloved public sauna here is Rauhaniemen Kansankylpylä, a lovely lakeside facility from the 1920s. To see (and feel) the difference between old and new saunas in Finland, pop over to **Pereensaaren sauna** (*pereensaarensauna.fi*) on the shores of Pyhäjärvi and **Kuuma** (*saunaravintolakuuma.fi*) by the city-centre rapids, which both represent the fancier, and even a spa-like, side of Finnish sauna culture.

former factory, where you can see Tampere from another perspective (*roofwalk.fi; from €30*). Check out also the **Finnish Labour Museum Werstas** (*tyovaenmuseo.fi; free*) and the Sulzer steam engine still in its original place.

Werstas also operates the new **Museum Nootti** (*museo nootti.fi; adult/child €10/8*) near Hämeenpuisto, dedicated to Finland's complex relations with Russia. The museum is located on the spot where the Russian Social Democratic Labour Party held underground meetings at the beginning of the 20th century, and where Lenin and Stalin met for the first time in 1905.

It's a five-minute stroll from the Finlayson Centre to **Tallipiha** (*tallipiha.fi*), where old stables now house a nostalgic cluster of little shops and cafes, charming in any season, but especially beautiful at Christmas time.

Magical Moomins

See Tove Jansson's beloved artwork

You don't need to have kids to be enchanted by the Moomins. The characters were created by Finnish-Swedish artist Tove Jansson in the 1930s, and they have since conquered the world in comic strips, books, TV shows and as toys.

The world's only **Moomin Museum** (*Moomimuseo; muumi museo.fi; adult/child €14,50/7*), and one of two Moomin-themed attractions in Finland, is framed around Tove Jannson's draw-

EATING IN TAMPERE: BEST CAFES

Vohvelikahvila: This cafe has a waffle menu of more than 20 sweet and savoury toppings. *10am-8pm Mon-Fri, to 7pm Sat, 11am-7pm Sun* €

Cafe Pispala: This cosy cafe also serves lunch, dinner and American-style brunch on the weekends. *10.30am-4.30pm Mon-Fri, 9.30am-5pm Sun & Sat* €

Kaffila: Quality coffee, lunches, brunches and sweet treats just off the city centre's main shopping street. *9am-7pm Mon-Fri, 10am-6pm Sat, to 4pm Sun* €

Kahvila Runo: Books and homemade cakes are always a good idea, and both are found here. *9am-8pm Mon-Fri, to 7pm Sat, 10am-8pm Sun* €

ings, which line the walls of the two-storey exhibition space. Much-loved quotes from the books are sprinkled around the space, reminding us of the characters' philosophical natures. The lighting is dim and the atmosphere magical, especially downstairs where small crystal-like threads hang from the ceiling. There are also miniature scenes from the books on display, crafted by Jansson's partner, graphic artist Tuulikki Pietilä. Photography is only allowed in a dedicated part of the museum. Closed on Mondays.

FOR MOOMIN FANS
Muumimaailma (p91) in Naantali is an idyllic island where you can visit the Moomins' and their friends' houses and interact with the characters. The island can be visited year-round, but the Moomins' homes are only open during summer season.

Amusement Central
Fun and art in one park

Located by Näsijärvi's shore, **Särkänniemi** (*sarkanniemi.fi; ride pass from €27*) amusement park is easy to spot due to its 168m-high observation tower, **Näsinneula**. The tower has a viewing deck at 120m, as well as a slowly rotating restaurant. Apart from the viewing tower, there are 32 different rides in the amusement park, including six roller coasters. Families with smaller children can visit the **Doghill Fairytale Farm**, with cute farm animals to pat, including mini-piglets, goats, puppies and alpacas, and a colourful cluster of small wooden houses with figures based on the popular Finnish *Koiramäki* children's books. The village also features shops, like a candy store set in an old pharmacy, and restaurants, such as the cute Kahvila von Guggelböö.

Visit also Särkänniemi's **Sara Hildén Taidemuseo** (*sara hildenintaidemuseo.fi; adult/child €15/5*), an art museum with a collection of more than 5000 works. As well as modern masters such as Joan Miró and Paul Klee, there is also an impressive range of modern Finnish art. The museum's summer exhibition is always a highlight of the season.

Island Idyll
Escape to trails and beaches

Beyond its urban amusements, Tampere has some great nature escapes. One such is **Viikinsaari** (*viikinsaari.fi*). From mid-May to early September, the island can be reached on a 20-minute ferry ride departing from Laukontori in the city

BEST VINTAGE SHOPS IN TAMPERE

Yesterday: Fab retro-flair is guaranteed, with clothes ranging from the 1950s to the 1980s, near the Moomin Museum.

Helga-Neiti: Tampere's oldest second-hand shop sells fabulous items from tuille skirts to cool jackets at reasonable prices, a few blocks away from the Railway Station.

OLDIE: Louboutin shoes, Gucci bags, Prada caps and more in the city-centre shop.

Kameratori: Pre-owned film cameras and camera gear in the Tammela neighbourhood – items are restored and tested for quality.

Sammakka: For vinyl records varying from Finnish rock to punk and metal, but also more mainstream rock from the 1960s onward.

DRINKING IN TAMPERE: OUR PICKS

G Livelab: A live-music venue in an industrial riverside setting, with drinks and food served on the summer terrace. *hours vary*

Ruby & Fellas: An Irish pub that serves food and hosts karaoke every weekend at 10pm before live music kicks in at 11.30pm. *hours vary*

Telakka: This bar has a outdoor terrace, a restaurant and live music. *11am-midnight Mon & Tue, to 1am Wed & Thu, to 3am Fri, noon-3am Sat, noon-midnight Sun*

Konttori: Beer-lovers gather in Konttori with more than 200 beers to choose from; ciders also available. *noon-midnight Mon, to 1am Tue & Sun, to 2am Wed-Sat*

SARA HILDÉN

One of Finland's Boss Ladies, Sara Hildén (1905–93) was orphaned at the age of 13. She began working as a maid and bus conductor before moving into fashion retail in the 1920s. In the 1950s, Hildén established her own boutiques. Around this time, she also married the artist Erik Enroth and developed a passion for collecting modern art. A decade later, the couple divorced, but Hildén continued her enthusiastic patronage of the arts, becoming one of Finland's most prominent contemporary art collectors. Her legacy endures through the donation of her 2700-piece collection to the Sara Hildén Foundation, leading to the creation of the Sara Hildén Art Museum.

Tampere viewed from Pyynikki

centre and operated by Suomen hopealinja (*hopealinjat.fi, adult €14, child €10-12*). The island is a protected area with short nature trails to explore. There are little beaches dotted around the island on which to grab some sun, and you can take a dip in the lake. The island also has multiple possibilities for activities, including miniature golf and SUP, rowing boat and kayak rentals. Or try the Finnish game Mölkky, a simple version of bowling, played with wooden logs. Take your own picnic basket (bringing alcohol to the island is not allowed) or enjoy a leisurely lunch at the island's summer restaurant, Viikinsaari.

EATING IN TAMPERE: OUR PICKS

Bistro C: Bistro offers international and Finnish dishes like whitefish and seabuckthorn. *4-10pm Tue-Thu, to midnight Fri, 2pm-midnight Sat* €€

Panimoravintola Plevna: German and Finnish pub grub. *11am-midnight Mon-Thu, to 2pm Fri, noon-2am Sat, noon-midnight Sun* €€

4 vuodenaikaa: Enjoy French cuisine, a glass of wine and the atmosphere of Tampere Market Hall. *9.30am-6pm Mon-Fri, 9am-4pm Sat* €

Pyynikin Brewhouse: Tasty food, craft brews and a terrace by Tammerkoski. *3-11pm Mon-Thu, to 2am Fri, 1pm-2am Sat, 1-10pm Sun* €€€

Kajo: Fine-dining set menu includes seasonal ingredients from hay and cloudberries to Nordic kimchi. *5pm-midnight Tue-Fri, from 3pm Sat* €€€

Public House Huurre: BBQ and gastropub food from ribs to fish and chips, plus the pub's own brews. *3-10pm Mon-Thu, 1-11pm Fri & Sat* €€

Muusa: Tampere's top spot for Sunday brunch. *4pm-midnight Mon-Thu, to 2am Fri, 1pm-2am Sat (kitchen closes 9.30pm), noon-4pm Sun* €€

Gastropub Tuulensuu: A warm-hearted living room with a selection of Belgian beers. *3pm-midnight Sun-Thu, to 2am Fri, 1pm-2am Sat* €€

SCENIC STROLL WITH A SAUNA

Explore the fringe of the city centre on this walk among art, views and some of the city's best baking.

START	END	LENGTH
Tampere Art Museum	Rajaportin Sauna	2.1km; 5 hours

Start from the ❶ **Tampere Art Museum** (tampereentaidemuseo.fi; adult/child €13/6) which contains Finland's second-largest art collection, including original drawings by Tove Jansson, the creator of the Moomins. Then walk one block north to find a sight straight from 19th-century Tampere. This is the ❷ **Amuri Working Class Quarters** (amurinmuseokortteli.fi; adult/child €9/6). Its wooden houses showcase working-class lifestyles in Tampere between 1882 and 1973. The Art Museum and the Working Class Quarters are closed on Mondays.

Continue southeast to ❸ **Pyynikki Hill**, the tallest longitudinal esker in the world, rising 80m above the surface of Pyhäjärvi lake. Atop the hill, there's an elevator to the tip of the ❹ **Pyynikki Observation Tower** (munkkikahvila.net; adult/child €2/1) to take in the views over the forest-covered hillsides and city scenes. At the foot of the tower, the popular ❺ **Pyynikin Munkkikahvila** is famed for its fresh doughnuts.

Wind down from the hill climb by continuing northeast to one of Finland's most famous saunas, ❻ **Rajaportin sauna** (rajaportinsauna.fi; adult/child from €7/4), which has been heated up regularly in Pispala neighbourhood since 1906. The sauna has separate changing and sauna facilities for men and women plus a common terrace on which to chat and cool down between *löyly* (the steam of a sauna).

See Tampere's most iconic tower, Näsinneula, with its revolving restaurant in Särkänniemi amusement park, from the Pyynikki observation tower.

Pause at Amuri's beloved neighbourhood cafe Amurin Helmi, serving freshly baked goods from buns to *pannukakku* (oven pancakes).

Take a stroll around the storybook-like Pispala neighbourhood to see its wooden houses lining the narrow, hilly streets.

Beyond Tampere

Shake off Tampere's urban buzz with artsy finds in a small town or on a hike through a national park.

Places
Mänttä-Vilppula p138
Helvetinjärvi National Park p139
Ruovesi p139
Laukko Manor p140

Tampere is very much Pirkanmaa region's urban hub, but there are some great spots to explore beyond the city. Helvetinjärvi (Hell's Lake) National Park is famed for its namesake lake edged by rocky cliffs, and Helvetinkolu, a 2m-wide, 40m-long canyon carved during the Ice Age. There are several walking trails, from a few hundred metres in length to an 11km hike that takes you from the top of the hills to the bottom of the gorges – the terrain is challenging but some sections have stairs. The national park can be visited throughout the year, while summer is the best time to visit Mänttä-Vilppula, a town renowned for its art galleries and summer arts festival.

Mänttä-Vilppula

TIME FROM TAMPERE: **75 MINS**

Art & art sauna

Dubbed an Art Town, Mänttä-Vilppula's city centre first developed around the 19th-century wood industry and its main sights are the **Serlachius Museums Gösta** and **Gustaf** (*serlachius.fi, adult/child €15/free*) – the former dedicated to the arts, and the latter to history. The lakeside art museum's old section is housed in a manor house, once the home of paper mill owner Gösta Serlachius. One of Finland's most influential art patrons, his collection of Finland's Golden Age art, as well as old European masters, forms the core of the museum and is one of the most important private fine-art collections in the Nordic countries. The Serlachius Museums operate a daily shuttle from Tampere to the museums between 1 June and 1 September. Outside that season, the bus runs from Tuesday to Sunday (*matkahuolto.fi; return adult/child €30/26*).

The Serlachius family's dedication to the arts is still commemorated today in an annual contemporary-art festival, Mäntän kuvataideviikot, taking place from mid-June to the end of August. But visiting in wintertime doesn't leave anyone cold, either. Book a spot to take the heat in the museum's award-winning **Serlachius Art Sauna** (*adult/child €13/10*), where the harmonious exterior conceals a round sauna room as well as artsy details from designer sauna towels to the mosaics in the showers. Afterward, you can enjoy a meal in the museum's restaurant.

GETTING AROUND

The best way to reach Helvetinjärvi National Park is by car or campervan, for which there are specific parking lots. A bus from Tampere runs two times a day, leaving you 10km from the park. In summer there's an Outdoor Express bus (*outdoorexpress.fi*) which runs from Tampere railway station to Helvetinjärvi National Park every third weekend. Mänttä-Vilppula can be reached by car or bus, which takes around two hours.

Helvetinjärvi National Park

Helvetinjärvi National Park

TIME FROM TAMPERE: **75 MINS**

On the gates of hell

Just over an hour's drive from Tampere, there's a gate made from two trees turned upside down, their roots forming an arch above the road, and with a sign reading 'To Hell'. This is Helvetin portti (Hell's Gate), one of two entrances to **Helvetinjärvi National Park**. This gate can be found on Helvetinkoluntie 775, Ruovesi (Kankimäki parking lot), but there's another gate on the park's west side in Ruovesi. There are various hiking options in the park, with camping and toilet facilities dotted along the trails, especially on the park's northern side. Pitch your tent near Haukkajärvi beach and witness beautiful sunsets over the lake, or stay at Ruokejärvi camping site, closer to the park's main sights. You can also book the rustic Hiedanmaja cottage, available as accommodation from May to October.

At the moment, the only circular hike leads from Kankimäki to Helvetinjärvi's two main sights: Helvetinjärvi lake and Helvetinkolu gorge, formed some 200 million years ago when the bedrock split. The 4km trail includes stretches of duckboard across marshland, pathways through forests and a few sets of stairs that climb and descend. Entry into the gorge itself is blocked for safety reasons, but it can be admired from a viewing platform above.

Just outside the national park, the duckboard trails at **Siikaneva** showcase Finland's marshy landscape. Here, you can also find **Ollinkivi**, a round glacial erratic that was one of Finland's first nature sights protected by environmental law.

Ruovesi

TIME FROM TAMPERE: **1¼HR**

A bookstore worth saving

A rarity in rural Finland, the 120-year-old **Vinhan Kirjakauppa** (*vinhankirjakauppa.fi*) bookshop makes a great pitstop for

---

MÄNTÄN KUVATAIDEVIIKOT

The Mänttä Art Festival, inaugurated in 1993, has evolved into one of Finland's premier art events and the country's largest exhibition of contemporary Finnish art. Each year, a new curator selects several dozen artists to feature, showcasing a diverse range of contemporary works. The main venue is called Pekilo after the former factory's main product, protein meant for animal consumption. But the closure of Mänttä's sulphite pulp mill in 1991 also ended the operations at the Pekilo mill as the factory ran out of raw material. Art took over, and today, every year, Pekilo factory houses Finland's largest exhibition of contemporary Finnish art. The festival takes place from mid-June to the end of August.

Laukko Manor

booky travellers in Ruovesi, a small village with about 4000 inhabitants. After being owned by the same family for four generations, the bookstore was close to being shut down but was saved by two book-loving Finns. The bookshop re-opened in 2023 freshly renovated. The lovely wooden building is on Ruovesi's main street and apart from books, you'll also find an art gallery and a good cafe here serving sweet and savoury snacks as well as drinks. Upstairs, four charming rooms accommodate one to four people – in one of them, dogs are also welcome.

Laukko Manor

TIME FROM TAMPERE: **40 MINUTES**

Summery stop for coffee & art

One of the Tampere region's most cherished destinations is **Laukko Manor** (*laukonkartano.fi; adult/child €15/5*), a centuries-old estate where Finnish history and culture blend into a charming whole. First mentioned in 1416, Laukko Manor has a storied past with many twists and turns. A particularly notable chapter began in 1824 when Elias Lönnrot, author of Finland's national epic *Kalevala*, started tutoring there. The manor was a popular social hub, and it was at Laukko that Lönnrot, of humble origins, acquired the manners of high society and formed lifelong friendships. Encouraged by the lady of the manor, Lönnrot became interested in poetry and the Finnish language, and began collecting Finnish oral poetry. One such piece, *Elinan surma* (Murder of Elina), was published in *Kanteletar* in 1840, the sister collection to *Kalevala*. The ballad tells the tragic story of Elina, whose jealous husband is tricked into burning her and her supposed lover alive. The plotline has European roots; however, some studies suggest the murderous husband is based on the medieval nobleman Klaus Kurki, who lived at Laukko Manor in the late 15th century. Today, you can enjoy Laukko Manor's less dramatic setting from late June to late August, by stopping for a coffee break in its cafe or a summery lunch buffet in the restaurant after checking the art exhibitions in the main building.

CULTURED RUOVESI

Ruovesi's cultural impact on Finland far exceeds its modest size, with a population of just around 4000. One of the country's most esteemed artists, Akseli Gallen-Kallela, built a wilderness atelier and family home Kalela nearby. This 13m-tall log house remains one of Finland's largest, though it is sadly not open to visitors. Another notable figure with ties to Ruovesi is Finland's national poet, Carl Ludvig Runeberg. In 1825–26, Runeberg worked as a teacher in Ruovesi, where he wrote the poem *Vid en källa* (By a Spring). You can still visit Runeberg's Spring, although it is not the same spring he wrote about.

Saimaa Lakeland

MEDIEVAL CASTLE | WATER ACTIVITIES | LOCAL FOOD

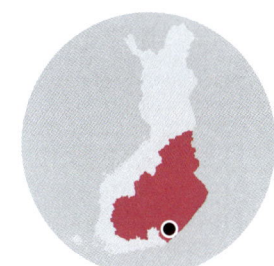

Saimaa's reputation in Finland is almost mythical. It seems like the labyrinth of lakes and islands has been here forever, though, in fact, it was created 11,000 years ago when the glaciers of the last Ice Age withdrew across Finland carving landmasses and leaving thousands of lakes behind. Around this time, a population of ringed seals separated from their pack in the Arctic Ocean and were left stranded in freshwater. These ringed seals are now endemic to Saimaa, and though they remain endangered, their numbers have risen from dozens to more than 400 in recent decades.

The seals are a lovely attraction, but Finns also flock to Saimaa to bask in the summer sun, staying in cottages lining the lakes' shores as the region's villages come to life with outdoor terraces and little festivals. Visit here in winter, and the lakes are covered with ice and snow – as well as locals ice-hole fishing, skating and skiing.

Savour Savonlinna
Saimaa's king of the castle

Savonlinna, with its medieval castle and busy summertime harbour, is the jewel of Saimaa. Located on its own island, **Olavinlinna castle** (*kansallismuseo.fi/fi/olavinlinna*; *adult/child €14/7*) dates from the 15th century when Sweden wanted to protect its eastern regions against the Novgorodians. Olavinlinna now hosts an annual **Opera Festival**, started by Finnish opera singer Aino Ackté in 1912. The castle is dimly lit and its slightly claustrophobic corridors and staircases are fun to explore. Guided tours in English run hourly from June to August.

Neighbouring **Riihisaari** used to harbour Olavinlinna's war boats until Finland's border shifted further east in 1617, making the castle's defences obsolete: Riihisaari came to house grain-drying kilns, known as *riihi* in Finnish, and the name stuck. Riihisaari holds **Savonlinna Museum**

GETTING AROUND

Saimaa has the world's longest lake coastline, 14,500km long, and the urban centres are few and far between. The area's is best explored by car – or from the waters – as trains and buses won't reach the best spots.

City-hopping between bigger hubs, such as Savonlinna and Lappeenranta, is possible by public transport. For example, the bus from Lappeenranta to Savonlinna takes three hours and 40 minutes, whereas the train takes just over two hours, with a change in Parikkala.

☑ TOP TIP

Contact local tourist offices about cycling trips in summer. There are two popular routes, Saimaa archipelago covering 154km and Puumala archipelago 60km. Both include ferry rides. There are also hotels, restaurants, cafes and spots for swimming along the routes.

SAIMAA LAKELAND TAMPERE, THE LAKELAND & KARELIA

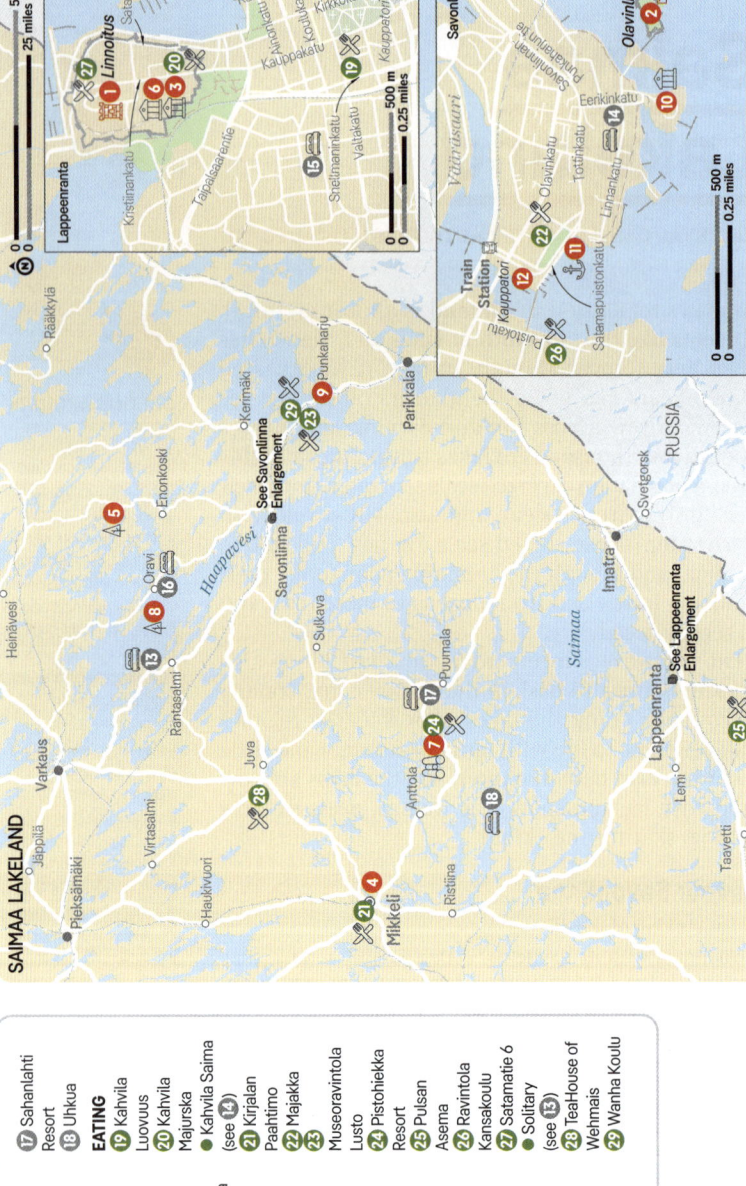

HIGHLIGHTS
1. Linnoitus
2. Olavinlinna

SIGHTS
3. Cavalry Museum
4. Kenkävero
5. Kolovesi National Park
6. Lappeenranta Art Museum
7. Lietvesi Scenic Road
8. Linnansaari National Park
9. Punkaharju
10. Riihisaari
11. Savonlinna Harbour
12. Savonlinna Market Square

SLEEPING
13. Hotel & Spa Resort Järvisydän
14. Hotel Saima
15. Hotelli Rakuuna
16. Oravi Village
17. Sahanlahti Resort
18. Uhkua

EATING
19. Kahvila Luovuus
20. Kahvila Majurska
- Kahvila Saima (see 14)
21. Kirjalan Paahtimo
22. Majakka
23. Museoravintola Lusto
24. Pistohiekka Resort
25. Pulsan Asema
26. Ravintola Kansakoulu
27. Satamatie 6
- Solitary (see 13)
28. TeaHouse of Wehmais
29. Wanha Koulu

(*savonlinna.fi/riihisaari*; adult/child €10/free) with various exhibitions, including History of Saimaa, featuring life-sized Saimaa ringed seals and some intriguing sailing and sea-life paraphernalia such as James Bond–like diving costumes from the 1950s.

Linnankatu is a cobblestoned street leading from the *linna* (castle) to Savonlinna's harbour. Grab lunch or coffee at **Kahvila Saima** (p143; *kahvilasaima.fi*), inside an old wooden villa and serving salmon soup and sweet treats.

Savonlinna's *kauppatori* (market square) and *satama* (harbour) sit side-by-side and are best experienced in summer when local delicacies such as fried vendace and *lörtsy* (pasty) are sold at stalls. The harbour holds a handful of old ships now transformed into restaurants, and pleasure boats offering slow rides to various parts of Saimaa. Jump aboard and take in the beauty of Saimaa. Cruises vary from one to eight hours (*visitsavonlinna.fi/sisavesiristeilyt*).

Unleash Your Island Explorer

Aquatic national parks

Kolovesi and **Linnansaari** National Parks are located on islands on Lake Saimaa. In summer, Järvisydän Resort provides kayak and boat excursions to Linnansaari. Another excellent starting point for exploring both parks is Oravi village, offering diverse accommodation options ranging from cosy cabins and tree tents on Linnansaari island to modern apartments and lakeside glass houses in the village. From Oravi, you can also take a boat taxi to Linnansaari.

When the lake is frozen, Linnansaari can be reached from Oravi and Järvisydän on marked trails, but don't stray from the path as it is important to provide a peaceful breeding period for the Saimaa ringed seals.

Linnansaari's landscape is created by the slash-and-burn techniques used by the island's farmers since the 16th century. Eventually, new deciduous forests grew from the burnt land, and now, the light-filled leafy forests create a safe haven for species from beavers to white-backed woodpeckers. There are trails of various lengths crisscrossing Linnansaari, the highlight being a climb to **Linnanvuori**, a rocky cliff with views of Saimaa's blue horizon.

Kolovesi National Park can only be visited during summer. Paddling quietly between the islets and tall cliffs rising from Lake Saimaa reveals the area's landscape at its most magical. Keep an eye on the small rocks, as it's possible to spot a ringed seal or two resting on them. From Oravi, it takes

---

WHY I LOVE SAIMAA LAKELAND

Paula Hotti, writer

Growing up near Saimaa Lakeland, the best thing about local road trips with family were the stops for ice cream.

It took me a couple of decades to appreciate what had always been there: a lakeland setting with its own archipelago, its endemic species of seal, and manor houses putting up feasts of local produce.

But most of all, amid all the hecticness of modern life, the calming effect of sitting atop a cliff, looking at the lakes dotted with small islands covered in pines, is unparalleled. Lapland might offer its oohs and Helsinki its aahs, but here, sitting on the shores of Saimaa, nature wraps you in a reassuring calmness.

 EATING IN SAVONLINNA: LOCAL FOOD

Kahvila Saima: Creamy salmon soup is served daily in Linnankatu street's charming villa near the castle. *9.30am-8pm Mon-Sat, to 6pm Sun summer* €

Market Square: Savonlinna's most iconic foodie spot – try *lörtsy*, a deep-fried pasty. For a sweet tooth, taste one filled with apple jam. *hours vary* €

Majakka: Fried vendace with mashed potatoes – or order the *sapas* plate, a tapas with a Savonian twist. *11-1am mon-fri, noon-1am Sat, noon-midnight Sun* €€

Ravintola Kansakoulu: A weekly changing lunch menu includes classics from herring in sour cream and vendace terrine to mushroom salad. *10am-3pm Mon-Fri* €

Saimaa ringed seal

A SONG THAT SAVED THE SEALS

Vanhojapoikia viiksekkäitä (Bachelors with Moustaches) by Juha Vainio is a beloved Finnish song from 1982, known for its heart-gripping nostalgic charm. The song's lyrics depict aging men with moustaches, one a human playing a harmonica on a lakeside, the other a seal, listening. The song's connection to the Lake Saimaa region helped rally public support for the conservation of the endangered Saimaa ringed seal. The seal's population had been dwindling, but the song brought attention to their plight. This cultural connection ignited efforts to protect the seals, ultimately contributing to their recovery. Today, you can see a statue of the man and the seal in Puumala.

one to two days to paddle to Kolovesi, with camping possibilities along the way.

Seal-Spotting

See the elusive ringed seals

Saimaa is home to one of the world's most endangered freshwater seals, the **Saimaa ringed seal**. These animals descend from ringed seals that were separated from the pack when the land rose after the last Ice Age, some 9500 years ago. Now, due to a tenacious protection campaign, there are about 400 seals living in Saimaa. The seals are typically under 1.5m and weigh 50kg to 90kg.

The best time to spot the elusive creatures is from May to mid-June, when the seals climb on top of rocks to moult, but you can make sightings till September.

As Saimaa ringed seals are protected, it's advised to try to view them on a guided tour. The professional guides also know the best spots for sightings. If you do venture out on your own, never go too close to the seals: the rule of thumb is to be at a distance at which you can seen them with binoculars.

One of the best ways to take in the beauty of Saimaa, and spot the seals, is to take an **eco-boat ride** (*lakelandgte.fi; adult/child €65/50*), silently gliding between Saimaa's many islands for an intimate feel of the landscape.

EATING IN LAPPEENRANTA: BEST CAFES

Kahvila Majurska: Located atop the fortress, Majurska's old-fashioned charms and cakes lure in plenty of people. *10am-7pm Mon-Sat, from 11am Sun* €

Pulsan Asema: A former railway station now cafe and design shop offering boutique B&B accommodation in summer. *11am-7pm Mon-Thu, to 4pm Fri-Sun* €

Satamatie 6: Award-winning cafe by the fortress steams up stellar flat whites and serves sweet and savoury treats and healthy snacks. *hours vary* €

Kahvila Luovuus: Cute and homey cafe with freshly baked cakes and buns just off the city's main shopping streets. *11am-5pm Tue-Fri, 10am-3pm Sat* €

An eco-boat trip from Puumala lasts 75 minutes and includes an informative narration given by the skipper. Binoculars – and coffee and buns – are available. In the end, you will hear a popular Finnish song telling the story of a lonely bachelor befriending a seal. The song made people fall in love with the seals and might have saved them from extinction, too.

ON THE WAY TO KOLI
If you're heading to **Koli National Park (p165)** from Helsinki, Lappeenranta makes a good pit stop before you continue deeper into the Karelian landscape. Lappeenranta is the capital of South Karelia whereas Koli is part of North Karelia.

Barracks & Borders
A hilltop fortress packed with museums

Lappeenranta's close proximity to the Russian border has shaped its history through the ages. In fact, the city is established on a **hilltop fortress** (Linnoitus) built here in the 1640s. Although Lappeenranta has since grown – it's now home to more than 70,000 inhabitants and a small harbour offering cruises to Saimaa Lakeland – the fortress is still the city's highlight, hosting a bundle of museums, from the **Lappeenranta Art Museum** to the **Cavalry Museum**. On and around the fortress there are also craft and boutique shops, cafes and views over Saimaa and the city.

A day is enough to explore Lappeenranta's main sights and it can be covered on foot, resting at some of the city's many restaurants or coffee shops along the way. You can also take advantage of the city's position as a gateway to Saimaa and enjoy a cruise on one of the slow boats operating from the harbour. The boats head to Saimaa's archipelago and all the way to Puumala and Savonlinna. Alternatively, cruise along the ill-fated Saimaa Canal connecting Finland's waterways to the Gulf of Finland via Russia. The 814km-long canal was built in the 1850s and has been an important waterway but today, since part of the canal is located in Russia, international cargo traffic has ceased and crossing the border via the canal is not possible.

OLAF'S CASTLE

Olavinlinna is one of the rare medieval castles in Finland that has survived to today. The castle was built in 1475 by Erik Axelsson Tott, a Dano-Swedish statesman. Designed to protect the region against Russia, the castle's strategic position on an island made it highly defensible – and striking to look at even now. Sixteen master masons were hired from Estonia, while locals paid their taxes by participating in the building and by providing materials. The castle is named after the Norwegian Viking king Saint Olaf (Olavinlinna means 'Olaf's Castle'), who is also the patron saint of knights.

EATING AROUND SAIMAA: OUR PICKS

Wanha Koulu: A summer restaurant and cafe cum design store is located in an old school. *10am-6pm Mon-Sat, from noon Sun* €€

Museoravintola Lusto: This museum restaurant serves local food from nearby lakes to mushrooms from the surrounding forests. *11am-7pm* €€

Kirjalan Paahtimo: A small cafe and roastery serves Mikkeli's best breakfast, the Taste Saimaa Breku. *7.30am-5pm Mon-Fri, 9.30am-3pm Sat* €

Solitary: Local flavours from mushrooms to currant leaves are served in a sleek fine-dining setting surrounded by treetops. *5-9pm* €€€

HELP ME PICK:

Saimaa Lakeland Boat Trips

Saimaa Lakeland is all about nature – a unique mix of serene waters, verdant forests and rocky islets. The true essence of the region is best savoured by embarking upon its waterways. Hop on a slow boat and cruise leisurely between charming towns, or participate in a quest to have a glimpse of the elusive ringed seals. For the more intrepid, a kayaking adventure is complete with the promise of pitching a tent onshore.

Where to paddle if you love...

Intrepid Expeditions

Saimaa Canoeing Self-guided kayak tours starting from Puumala. Along the way, you can camp or stay in Saimaa Canoeing's rustic lodgings scattered around the islands. In winter, try ice water kayaking.

Seal Trail Take on the 130km circular waterway to explore both Linnansaari and Kolovesi National Parks. Navigation skills and experience in long-distance kayaking are essential. The unmanned kayak rental is located at Kirkkorannantie 200 in Enonkoski, near Savonlinna, so pre-booking is necessary.

Chilled City Hops

Karelia Lines Hop aboard Karelia Lines' M/S *Camilla* in Lappeenranta (*karelialines.fi*) and see the historic Saimaa Canal which, until recently, connected Saimaa's lakes with the Gulf of Finland via Russia. While commercial traffic on this canal has ceased, you can enjoy a two-hour cruise to the canal and back (*adult/child €24/12*).

Sääminkiseura Experience Savonlinna the traditional way by renting a rowing boat from Sääminkiseura. You can book one using its online form (*saaminkiseura.fi/kaupunkiveneet*). The boats are free to rent for three hours, though donations are welcome.

Archaeological Sites

M/S Aino Cruise back in time with M/S *Aino*, dating back to 1893 (*ainosaimaa.fi*). As part of Mikkeli's hop-on, hop-off bus and boat service (*visitmikkeli.fi*), you'll first take a bus from Mikkeli to Ristiina or Puumala. From there, *Aino* continues to the ancient Astuvansalmi Rock Paintings, adorning the cliffs rising from Lake Yövesi since 4000–2200 BCE.

Seal Tours

Oravi Village Accessible seal safaris, sunset safaris and early-morning safaris: Oravi Village near Savonlinna is Saimaa's 'Seal Central' (Norppakeskus) and offers various boat tours to see the Saimaa ringed seals from May to September.

Nature Hotel & Spa Resort Järvisydän A nostalgic wooden boat takes you from Hotel Järvisydän to Linnansaari National Park to spot seals. The cruises come with coffee and snacks included, and you don't need to be a guest at the hotel to book one.

Saimaa Canal

HOW TO

When to go Many slow boats operate from June to mid-August; equipment rentals are open from around April to October.

Book ahead June and July are holiday months in Finland, so book in advance. Some more remote boat trips won't depart unless enough people are participating.

Budget Renting a kayak or canoe and sleeping in your own tent won't break the budget. Canoeing and camping also give a unique perspective of Saimaa.

Top Tip The 'Everyone's Rights' law guarantee that you can pitch your tent in the wild. Be sure to respect the rights and never leave a trace of your visit.

DIY or Guided Tour

Exploring Saimaa Lakeland's waterways at your own pace, enhanced by the joy of Finland's 'Everyone's Rights' to camp and forage, offers a profound sense of freedom. However, planning and expert map reading are crucial, especially for lengthy kayak or canoe expeditions. If uncertain, consider using local tour operators with in-depth area knowledge or start with a short paddling excursion to test your skills.

The daily price for a double kayak in Saimaa Lakeland typically ranges from €60 to €90, while canoes are around €50. In winter (from October to spring), some providers offer ice water kayaks, costing €80 for a single and €120 for a double. For example, self-guided three-day (two-night) expeditions with Saimaa Canoeing (*saimaacanoening.fi*) start at €180, with four-night trips priced at €260. Most rental places offer transportation for the equipment to the nearest town or city for an additional €50 to €80.

The easiest way to enjoy Saimaa on the water is by hopping on a slow boat, available in major cities like Savonlinna and Lappeenranta; *outroodactive.com* provides a comprehensive list of the best routes around the Saimaa region. *Visitsavonlinna.fi* has a map of rental spots near Savonlinna.

In winter Saimaa freezes over and there are very little, if any, kayaking possibilities and slow boats don't operate.

SERENE ROAD TRIP AROUND SAIMAA LAKELAND

Explore Saimaa's best spots for scenery, food and local lifestyle with this road trip around the Lakeland.

START	END	LENGTH
Savonlinna	Punkaharju	318 km; 3 days

After exploring ❶ **Savonlinna and its castle** (p141), take road 14 and 464 towards ❷ **Hotel & Spa Resort Järvisydän**. Relax in the lakeside spa or join a boat tour to the nearby ❸ **Linnansaari National Park** (p143) *(jarvisydan.com; adult/child €32.90/16.45)*.

Next, continue toward Juva on roads 464, 467 and 14. The rural landscape hides an English tearoom with a Finnish twist. After a refreshing break at the ❹ **TeaHouse of Wehmais** *(teahouse.fi)*, continue to ❺ **Mikkeli**, where you'll find a hospitable manor house ❻ **Kenkävero** *(kenkavero.fi)*. Kenkävero hosts a restaurant, cafe and boutique shops selling local designs, from jewellery to kitchenware.

Continue from Mikkeli on road 62 towards Sahanlahti Resort and you will pass a winding ridge with views over rocky islets scattered around the lake. This is the ❼ **Lietvesi Scenic Route**, part of the Saimaa Geo Park, located just before ❽ **Pistohiekka Resort** *(pistohiekka.fi)* and beach.

Stop at the nearby ❾ **Sahanlahti Resort** *(sahanlahtiresort.fi)*. Spend the night and immerse yourself in Sahanlahti's history as a 19th-century sawmill community.

Finally, head back past Savonlinna to Punkaharju and ❿ **Punkaharju ridge**, the most famous of Saimaa's eskers.

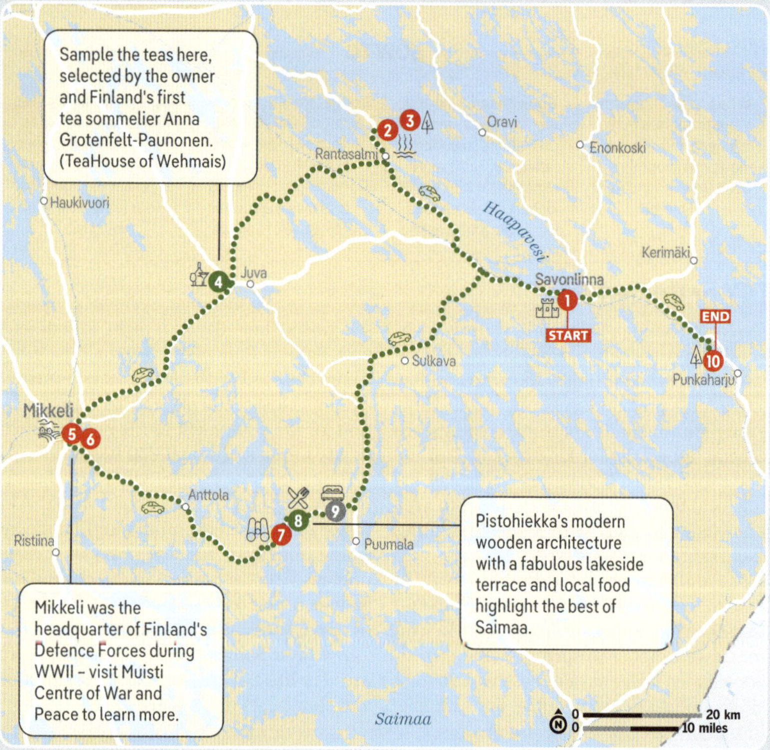
Sample the teas here, selected by the owner and Finland's first tea sommelier Anna Grotenfelt-Paunonen. (TeaHouse of Wehmais)
Oravi
Enonkoski
Rantasalmi
Haukivuori
Haapavesi
Kerimäki
Juva
Savonlinna
START
END
Sulkava
Punkaharju
Mikkeli
Anttola
Puumala
Ristiina
Pistohiekka's modern wooden architecture with a fabulous lakeside terrace and local food highlight the best of Saimaa.
Mikkeli was the headquarter of Finland's Defence Forces during WWII – visit Muisti Centre of War and Peace to learn more.
Saimaa
0 20 km
0 10 miles

Beyond Saimaa Lakeland

Explore Salpausselkä Geo Park's Ice Age marvels, or get curious over arts and sports in Lahti, Finland's leading green city.

Places

Lahti p149

Salpausselkä Geopark p150

Repovesi National Park p150

The strap of land between the Saimaa Lakeland and Helsinki makes a great area to explore in southern Finland. Like everywhere in the south, the landscape is dominated by forests and lakes: here, the main water is called Päijänne. Surrounded by the recently anointed Salpausselkä Geo Park, the region's main city Lahti is also unsurprisingly Finland's leading city in sustainability.

With three ski-jump towers and plenty of cross-country tracks, Lahti is also known for its winter sports. But it's not all about wintry fun here: in summer, there's an outdoor pool at the foot of the tallest tower, and the city centre has sights from a cute harbour to impressive museums to keep you busy.

Lahti

TIME FROM SAVONLINNA: **2HR 50MIN**

Lahti's artful reinvention

Long known as a winter sports centre, primarily for its ski jumping and cross-country skiing, Lahti, the European Green Capital of 2021, has been reinventing itself, tackling sustainability issues with success and establishing a flashy new **Museum of Visual Arts** *(Malva; malvamuseo.fi; adult/child €15/free)* in a former brewery building. After exploring the exhibitions, which vary from poster art and interior design to sculptures and paintings, take a break in the modern cafe Kahiwa, the Malski bistro, or the downstairs brewery restaurant Ant Brew.

Then stroll to **Lahti harbour**, lined with cafes and restaurants, to visit the small art gallery **Pro Puu** *(propuu.fi)*. *Pro Puu* means Pro Wood, and showcasing Finnish wood design helps you to understand more of the key elements of forests and wood in Finland. The gallery is free and open on weekdays, and its boutique sells outstanding wooden artefacts from Finnish designers.

Ski jumping

To get acquainted with one Finnish obsession, visit Lahti's three imposing ski towers, which are a 15-minute stroll from

GETTING AROUND

Lahti makes a convenient train trip from Helsinki. The journey takes about an hour, with one or two departures every hour. Lahti railway station is a 15-minute walk from the city centre.

Lahti's sights are easily explored on foot but you can also use the city bikes, called *Mankeli*, after downloading the Freebike 2.0 app or using a contactless payment card *(20 cents per minute)*.

To visit Lahti's surroundings, a car is the best option.

the city centre in Salpausselkä. The towers were built in the 1970s, and there is a **viewing platform** on top of the tallest one that can be visited from early June to late August. If you're lucky, you might see jumpers floating in the air like feathers as they practise their craft. If you are intrigued, step inside the Lahti **Ski Museum** (*hiihtomuseo.fi; adult/child €10/ free*) located by the ski-jump towers. The museum, which is closed on Mondays, details the history of skiing in Finland – the highlight is the 3D ski-jump simulator. In summer, there is an outdoor swimming pool at the foot of the tallest tower, making it an extraordinary spot for a day out.

Salpausselkä Geopark   TIME FROM SAVONLINNA: 3HR
Ice-sculpted landscapes

A unique landscape shaped by ice and water, the **Salpausselkä** area near Lahti was granted UNESCO Global Geopark status in 2022, highlighting the region's internationally significant geological formations.

The two Salpausselkä ridges – terminal moraine formations left by the Ice Age some 12,000 years ago – run the length of southern Finland and are at their most stunning near Lahti. Altogether, the formation is almost 500km long, rising at times as high as 80m. There are plenty of nature activities here, ranging from marshland walks to bike tours (see *visitlahti.fi* for details), but the main sights are the **Kelvenne** esker island and **Pulkkilanharju** esker, both part of **Päijänne National Park**. Kelvenne island is located in the southern part of Päijänne and can only be accessed by boat, such as M/S *Jenni Maria* from Padasjoki harbour, from the end of June till early August (*kulkeevettenhalki.fi; adult/child €35/20*)

Pulkkilanharju is best reached by car – it's 40 minutes from Lahti. The esker is about 8km long and includes a small patch of Päijänne National Park. Apart from the photogenic esker and bridges connecting small islands, there's a cute canal-side town, Vääksy. **Vääksy's channel** was built in 1871 and today it's Finland's busiest canal. The area is dotted with lovely cafes and restaurants in which to spend an hour or two.

Repovesi National Park   TIME FROM SAVONLINNA: 2¼HR
Climb, paddle, explore

Between the heartlands of Saimaa Lakeland and Lahti lies Repovesi National Park. Repovesi is most famous for the vertical rock wall **Olhavanvuori**, rising 50m directly from a pond below.

BEST ART FESTIVALS

Soundfest: A new addition to Finland's summer festivals brings Finnish pop and rap artists on stage in early June.

Lahti Organ Festival: For a week in August, Lahti fills up with Finnish and international organ music enthusiasts.

Lahti International Film Festival: In April, cinema Kinos shows short films in genres varying from music videos to drama, sci-fi and artsy flicks.

Lahti Sibelius Festival: The Lahti Symphony Orchestra's 26th International Sibelius Festival takes place at the end of August 2025, conducted by Hannu Lintu.

Jazztori: Jazzy tunes – with some big bands thrown in – have taken over Lahti for some 35 years for a week every September.

EATING IN VÄÄKSY: OUR PICKS

Ranskalainen kyläkauppa: French breakfasts, brunch and lunch. *9.30am-8pm Mon-Fri, 9am-9pm Sat, 10am-6pm Sun* €

Kanavan panimo: Vääksy's craft brewery opens its terrace in June and July, and the shop and tours run all year. *11am-6pm Mon-Sat, to 3pm Sun* €

Kanavan helmi: Artisanal ice creams, sumptuous doughnuts and other sweet treats by the idyllic Vääksy canal. *9am-9pm Jun-Aug, May varies* €

Wine & Cafe Jokiranta: A 1920s wooden house to enjoy savoury waffles, tapas plates or typically Finnish snacks. *11am-6pm Sun-Wed & Fri, to 8pm Thu & Sat* €€

Olhavanvuori

This is Finland's main destination for rock climbers, and a dramatic sight for everyone. It's also a good place for bird-watchers, as flocks of red-throated loons live by the cliff. The national park can be explored by foot, bike or kayak, which are available to hire at the park's service points (*tervarumpu.fi*) – Olhavanvuori, however, is out of reach for cyclists. Another popular sight is the 55m-long Lapinsalmi suspension bridge, but at the time of writing it was temporarily out of use.

Repovesi National Park is open all year round, but as with many other forest walks, the pathways here are not maintained during winter months, though they get tramped by visitors. There are also many private cottages here, which are off-limits even under Finland's Everyman's Rights. Repovesi's Valkjärvi Group Camp cottage can be pre-booked from April to October (*luontoon.fi*).

The easiest way to get to Repovesi National Park is by car (use Saarijärvi or Tervajärvi parking areas), but from mid-June to the end of October, bus 15 from Kouvola runs to the park on weekends. Alternatively, jump off the train in Mäntyharju and canoe, kayak or cycle the remaining 47km to Repovesi.

FINLAND'S WATERWAYS

With around 188,000 lakes and over 70,000km of rivers and streams, Finns have long known how to utilise their waterways to transport goods, especially timber. The earliest canals were built in the 18th century to connect Finland's inland waters to the sea. The most famous, the Saimaa Canal, opened in 1856, linking Lake Saimaa to the Gulf of Finland, enhancing trade with Russia and Europe. Today, many of these historic canals remain operational, combining heritage and modern use. The summer-time Vääksy canal is one of the liveliest, with 5000 vessels passing through it yearly.

 EATING IN LAHTI: OUR PICKS

Teerenpeli: A classic since 1994 includes a brewery, distillery and a deli. *2pm-midnight Sun & Mon, to 2am Tue-Thu, to 3am Fri & Sat* €

Gastropub Mylly: Good-value lunch available on weekdays and a touch flashier dinner options in gastropub style. *hours vary* €€

Bistro Popot: International dishes from mussels to the Swedish toast Skagen. *1-9.30pm Tue-Thu, to 10.30pm Fri & Sat* €€

Roux: A fine-dining, Chaîne des Rôtisseurs restaurant with set menus (including vegan) as well as à la carte. *4-10pm Tue-Thu, to 11pm Fri, 1-11pm Sat* €€€

Jyväskylä

ALVAR AALTO ARCHITECTURE | VIBRANT STUDENT CITY | LAKESIDE SETTING

Jyväskylä is dubbed the Athens of Finland due to its university campus and thriving creative spirit. The city centre is concise and clustered around the main shopping street, Kauppakatu, which runs 2km from 'Yläkaupunki's' (Upper Town) university area, dotted with Alvar Aalto's architecture, to 'Alakaupunki' (Lower Town). In Upper Town, there are bars, restaurants, museums and galleries, whereas approximately in the middle of Kauppakatu, you'll find Kirkkopuisto (Church Park), the city centre's main area of greenery. More restaurants and high-street shops line Kauppakatu in the Lower Town.

Ascend a block uphill from Kauppakatu and you are at the foot of a city-centre hill, Harju, where Jyväskylä's inhabitants go walking, running and occasionally partying. A view down towards the harbour shows Jyväskylä in another light: not only a studious academic hot spot with a youthful spirit, but also a calm lakeside city with an abundance of nature activities on offer.

GETTING AROUND

Jyväskylä is easy to explore on foot and you won't need public transportation for the main sights.

For quicker travel, rent a bike from the city center Polkupyörätori (*polkupyoratori.fi*) or hop on an e-scooter using the Tier, Voi or Ryde apps.

Ride-hailing apps such as Uber or Bolt don't operate here, so download the local JYTAKSI app or call 01006900.

If arriving by car, ample outdoor and indoor parking is available, and the roads are easy to navigate.

The bus and train center, Matkakeskus (Travel Centre), is just a five-minute walk from the city center.

☑ TOP TIP

Rent a bike and cycle around Jyväsjärvi, the lake at the centre of the city, to get a glimpse of Jyväskylä's urban and nature-driven lifestyles.

Alvar Aalto's Jyväskylä

Aalto overload

Jyväskylä has the largest number of Alvar Aalto–designed buildings of any city in the world. There are 29 in total, with the architect living and starting his career here, where he also married Aino Aalto, a designer and architect of her own standing. Get insight into Aalto's Jyväskylä at **Alvar Aalto Museo** (*aalto2.museum; adult/child €17/3*), dedicated to architecture and design inside a building designed by Aalto in the early 1970s. Next door, see the Aalto-designed **Keski-Suomen Museo** (*jyvaskyla.fi/keskisuomenmuseo; adult/child €17/3*). Then, walk uphill to the university campus and pop inside the red-brick **Capitolium** (*free*), built in 1955. From the campus area, which is dotted with Aalto's work from the 1950s, stroll down Kauppakatu to Kirkkopuisto and you'll recognise Aalto's style in the white **Jyväskylä City Theatre** (*jklteatteri.fi*)

SIGHTS
1. Alvar Aalto Museo
2. Capitolium
3. Craft Museum of Finland
4. Harju
5. Jyväskylä City Theatre
6. Jyväskylän Art Museum
7. Keski-Suomen Museo
8. Kirkkopuisto
9. Natural History Museum of Central Finland
10. Workers' Club Building

ACTIVITIES, COURSES & TOURS
11. Viilu

SLEEPING
12. Hotel Yöpuu
13. Time Hostel Jyväskylä
14. Verso Hotelli

EATING
15. Bistro Kirkkopuisto
- Kahvila Valkoinen Puu (see 18)
16. Lounaispuiston Grilli 21
- Pöllöwaari (see 12)
17. Teeleidi

SHOPPING
18. Toivolan vanha piha

TRANSPORT
19. Passenger Harbour

facade on the opposite side of the park. Continue down Kauppakatu until you come to the corner of Väinönkatu, where Aalto's first significant public building, the **Workers' Club** (*aaltosali.fi*), dating from 1924–25, stands.

Other Aalto highlights include the **Muuratsalon Koetalo** (*Muuratsalo Experimental House; aalto2.museum; adult/child €30/15*) and **Säynätsalon Kunnantalo** (*Säynätsalo Town Hall; tavolobianco.com; adult/child €10/free*), outside the city. Muuratsalo Experimental House was Elissa and Alvar Aalto's self-designed summer home and atelier, inspired by the idea of an Ancient Roman atrium. The Aaltos discovered the lovely lakeside spot while building the nearby Säynätsalo Town Hall in the early 1950s, and decided to construct a

---

LIVE MUSIC

Vakiopaine Becomes a stage for bands in the evenings.

Ylä-Ruth Bar favoured by musicians and underground artists.

Lutakko & Musta kynnys The city's best live-music venues.

Poppari Musicians gather for jam sessions.

BEST FAMILY FUN IN JYVÄSKYLÄ

Laajavuori: Laajavuori's slopes *(laajis.fi)* offer activities in all seasons, from downhill skiing to Frisbee golf and fat biking.

Spa Hotel Scandic Laajavuori: Located near Laajavuori, this small spa hotel delivers relaxation and fun for the whole family.

Pandan tehtaanmyymälä: This Finnish candy manufacturer's outlet store is a sweet-tooth's paradise and a good spot to try to buy some liquorice.

Spa Hotel Peurunka: 25km out of the city, you'll find a fun spa with a 130m-long slide, a bowling alley and more.

Mäki-Matin perhepuisto: A playground is always a good idea – especially if it is conveniently located near many of the city's sights, such as this quaint one.

---

summer house with multiple architectural experiments. One test was the use of various kinds of brick and ceramics in the walls – some bricks being leftovers from the Town Hall. The Experimental House can be visited by tour *(alvaraalto.fi)* from the beginning of June to the end of August. Säynätsalo Town Hall is open daily from June to August, with tours in English starting around noon. Outside those months, bookings can be made two days before your visit. There is also accommodation available inside Säynätsalo Town Hall.

Visit Jyväskylä *(visitjyvaskyla.fi)*, the city's tourism organisation, also organises Alvar Aalto tours; see options on the webpage.

Harbour Life, Lakeside Vibes

Fun by the water

In recent years, Jyväskylä's **harbour** has gone through rapid modernisation. Sprinkled with cafes, cruises and a modern sauna, the waterside area is now a popular spot for locals and visitors.

The harbour is easy to reach from the city centre: walk downhill, cross the train tracks and you'll find yourself by Jyväsjärvi's shores in a neighbourhood called Lutakko, mostly known for its namesake music venue.

The latest addition to the harbour is a modern sauna and restaurant, **Viilu** *(satamanviilu.fi; 2hr adult)*. There are three different types of saunas, two with panoramic lakeside views and one *savusauna* (smoke sauna). All saunas are mixed so bring your swimsuit. The changing rooms for men and women are separate. After, or in between saunas, it is possible to cool off on the terrace, plunge into a pool or relax in a jacuzzi. The pool uses water from the lake, so in winter, this is a fab spot to try ice swimming – alternatively, enjoy a brisk wintry evening in one of the heated jacuzzis. The saunas are warm from Sundays to Thursdays between 9am and 10.30pm and on Fridays and Saturdays from 9am to 11.30pm.

If you prefer a more private and unique sauna setting, you can also rent a **sauna float**, with Jyväskylä having many providers. Many **slow-boat tours** also depart from the Lutakko harbour to cruise on the calm waters around Jyväskylä.

Be sure also to check out **Alvar Aalto's old boat**, which is now permanently docked next to Viilu.

The harbour isn't only a summertime hangout. In winter, the frozen lake becomes a scene of **ice skating**, **skiing** and **walking tracks**.

EATING IN JYVÄSKYLÄ: OUR PICKS

Teeleidi: The best tearoom in central Finland is located in a cute town mansion (coffee also available). *11am-7pm Tue-Fri, to 4pm Sat* €

Lounaispuiston Grilli 21. A classic for after-party burgers, curly fries or *lihapiirakka* (minced meat inside a savoury doughnut dough). *hours vary* €

Pöllöwaari: Boutique Hotel Yöpuu's fine-dining restaurant offers international and Finnish dishes. *11am-3pm & 4-11pm Mon-Fri, 2-11pm Sat* €€€

Bistro Kirkkopuisto: A glitzy spot is in the central Church Park – people-watching and fab drinks. *9am-9.30pm Mon-Fri, from 10am Sat, 11am-8pm Sun* €€€

VIEWS, VAULTS & FEMINISTS

Wander through Jyväskylä, where Harju Hill offers sweeping vistas, and art, history and charming cafes will keep you entertained.

START	END	LENGTH
Harju	Kahvila Valkoinen Puu	2km; 2 hours

Start from ❶ **Harju**, the 34m-high hill in the city centre. Climb the stone-walled stairs and take in the view over the city and the lake. On top is the ❷ **Vesilinna observation tower**, featuring a scenic cafe and restaurant *(vesilinna-restaurant.fi)* and the small ❸ **Natural History Museum of Central Finland** *(tiedemuseo.jyu.fi)*.

Then, descend to the city and visit ❹ **Jyväskylä Art Museum** *(jyvaskyla.fi/taidemuseo)* and the neighbouring ❺ **Craft Museum of Finland** *(craftmuseum.fi)*. The art museum (closed Mondays) showcases Finnish and local art on two floors; those under 24 have free entrance. In the Craft Museum, admire Finnish traditional costumes and learn about the world of crafts through smells, sounds and tastes. Both museums line ❻ **Kirkkopuisto** (Church Park). A red-brick church from 1880 stands in the middle of the park. The park also has uplifting light installations during the Christmas season. From here, it's a few blocks walk to ❼ **Toivolan vanha piha** *(toivolanpiha.fi)*, a lovely courtyard lined with wooden buildings containing boutiques and craft workshops. Don't miss the charming ❽ **Museum Shop Sparvin**, located in Jyväskylä city centre's oldest building, dating from 1861. Finish your walk in the courtyard's ❾ **Kahvila Valkoinen Puu** *(valkoinenpuu.fi)*, a cosy cafe in a cellar with red-brick vaults.

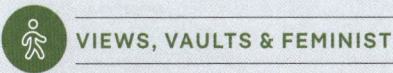

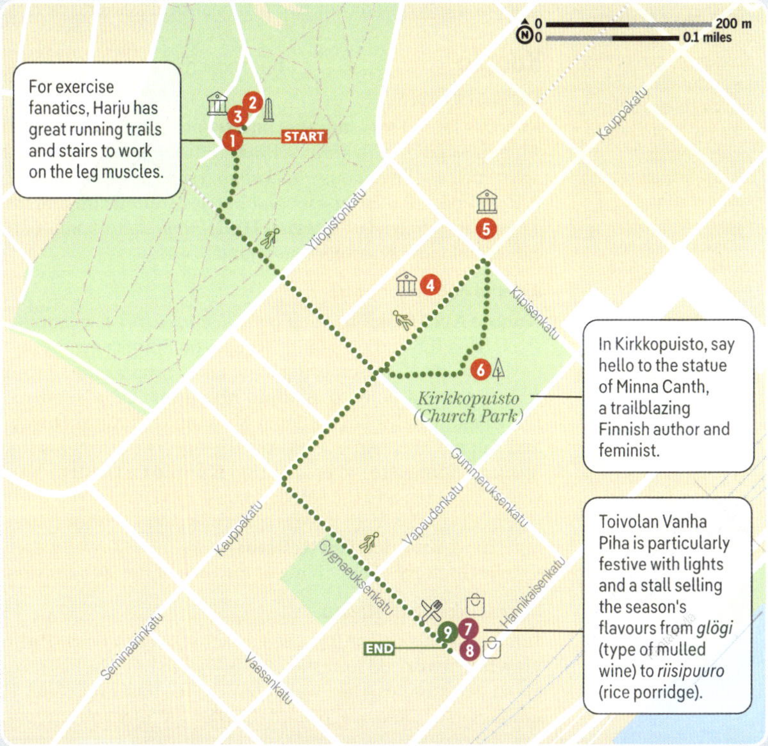

0 200 m
0 0.1 miles
For exercise fanatics, Harju has great running trails and stairs to work on the leg muscles.
START
1
2
3
4
5
6
7
8
9
END
Kauppakatu
Yliopistonkatu
Kilpisenkatu
Kirkkopuisto (Church Park)
Gummeruksenkatu
Vapaudenkatu
Cygnaeuksenkatu
Hannikaisenkatu
Seminaarinkatu
Vaasankatu
In Kirkkopuisto, say hello to the statue of Minna Canth, a trailblazing Finnish author and feminist.
Toivolan Vanha Piha is particularly festive with lights and a stall selling the season's flavours from *glögi* (type of mulled wine) to *riisipuuro* (rice porridge).

Beyond Jyväskylä

For more city life, head northeast to Kuopio, the affable capital of Northern Savonia, renowned for its traditional cuisine.

Places
Kuopio p156

Known for their distinctive dialect, the people of the Savonia region tend to have a cheeky twinkle in their eye. And no wonder – with Savonia's towns and cities located on lakeshores and surrounded by dense forests, the area is all about calm lifestyle. Kuopio is the capital of Northern Savonia, known for its lively summer market square and year-round market hall selling traditional foods. Kuopio and Northern Savonia was the first area in Finland to receive the European Region of Gastronomy Award, which it won in 2020–21. Apart from foodie finds, Kuopio, with its varied museums, makes a great stop for a relaxing day or two in a beautiful lakeside setting.

GETTING AROUND

Kuopio city centre can be explored on foot, and city buses will take you to outlying sights such as the Jätkänkämppä smoke sauna and Puijo's observation tower.

You can also rent an electric city bike from Vilkku-fillari via the Freebike app *(kaupunkipyorat.kuopio.fi)*. For €5 per day, you will have an unlimited number of 30-minute rides.

By train, Kuopio is two hours from Jyväskylä and about five hours from Helsinki, passing Lahti and Mikkeli.

Kuopio
TIME FROM JYVÄSKYLÄ: **1HR 50MIN**

Taste of Kuopio

Kuopio's famed *tori* (**market square**) is at its liveliest from June to August, with stalls selling traditional foods from the area, such as the famous *kalakukko* (rye-crusted bread with fish and pork baked inside) and berries from nearby farms. The square's Jugendstil **Market Hall** (*kuopionkauppahalli.fi*) caters to foodie cravings year-round.

Art and culture central

Kuopio Art Museum (*kuopiontaidemuseo.fi*), a few minutes' stroll from the market square, focuses on Finnish art. Almost next door rises an imposing Jugendstil mini-castle, dating from 1904 and housing **Kuopio Museum** (*kuopionmuseo.fi*), which includes both Kuopio Museum of Natural History and Kuopio Museum of Cultural History. The museums line Snellmanninpuisto, where the 1816 **Kuopio Cathedral** is located. The area and the wooden-house quarters on the south side of the park are an integral part of Kuopio's cultural heritage. Here, **Kuopion Korttelimuseo** (*kuopionkorttelimuseo.fi*) tells the story of city living at the turn of the 19th century.

Peaks, lakes and slopes

Jump onto bus 6, 7 or 9 at the market square to reach **Puijo viewing tower** and its restaurant (*puijopeak.fi*). The bus takes about five minutes, then walk uphill to the tower for about 15 minutes – the views will reward the effort. At Kuopio's harbour,

Jätkänkämppä sauna

board a **Roll boat** (*roll.fi*) and enjoy the scenic lakeside setting of Kallavesi from June to late August. In snowy months, visit **Tahko** (*tahko.com*), a 45-minute drive north of Kuopio, for a day out on its slopes for downhill skiing or snowshoeing.

Jätkänkämppä smoke sauna

A traditional smoke sauna is an out-of-the-ordinary experience, even for Finns. **Jätkänkämppä sauna** (Lumberjack's sauna) is one of the most lauded of these – it's located on the shore of Kallavesi in Kuopio. Take bus 7 from Kuopio's market square and jump off at Spa Hotel Rauhalahti. There is a sign to the sauna, a short walk away through the forest.

Pay for the sauna in the sauna's main building (*rauhalahti.fi; adult/child €17/8.50*), where a buffet dinner, accompanied by traditional tunes from an accordion, is served. Booking ahead for the buffet is advised. Here, you can also buy cold drinks to take to the sauna and enjoy on the terrace outside with views towards the lake.

Bring a swimsuit, as the sauna is mixed. Changing rooms are separate for men and women, and the receptionist will give you a towel. There are also special sauna towels on which to sit. Have a shower, step inside and relax.

It might take an acquired taste to enjoy the smokiness, but the experience is memorable: the scene inside, with people wrapped in a dim husk, is like something from an old Flemish painting.

TRAILBLAZING FEMINIST

Minna Canth (1844–97) was Finland's first female writer and journalist writing in Finnish, as well as a pioneering feminist. Widowed at the age of 35 with seven children, Canth was an advocate for women's education and equality, causing a stir with her critical plays. Although an applauded celebrity of her time, she was also verbally attacked by those opposing her views. Today, Canth is the first Finnish woman to be honoured with her own flag day: 19 March is Minna Canth Day and celebrates social equality. Minna Canth's salon in Kuopion korttelimuseo is furnished with items that belonged to the writer, such as the Neo-Rococo sofa and chairs.

 EATING IN KUOPIO: OUR PICKS

Kahvila Kaneli: Bossa Nova sets the mood in this cute cafe with simple lunches, cakes and pies. *11am-6pm Mon-Fri, from noon Sat* €

Sampo: Smoked, fried, rolled in rye flour...the vendace comes in many forms in this classic restaurant from 1931. *hours vary* €€

Sorrento: Awarded for its Neapolitan pizzas; pasta-freaks dine at Pasteria Sorrento, located in a Mill from 1776. *hours vary* €€

Musta Lammas: This cellar restaurant serves fine-dining plates inspired by the surrounding nature. *4.30-10pm Tue-Thu, to 11pm Fri, 3-11pm Sat* €€€

Hämeenlinna

CASTLE IN THE CITY | SIBELIUS'S HOME | CHARMING VILLAS

GETTING AROUND

Hämeenlinna is a very walkable city: it's barely a 15-minute walk from the medieval castle to city centre and its sights. To make it quicker, download the Joe Scooter or Bird app and use their e-scooters.

If you come by car, parking is simple as there are plenty of free roadside spots available.

Hämeenlinna is located between Helsinki and Tampere, and can be easily reached from both cities by train, bus or car. The bus station is in the city centre, while the railway station is a short walk away.

☑ TOP TIP

For a picturesque stroll, take a peek at the city centre, cobbled Linnankatu and its side streets, where many charming villas date from the 19th century.

Renowned for its mighty medieval castle, Hämeenlinna is Finland's oldest inland city. Officially founded in 1639, the city's roots date back to the turn of the 12th century, when a community settled here soon after the Swedish rule was established in Finland. In those days, Hämeenlinna was a crucial trading point passed by two important roads: one to the coastal Turku and the other to Vyborg, now in Russia. In 1777, King Gustav III of Sweden relocated the city centre, commissioning a charming neoclassic church reminiscent of the Pantheon, near the market square. The church survived a fire that razed three-quarters of the city in 1831. Subsequently, the German architect CL Engel, known for creating Helsinki's empirical look, redesigned Hämeenlinna to cater to the growing bourgeoisie – though few of his buildings remain. Modern Hämeenlinna is an eclectic mix of old and new, with fanciful villas rubbing shoulders with 1960s blocks of flats.

Castle Dreams, Prison Nightmares
Centuries of history

A 20-minute stroll from Hämeenlinna's central railway station brings you to the city's main attraction, **Häme Castle** (*Hämeenlinna; kansallismuseo.fi/fi/haemeenlinna, adult/child €14/7*), perched on the shores of Vanajavesi. Dating back to the late 13th century, Häme Castle is one of Finland's three remaining medieval brick buildings.

The castle's narrow corridors, small windows, and exhibits ranging from knightly harnesses to pilgrims' costumes make it a fascinating visit for the whole family. Be prepared to push prams over the cobbled courtyard, though. Inside, the castle's vaulted rooms and halls display its rich history through a variety of artefacts, including swords and exquisite tapestries.

In addition to its role as a castle, the building has also served as a prison and Finland's only women's convict prison. **The prison wing** (Vankilamuseo), open during summer, is

HIGHLIGHTS
1 Häme Castle
2 Palanderin Talo

SIGHTS
3 Hämeenlinna Art Museum
4 Museo Skogster
5 Sibeliuksen syntymäkoti
6 Vankilamuseo

SLEEPING
7 Matin ja Maijan Majatalo

EATING
8 Piparkakkutalo
9 Vanai Bistro & Bastu
10 Villa Marenki

DRINKING & NIGHTLIFE
● Nooran Viinibaari (see 4)

accessible to children with parental guidance, though some cell walls bear sexist and racist graffiti.

For those interested in military history, the **Artillery, Engineer, and Signals Museum of Finland** is located adjacent to the castle. In August, Finland's only **Medieval Fair** (*keskiaikafestivaali.fi*) brings another era alive in the park next to the castle. To visit the castle, prison and military museum, buy a combined ticket (*adult/child €23/12*).

A Colonel's Garden

Views from the top

The history of **Aulanko Nature Reserve** spans more than 10,000 years, to a time when the first people of Häme region were living in the area. But the resident who most shaped Aulanko was colonel Hugo Standertskjöldlived, who lived here in the late 19th and early 20th centuries, modifying Aulanko's landscape to create an English-style garden with artificial ponds, roads and leisure pavilions. He also planted foreign flowers and trees in the area.

Finland's government acquired the land in 1963, and in 1991 it became protected by the law. Now, there are several easy walking paths crisscrossing the park, the longest one stretching for 7km. In winter, there are two cross-country skiing tracks (4.5km and 6.5km) that are lit up, as well as an unlit 10km track around Aulangonjärvi lake. But the main sight here is a 33m-high granite viewing tower. The view from the top looks over the dark forests and lakes, and the tower's interior features make climbing the stairs a joy.

Descend from the tower using the stone staircases. Here, you will be greeted by a family of bears in their cave – this is *Karhuluola* (Bear Cave), a sculpture carved by Robert Stigellin in 1906.

JEAN SIBELIUS, NATIONAL COMPOSER

Born in Hämeenlinna in 1865, Jean Sibelius received piano lessons from his aunt and, more importantly, his uncle gave him a violin, which Sibelius loved.

Although the Sibelius family was Swedish-speaking, Jean (known as Janne in his boyhood) also spoke Finnish and attended Hämeenlinna's Finnish-language Normal Lyceum.

Later, he would become one of the greatest influences in creating Finland's national identity as the country struggled to free itself from Russian rule. Today, Sibelius, celebrated all over the world, has a special status in Finland as the country's national composer.

HÄME CASTLE

Häme Castle began as a single-storey stone camp in the late 13th century, fortifying Swedish rule. After defending against a Novgorodian raid in 1311, a second brick storey was added. Faced with disasters from fires to collapses and conquerors, Häme Castle also experienced grand times, particularly when the influential Lady Ingeborg was the castellan in the early 16th century. Briefly Danish in the 1520s, the castle changed hands between Sweden and Russia until in 1809 when Russia defeated Sweden for good, and Finland became part of the Russian Empire. In the 1950s, when Finland had been independent for decades, restorations begun.

Palanderin Talo

City Museums
Birthplace of a composer

Just around the corner from Hämeenlinna's central market square, an unassuming plaque decorates a yellow wooden building. This is the birthplace of Finland's most celebrated composer, Jean Sibelius (1865–1957), and now one component of Hämeenlinna's excellent collection of museums. Sibelius lived his first 20 years in the building with his family, and it was in this home that the young boy started his career in music. The **Birthplace of Jean Sibelius museum** (*Sibeliuksen syntymäkoti; hmlmuseo.fi; adult/child €10/free*), closed on Mondays, includes a beautiful music room with two pianos and a small bed chamber, believed to be the place where Sibelius was born. If you ask, the receptionist will play your favourite piece of Sibelius music from a CD during your visit.

Elsewhere in the city, the **Hämeenlinna Art Museum** (*hameenlinnantaidemuseo.fi; adult/child €12/free*) features an art collection that was saved from Vyborg in the 1930s, and exhibits Finnish and foreign art in its two buildings. **Museo Skogster** (*hmlmuseo.fi; adult/child €7/free*), located in a striking city-centre Jugendstil building, drills into Hämeenlinna's history across two floors, while **Palanderin Talo** (*hmlmuseo.fi; adult/child €8/free*) is a fabulous example of a 19th-century bourgeoise home and the accompanying lifestyle in Hämeenlinna. Booking ahead for guided tours is advised – check opening times online as they change every season.

EATING IN HÄMEENLINNA: OUR PICKS

Villa Marenki: This cute and cosy cafe serves hefty breakfasts to start the day. *8am-8pm Mon-Fri, 9am-5pm Sat, to 3pm Sun €*

Vanai Bistro & Bastu: A new bistro using Finnish ingredients to dish up magical plates in the city's old barracks. *3-10pm Tue-Thu, from 1pm Fri & Sat €€*

Nooran Viinibaari: For an after eightseeing hangout or evening tipple, sit down at Noora's Winebar. *4-10pm Wed-Thu, 5pm-midnight Fri & Sat €*

Piparkakkutalo: In a quirky wooden house (hence the name, 'Gingerbread House') serving fine-dining dishes. *5-10pm Tue-Thu, to 11pm Fri, noon-11pm Sat €€€*

Beyond Hämeenlinna

Hämeenlinna's surrounds are dotted with artsy finds, from world-class glass-blowing to fun naïve art. Take a day and tour around.

Places
Iittala Village p161
Visavuori p162

Many people know the stern granite statues carrying spherical lamps in their hands that guard Helsinki's Central railway station, and even more will have seen the wavy Aalto vase, adorning many homes since the 1930s. The former are works by the sculptor Emil Wikström, and the latter was designed by the world-renowned architects and designers Aino and Alvar Aalto. Today, Wikström's home and *ateljé* (studio) can be visited near Hämeenlinna in Visavuori, and pioneering items of Finnish glass design can be seen and bought at Iittala Village, where you can also watch glass-blowers at work. Iittala Village's playful naïve art exhibition is another must-visit.

Iittala Village
TIME FROM HÄMEENLINNA: 20MIN

Glass design hub
Finland is famed for its design, especially glasswork, with much of the fame due to **Iittala** (*iittalavillage.fi*), a glass-manufacturing village that has been making waves in the glassware world since 1881. After kicking off the business with Swedish designers, Iittala started to produce glass and crystal items designed by Finns during the 1920s and '30s. Then, Aino and Alvar Aalto brought their functionalist style to Iittala, with such items as Aino Aalto glasses and the curvy Aalto vase. Later designers included Tapio Wirkkala, Timo Sarpaneva and Kaj Franck.

Today, you can visit the viewing platform at the **glass-blowing factory** and witness the magic as skilled artisans practise their craft. The platform is free and open on weekdays but closed in July. Other spots to visit in Iittala Village include the **Iittala Glass Museum** (*iittala.com; adult/child €5/free*) set in an old barn (open June to August daily except Monday; otherwise open on weekends). The museum showcases Iittala's glass designs from mass-produced classics to unique art pieces, with an emphasis on contemporary glass designers, too. Nearby, the colourful paintings at the **Iittala Naïve Art Exhibition** (*naivistit.fi; adult/child €14/free*) create a welcome contrast to Iittala's glass products' sleek and controlled lines.

GETTING AROUND

Exploring the region around Hämeenlinna is easiest by car. Iittala is also accessible by train (12 minutes from Hämeenlinna, departures almost every hour). From Iittala's station, it's an 800m walk to the village. The bus from Hämeenlinna to Tampere stops at Uittamo (Uittamo crossroad), 1km from Visavuori. The bus trip takes 23 minutes and there are a couple of departures daily. In summer, hop aboard a Hopealinja boat (*hopealinjat.fi*), slowly shuttling between Hämeenlinna and Tampere and stopping at Visavuori in between.

EMIL WIKSTRÖM

If you've admired the tall granite statues holding spherical lanterns at Helsinki Central Railway Station, you're familiar with the work of Emil Wikström (1864–1942). After losing his father at an early age, Wikström and his three brothers were raised by their mother in Turku. Young Wikström's talent for sculpting was noticed and local benefactors sent him to study in Helsinki. Later, Wikström continued his studies in Vienna and Paris. He built his home and studio, Visavuori, in 1893-1912. He became the leading sculptor of public works in Finland and a key figure in the country's artistic Golden Age – although today he's overshadowed by his friends, painters such as Akseli Gallen-Kallela and Eero Järnefelt.

There are also many boutique shops in the area, including Iittala's classics and modern designs in the **Iittala outlet**, ceramics and little souvenirs at **Keramiikkapaja Anubis**, and bow ties made of leather recycled from old boxing gloves at **Naskali Leather**.

Visavuori

TIME FROM HÄMEENLINNA: **25 MINS**

A sculptor's studio

Be ready to be charmed by **Visavuori** (*visavuori.com, adult/ child €12/2*) in Valkeakoski, the Art Nouveau domicile of the sculptor Emil Wikström (1864–1942) and his grandson, the beloved Finnish cartoonist Kari Suomalainen (1920-99). The national romantic-style house was designed by Wikström, with plentiful Art Nouveau details inside. The bedrooms are serene, or even austere, but the kitchen and salon have definite wow factors, with most of the furniture bought from Paris. Surrounded by tall pine trees, planted by Wikström as a young boy, the house is also a prime example of Karelian building design.

Next door is Wikström's studio, its curved windows hiding behind Wikström's garden creating a Hobbit-like outlook. Inside, a somber atmosphere prevails, and you can see almost a hundred of Wikström's works on display. The studio is fun to explore with many details so allow yourself some time to linger – make sure to climb up to the small observatory, too. Downstairs, there is a summer cafe.

To get a glimpse of Finnish political history before the 1990s, visit also Kari's Pavilion. Kari Suomalainen was a prolific – and polemic – political cartoonist, and his strips are exhibited here. Suomalainen was a product of his times, and many of his strips have not lasted the test of time when it comes to political correctness. From June to August, Visavuori is open daily; closed in January and February, other months from Wednesday to Sunday.

Emil Wikström scultures, Visavuori

Koli National Park

ICONIC VIEWS | WINTER MAGIC | VARIABLE TRAILS

Located on the shores of Pielinen, Finland's fourth-largest lake, Koli National Park is the heart of the north Karelia region.

Koli's highest peak, 347m Ukko-Koli, is southern Finland's highest point. From the bare summit, the views sweep over forest-covered slopes to the shores of Pielinen, which is dotted with small islands. This is also Finland's best-known landscape, immortalised in Eero Järnefelt's paintings and inspiring his travel companion, the composer Jean Sibelius.

But you don't need to have an art degree to appreciate Koli's beauty. In winter, the national park is the southernmost point in Finland to witness the magic of crown snow-load, which transforms the foliage into a magical sight, heroically carrying the weight of snow. Winter is also the time to tackle Koli's slopes on skis or snowshoes.

The region's towns are sparsely scattered and offer few accommodation, restaurant and sightseeing options. Here, everything is about nature.

Hiking in Koli National Park
Southern Finland's highest points

Koli National Park has more than 60km of marked trails, ranging from an accessible (albeit slightly tricky) 800m route to a multiday 60km hike.

A classic is the 1.4km **Huippujen kierros** trail, taking in Koli's most famous peaks, **Ukko-Koli**, **Akka-Koli** and **Paha-Koli**. Here, the mountaintops are bare, pale grey and white quartzite, and the views sweep over lake Pielinen and its islands. Twisted and barren tree trunks mix with lush pine trees.

Another good route along the peaks is the 7.5km **Mäkrän kierros**, which heads to pristine forests and glades and has a spot for a campfire. This route has some steep climbs but the views from 313m Mäkrä hill, rising 219m above Pielinen, make the effort worthwhile.

GETTING AROUND

The best way to reach the remote Koli National Park is by car, with several parking possibilities near the trails. Joensuu, the closest city, is 63km away. From Joensuu, you can take a bus to Ahmovaara (9km from the park). When booking, search for the destination 'Ahmovaara (Juuka)'. Or book the recently opened shuttle/taxi from the train station to Koli. Pre-booking is required *(liput. matkahuolto.fi or vr.fi)*. Joensuu is a four-hour train ride from Helsinki, with the shuttle bus/taxi synchronised with the train schedule. The local taxi is called Kolin taksi *(kolintaksi.fi)*.

☑ TOP TIP

In winter, when Pielinen is frozen, you can get off the train at Vuonislahti village and take a taxi across the 7km ice road to Koli.

SIGHTS
1. Koli Nature Centre Ukko
2. Pirunkirkko

SLEEPING
3. Kolin Keidas
4. Vanhan Koulun Majatalo

EATING
5. Kahvila Kolin Ryynänen
6. Kahvila Lentävä Luuta
7. Kolin Satamaravintola

BEST WINTER EXPERIENCES IN KOLI NATIONAL PARK

Snowshoeing: Tackle Koli's snowy slopes on snowshoes on a self-guided or guided tour, organised by many hotels and companies, such as Koli Active.

Dogsled ride: Whizz across the frozen Pielinen lake pulled by frisky huskies.

Downhill skiing: Koli has a downhill-skiing centre with four lifts and seven slopes of varying difficulties.

Ice fishing: Thanks to Finland's Everyone's Rights law, people can ice fish freely.

Ice swimming: Dip into an ice hole for an unforgettable experience in Koli; see local providers at *koli.fi*.

The longest hike winds around **Herajärvi** lake, covering 60km and taking four days. It can also be cut almost in half, making it a three-day, 35km walk. The Herajärvi route isn't open in winter, but the shorter and more popular routes have tramped trails, left behind by a stream of other hikers.

In winter, Koli is Finland's southernmost spot to see *tykkylumi*, snow-crowned trees which create a picturesque setting. Another stunning sight is **Pirunkirkko** (Devil's Church). It is a narrow, rocky crevice approximately 34m long and 1m to 7m wide. This cave is steeped in folklore, with stories suggesting it was once a place for rituals and a favoured spot by witches. The name 'Devil's Church' reflects these eerie legends. The spot can be found about 12km south of Koli's peaks.

Koli Nature Centre Ukko is accessible by a funicular and there's car parking nearby. The centre has a little museum and maps of the area. Many walks begin from the centre, while others start from Koli village and Koli harbour. Longer trails also set out from nearby towns such as Lieksa.

EATING & DRINKING IN KOLI: OUR PICKS

Kolin Ryynänen: Unmissable red wooden house on Koli's main street serves the best dishes in the area. *hours vary* €€€

Kolin Satamaravintola: A harbourside restaurant serving pizzas with vendace, salmon and beetroot toppings. *11am-6pm* €

Kahvila Lentävä Luuta: Local produce and home baking, including Karelian specialties, in a cafe including a souvenir shop. *11am-5pm* €

Kolin Panimo: IPAs, Belgian ales and brunettes, as well as seasonal beers and ciders made of local apples are sold in the brewery's shop. *hours vary* €

Beyond Koli National Park

Koli's surroundings offer some of Finland's best wilderness scenery. Grab the camera or binoculars and go wildlife-spotting.

Places
Kuhmo p165

Home to Finland's highest number of bears and wolves, remote Kuhmo has also been at the crossroads of many of the country's historic events, mainly due to its proximity to the Russian border, with Swedish and Russian monarchs fighting over their possessions. In 1809, when Finland became part of Russia as a Grand Duchy, Kuhmo's businesses started to thrive. In the winter of 1940, Kuhmo witnessed heavy fighting during the Winter War against Russia, and the Talvisotamuseo, dedicated to this war, is now one of the town's main sights. Kuhmo is home to less than 10,000 inhabitants, and instead of bustling city life, it's a place that's all about nature.

Kuhmo
TIME FROM KOLI NATIONAL PARK: 2HR

Wilderness and wildlife

Around Kuhmo, the visitor experience is all about wildlife. It's an area dubbed as 'Wild Taiga', in reference to the landscape's untouched feel and the evergreen coniferous forest, which stretches all the way to Asia. Kuhmo's wilderness is a natural habitat for many of Finland's biggest carnivores, such as bears, wolves and wolverines. There are plenty of wildlife huts and tour operators in the area. Many visitors stay overnight in rented hides and cottages – with the sun barely setting around June and July in these latitudes, it makes an ideal setting for wildlife observation and photography. The season for bear-spotting begins around April and lasts till September or October when the animals start getting ready for hibernation. Wolverines and wolves move around the area throughout the year.

Wild Taiga (*wildtaiga.fi*) has huts for wildlife-watching in Kuhmo and nearby Suomussalmi. Located some 60km northeast of Kuhmo, **Bear Centre** (*bearcentre.fi*) has a large viewing cottage with beds and bathrooms as well as more private luxury cottages and small hides dotted around marshland that's roamed by bears and wolverines. **Wildlife Safaris** (*wildfinland.org*) offers versatile services and tours that range from wild-

GETTING AROUND

Kuhmo, located at the southeastern corner of the Kainuu region, is pretty much surrounded by wilderness and you'll need a car to move around here – the city itself is small. Helsinki is 600km away, and the nearest airport is in Kajaani, 100km west of Kuhmo. Kajaani has railway and bus stations, with buses running to Kuhmo multiple times a day. Buses between Kuhmo and Nurmes, 80km to its south, run on Fridays and Sundays.

SISU

Sisu is a uniquely Finnish concept that embodies resilience, determination and the ability to persist in the face of adversity, even when the odds seem insurmountable.

Often described as a form of inner strength, *sisu* goes beyond mere perseverance – it's about pushing forward with grit and courage (some might say stubbornness), even when the journey is difficult.

Rooted in Finland's history, particularly during tough times like the Winter War, *sisu* reflects the nation's spirit of overcoming challenges. To catch a glimpse of a modern-day, action hero–like personification of *sisu*, watch the film *Sisu* directed by Jalmari Helander.

life-watching in hides, to Northern Light hunts, to snowshoeing, with the possibility of finishing with a sauna or smoke sauna.

Chamber music and epic poetry

Combine wilderness and culture by visiting Kuhmo in July, when the city bursts into life for two weeks as it hosts the world's oldest and biggest chamber music festival, **Kuhmon Kamarimusiikki** (*kuhmofestival.fi*), attracting thousands of visitors. Kuhmo is also Finland's only UNESCO City of Literature due to its importance for the country's national epic poem, *Kalevala*. Elias Lönnrot, who penned the poem and roamed area writing down the area's oral folk poetry, would often stay in Kuhmo. Today, Finland's national Kalevala Centre **Juminkeko** (*juminkeko.fi; adult/child €5/free*) is located in Kuhmo and features one of the biggest *Kalevala* collections in the world. The log building housing the Centre is worthwhile to see, too, with its peat roof covered with heather.

The Arctic version of David and Goliath

If you know anything about Finnish history, it most likely concerns the **Winter War** (*talvisota*), fought between Finland and the Soviet Union in 1939–1940 and sparked by the Soviet invasion of Finland on 30 November 1939. Despite being vastly outnumbered, Finnish forces used their knowledge of the terrain, guerrilla tactics and sheer *sisu* (resilience) to resist Soviet advances. The winter was harsh, with temperatures plummeting to -40°C, and the **Talvisotamuseo** (Winter War Museum) hauntingly captures the essence of the times through photographs, original artefacts, maps, diaries and other materials. As a border city, Kuhmo's civilians also bore the burden of the war, with many being evacuated to western Finland.

Adjacent to the Talvisotamuseo is a digital exhibition about Arctic warfare based on the award-winning documentary series *Untold Arctic Wars*. The exhibition and documentary reveal lesser-known aspects of the war, with its crushing events intensified by the harsh surroundings. The digital exhibition is free to enter, and you can get the door code from the Talvisotamuseo.

Talvisotamuseo

Places We Love to Stay

€ Budget €€ Midrange €€€ Top End

Tampere MAP p133

Dream Hostel € Cool, clean and conveniently located by the Moomin Museum, Dream Hostel has dorms for 10 to 16 people and rooms for one to four people.

Hotelli Ville €€ A 10-minute bus ride away from the city centre, Hotel Ville is great value for your bucks and comes with a charming bistro downstairs.

Unity Tampere €€ Rooms come with a kitchenette in this convenient hub in Pyynikki with a gym and pizzeria-cum-brewery in the same building.

Solo Sokos Hotel Torni Tampere €€€ For the best city views head to the top-floor bar with a terrace – but don't forget to visit the sauna below the ground, too.

Saimaa Lakeland MAP p142

Oravi Village €€ Located between Linnansaari and Kolovesi National Parks, Oravi has an eco-hostel and tree tents on Linnansaari island as well as budget-friendly apartments on the mainland.

Hotel Saima €€ This lovely wooden villa in central Savonlinna has six rooms with vintage furniture – the suite is particularly spacious, while the castle-view room offers a vista of the castle.

Hotelli Rakuuna €€ The building used to house Lappeenranta's dragoons, and the military theme still shows in the simply furnished corridors and rooms.

Pulsan Asema €€ Charming set of traditional wooden cottages and villas in the yard of a former train station 13km from Lappeenranta city centre.

Uhkua €€€ The essence of Saimaa shines in Uhkua's floating cottage and sauna and its nature-driven activities from kayaking to foraging tours.

Lahti

Hostel Matkakoti Patria € Small, budget-friendly single and double rooms with shared bathrooms near the railway station.

GreenStar Hotel Lahti €€ Located in an unassuming block of flats next to Lahti's railway station, this hotel's ecological ethos counters its lack of flashy design.

Jyväskylä MAP p153

Time Hostel Jyväskylä € Unisex dorms and private rooms with colourful splashes for one to four people, as well as a shared kitchen and lounge.

Verso Hotelli €€ Located on the main shopping street, the interior is a touch worn-out but the fresh-looking, toiletries-packed sauna and the Jopo-bikes for guests are a treat.

Boutique Hotel Yöpuu €€€ This award-winning boutique hotel has rooms decorated with Finnish designs, such as Aalto, and fabulously Finnish breakfast items.

Kuopio

Lapland Hotels Kuopio €€ Centrally located hotel with a few touches of Lapland in the decor, as well as saunas for guests every evening.

Kylpylähotelli Rauhalahti €€ A popular spa on the shores of Kallavesi with indoor and outdoor pools as well as a traditional Jätkänkämppä smoke sauna tucked away in the forest.

Hämeenlinna MAP p159

Matin ja Maijan Majatalo €€ Quaint city-centre villa with plenty of homey characteristics, from wooden floorboards to an upstairs lobby with a small library and Nespresso machine.

Koli MAP p164

Vanhan Koulun Majatalo € Rooms with shared bathroom and kitchen, and two small ensuite apartments with kitchenettes, all in an old school building among lush forest.

Kolin Keidas €€ Rooms in the barn are more rustic than in the main building, but all come with a great atmosphere – the breakfast buffet is fantastic as is the sauna in a log building.

Above: Oulanka National Park (p197); Right: Market square (p190), Oulo

West Coast & Northern Ostrobothnia

HARBOURS, BOATS, ISLANDS & CITIES

Explore historic and contemporary maritime towns, intriguing archipelagos and lake-strewn inland forests.

As you drive north from Turku along the coastal roads that run parallel to the Gulf of Bothnia, historic harbour towns link to buzzing university and tech hubs facing tens of thousands of islands scattered in the waters that separate this part of Finland from Sweden. Despite their differences, many of Finland's western cities have suffered a similar fate in the past – ravaging fires have torn down wooden urban centres multiple times. UNESCO-listed Rauma has managed to keep some of its medieval architecture intact, but cities like Pori, Vaasa and Oulu have all been reconstructed, leaving few traces of their ancient roots. The transformation of this part of the country through the ages is best observed in nature – this is a coastline with a profile that has been continuously changing for millennia, thanks to the phenomenon of post-glacial uplift, which in some places has pushed the sea back as much as 100km since the last Ice Age. This unique phenomenon can be seen in the Kvarken Archipelago, partially connected to the mainland thanks to Finland's longest bridge. The city of Oulu, European Capital of Culture in 2026, is capital of the region of Northern Ostrobothnia (Pohjois-Pohjanmaa), which stretches below Lapland to the Russian border. Its eastern forests and hills are home to some remote national parks, chief among them Oulanka, the rivers and canyons of which form some of the country's most dramatic scenery.

THE MAIN AREAS

RAUMA
Charming old wooden town. **p174**

VAASA
Buzzing university city and port. **p182**

OULU
Growing cultural capital and tech hub. **p190**

OULANKA NATIONAL PARK
Dense forests and raging rivers. **p197**

Find Your Way

The 600km of coast from Uusikaupunki to Oulu is home to many attractive towns and thousands of islands. Across Finland's central 'waist' lie remote forests, canyons, lakes and rivers. From four hubs you can explore this diverse slice of Finland.

Oulanka National Park, p197
Forests, canyons, waterfalls, rapids, hanging bridges – Oulanka is one of Finland's top destinations for hikers, canoeists, rafters and all nature-lovers.

Oulu, p190
The likeable 'capital of the north'; spread over several islands, with plenty of good food, drink, music, art and quirky humour.

THE GUIDE

WEST COAST & NORTHERN OSTROBOTHNIA

CAR & MOTORCYCLE
Your own wheels are by far the most convenient way of getting around the region. There are car rentals at all four airports (Pori, Vaasa, Oulu and Kuusamo) and in several town centres.

TRAIN
Railways reach Pori, Vaasa, Seinäjoki, Jakobstad and Oulu, but for intra-regional travel they are only really useful on the northern section between Seinäjoki and Oulu – plus the Vaasa–Oulu route, which is better served by trains than buses.

BUS
Buses are the only public transport between many towns – frequent on some routes, scarce on others. They also helpfully reach some very out-of-the-way places, such as Hailuoto island near Oulu and the Karhunkierros trailheads around Oulanka National Park.

Vaasa, p182
A bright modern seaside city from which you can easily journey out to some remarkable islands and quaint historic towns.

Rauma, p174
This charming, UNESCO World Heritage-listed old wooden town is very much alive, with a multitude of good eateries, bars and shops.

Plan Your Time

As you travel this coast, enjoy the varied towns but be sure to get out to some of the islands. Check opening dates for anywhere you want to visit: some places have extremely short seasons.

Vanha Raatihuone(p174), Rauma

Just a Couple of Days

● Head to **Rauma** (p174), which arguably best preserves the coast's unique flavour. Start on the old wooden town's market square, **Kauppatori** (p174) and have a wander, visiting landmarks such as the **Vanha Raatihuone** (p174), with a museum and crafts shop within, and the **Marela** (p176) house museum. Lunch at bistro **Sydvest** (p177), visit **Pits-Priia** (p177) with its delightful lacework, and dine later at traditional, wood-beamed **Wanhan Rauman Kellari** (p177).

● On your second day, take a trip to **Kuuskajaskari** (p180) island, exploring its forests and old fortifications on the walking trail and enjoying lunch in the cafe in the old barracks. Alternatively, drive out to the **Noormarkku Ahlström Works** (p179) to admire Alvar Aalto's Villa Mairea and other notable architecture dotting the manicured gardens of this former industrial area.

Seasonal Highlights

Almost throughout the region, the ideal months to visit are June to September. The weather is at its best, daylight is long and almost everything is open.

JANUARY
A good month for winter sports at Ruka: New Year crowds have gone and the **Polar Night Light Festival** brightens everything.

MARCH
Mainly classical and jazz concerts welcome the spring in the two-week **Oulu Music Festival**.

JUNE
Schools break up and the summer season starts; the nights are bright, and the eastern lakes and trails have unfrozen.

A Few Days to Travel Around

● Spend a day and night in old **Rauma** (p174) and discover the town's maritime heritage at the local **Maritime Museum** (p176). Then head out to the UNESCO-listed Stone Age mounds of **Sammallahdenmäki** (p180) and down to **Uusikaupunki** (p000) to check out the quirky **Bonk** (p181) museum and a couple of restaurants and bars. The following day, cycle the **Velhovesi Ring** (p180).

● Day four: travel up to Vaasa, breaking the journey at charming old **Kristinestad** (p188). Spend a day exploring **Vaasa** (p182) and its lively restaurants and bars, then venture out to the **Kvarken Archipelago** (p186) by crossing Finland's longest bridge, Replot. See post-glacial uplift in action on the **Bodvattnet nature trail** (p187) and climb the Saltkaret observation tower for a bird's-eye view of the archipelago's thousands of islets. Round things off with a meal at **Cafe Arken** (p187).

Exploring in Greater Depth

● Do everything in the previous itinerary then continue north to the interesting old-meets-modern town of **Jakobstad** (p187) and the nearby **Nanoq Arctic Museum** (p188), where you'll get to know the stories and living conditions of some of the best-known explorers of the extreme north. Head on to laid-back **Oulu** (p190) to enjoy a day of city life in northern Finland's biggest metropolis, titled European Capital of Culture 2026.

● Take a day trip to the island of **Hailuoto** (p194) for an organic beer-tasting and a visit the red village of Marjaniemi. Continue to the forests of **Oulanka National Park** (p197) near the Russian border for a couple of days' hiking along the famous Bear's Trail and maybe a day of gentle canoeing or thrilling white-water rafting.

JULY	AUGUST	SEPTEMBER	NOVEMBER
Finland's peak holiday month: coastal towns fill, and festivals like **Pori Jazz** and **Rauma Lace Week** are celebrated. Also peak mosquito month (bad for hiking).	Schools go back in the second week, so it's a more tranquil time to travel, still with decent weather.	Best month for Oulanka and Hossa national parks: autumn colours, few insects and reasonable weather.	Oulu's **Lumo Light Festival** fends off the darkness; ski jumpers and cross-country skiers flock to **Ruka Nordic** weekend; and you might see the aurora borealis.

Rauma

MARITIME HERITAGE | MEDIEVAL ARCHITECTURE | MARKETS & CRAFTS

GETTING AROUND

There is no direct connection to Rauma by train, but buses run frequently from Turku, Tampere, Helsinki and towns along the coast. Once you get there, Old Rauma is easily explored on foot. There's very limited parking in the old town, but plenty of spaces just outside it. Rauma's very professional tourist information service (*visitrauma.fi*) is normally based just outside the old town at Valtakatu 2, but from June to August it opens an office in the Vanha Raatihuone (the old town hall) in the heart of old Rauma.

☑ TOP TIP

The best time to visit Rauma is in the second half of July, when the city celebrates its Lace Week with markets and public performances for the whole family all around the old town. Check the program on *visitrauma.fi*.

Rauma preserves the imprint of the past like few other places in Finland. Its charming old quarter, Vanha Rauma (Old Rauma), with some 600 old houses, has UNESCO World Heritage listing as an outstanding example of an old Nordic wooden city. Though Rauma got its charter in 1442, it burned down twice in the 17th century, so the old town mostly dates from the 18th and 19th centuries, when Rauma became one of Finland's biggest trading ports. It remains intimately linked with the sea. The making of fine lace also plays a big part in Rauma's story: in the early 19th century, when this cottage industry peaked, almost all Rauma women engaged in it. Vanha Rauma remains the lively hub of town life, with over 100 shops, restaurants and cafes. The largest and most atmospheric of a few old wooden towns on Finland's west coast, it's also a base for some excellent mainland and island excursions.

Exploring Old Rauma

A living past

Covering a surface of 29 hectares, Old Rauma is one of the best-preserved collections of urban wooden architecture in the Nordics. Its picturesque cobbled streets branch out from the central market square, Kauppatori, still active year-round in its original function with colourful flower and produce stalls. The Baroque old town hall, the **Vanha Raatihuone**, dates from 1776 and it's Rauma's most prominent historic building.

Two blocks north of Kauppatori rises the beautiful **Pyhän Ristin Kirkko** (Holy Cross Church), built in the early 16th century, originally as part of a Franciscan convent. The vivid east-end murals date from the church's early years and present the biblical story of salvation. It's Rauma's oldest building and Finland's only still-functioning church built by Franciscans.

As you stroll through the streets, notice the porcelain dogs sitting on many of the windows. It's an old tradition – when the dogs looked outwards it meant that the man of the house was

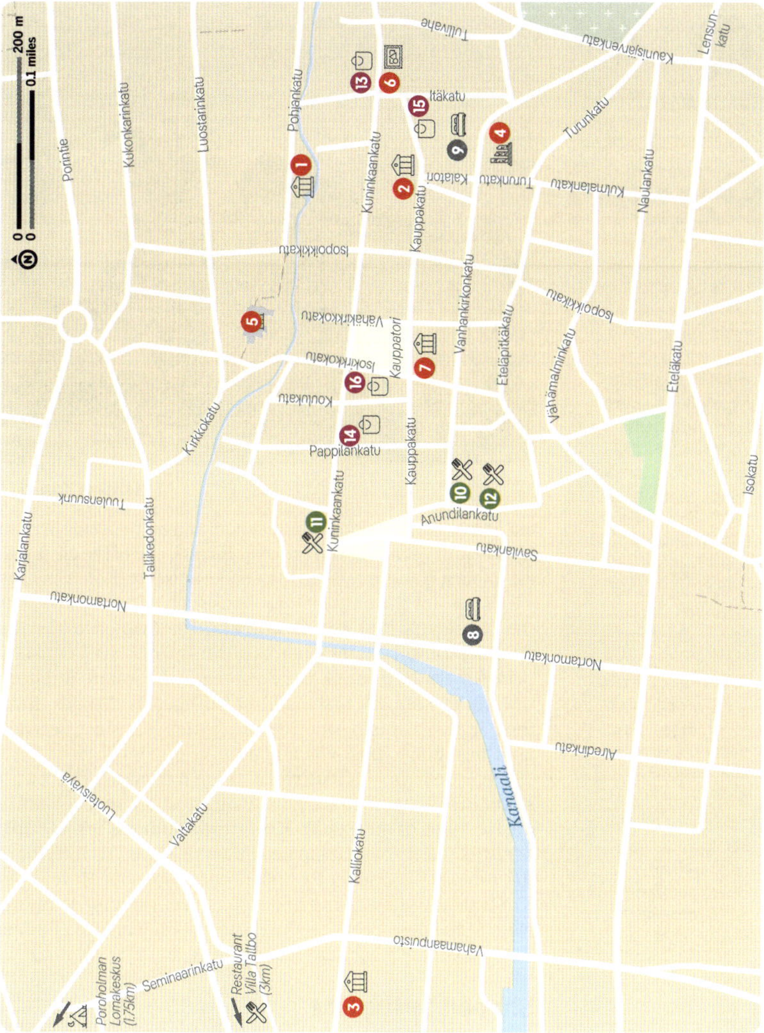

WEST COAST & NORTHERN OSTROBOTHNIA RAUMA

SIGHTS
1. Kirsti
2. Marela
3. Maritime Museum
4. Pyhän Kolminaisuuden Kirkko
5. Pyhän Ristin Kirkko
6. Rauman Taidemuseo
7. Vanha Raatihuone

SLEEPING
8. Hotelli Cityhovi
9. Hotelli Vanha Rauma

EATING
10. Savila
11. Sydvest
12. Wanhan Rauman Kellari

SHOPPING
13. Heikkilän taidepiha
● Kistupuad (see 2)
14. Kultaseppä Laiho
15. Pits-Priia
16. TaruLiina

Maritime Museum

RAUMA'S LACE WEEK

Usually starting in the last week in July, Rauma's most awaited event celebrates the town's lacemaking heritage, with a contemporary twist. Three different markets – one dedicated to international street food, the other to crafts and the last to lace – liven up the town's central streets for seven consecutive days. During the days of the festival, local artisans open their workshops for people to visit and learn about the craft legacy of this maritime town. A rich programme for children makes the event especially family-friendly – live performances are held on the big stage set up in Rauma's central square. Check out the full programme on *visitrauma.fi*.

out at sea. To get an idea of how sailors and craftspeople lived in 19th-century Rauma, you can visit **Kirsti**, one of the city's oldest wooden houses preserved as a home museum on Pohjankatu.

Kirsti is not the only historic house you can visit. Towards the old town's east end is **Marela**, the former home of a late-19th-century shipowner, beautifully preserved in grand period style. In front of Marela spreads the square Kalatori, the site of Rauma's first buildings in medieval times. Back then Kalatori was beside the sea, which has since receded 2km west due to post-glacial uplift.

East of Marela is **Kitukränn**, often named the narrowest street in Finland with its 2.6m width, and at a short distance are the ruins of the **Pyhän Kolminaisuuden Kirkko** (Holy Trinity Church), which burned down in 1640. The interior of the Town Hall is currently under renovation, but Marela and Kirsti can be visited with a joint €8 ticket valid for 48 hours, which includes access to the Rauman Taidemuseo (Rauma Art Museum). Check seasonal opening hours at *rauma.fi*.

Shaped by the Sea

Learn about Rauma's seafaring history at the Maritime Museum

If you've ever considered a career as a ship's captain, Rauma's **Maritime Museum** (*rmm.fi; adult €9*) is a good place to start. Dating from 1900, the towering building now housing the exhibition functioned as the training centre for the crews setting off to cross the Gulf of Bothnia and the Baltic Sea to export Finland's coveted timber. As the many artefacts on display show, Old Rauma has been shaped by its relationship with the water – seafaring brought prosperity, influenced the local dialect and attracted enemies. The local naval industry reached its peak at the end of the 19th century, when Rauma boasted Finland's largest fleet of sailing vessels. While the

Nautical College has now moved to more modern premises, there is still much to learn around here. Besides the rich collection of Romantic paintings depicting rough seascapes and the models used to teach young shipbuilding students the tricks of the trade, you can test your hand at navigating a ship through Rauma's archipelago with the Jenny simulator. The museum's guide will run you through the switches and gears before letting you attempt a docking at Rauma's port.

Lace & Other Crafts
Keeping old traditions alive

Lace-making has been central to Rauma's economy for centuries. Lace models were brought to Rauma by sailors from abroad, and from the 18th century the production of lace became the main source of income for women in the town. A few artisans still operate in the city – **Pits-Priia**, the shop of the local Lacemakers Association in Kauppakatu, sells all sorts of lace products and equipment to make your own. If you're lucky you may even see some artisans at work there. **Kistupuad**, in the home-museum Marela, has a good selection of local crafts, including lace items; and jeweller **Kultaseppä Laiho** (*kultaseppalaiho.fi*) makes some wonderfully intricate silver items based on Rauma lace designs.

Lace isn't the only craft that defines Rauma today – in fact, the old town is full of workshops and atelier worth stepping into. Opening hours vary from season to season. As well as classic all-Finland design houses such as Pentik and Marimekko, you'll find numerous small-scale local enterprises. **TaruLiina** (*taruliina.fi*), on Kuninkaankatu, has an eclectic collection, including some silver knives and key rings recycled from old spoons. Off the east end of Kuninkaankatu, you'll find **Heikklän taidepiha** (Heikklä art yard), a historic courtyard hosting the studios or galleries of five different artists.

Art Discoveries
Paintings of the Finnish golden age

Behind the pink walls of a late-18th-century building on Kuninkaankatu, find the collection of Rauma's **Taidemuseo** (*Art Museum; rauma.fi; adult €7*), stretching on both sides of the courtyard of one of the first stone houses built in the city. The permanent exhibition of the museum showcases a small selection of paintings produced by Finnish golden-age artists such as Albert Edelfelt, Akseli Gallen-Kallela and Eero Järnefelt between the late 19th century and the early 20th century. There is also a section dedicated to temporary exhibitions changing throughout the year.

MEETING THE LOCALS

Aino Koivukari, World Heritage coordinator in Rauma, shares her tips.

Everybody meets up in Old Rauma. It offers various charming cafes to treat yourself with delicious traditional pastries. Do it like the locals and get your coffee and a doughnut at the market square – enjoy them standing by the kiosk in the morning. *Pystökaffe* (standing-up coffee) is a traditional way to start the day.

The residents of Old Rauma are friendly: ask permission to have a peek into courtyards behind closed gates. The private courtyards are open for visitors also during the Lace Week festival in July. You'll get an authentic insight into people's daily lives!

 EATING IN RAUMA: OUR PICKS

| **Restaurant Villa Tallbo:** Villa Tallbo offers a generous lunch buffet of cold fish cuts and warm dishes. *10.30am-2pm Mon-Fri, noon-4pm Sat & Sun* €€ | **Sydvest:** Internationally inspired salads, or live on the edge and order a five-course 'chef's surprise menu'. *11am-2pm & 5-10pm Tue-Fri, 4-10pm Sat* €€ | **Wanhan Rauman Kellari:** The restaurant expands onto the sunny terrace in the summer. *11am-10pm Mon-Thu, to 10.30 Fri & Sat, noon-9pm Sun* €€ | **Savila:** Big gourmet burgers, salad and tasty desserts. Veg options available. *10.30am-9pm Mon-Thu, to 10pm Fri & Sat* €€ |

Beyond Rauma

Exploring the areas around Rauma you'll find Islands, lighthouses, beaches, seafaring towns and dense forests wait to be discovered.

Places
Pori p178
Sammallahdenmäki p180
Uusikaupunki p180

The labyrinthine archipelagos of Finland's southwest coast beg to be explored: hundreds of low-lying islands large and small, some little more than bare rocks, others with forests, beaches, lighthouses, accommodation and restaurants. You can reach them by summer water buses, on boat taxis, by paddling your own canoe or kayak or, in the Velhovesi Ring islands, by cycling or driving across small dams and bridges. The Bothnian Sea National Park groups dozens of separate tracts of sea and land strung along 160km of this coast. On land, the laid-back port of Uusikaupunki and the larger city of Pori, with the superb sweep of Yteri beach nearby, are within an hour's drive of Rauma.

GETTING AROUND

Having your own vehicle certainly makes things easy. Parking is straightforward everywhere. Otherwise, there are frequent buses between Rauma and Pori (where the bus station, the Matkakeskus, is 1.2km south of the city centre); and six each way (Monday to Friday only) between Rauma and Uusikaupunki. Pori city buses 34, 34M, 34R or 34W, which run about hourly, link the Matkakeskus with the central Kauppatori square and Yteri (a 50-minute trip).

Pori

TIME FROM RAUMA: **40MINS**

Nordic dunes

A 20-minute drive from Pori's city centre are some of the largest sand dunes you can find in Northern Europe. During long summer weekends, locals flock to the 3km beach of **Yteri**, reached through the a wooden walkway that climbs over the sand and then down into the Gulf of Bothnia. Despite it's popularity, Yteri remains fairly relaxed and family-friendly, but if you are looking for some action you have plenty of options in the area. You can rent a fatbike from the **Huikee Adventure Park** (*seikkailupuistohuikee.fi*) to explore on two wheels, or follow the hiking paths that cut through the forested areas surrounding the sand. The Lietteiden Reiten, a 4.5km (one-way) route from the south end of the main beach, traverses coastal wetlands, mainly on boardwalks, via several birdwatching platforms. A new, modern visitor centre was set up in 2024 in Yteri – stop by to pick up a map of the trails and choose your adventure.

Nine times on fire

Besides the pleasant Kokemäenjoki riverbank area dotted with stone buildings and parks, the grid-shaped city centre of Pori (Swedish: Björneborg) may not look that appealing at first glance – most of its historic buildings had to be rebuilt in the 19th century following the most recent of a long string of fires that have burned down the city throughout its history.

In 1852, 295 of the town's 392 plots were destroyed – this was only the last of the nine recorded fires that have damaged the town since the 16th century. Yet, while some traces have disappeared, the history of this region is long and convoluted, as you'll learn in the excellent **Satakunnan Museo** (*satakunnanmuseo.pori.fi; adult/child €8/4*). Starting from the arrival of the first humans in the region around 9000 years ago, the museum tells of the evolution of the Satakunta province where Pori is found through many thousands of exhibits spread across three floors. You'll learn about the founding of Pori in 1558 and its development as Finland's northernmost town (until the 17th century) during the Swedish era, moving all the way to the 20th century and the impact of WWII.

How stuff was made

It is quite impressive to think that in the 19th and 20th centuries a single brand, the Rosenlew Company, managed to provide so many different kinds of machinery to Pori's expanding population. From steamships to household appliances to agricultural equipment, the Rosenlew family knew how to play the supply-and-demand game. The **Rosenlew Museo** (*rosenlewmuseo.pori.fi; adult/child €7/2.5*), housed inside a former brick granary dating back to the 1860s, tells the story of how dozens of essential items were produced by what became one of the largest industrial companies in Finland.

The last ironworks

A 15-minute drive from Pori, in the area of Noormarkku, are the manicured grounds of the **Noormarkku Ahlström Works**, the last ironworks established in Finland under Swedish rule. Set up by General Carl Constantin De Carnall in 1806, only three years before Finland would become part of the Russian Empire, the grounds were eventually purchased by Antti Ahlström, who expanded and transformed the area into a picturesque space for aristocratic residences. Besides the remnants of the industrial era, connected by bridges that cross streams and ponds, in Noormarkku you'll find important pieces of 19th- and 20th-century architecture surrounded by beautifully kept gardens. Among the most prominent examples are the castle-like Isotalo, designed in 1881 by architect Evert Lagerspetz, standing in contrast to the minimal **Villa Mairea**, designed by Alvar and Aino Aalto in 1939. You can walk freely through the gardens of Noormarkku but to visit the interior of Villa Mairea you'll need to join one of the frequent group tours (*€30, book via villamairea.fi*). A restaurant and a number of boutique hotel rooms are also available on the grounds.

PORI JAZZ

The city of Pori bursts into life in the first half of July for Pori Jazz, one of Finland's biggest festivals of any kind. Well over 300,000 people have attended some recent editions. The focus of the musical action is leafy Kirjurinluoto park, where dozens of free concerts happen during the first six days of the nine-day festival. The final three days see the big-name acts playing in a ticketed area, also in Kirjurinluoto. Finnish jazz gets a big piece of the action, but the line-ups are broad. Megastars such as Elton John, Miles Davis and Björk have played Pori in the past, and recent editions have hosted the likes of Nick Cave, Brian Wilson, Toto and Emeli Sandé.

 EATING IN PORI: OUR PICKS

Hellulan Kaffila: Homemade *kanelipullat* (Finnish buns) and other treats are served in this cozy cafe. *10am-6pm Wed-Fri, to 4pm Sat* €

Porinna: This summer ship-restaurant docked by the Porinsilta Bridge is a relaxing spot. Vegan options available. *11am-8pm Tue-Sun May to Aug* €€

Borg Kitchen & Bar: Modern ambience and contemporary international cuisine. *11am-9pm Tue-Thu, to 10pm Fri, noon-10pm Sat* €€

Raatihuoneen Kellari: Probably the best restaurant in Pori, serving fish- and meat-based menus. *11am-3pm Mon, to 11pm Tue-Thu, to midnight Fri, 1pm-midnight Sat* €€€

OFF TO THE ISLANDS

In summer, explore Rauma's islands via water buses from Suvitien Merijakamo harbour. Kuuskajaskari, 6km offshore, features a 3km walking circuit with historic guns, watchtowers, and trenches. Kylmäpihjala, 10km away, boasts a 36m lighthouse and diverse bird species. Both islands offer dining and accommodations. From mid-June to late August, you can visit both in a day. For a natural retreat, head to Reksaari, northwest of Rauma, accessible by boat taxi or a mix of transport modes. The island has 6km of trails and a summer cafe. Alternatively, paddle to Nurmes Island, 9km from Rauma, in a canoe or kayak. Local companies like Eräheppu and Luontotaival offer guided tours and rentals.

Sammallahdenmäki

TIME FROM RAUMA: **20MINS**

Bronze Age burial sites

One of the largest archeological sites to show Nordic Bronze Age culture, the UNESCO-listed site of **Sammallahdenmäki** sits a short drive from Rauma, in the middle of a forested area. From the first discovery in the 1880s, 36 cairns have been excavated here showing stone circles and dry stone walls that were used as graves and coal stoves starting from the early Bronze Age. From the parking lot a 1.5km trail takes you to the heart of the site where human bones dating back to 1300–1000 BCE have been found, pointing to the funerary practices of some of the first communities to settle in western Finland.

Uusikaupunki

TIME FROM RAUMA: **45MINS**

The Velhovesi Ring

Northwest of Uusikaupunki (Nystad in Swedish), an arc of islands around the Ruotsinvesi and Velhovesi bays is joined by short dams and bridges to create a circuit of country roads, the Velhovesi Ring (Velhoveden kierros in Finnish). It makes a great trip for cyclists or drivers: the basic loop, from Santtioranta Camping on the edge of Uusikaupunki, is 55km. It runs through plenty of forest, with bays, inlets and a few beaches, and scattered settlements opening up at regular intervals. The route is marked by little brown signs with an orange circle for the main circuit, and a green circle for detours.

One particularly good detour is to the pretty village of **Pyhämaa**, with a cafe-restaurant, a shop, a guesthouse and two old churches side by side – the smaller, wooden one is the 17th-century Uhri Kirkko (Sacrifice Church), the entire interior of which is covered in colourful biblical-theme murals. From Pyhämaa a further scenic detour continues 8km to the remote fishing harbour of **Pitkäluoto**.

You can rent bikes and e-bikes at Santtioranta Camping or Uusikaupunki's tourist office – or from late May to mid-September, M/S *Kerttu* does day trips from Uusikaupunki to beautiful **Isokari island** (*isokari.fi*), 22km southwest of Uusikaupunki. Within the rocky shoreline of the 2.4km-long island are forests, meadows, a lake, a 19th-century lighthouse, a 2.2km nature trail and a restaurant. The *Kerttu* also offers seal safaris, birdwatching trips and sightseeing cruises.

 EATING IN & AROUND UUSIKAUPUNKI: OUR PICKS

| **Gasthaus Pooki:** Town-centre restaurant with very good dishes inventively prepared from local ingredients. *noon-8pm Tue-Sat* €€ | **Bistro Bay:** Straightforward but well-done fare (pizzas, burgers, beef, octopus). *11am-10pm Mon-Thu, to 2am Fri, to 4am Sat, noon-10pm Sun* €€ | **Pyhämaan Pirtti:** Excellent little stop, doing buffet lunch with local fish and veggies. *11am-5pm Mon-Sat, from noon Sun* €€ | **Wiku:** This waterfront cafe serves generous burgers, pizzas and salads overlooking the river. *10.30am-11pm Mon-Thu, to 2am Fri, to 3am Sat, noon-10pm Sun* €€ |

TOP EXPERIENCE

Bonk

As you step into the former headquarters of the Bonk Business Inc, a lab-coat-wearing member of the museum's staff will welcome you and guide through the collection of machines invented by Uusikaupunki entrepreneur Pär Bonk and his heirs. From a paranormal gun to a cosmic therapy unit, you'll get up close and personal to world-changing inventions you've never heard of.

Origins of Bonk

Pär Bonk made a breakthrough in business by selling anchovy oil, a substance useful in both mechanical machines and medicine. From distilled anchovy oil he also produced garum, a hallucinogenic drug that made Bonk millions thanks to its popularity among the Russian Empire's elite. After the October Revolution, garum was made free for all in Soviet Russia. See the original garum distiller in the first hall.

Bonk Electricity

Garum became so popular around the world that Baltic anchovies ran out. Bonk began importing giant anchovies from Peru to make up for the demand and discovered that the fishes' movement in the Baltic water could generate electricity. Soon, the whole of Uusikaupunki was electrified thanks to Bonk's Peruvian anchovies.

Bonk Goes to America

Bonk's grandson Pärre took hold of the company after the founder's death, relocating to California during WWII. Pärre produced award-winning films such as *Anchovies from Outer Space* and continued to invent machines. He realised that it is not essential for a machine to function in order to sell. Bonk's 'dysfunctional machines', whose sole purpose was to exist, became a success in post-war America, keeping the legacy of the Bonk industries alive.

TOP TIPS

● Don't believe everything you hear, even if the knowledgeable guides of the Bonk Museum are wearing very professional-looking lab coats!

● Below the main museum halls find the Bonk Mausoleum, where the remains of Pär Bonk, found after an explosion killed him in Siberia, are exhibited.

● The entrance ticket includes a 20-minute tour of the museum in Finnish or English.

PRACTICALITIES
Scan this QR code for more information.

Vaasa

ARCHIPELAGO GATEWAY | COSMOPOLITAN STUDENT CITY | HARBOUR WALKS

Surrounded by the ever-rising Kvarken archipelago and combining its industrial heritage with a vibrant international student culture, bilingual Vaasa (Vasa in Swedish) is the liveliest city on Finland's central coast. Vaasa was originally founded by Swedish king Karl IX in 1606 – 7km southeast of the current city centre, in a location that, at the time, had a sea harbour (since dried up). Old Vaasa burnt down in 1852 and was rebuilt in its current location following an urban plan designed by Swedish-born Finnish architect Carl Axel Setterberg, taking the name Nikolaistad – a tribute to Russian Tsar Nicholas I – until the fall of the Empire. Functioning as an important hub for energy companies serving both Finland and Sweden (Umeå is only 105km away opposite the Gulf of Bothnia), Vaasa's Swedish imprint remains strong. The city now hosts six university faculties and nearly a sixth of its population is made of students, who add to the cosmopolitan atmosphere. There's plenty of eating, drinking and shopping action around the large market square, Kauppatori, and its nearby streets.

GETTING AROUND

It's only a little over 1km from Vaasa's picturesque old railway station to its inner-harbour seafront, passing through the bustling city-centre area as you go – so a pair of legs or a rented bicycle are the perfect ways to get around. City buses serve outlying areas and the Wasaline ferry runs to Umeå in Sweden daily.

☑ TOP TIP

To explore beyond the city centre, take the Vaasa Summer Bus, introduced in 2024. Departing from three locations in the city – Top Camping Vaasa, Hotel Scandic Waskia and Sokos Hotel Vaakuna – the tourist bus runs to the Kvarken Archipelago on Tuesday, Wednesday and Sunday, while on other days it travels to city sights and Strömsö. Book tickets (adult €10) via the visitor centre in the market square or online (*vaasa.fi/en/summer-bus*).

Vaasa's Origins
Touring the remains of the original city

While the area of Vaasa is known to have been inhabited since at least the 14th century, the actual city was founded in 1606, when King Karl IX of Sweden gave Mustasaari official town status. Five years later, Mustasaari changed its name to Vaasa – a tribute to the Swedish Wasa dynasty – and the settlement began to expand around the stone-built St Mary's Church. The town's fate, however, would reflect that of many Finnish urban settlements along the west coast. Vaasa burned down almost completely in 1852. In the period between Vaasa's construction and its destruction the land had risen so much that Vaasa was no longer a coastal town. A decision

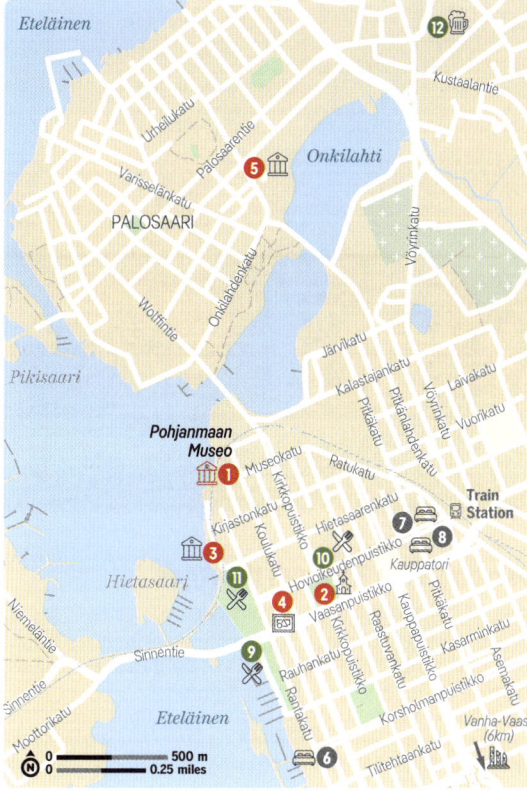

HIGHLIGHTS
1. Pohjanmaan Museo

SIGHTS
2. Holy Trinity Church
3. Kuntsin Modernin Taiteen Museo
4. Tikanoja Art Museum
5. Vaasa Museum of Labour

SLEEPING
6. EC Hostel
7. Forenom Aparthotel
8. Hotel Astor

EATING
9. Faros
● Fröj (see 7)
10. Pharmacy House
11. Strampen

DRINKING & NIGHTLIFE
12. Bock's Corner Brewery

was made to rebuild new Vaasa 7km west of the original settlement, leaving the ruins of **Vanha Vaasa** (Old Vaasa) in their place as a testament to a past chapter of the city's history. Busses 341 and 360 running in the direction of Närpiö stop near the ruin park of Vanha Vaasa, where the remains of the few buildings that survived the great fire – St Mary's Church, the bell tower, the school and the town hall – stand surrounded by greenery.

Setterberg's Neo-Gothic Church

Visit the city's main religious building

The cherry on top of Carl Axel Setterberg's urban design cake was Vaasa's **Holy Trinity Church**, the neo-Gothic red-brick structure functioning as the inner city's main architectural monument. Setterberg completed the structure in 1869 as the centrepiece for new Vaasa, surrounding the church with tall trees. It's worth stepping inside – besides the intricate pattern covering the sky-blue ceiling, the Lutheran church houses the only altarpiece produced by Finnish national painter Albert Edelfelt. Knowledgeable guides work inside the church and are usually happy to show visitors around free of charge.

WHEN A METEORITE HIT VAASA

Ten kilometres south of Vaasa's city centre the thick forests of coastal Finland open up around a massive crater created by a meteorite collision that occurred 520 million years ago. One can only imagine how the impact of the flying rock with the ground changed the landscape of the region – while the circular crater, 6km in diameter, is visible from the sky, there is not much to see in the Söderfjärden Crater Valley from ground level, as the area is mostly covered in cultivated agricultural fields. In the Meteoria Visitor Centre, in the middle of Söderfjärden, you can learn what happened in the area during and after the apocalyptic event.

Ostrobothnia Through the Ages
Tour the halls of the regional museum

Located in a functionalist building in Marianpuisto Park, a 15-minute walk from Kauppatori, the **Pohjanmaan Museo** (*Ostrobothnian Museum; vaasa.fi; adult €12*) serves as regional historical centre. Temporary exhibitions change frequently, but the permanent collection alone is worth a visit to better understand both the 400 years of Vaasa's development as a city and the natural phenomenon causing the Kvarken World Heritage site to rise year after year.

Art Wanders
Step into Vaasa's galleries

The waterfront **Kuntsi Museum of Modern Art** (*adult €12*), Vaasa's main art institution housed in the former Customs House, exhibits top-rank modern Finnish and international art. The core of the exhibits was donated by collector Simo Kuntsi, who had acquired a varied collection of Finnish art spanning the whole 20th century. Local dentist Lars Swanljung followed in Kunsti's footsteps and gifted the city of Vaasa with 900 works of Nordic artists in 2018, doubling the museum's artworks.

EATING IN VAASA: OUR PICKS

Choose between 'short' and 'long' tasting menus!

Pharmacy House: The atmosphere of the old pharmacy welcomes those who enter this bakery and cafe. *10am-6pm Mon, 9am-6pm Tue-Fri, 11am-4pm Sat* €

Faros: Partly installed in an old sailing ship, Faros is a scenic spot for gourmet burgers, beetroot soup and reindeer steaks. *4-10pm Tue-Thu, to 11pm Fri* €€

Strampen: Wonderful 1860s pavilion with a large terrace overlooking the bay; go for an economical lunch or à la carte dinner. *11am-2.30pm & 4-11pm Mon-Fri* €€

Fröi: Beautifully composed creations from Nordic ingredients; book ahead and consider a tasting menu. *4.30-11pm Tue-Sat, 11am-3pm Fri* €€€

Kuntsi Museum of Modern Art

Those looking for a more international art exhibition can walk to the **Tikanoja Art Museum** (*adult €12*), a block inland from the monumental Court of Appeal. The museum combines works of Ostrobothnian artists dating as far back as the 17th century, with rare pieces by French modernists and Persian painters.

History of the Labour Movement
Learn about the workers who built Vaasa

Hidden on a side street removed from the city centre, the **Vaasa Museum of Labour** (*€4, cash only*) offers a glimpse into a little-talked-about part of the local history. Together with its vast industrial plants, an active labour movement flourished in the city starting from the late 19th century. Through photographs, archival documents and a library of thousands of books and newspapers, this little museum sheds a light on the development of the workers' associations over 150 years.

Brewing Revival
Taste Bock's craft beer

About 3km north of the city centre, the independent **Bock's Corner Brewery** (*bockscornerbrewery.com*) has a long history of beer-making. The brand's name tributes Johan Leonard Bock, one of Vaasa's beer pioneers who set up one of the city's first breweries in the late 19th century. Bock's brewery operated for over a century until it shut down in the 1980s. In 2015, a group of independent beer enthusiasts acquired the facilities to revive the old tradition – Bock's Corner Brewery is now a welcoming gastropub serving beers, ciders and soda made on-site on its summer terrace.

BEST FESTIVALS IN VAASA

Vaasa Choir Festival: Finland's largest celebration of choral music takes place in Vaasa in May, with concert halls and churches hosting performances of all sizes.

Vaasa Festival: The biggest music festival in the city may not have the most original name, but draws thousands to the inner harbour with a week of top Finnish acts and an international food village in late July.

Vaasa Wildlife Festival: Every two years in September, Vaasa screens over 50 nature-inspired films from all around the world during its international documentary film festival.

ZINC Festival: In mid-July, 17 breweries from all over Europe gather in Vaasa's market square to showcase their hoppy creations.

Beyond Vaasa

Explore the unique islands of the Kvarken Archipelago and roam charming historic wooden towns up and down the coast.

Places
Kvarken Archipelago p186
Kokkola p187
Jakobstad p187
Alajärvi & Seinäjoki p188
Kristinestad p188
Närpes p189

Vaasa is perfectly positioned for forays out to several appealing destinations along the coast and inland. The main draw of the central coast is the mesmerising Kvarken Archipelago, a UNESCO World Heritage site that has been slowly emerging from the Gulf's waters for millennia. Thanks to Finland's longest bridge, you can drive to this geologically unique collection of islands in less than half an hour. But that's not all – the wooden architecture of quaint coastal towns such as Kokkola, Jakobstad, Kristinestad and Närpes sits in sharp contrast with the interior's ground-breaking modern constructions of Alvar Aalto in Alajärvi and Seinäjoki. All are within comfortable range for a day trip – each one is one to 1½ hours' drive away, though in different directions.

Kvarken Archipelago
TIME FROM VAASA: **30MINS**

The still-rising Kvarken Archipelago

The 5600 islands of the Kvarken Archipelago, together with Sweden's Höga Kusten (High Coast), comprise a UNESCO World Heritage site as the best place in the world to observe post-glacial uplift. The beautiful, low-lying islands, with countless inlets, bays and islets, forests, fields and scattered homesteads, make a lovely day's (or longer) outing from Vaasa.

The 1km-long Replot Bridge, 16km northwest of Vaasa, crosses to Replot island, with the **World Heritage Gateway Visitor Centre** at its far end. The World Heritage Gateway is worth a stop: besides serving coffee with a view of the Replot Bridge – the longest in Finland – crossing the sea, there is an interactive exhibition explaining in detail the geological phenomenon that characterises this part of the world.

The main road continues to Björkö island by causeways. Svedjehamn, on Björkö's north coast, is a picturesque little harbour with rust-painted boathouses and a summer cafe over the water. The **Bodvattnet nature trail**, a 4km loop starting here, passes the Bodback fishing harbour, abandoned in the 1940s after land uplift rendered it useless, and the Saltkaret observation tower overlooking glacially formed ridges known as De Geer moraines, which almost seem to be rising out of the sea as you watch.

GETTING AROUND

Your own vehicle makes travel easiest, especially if you plan to visit the islands and smaller towns. At €10, the Vaasa Summer Bus (*vaasa.fi/en/summer-bus*) is a convenient option for a day trip to the archipelago from the city. Buses run from Vaasa to Kristinestad, Jakobstad, Kokkola and Seinäjoki, although traffic slows down on weekends. For Seinäjoki the train is faster, more frequent and cheaper.

In summer you can rent bicycles at the World Heritage Gateway and Svedjehamn. If you'd prefer to see the archipelago by boat, **M/S Tiira** (*from Vaasa; jannensaluuna.com/boats; adult/child €20/10*) does short cruises in the inner islands between late June and August.

Kokkola

TIME FROM VAASA: 1½HR

A stroll through Neristan

The main reason to make a stop in Kokkola is to take a stroll through the colourful architecture forming the historic heart of the town, **Neristan**. Hundreds of wooden houses once inhabited by sailors and artisans line up one after the other, dating as far back at the 18th century. After the fire that destroyed Kokkola in 1664, architect Johan Persson Gädda redesigned the urban plan inspired by Renaissance ideals – the area extends around Isokatu, between the market square and the modernist church of Kokkola. Besides the classic wooden houses, some non-residential buildings stand out: the 1909 Renlund Art School with its semicircular exterior; the more recent Orthodox Prayer Room, built in the mid-1950s and topped by a copper onion dome; and the 1842 Town Hall designed by Carl Ludvig Engel in Mannerheim Sq, Kokkola's former market square.

Museum quarter

Kokkola's Museum Quarter stays true to its name with a good blend of art, history and science split between two exhibition spaces, the **Kieppi Natural History Museum** and the **KH Renlund Museum** (*kokkola.fi*). Besides the expected stuffed animal collection, Kieppi houses a rich exhibition of minerals – 1500 pieces collected from all over the world – and more than 20,000 butterflies and moths collected by local lepidopterist Armas Järvelä (1918–2002) over the course of his life. The other section of the museum is dedicated to Karl Herman Renlund (1850–1908), who donated his precious collection of Finnish paintings to the city, now exhibited in the Roos House. It must be said that while the cultural offer is indeed fascinating, the main draw of the Museum Quarter for locals, at least during summer, is the **Vohvelikahvila** (Waffle House), which serves both sweet and savoury waffles in the garden of the Museum Quarter's courtyard.

Jakobstad

TIME FROM VAASA: 1¼HR

Stories from Arctic lands

The Swedish-speaking majority town of Jakobstad (Pietarsaari in Finnish) boasts another large old wooden-house quarter,

POST-GLACIAL UPLIFT

The land on the Kvarken islands is rebounding (slowly) upward after being squashed under 3km of ice during the last Ice Age, which ended around 10,000 years ago. The rate of uplift is currently nearly 1m per century, which can make a significant difference in a person's lifetime, as Björkö island's **Bodvattnet nature trail**, for example, bears witness. The whole of Finland's west coast is a case study in post-glacial uplift: islands such as Björkö, and Kylmäpihjala off Rauma, didn't even begin to emerge from the sea till about 1200 years ago, and Vaasa and Rauma themselves were founded just a few centuries ago on coastlines that have since retreated 2km or more. Ten thousand years ago, these towns' locations were 80km or more out to sea. For a fascinating animation, check out *landupliftanimation. highcoastkvarken.org*.

EATING IN KVARKEN ARCHIPELAGO: OUR PICKS

Cafe Arken: Excellent soups, seafood, burgers and coastal views on the Kvarken island of Replot. *noon-7pm Mon-Fri, to 9pm Sat & Sun* €€

Berny's Café & Restaurant: Restaurant by the water that serves an excellent lunch. *9am-8pm Mon-Thu, to 10pm Fri, 10am-10pm Sat, 10am-8pm Sun* €€

Café Salteriet: Rustic Salteriet offers excellent soups and pastries in the village's historic fishing harbour. *10.30am-8pm Jun to Aug* €€

Kvarken Brewery: A selection of local beers are served next to pizzas and burgers. *11am-8pm Mon-Thu, to 9pm Fri, noon-9pm Sat, noon-7.30pm Sun* €

A FORGOTTEN OSTROBOTHNIAN ACROPOLIS

Little information is available on the story behind the obscure collection of temples and statues left to be eaten by vegetation on a hill in the village of Vörå, 35km from Vaasa. Ehrs Parken (marked on Google Maps as Bergpark for no clear reason) is an abandoned Ancient Greece-inspired sculpture park created by the late architect Ernst Ehrs in the 1980s. Park your car in front of the local library and climb up the hill to find yourself surrounded by modern ruins overtaken by vegetation. The site has not received maintenance in decades, which contributes to the allure of this odd open-air museum.

Skata, which is worth a stop if you are passing by. The main reason to visit, however, is out of the town centre. Any traveller will be fascinated by the exhibits of the **Nanoq Arctic Museum** (*nanoq.fi; adult/child €10/5*), a space dedicated to Arctic cultures founded by local explorer (and firefighter) Pentti Kronqvist. Inside the main hall, read the stories of people who have lived and researched some of the most remote (and climatically extreme) corners of the world – including biologist Anders Haggblom, who frequently visited Svalbard to research ocean currents through the analysis of driftwood in the 1950s; Soviet professor Ivan Papanin, who joined the 1932 expedition to Novaja Zemlya; and Greenlander Avataq Kernaq, who shot over 100 polar bears during his career as a hunter. Outside, a collection of buildings shows the way of life of Arctic explorers – including a copy of the hunting cabin of Henry Rudis, the 'Polar Bear King' who hunted 713 polar bears over 27 years of trips to Svalbard.

Alajärvi & Seinäjoki

TIME FROM VAASA: 1HR

On the Aalto trail

Modernist architecture enthusiasts have a lot to see on a day trip from Vaasa. Start from Alajärvi, an hour's drive east from Vaasa, where you'll find the **Administrative and Cultural Centre**, consisting of a collection of buildings designed by Alvar Aalto. Aalto spent his childhood summers in Alajärvi: he developed his first public structure here – the Youth Association Building (1918) – and returned to construct the Town Hall at the end of his career. Inside the Town Hall, find the exhibition dedicated to Aalto's glass designs. A few steps away is **Villa Väinölä**, built for Aalto's brother Väinö. Before leaving, pay a visit to the 1836 **Alajärvi Church**, a project by another Finnish starchitect, Carl Ludvig Engel. An hour southwest of Alajärvi is Seinäjoki, whose skyline is dominated by the bell tower of Aalto's **Lakeuden Risti Kirkko**, the Cross of the Plains Church. In front of it is the **Aalto Centre**, comprising some of the projects that epitomise Aalto's style and philosophy – the city hall, the theatre, and the beautiful library with a transparent glass wall for everyone to look inside. Learn more at *visit.alvaraalto.fi*

Kristinestad

TIME FROM VAASA: 1HR 20MINS

Wooden house tradition

As you drive south from Vaasa, it's worth making a stop in Kristinestad (Kristiinankaupunki in Finnish), the most charming town on this part of the coast. It's an easygoing estuary-side

EATING IN KOKKOLA: OUR PICKS

Café Kahvipuu: Freshly baked *mukki* and cinnamon rolls every morning. *8am-8pm Mon-Fri, 10am-5pm Sat, 11am-5pm Sun* €

Nera: Probably the best restaurant in town, this steak house sits in the heart of the Old Town, with windows overlooking the street. *4-10pm Mon-Sat* €€

Roja Kitchen: The menu is mostly Spanish-inspired, but there are also pizzas and a good selections of salads. Good wine selection. *11am-7pm Tue-Sat* €€

Rock 'n' Roll Diner: This American-style diner brings the 1950s to Kokkola. *11am-8pm Mon-Fri, noon-9pm Sat, 1-7pm Sun* €€

Ulrika Eleonora Kyrka

town of just 2700 people, with around 300 mostly 19th-century wooden buildings protected as heritage architecture. Don't miss the beautiful leaning-towered church **Ulrika Eleonora Kyrka**, built in 1700, and if you are driving through be careful in the Cat Whipper's Alley, named Finland's narrowest two-way traffic road (apparently).

Närpes

TIME FROM VAASA: **1HR**

Horse stables as far as the eye can see

The core of **Närpes Church** dates back to 1435, and while it has expanded and transformed over the centuries, some traces of its medieval roots are still visible, such as the 15th-century crucifix found inside above the altarpiece, painted by the Swedish court painter Pehr Hörberg. What will catch your eye as soon as you get close to the church, however, are the 150 red horse stables that surround the building. Most date back to the 18th century and were built to shelter the animals of those who reached Närpes (Närpiö in Finnish) from the countryside during celebrations. Behind Närpes Church is the Öjskogsparken, a free-to-visit open-air museum preserving 20 historic buildings, including an 18th-century pharmacy and a windmill.

ARCHAIC SWEDISH

The vast majority of Närpes' inhabitants speak Swedish. The Swedish spoken here, however, is very different from the language spoken on the other side of the Gulf of Bothnia, and even from the Swedish spoken in the rest of Finland. This town has managed to maintain a dialect that can be traced back to ancient Swedish, keeping idioms and pronunciation that have disappeared elsewhere, as the language evolved into its modern form. The archaic Swedish spoken in this corner of Ostrobothnia has shown similarities to Icelandic and can be difficult to comprehend for Swedes. This said, everyone in Närpes also speaks modern Swedish and Finnish, and English is also widespread, so communication shouldn't be difficult.

EATING IN JAKOBSTAD & KRISTINESTAD: BEST LUNCH SPOTS

After Eight: Chilled Jakobstad cafe and cultural centre, with a great courtyard-garden and top-value lunch. Rents bicycles. *10am-3pm Mon-Fri* €

Café Fäboda: Fresh fish, gourmet burgers, baked goods and fab views to Fäboda's sands. *11am-9pm Mon-Sat, from noon Sun* €€

Jungman: Uplifting Kristinestad estuary panoramas and good lunch buffet, plus à la carte steaks, salmon and pizzas. *11am-3pm Mon-Fri* €€

Eleonora's Bed & Breakfast: Perfect cafe with salads, waffles, coffees and lemonade. *11am-3pm Mon-Wed & Sat, to 6pm Thu & Fri* €

Oulu

CULTURE HUB | QUIRKY FESTIVALS | NORDIC CUISINE

GETTING AROUND

Oulu's train and bus stations are conveniently placed on the city centre's eastern edge, 1.5km from the waterfront market square, Kauppatori. The airport is 14km southwest, linked to the centre by buses 8 and 9. Bus 15 links Nallikari beach with the centre (Kaupungintalo stop). A great network of cycling paths connects the various islands in Oulu, making it easy to explore on sunny days.

☑ TOP TIP

To learn more about Oulu's history and culture, it's worth booking a tour with certified guide Sirpa Törmä (*tonttutarmonpaja.fi*), who'll be able to take you to the city's big and lesser-known attractions both in summer and winter, either walking or on a fatbike. Sirpa can also organise transport to Hailuoto and Turkensaari, which can be difficult to reach without a car.

This is the time to visit Oulu. Earning the title 2026 European Capital of Culture, the largest city in northern Finland has been working hard over the past few years to show the world its rich heritage and vision for the future. Oulu (Uleåborg in Swedish; Oula in North Sámi) expanded in the 18th century as one of the world's most important tar production centres, developing in the contemporary era as a tech hub with an artistic soul. This is the city where Nokia rose to dominate the global cellphone market in the early 2000s, although Oulu's relaxed residents don't seem to take the 'Silicon Valley of the North' label too seriously. Perhaps it's because the city has been rebuilt multiple times after fires razed it to the ground, that fixed categorisations don't stick well here. Oulu has been evolving since its origins, both geologically – the land on which it is built rises 8mm per year – and creatively. It continues to do so, often with a touch of self-irony, between sauna sessions and Air Guitar World Championships. The events calendar is packed in 2026, but whenever you visit, Oulu is bound to surprise you.

The City's Mascot
In and around Oulu's market square

The best place to start your exploration of Oulu is in the city's market square, carefully guarded by the 2.2m chubby **Toripolliisi**. Designed in 1987 by sculptor Kaarlo Mikkonen to thank the local police force for their patrolling service, the statue that has become Oulu's most recognisable symbol. Next to the policeman stands Oulu's brick **Market Hall**, one of the oldest in Finland continuously operating since 1901. During the summer most of the action takes place outdoors, and historic wooden storehouses converted into restaurants line up on the waterfront. To see the city from the Oulujoki River you can jump on the Sea Oulu Water Taxi (opposite the theatre), running between 2pm and 10pm from June to August.

SIGHTS
1. Korkeasaarensilta Bridge
2. Merimiehen Kotimuseo
3. Nallikari Lighthouse
4. Oulu Castle
5. Oulu Theatre
6. Pikigalleria
7. Toripolliisi

ACTIVITIES, COURSES & TOURS
8. Kesän Sauna
   - Nallikari Safaris (see 11)

SLEEPING
9. Lapland Hotel Oulu
10. Lasaretti Art Hotel
11. Nallikari Aalto
12. Nallikari Camping

EATING
13. 1881 Uleåborg
14. Alfred Kitchen & Bar
    - Bistro Lasaretti (see 10)
15. Kauppuri 5
16. Kitchen & Bar Oula (see 9)
17. Outun Kauppahalli
18. Rooster
19. Sokeri-Jussin Kievari

DRINKING & NIGHTLIFE
19. Mallassauna
20. Tähtitornin Café (see 4)
21. Viinibaari Vox

TRANSPORT
22. Pikisaari Forest Path

AIR GUITAR WORLD CHAMPIONSHIP

Oulu has long been known as one of Finland's musical hubs, with many of the country's best-known metal bands emerging from the northern city, and the yearly Qstock Music Festival, held in July, typically sold out months in advance. Yet it's the lack of instruments that draws thousands to Oulu's main square every August. The Air Guitar World Championships (*airguitarworldchampionships.com*) is a quirky and celebrated event that turns the world's lightest musical instrument into a global spectacle. Since its inception in 1996, this competition has hosted performers from all around the world, all competing to be crowned the best air guitarist. Participants 'play' an imaginary guitar to rock music, showcasing wild acting skills, elaborate costumes and exaggerated stage presence.

Taste the Arctic
Seek new flavours through the Arctic Food Lab network

You might believe that few ingredients grow at this latitude, but the Arctic Food Lab initiative, started as part of the Oulu2026 program, is here to make you think again. Many of Oulu's best restaurants are developing menus that celebrate Nordic Cuisine, using only local produce to provide an unexpectedly diverse culinary experience to visitors. Look out for the green logo marking dishes that include ingredients ranging from tart cloudberries to smoky tar syrup. Among the restaurants that have developed and Arctic Food Lab menu are the fashionable **Alfred Kitchen & Bar**, the **Kitchen & Bar Oula**, the **Bistro Lasaretti** and the **Sokeri-Jussi Kievari**. The full list is available at *oulu2026.eu/en/arctic-food-lab*.

Volunteer-run Sauna
A quintessentially Finnish social spot

People line up in front of the floating **Kesän Sauna** (*kesansauna.fi; adult/child €9/7*) before opening hours – that's how popular this volunteer-run, wood-burning sauna on the Oulujoki River is. Compensated in unlimited sauna sessions, the friendly staff will welcome you onboard by pulling the moving platform from the river bank to the sauna. Enter the unisex steam room (wear a bathing suit) then jump in the river to cool off. Open May to September.

A Kayak Excursion in Nellikari
Experience Oulu's natural surroundings from sea level

Join one of the kayaking expeditions in the Oulu River Delta run by **Nallikari Safaris** (*nallikarisafaris.fi; from €49*), whose expert guides will take you from the Nallikari Experience Center, right by the Nallikari beach, through the Mustasalmi channel to the diverse landscapes of the River Oulu Delta. Enter the water from the sandy beach of Nallikari then take a left to enter the channel leading to the river delta, and all the way to Oulu's market square.

Many veg options available!

EATING & DRINKING IN OULU: OUR PICKS

Viinibaari Vox: Cosy wine bar with vintages by the glass; cheeses and tasty nibbles. *3pm-midnight Mon-Fri, to 2am Sat & Sun* €€

1881 Uleåborg: Classy spot with creative French-influenced Finnish fare in an old wooden waterside warehouse off Kauppatori. *5-11pm Tue-Sat* €€€

Kauppuri 5: Casual spot with delicious handmade burgers and good craft beers. *11am-midnight Sun-Thu, to 2am Fri & Sat* €

Rooster: Satisfying speciality burgers, plus pita breads and salads. *10.30am-9pm Mon & Tue, to 10pm Wed & Thu, to 11pm Fri, noon-11pm Sat* €

CYCLING ON THE PIKISAARI ART TRAIL & BEYOND

From Oulu's best-known beach cycle into the open-air museum of Pikisaari and onward to the city centre through bridges and dedicated lanes.

START	END	LENGTH
Nallikari	Nallikari	9km; 2 hours

Pick up a Jopo bike for rent at Nallikari Safaris and start cycling east toward the island of Pikisaari. After about 1.7km you will get on the ❶ **Korkeasaarensilta Bridge** overlooking the Hietasaari marina. Once you've crossed the bridge you're in Pikisaari, home of a wooden old town set up by shipbuilders in the 18th century. Today, the island is home to the Pikisaari Art Hub, an artists' community that produced many installations scattered around the ❷ **Pikisaari Forest Path** stretching for 350m amid spruces. Follow the cycling path to the ❸ **Pikigalleria**, where resident artists set up exhibitions during the summer, and continue to the ❹ **Mallassauna**, an extension of the Hailuoto Organic Brewery, for a beer and sauna combo. Next is the ❺ **Merimiehen Kotimuseo** (Sailor's Home Museum), the oldest house on the island, then lunch in the historic ❻ **Sokeri-Jussin Kievari** (p192; try the tar and licorice dessert). Leave Pikisaari behind by crossing the Pikisaarensilta Bridge and cycle next to the brutalist ❼ **Oulu Theatre** to reach the Market Square Cross another bridge to reach the island of Linnansaari where you'll find the remains of the 16th-century ❽ **Oulu Castle** (Oulun Linna). Get back on Pikisaari to return to your starting point. Climb the ❾ **Nallikari Lighthouse** before dropping off your bike.

The remains of the Oulu Castle sit below the towering **Tähtitornin Café**, where you can stop for a coffee before continuing.

Check out @pikigalleria on Instagram for upcoming shows in Pikisaari's contemporary art gallery, **Pikigalleria**.

As you reach the Market Square, step into the **Oulu Market Hall**, one of the oldest buildings in the city, dating back to 1901.

Beyond Oulu

Take a ferry out to one of Finland's biggest islands, or head inland to relive lifestyles of the past.

Places
Turkansaari p194
Kierikki p195

The top excursion from Oulu is to Hailuoto, the biggest island in the Bothnian Bay (the northern part of the sea between Finland and Sweden). At 200 sq km and 30km from end to end, with a population of just 950 people, Hailuoto is like a microcosm of old Finnish rural life with its red-painted houses, wooden barns, occasional windmills, and open fields between dense pine forests. Also endowed with a picturesque coastline and some good sandy beaches, it's a favourite escape for Oulu city dwellers. Up the rivers inland from the city in summer, you can try your hand at Stone Age life at Kierikkikeskus, or walk among centuries-old wooden buildings on river islands at Turkansaari.

GETTING AROUND

The ferry to Hailuoto (finferries.fi) takes 25 minutes and sails about hourly from Oulunsalo. Bus 59 from Oulu bus station runs to the island (as far as Marjaniemi, 1½ hours) up to three times daily. Buses and island residents have priority on the ferry. You can rent bikes on Hailuoto at Marjaniemi, Ailosto and from the firm Luotorent. There's no public transport to Kierikkikeskus; Saaga Travel runs day trips some summer Saturdays. Turkansaari is a nice bike ride from Oulu, or city bus 41 goes to within 1.6km of the museum.

Turkansaari

TIME FROM OULU: **25MINS**

Traces of the tar trail

The Nordic open-air museum tradition is well represented on the outskirts of Oulu thanks to **Turkansaari** (*turkansaari.fi; adult €10*). Scattered across three islands in the Oulujoki River 12km east of Oulu, this museum celebrates the northern heritage through a showcase of the wooden architecture that used to house the remote communities living along the tar-transportation route over a century ago.

From the 17th to the 19th centuries, the Oulu area became known as the 'tar capital of the world' due to the abundance of the viscous substance in its forests. Tar, essential for waterproofing wooden ships, was transported from inland forests to Oulu via rivers and land routes, to then be exported all over Europe and allow the city to flourish. Villages like Turkansaari emerged along waterways as a result of tar trade that took place over the course of two centuries, and while technological advancements and the adoption of iron as a primary building material for ships brought tar exports to an end, traces of this pivotal period of Oulu's history are still visible all around.

Open in summer only (early June to the end of August), Turkansaari is worth the detour for its 17th-century church, huts and wooden homes that have been preserved to this day in this idyllic rural setting. During weekends, regular live demonstrations, markets and performances take place, showing the types of jobs people used to do here in the past – from tar-pit burning to woodcarving – before Oulu became a tech hub. In 2025, Turkansaari Open Air Museum celebrates 100 years of operation. On a sunny day, the museum can also be reached by bike thanks to the paths that link it to Oulu's city centre.

Kierikki

TIME FROM OULU: **50MINS**

Back to the Stone Age

Kierikkikeskus (*Kierikki Stone Age Centre; kierikki.fi; adult/child €10/7*), 55km northeast of Oulu, is set on the site of a large Stone Age village occupied around 6000 years ago. Housed in an architecturally striking modern log building, the Centre for Ancient Times offers an engaging glimpse into prehistoric life. Inside, you can explore a range of fascinating artefacts uncovered from the site, watch films detailing ancient lifestyles, and learn about archaeological methods used by research to uncover how our ancestors lived in this remote corner of Europe. Outside, the experience becomes hands-on: walk to a meticulously recreated Stone Age village by the scenic Iijoki River, where you can practice archery, craft stone tools, or participate in experimental archaeology workshops. In summer, it is also possible to join a canoeing trip with a vessel carved directly from a tree trunk and experience the mode of transport used thousands of years ago.

WHY ARE ALL THE HOUSES RED?

In villages like Marjaniemi, in the western edge of Hailuoto, you'll notice that all wooden houses are painted the same colour red. Not any red, but a specific variety of red known as falu (or *punamulta*, in Finnish). Falu red houses are a common sight not just in Finland, but across the Nordics. The pigment originates from the copper mines of Falun, in Sweden, where a byproduct of copper extraction became a cheap coating for wooden structures. Over time, Falu Red has become part of the heritage of many rural areas across Finland, Sweden and Norway, and it's still a symbol of countryside Nordic living.

Turkansaari

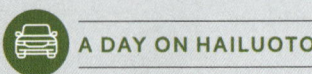

A DAY ON HAILUOTO

Hop on the ferry to explore the island of Hailuoto, where modernist architecture, organic beer and an old fishing village hide amid the peaceful forests.

START	END	LENGTH
Haliuoto Harbour	Haliuoto Harbour	60km; 3-4 hours

Get off the ferry at ❶ **Hailuoto harbour** and start driving west – there is only one main road, so you can't get it wrong. Less than 1000 people live on this peaceful, police-free island. The first stop is the triangular ❷ **Hailuoto Church**, the first glass-and-concrete modernist church to be built in the Nordics, erected after the island's former church burned down in 1968. Continue to the western edge of the island and take some time to explore Marjaniemi on foot. Park by ❸ **Marjaniemi Lighthouse** (partly converted into a hotel) and stroll through the red wooden houses that make up this picturesque fishing village overlooking the Gulf of Bothnia. A short boardwalk ❹ **Nature Trail** starts from the village, taking you along the beaches that 300 species of birds visit every year, including Arctic terns that come and nest here in the spring. Lunch at ❺ **Haili**, then on your way back to Hailuoto Harbour stop for a tasting at the ❻ **Hailouto Organic Brewery**, one of the best in Ostrobothnia. Opposite the brewery, ❼ **Luovon Puoji Osk** sells locally produced handicrafts and hosts an exhibition dedicated to Hailuoto's traditional knitwear. And if you decide to spend the night in Hailuoto, get a taste of the local nightlife at the ❽ **Dancing Bobcat Bar**, likely the only farm-club you'll visit on your trip.

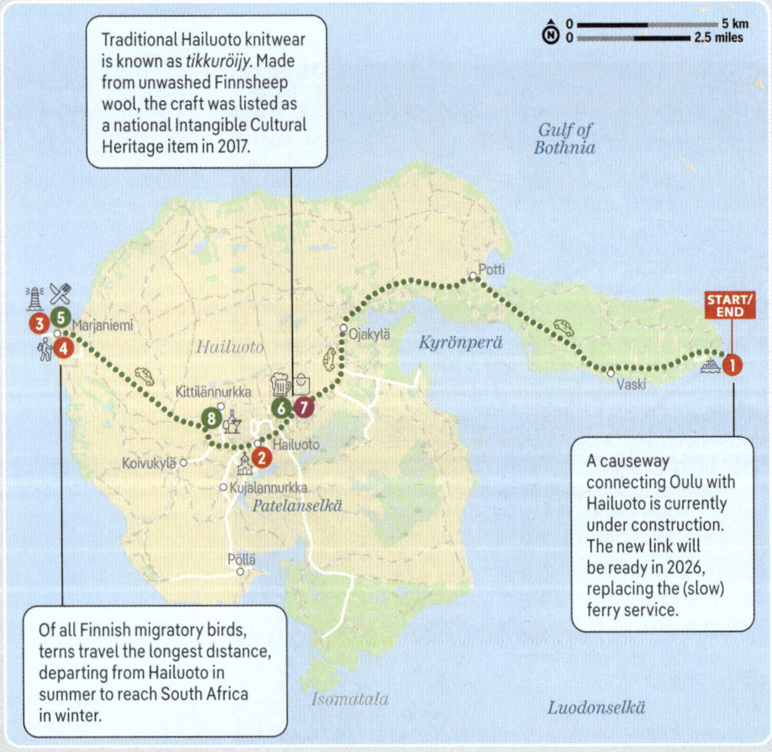

> Traditional Hailuoto knitwear is known as *tikkuröijy*. Made from unwashed Finnsheep wool, the craft was listed as a national Intangible Cultural Heritage item in 2017.

> A causeway connecting Oulu with Hailuoto is currently under construction. The new link will be ready in 2026, replacing the (slow) ferry service.

> Of all Finnish migratory birds, terns travel the longest distance, departing from Hailuoto in summer to reach South Africa in winter.

Oulanka National Park

LONG-DISTANCE HIKING | CANYONS & RAPIDS | WILDLIFE

On the east side of Finland's central 'waist', Oulanka is one of the country's most beloved national parks – in large measure for the rugged scenery of canyons, rapids, waterfalls, cliffs and lakes carved among the dense forests by its two main rivers, the Oulankajoki and the Kitkajoki, which meet close to the Russian border. It's a wonderful place for a walk – most famously along the 82km Karhunkierros (Bear's Ring) trail, which crosses the park from north to south, but also for many scenic shorter routes. But Oulanka is not just for hikers: the rivers are good for canoeing, kayaking and white-water rafting, and in winter there are snowshoe and cross-country skiing trails. Sleeping and eating options in and near the park are limited but there are plenty at Ruka.

Karhunkierros: The Bear's Ring
Finland's most popular long-distance trail

Despite its name, the **Karhunkierros** is a linear route: 82km for the full hike from Hautajärvi, just north of Oulanka National Park, to Ruka, south of the park. Also, despite the name, you are highly unlikely to meet a bear. It takes most people four to six days to complete the itinerary. Dense, silent forests are interspersed with rivers, lakes, waterfalls, rapids, canyons, cliffs and hanging bridges. The trail is normally snow-free from about the beginning of June to mid-October. July is peak mosquito season. September, with autumn colours, is an ideal month. There are six wilderness huts for sleeping on the main trail, plus a campground near the park visitor centre and accommodation options at Juuma.

Day Hikes in Oulanka
The Little Bear's Ring and other day hikes

The highly popular **Pieni Karhunkierros** (Little Bear's Ring) incorporates some of Oulanka's most spectacular scenery in a 12km loop (3½ to four hours) from Juuma village. It's walkable almost year-round and it is one of the best day hikes in the country. Highlights include the Myllykoski and Aallokkokoski rapids, the

GETTING AROUND

The airport at Kuusamo, 26km south of Ruka, is many people's entry point to the area. It has car-hire desks. An airport bus (*pohjolanmatka.fi*) runs to and from Ruka for all arriving and departing flights, with some services extending to/from Hautajärvi. A taxi from the airport to Ruka/Hautajärvi costs around €65/140. There's a daily morning bus from Ruka to Hautajärvi, and a service also calling at Juuma and the national park visitor centre. Check *ruka.fi* for schedules.

☑ TOP TIP

A great deal of very good practical and background information on the park, the Karhunkierros and other activities, including route maps and descriptions, is published at *nationalparks.fi*. The national park's visitor centre, in Oulanka's heart, is excellent.

SIGHTS
1. Kiutaköngäs Falls

ACTIVITIES, COURSES & TOURS
- Könkään keino (see 6)
- Pieni Karhunkierros (see 4)

SLEEPING
2. Basecamp Oulanka
3. Juuman Leirintäalue
4. Lomakylä Retki-Etappi
5. Oulanka Camping

EATING
- Kahvila Retkietappi (see 4)
- Napapiiri Café (see 7)
6. Ravintola Talonpöytä

INFORMATION
7. Karhunkierros Visitor Centre

OULANKA NATIONAL PARK

WHAT'S IN A BEAR'S NAME?

There are hundreds of names for 'bear' in Finnish – according to estimates, between 200 and 300. Calling the animal with the proper name *karhu* was believed to attract the bears in old times, and communities of the past came up with all sorts of words to avoid inviting bears too close to their home. Some of these terms have stuck around, others have disappeared from the contemporary language.

thundering Jyrävä falls and two hanging bridges. Another excellent, much less frequented circuit is the 6km **Kanjoninkurkkaus** (Canyon View) trail in the park's north, with views into the impressive Oulankajoki canyon. Walkable June to October, it starts at the Savilampi parking area, 10km off Rd 950. The dramatic **Kiutaköngäs Falls** are an easy 1km walk from the park visitor centre. For a longer hike take the **Könkään keino** forest circuit (8km).

Running the Rivers
Rafting and kayaking in Oulanka's waterways

When they're unfrozen, Oulanka's rivers make for excellent paddling. The main paddle is a 25km canoe and kayak route down the **Oulankajoki** from Matarániemi to Jäkälämutka. This usually takes five to seven hours and is fine for beginners. Ruka-based Kuusamo Safaris will provide all the gear and bring you back to Matarániemi at the end (€35 to €40 per person).

The rafting river is the **Kitkajoki**, with three sections. The 14km 'family route' extends from Rd 950 near Käylä to Juuma, with seven rapids (class I to III). Then there's the 'wild route' from Juuma to just before Jyrävä falls, with three rapids, including the thrilling class IV Myllykoski and Aallokkokoski (minimum age 18). Firms offering these routes include Basecamp Oulanka and Retkietappi at Juuma, and Ruka-based Stella Polaris and Ruka Safaris.

EATING IN & AROUND OULANKA NATIONAL PARK: OUR PICKS

Basecamp Oulanka: Hearty, well-prepared, local-produce meals in the lodge's bright, wood-beamed dining room. *8am-10pm* €€

Ravintola Talonpöytä: The restaurant at the visitor centre serves soup lunches, reindeer sausage and veggie burgers. *10am-6pm* €

Kahvila Retkietappi: Tempting baked goods at a lakeside cafe at the start of the Pieni Karhunkierros. *11am-5pm* €

Napapiiri Café: The northern Karhunkierros Visitor Centre, near Salla, sits on the Arctic Circle and hosts a rustic cafe at the trail's entrance. *9am-4pm* €

Beyond Oulanka National Park

A top ski and summer resort and a less-visited national park are within reach, plus there's summer bear-spotting.

About 20km southwest of Oulanka National Park lies Ruka, one of Finland's most popular ski resorts and a base for other winter activities such as snowmobiling and ice fishing. Many outdoor activities are available in Ruka during the summer, but a regional highlight is found in the surroundings of Kuusamo, south of Ruka, where you have the opportunity to see brown bears in the wild in the forests stretching across the Russian border. Around 80km south of Kuusamo is Hossa National Park, considerably less visited than Oulanka and with an expanse of forest, lakes and rivers with famous rock paintings and good hiking, cycling and canoeing.

Kuusamo
TIME FROM OULANKA NATIONAL PARK: **45MINS**

An evening with the bears

Every spring, as bears exit hibernation, Pekka Veteläinen sets up his remote observation huts to welcome visitors in one of the best spots to observe the animals in the wild. An estimated 2000 brown bears roam Finland's forests, although numbers can hardly be precise given that most of these large mammals move frequently across the Russian border. Once you reach the meeting point, Veteläinen – who has been running **Karhu-Kuusamo** (*karhujenkatselu.fi*) for the past two decades – will escort you to the huts, equipped with binoculars and holes for large camera lenses. He will then drive around the swampy field in front of you to drop some fish bones and carcasses, which will entice the bears to exit the thick forests and come out in search of food. It's an exhilarating experience. Bear-watching sessions start at €120 for four hours (between 6pm and 10pm, May to September), but it is also possible to stay overnight for €170. Book via the website.

Places
Kuusamo p199
Hossa National Park p200

GETTING AROUND

Winter Skibus services link the centre of Ruka Village with Ruka Valley and other outlying areas of Ruka. To head further afield, your own vehicle is by far easiest. Kuusamo airport, 26km south of Ruka, has car-hire desks. From early June to early August (except Sundays) Hossa Bussi runs from Ruka to Hossa National Park in the morning and back in the evening.

WINTER FUN IN RUKA

With over 200 days of skiing a year on 39 varied slopes, and a lively après-ski scene, carbon-neutral Ruka, 20 minutes' drive from Oulanka, is among Finland's top ski destinations. The resort divides into Ruka Village (Rukan Kylä) and Ruka Valley (Rukan Laakso), with the slopes on Rukatunturi hill between the two. Only six slopes are black-rated but the 600m FIS is a worthy challenge for advanced skiers. Also at Ruka are an outstanding snow park (Ruka Park), the Rosa & Rudolf Family Park for beginners, and 88km of cross-country trails. PisteVuokraamo, in Ruka Village and Ruka Valley, is a one-stop shop for ski passes, equipment rental and ski school bookings; you can also book everything at *ruka.fi*.

Hossa National Park

TIME FROM OULANKA NATIONAL PARK: 1½HR

Hiking around ancient art

A recent addition to Finland's national park portfolio, **Hossa National Park** draws in a lot less people than Oulanka, allowing for many solitary walks on the routes that run through the 110-sq-km reserve. The excellent visitor centre (Hossan Luontokeskus) provides maps and information on the trails available and can rent canoes for exploring the lakes. The Karhunkainalon campground, with modern cabins and apartments, is next door. The easiest way to access the park is via the 3km **Nature Trail** that starts outside the visitor centre and takes you around the Huosilampi Lake and up to the fells, offering great views of the surrounding landscapes. The 8km **Värikallion kaarros Trail** runs from Lihapyörre to the Värikallio Cliffs, where Finland's largest group of prehistoric rock paintings are found. The ochre-toned paintings, on a cliff face directly above the waters of Somerjärvi, date back at least 3500 years and mainly depict animals and human-like, possibly shamanic, figures. The more demanding **Ölökyn ähkäsy Trail** (10km, about five hours) starts from the Julma-Ölkky parking lot 15km northwest of the visitor centre and stretches north around the impressive canyon that forms around the Julma-Ölkky lake.

Hossa National Park

 EATING IN RUKA: OUR PICKS

Pizzeria Ruka: Pleasant ambience and very tasty pizzas, 600m south of central Ruka Village. *11am-11pm* €€

Restaurant KaltioKivi: Nicely done fish, reindeer, burgers, pasta and soups in the middle of Ruka Village. *4-10pm* €€

Riipisen Riistaravintola: This log-cabin-style restaurant is the place to come for game classics – elk, reindeer and, yes, bear. *1-9pm* €€€

Zone: Open from breakfast to the early morning hours, this grill restaurant also has frequent live music gigs during the winter. *8am-4am* €

Places We Love to Stay

€ Budget €€ Midrange €€€ Top End

Rauma MAP p175

Hotelli Cityhovi €€ Small, comfy hotel in greys, whites and silver, just outside the old town.

Poroholman Lomakeskus €€ Large RV/camping park on a picturesque bay with two-bedroom chalets and loads of facilities.

Hotelli Vanha Rauma €€€ The only old town hotel, with comfortable, tasteful rooms and a top restaurant.

Uusikaupunki

Santtioranta Camping € Idyllic campground near the water, with cabins, a cafe and cheap hostel dorms available for solo travellers.

Hotelli Aittaranta €€ Good, medium-size hotel overlooking the inner harbour with classically Nordic clean-lined rooms.

Gasthaus Pooki €€ Four tastefully old-fashioned rooms upstairs from one of the town's best restaurants. Centrally located.

Pori & Yyteri

Hostel River € Friendly and comfy hostel with private rooms and three-person dorms not far from central Pori.

Yyteri Spa Hotel €€ Large spa-resort-type hotel with loads of facilities at the north end of Yyteri beach.

Vaasa MAP p183

EC Hostel € Student-like accommodation in plain but clean, comfy private rooms; shared kitchens.

Forenom Aparthotel €€ Anonymous but fully equipped and super-central budget apartments with self check-in.

Hotel Astor €€€ A touch of old-fashioned class: rooms are modestly sized but very cosy and the breakfast spread is superb.

Kristinestad

Eleonora's Bed & Breakfast €€ Charming, recently made-over B&B in an old Kristinestad house.

Oulu MAP p191

Nallikari Camping € Endless summer days are best spent by the beach where the sun never sets. Rent a cabin or pitch your own tent in this fully serviced campground.

Lasaretti Art Hotel €€ With 500 works of Nordic art hanging from the walls, an 'aurora room' and thick curtains for nightless nights, you'll love your stay here.

Nallikari Aalto €€ Opened in 2024 right in front of Oulu's favourite beach, Nellikari Hotel overlooks the ocean, making for an ideal base for outdoor activities and water sports.

Lapland Hotel €€€ Worth a visit even just for a meal at its fine-dining Oula restaurant, this high-end hotel by Oulu's cathedral doesn't disappoint.

Hailuoto

Arctic Lighthouse Hotel €€ Most of the attractive, blond-wood rooms in this hotel in Marjaniemi's old lighthouse-pilot station provide wonderful sea views; the restaurant emphasises local fish.

Frans Bistro €€ Comfy old lighthouse-keeper's cottage and similar lodgings at Marjaniemi; also has budget rooms available.

Terwaluoto €€€ Newly built, fully equipped family cabins in front of an isolated beach, complete with sauna and kitchen. Great spot for a retreat in Hailuoto's nature.

Oulanka National Park MAP p198

Oulanka Camping € National-park summer campground near the visitor centre, with 10 simple four-person cabins, a food-and-drink kiosk, and plenty of tent and RV space.

Juuman Leirintäalue € Juuma summer campground with sauna-equipped, year-round cottages, a cafe, rowing boats and SUPs.

Basecamp Oulanka €€ Well-run, cosy lodge near Juuma: good food, warm welcome, free sauna.

Lomakylä Retki-Etappi €€ Three solidly comfy log cabins, plus camping space and a lakeside cafe, at Juuma.

Ruka

Iisakki Village €€ Charming recreation of an old Karelian village with cosy rooms on a lakeside 7km southeast of Ruka Village.

Arctic Zone Hotel €€ Well-kept, reasonably priced, sparsely decorated rooms in the heart of Ruka Village.

Lapland

THE ARCTIC NORTH

A vast land of vast extremes, where in summer there's no night, and in winter no real day.

Lapland is the country's largest and northernmost region, stretching for over a quarter of Finland's surface. This is one of Europe's best-preserved wilderness areas, where trees appear to be shrinking as you cross the Arctic circle and drive up toward the sparsely populated northern edges of the country. With vast national parks preserving much of these pristine lands, nightless summers offer exceptional hiking opportunities, thanks to an excellent system of huts and information centres scattered across the region. In winter, when darkness is constant and temperatures drop far below freezing point, the magical aurora borealis reflects its green hues on frozen lakes.

But nature isn't all there is. While Finland's national borders overlap with the natural frontiers formed by the Teno and the Tornio rivers, Lapland shares its cultural heritage with the broader region of Sàpmi, the historic home of the indigenous Sámi people stretching across the Arctic region, from the Norwegian coast to Russia's Kola Peninsula. Many tangible traces of Sámi history dating back millennia were destroyed at the end of WWII, when German troops scorched much of Lapland's territory while retreating from Finland. Reindeer husbandry is still central to the local economy – as anyone who travels on Lapland's roads will inevitably notice – but Sámi culture extends well beyond traditional livelihoods and finds expression in the arts, the celebration of nature and the preservation of the three endangered languages spoken in the far north.

THE MAIN AREAS

ROVANIEMI
Regional capital and busy tourism hub. **p208**

INARI
The Centre of Sámi culture. **p224**

KILPISJÄRVI
Remote outpost with great hiking. **p234**

For places to stay in Lapland, see p237

THE GUIDE

LAPLAND

Left: Walkers in Arctic beauty; Above: Aurora borealis, Rovaniemi (p208)

Find Your Way

Easily Finland's biggest region, Lapland stretches 500km from north to south. The few larger towns are all in the south: beyond the Arctic Circle it's villages (and a few ski resorts) only.

Inari, p224
The cultural capital of the Sámi in Finland, with a beautiful lakeside setting and access to some of the country's biggest, most spectacular national parks.

Kilpisjärvi, p234
This very remote village at the top of Lapland's northwest arm, almost in Norway, is a great base for wilderness hiking.

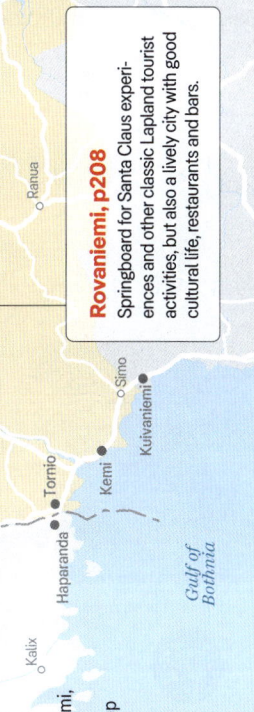

Rovaniemi, p208

Springboard for Santa Claus experiences and other classic Lapland tourist activities, but also a lively city with good cultural life, restaurants and bars.

CAR & MOTORCYCLE

Unless you're just visiting one place, with limited excursions, having your own vehicle is the easiest way to go. Just watch out for reindeer on the roads, know where the next filling station is, and in winter use snow tyres and check the weather.

BUS

Buses fan out to the main towns and villages from Rovaniemi, but most services are not very frequent. Just two or three buses a day head up to Inari (one continues on into Norway) and Kilpisjärvi.

CAR RENTAL

All Lapland's four airports – Rovaniemi, Kemi-Tornio, Ivalo and Kittilä – have car-rental desks. You can also pick up cars at Rovaniemi railway station.

Plan Your Time

Visiting Lapland is all about getting out into the countryside and visiting reindeer farms, hiking or skiing the forests and fells, husky-sledding or gaping at the aurora borealis.

Lemmenjoki National Park (p228)

If You Only Visit One Place

● Basing yourself at **Inari** (p224) will give you a taste of the north, which some consider the 'real' Lapland. If you have just two days, spend one visiting the brilliant Sámi museum **Siida** (p226) and **Sámi Cultural Centre Sajos** (and Parliament; p224) for a great introduced to Sámi culture and history.

● After that, either take a boat trip on **Inarijärvi** (p224) or walk out to the **Pielpajärven Erämaakirkko** (p224), one of the oldest churches in the region, nestled in the pristine forests surrounding Inari.

● On the second day get yourself out early to **Lemmenjoki National Park** (p228) and, if it's summer, ride the river boat along the Lemmenjoki and take a hike among the hilly forests.

Seasonal Highlights

Seasonal changes are certainly extreme. There's no night in summer and little light in winter. It gets more pronounced heading north: Rovaniemi has 30 days of midnight sun, Utsjoki has 70.

MARCH
Usually a good month for snow-based activities, as there's plenty of snow but also daylight, and temperatures are climbing.

MAY
The snowmelt makes streams overflow and the wetlands wetter, curtailing activities in the countryside.

JUNE
The midnight-sun season starts in most of Lapland; it's party time, as Finns soak up the blessed rays.

A Few More Days

● Start at **Rovaniemi** (p208), the regional capital and 'official hometown of Santa Claus'. In two days you can visit the excellent **Arktikum** (p208) and **Pilke Science Centre** (p210) museums, enjoy a spot of shopping, a riverside walk and some of the town's excellent restaurants and bars, and take a trip out to meet the man himself at **Santa Claus Village** (p211).

● Days three and four: head up to **Saariselkä** (p229) for some hiking in the endless hilly expanses of **Urho Kekkonen National Park** (p229) or (if it's winter) some skiing. Discover the history of Finland's gold rush at the **Kultamuseo** (p230) before continuing to **Inari** (p224) and then further north to the Norwegian border to see the mighty Teno river from the northernmost point in the EU.

Two Weeks

● Now we're talking. Do everything in and around **Rovaniemi** and **Saariselkä** in the previous itinerary, and give yourself an extra day based in **Inari** to visit the Sámi home of **Tuula Airamo** (p227). Add in a one- or two-day driving trip to Finland's northernmost extremities along the beautiful Tenojoki, and stay overnight at **Lemmenjoki National Park** (p228) to allow for lengthier explorations.

● Then head to remote **Kilpisjarvi** (p234) at the northwest tip of the country for some superb wilderness hiking, including another extremity of mainland Finland, the **Three-Country Cairn** (p236) where Finland, Norway and Sweden all converge. As you return south, stop in the village of **Kukkola** (p217) to learn about ancient fishing traditions on the rapids of the Torne River, then conclude with a break in **Kemi** (p214) before looping back to Rovaniemi.

JULY
Still high summer, the main Finnish holiday month, but also peak mosquito season, so not a great time for hiking.

SEPTEMBER
Magnificent autumn colours, moderate temperatures, no mosquitoes: ideal for hiking and other countryside pursuits.

OCTOBER
First snows normally arrive over northern Lapland in the second half of the month (early November in the south).

DECEMBER
Peak season (continuing into January) at winter tourism destinations Rovaniemi and Saariselkä: prices go up, crowds thicken. Little daylight.

Rovaniemi

LAPLAND'S CAPITAL | SANTA'S HEADQUARTERS | ARCTIC HISTORY

GETTING AROUND

Rovaniemi airport is 8km northeast of the city centre. City bus 11 runs to/from the city centre (Ruokasenkatu) every 40 minutes daily from December to February (departures from the airport: 8.40am to 8pm). Airport Express minibuses (*airportbus.fi*) run into the centre. A taxi from airport to city costs €20 to €30. The city is walkable: the train and bus stations are within a 20-minute walk of the central square Lordinaukio. City bus 9 serves the Ounasvaara ski station and Santasport, and bus 10 serves Santasport. No buses go to the top of the hill.

☑ TOP TIP

There's usually snow here from about mid-November to late April. In December and the first half of January the sun is up less than four hours a day. Peak season is December and January. Book ahead for accommodation and activities at that time.

From Helsinki, a double-decker train nicknamed Santa Claus Express travels overnight – when night is available – through the changing scenery of western Finland, reaching Rovaniemi (Roavvenjárga in Northern Sámi) in 12 hours. Rovaniemi is often referred to as 'Lapland's capital', although many people think Lapland proper only begins some 150km further up. Rovaniemi's calling card is – you guessed it – Santa Claus, who resides year-round in the village 8km northeast of town and magically multiplies in winter to greet the tens of thousands of visitors who visit during peak season. If you've misbehaved, don't worry – Rovaniemi will reward you anyway. While the city's utilitarian core – rebuilt to a plan by Alvar Aalto after it was razed to the ground by the retreating Wehrmacht in 1944 – may appear a bit plasticky at first glance, but it contains some of the best museums of the North, a lively restaurant scene, and easy access to any outdoor activity you can think of, from snowmobiling to berry foraging.

Arctic History

Your intro to the North

Arktikum (*arktikum.fi; adult/child €18/5*) is the best place to start your Lapland journey. Housed inside one of Rovaniemi's most iconic buildings, a two-storey gallery covered by a glass ceiling resembling a frozen finger pointing to the North Pole, Rovaniemi's main cultural institution takes you on a journey through the history of the region, starting from the Iron Age to the contemporary era. After learning about the early historiography produced by Swedish archbishop Olaus Magnus, author of the *Carta Marina* (1539) and *History of the Northern Peoples* (1555), and the introduction of Christianity in the Arctic. Then discover the story of how Rovaniemi evolved from an agricultural settle-

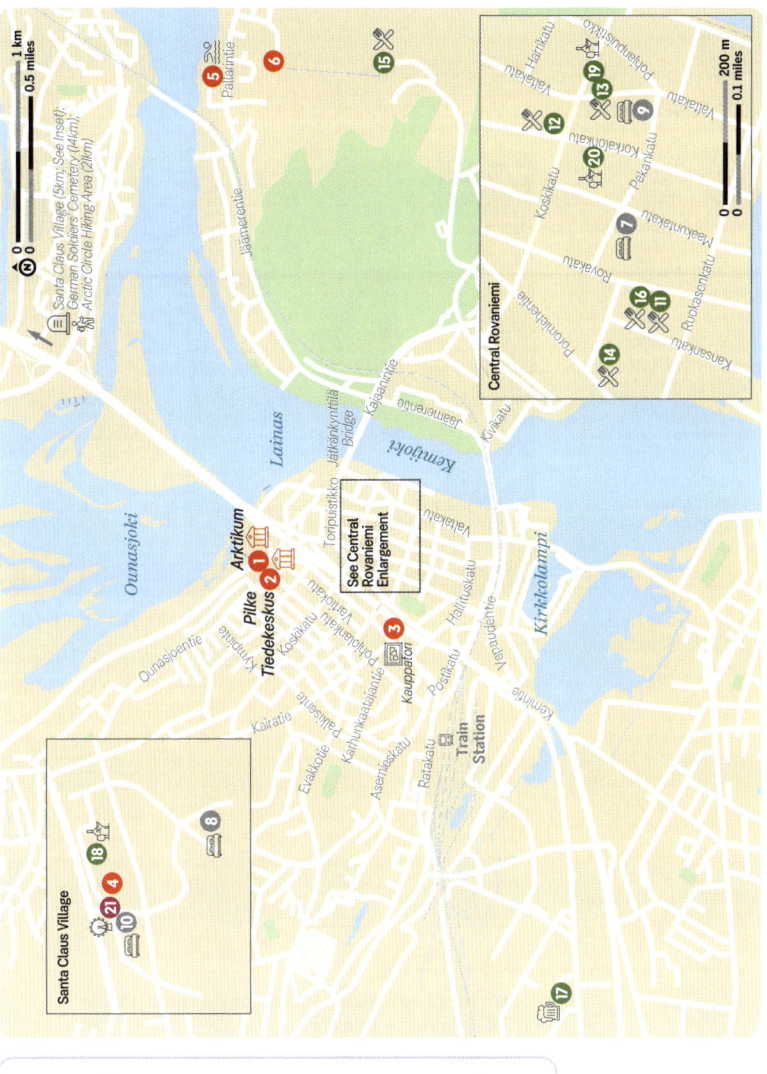

HIGHLIGHTS
1. Arktikum
2. Pilke Tiedekeskus

SIGHTS
3. Rovaniemen Taidemuseo
4. Santa Claus Post Office

ACTIVITIES, COURSES & TOURS
5. KesäRafla Restaurant & Sauna
6. Ounasvaara

SLEEPING
7. Arctic City Hotel
8. Glass Resort
9. Hostel Cafe Koti
10. Santa Claus Holiday Village

EATING
11. Cafe & Bar 21
- Café Koti (see 9)
12. Gustav Kitchen & Bar
- Monte Rosa (see 7)
13. Nili
14. Roka
15. Sky Kitchen & View
16. Taqueria Yuca

DRINKING & NIGHTLIFE
17. Lapland Brewery
18. Loft Cocktail Lounge
19. Paha Kurki
20. Uitto

ENTERTAINMENT
21. Santa Claus Village

THE GUIDE

LAPLAND ROVANIEMI

Rovaniemi viewed from Ounasvaara

SCORCHED EARTH

The final stage of WWII in Finland began with the signing of an armistice with the Soviet Union in September 1944. The terms required Finland to expel all German forces, which had been allies up that point. About 200,000 German soldiers were stationed in northern Finland, with headquarters in Rovaniemi. As Finland pressured the Nazi troops to leave, engaging in what became known as the Lapland War, German General Rendulic gave the infamous orders to raze all buildings in the region. On 27 April 1945, the last German troops withdrew across the border, signalling the end of the Lapland War. But the German scorched earth policy caused the destruction of nearly every building in Rovaniemi.

ment first mentioned in 1453 to official town in 1960. Special attention is given to the loss of Petsamo during the Winter War. Petsamo (Pechenga in Russian, Beahcán in Northern Sámi, Peäccam in Skolt Sámi) was an area extending northeast from the current Finnish border to the Arctic Ocean. It was joined to Finland in the Treaty of Tartu in 1920, but was captured by the Soviet Union in 1944. Besides regional history, Arktikum also features a new permanent science exhibition launched in late 2024 titled Arctic Opposites, which focuses on the seasonal extremes that can be experienced in the polar regions of the world.

Forest Living

Learn how Lapland's people coexist with nature at Pilke Science Centre

The **Pilke Science Centre** (*Pilke Tiedekeskus; tiedekeskuspilke.fi; adult/child €7/5*), located right next door to Arktikum, is an entertaining exhibition on Finnish forestry with a sustainable focus. Kids of all ages can climb up into a giant logging vehicle or a birdhouse. There is an infor-

 EATING IN ROVANIEMI: BEST LIGHT BITES & CAFES

Roka: Communal tables, exposed-brick walls and imaginative bistro-style fare. *noon-9pm Sun-Thu, to 10pm Fri & Sat* €€

Cafe & Bar 21: Stylish haunt for lunch serving waffles, salads and bao buns; also wine later in the evening. *11am-9pm Sun-Thu, to 10pm Fri & Sat* €€

Café Koti: Housing the reception of the homonymous hostel, a welcoming cafe filled with natural light. *7am-5pm Mon-Fri, 8am-3pm Sat, 8am-noon Sun* €

Taquería Yuca: Perhaps you don't expect good Mexican street food in the Arctic Circle, but, well, here it is. *11am-9pm Mon-Thu, to 10pm Fri, 2-10pm Sat* €€

mation centre and shop of Metsähallitus, the forest administration, where you can pick up walking leaflets and buy maps useful for hiking.

Northern Art Discoveries
Installations, paintings and sounds at Culture House Korundi

Housed inside the former post office depot, the Culture House Korundi (*korundi.fi, adult/child €11/5*) is where Rovaniemi's art scene comes to life. Split between the **Rovaniemi Art Museum** (*Rovaniemen Taidemuseo*) and the Lapland Chamber Orchestra, Korundi hosts exhibitions and concerts year-round, with a focus on local artists to whom temporary shows are dedicated.

Rovaniemi's Action Playground
Ounasvaara for summer and winter

Ounasvaara (*ounasvaara.fi*), the forest-clad fell across the river just east of Rovaniemi, is where the city lets off steam. On its northern side, the Ounasvaara Ski Resort has 10 varied downhill slopes (including freeride), a snow park and an area for beginners. There are also 200km of cross-country ski tracks on Ounasvaara and around Rovaniemi. In summer (late June to mid-August) the ski station operates a summer bobsleigh run and a bike park with downhill runs.

Santa's Headquarters
Meet Father Christmas at Santa Claus Village

About 8km northeast of Roveniemi's city centre is the official residence of Santa Claus, open 365 days a year for the half a million people that come to visit him from all corners of the globe. Christmas is serious business in Finland – surrounded by forests, the red village is part shopping centre, part theme park, with restaurants serving slow-cooked reindeer stews, souvenir shops brimming with all-things Arctic, and design stores of Finnish brands such as Marimekko and Pentik. Different companies operate in the Christmas playground and – sorry to break the magic – there are at least two competing Santas you can meet, one in Santa's Office and the other in the Christmas House. The most popular Santa is at the Office (enter under the 'Meet Santa' sign). Taking photos inside isn't permitted, but your three-minute chat will be photographed and videoed by elves and you can download the results for €50 (or

SANTA'S ORIGINS

The figure of Santa Claus is a feature of many cultures that celebrate Christmas, but few parts of the world cherish it as much as Finland. According to tradition, Santa Claus visits children in their homes on Christmas Eve, bringing gifts to those who have behaved well. Santa's origins are typically tied to St Nicholas, a 4th-century Greek bishop from Myra, although Finland's Santa has been influenced by the pagan myth of Joulupukki, the 'Yule Goat' of mid-winter celebrations that used to roam the Finnish fells asking villagers for alcoholic donations. It was only in the 19th century that it began blending with the Christian tradition, turning from a menacing creature to a gift-giving, loving old man.

EATING IN ROVANIEMI: BEST UPSCALE RESTAURANTS

| **Nili:** Hunting-lodge-style interior; very well prepared Lapland classics, such as lake fish, reindeer, elk and salmon soup. *4-11pm Tue-Fri, from 2pm Sat* €€€ | **Sky Kitchen & View:** Sky Ounasvaara hotel's restaurant serves wild-mushroom risotto and reindeer of the day. *5-10pm Sun-Fri, to 11pm Sat* €€€ | **Monte Rosa:** Wooden booths and candles enhance the experience at this long-established steak specialist. *11am-2pm Mon-Fri, 5-10pm Tue-Sat* €€€ | **Gustav Kitchen & Bar:** Internationally inspired, fashionable restaurant. *11am-3pm Mon, to 11pm Tue-Thu, to midnight Fri & Sat* €€€ |

WHERE IS THE ARCTIC CIRCLE?

Running through Santa Claus Village is the line that marks the border of the Arctic Circle, the southernmost latitude at which the Sun will not rise all day during the winter solstice. While the boundary makes for a great photo op, you may not be standing in the right spot when visiting Rovaniemi. This is because the Arctic Circle is not fixed, but moving slightly season after season. Because of variations in the Earth's axial tilt caused by gravitational interactions with the Moon and other celestial bodies, the actual Arctic Circle shifts north or south by several metres each year.

pay €35 for an A4 print). In the middle of the village you'll also find the **Santa Claus Post Office**. Any mail sent from here will be stamped with a special Arctic Circle/Santa/Reindeer postmark. Post it in special boxes for it to arrive just before Christmas. The office receives around 500,000 letters a year to Santa from around the world. A historical curiosity is the Roosevelt Cottage, a log cabin built for a visit by Eleanor Roosevelt in 1950. It's now a reindeer-horn souvenir workshop. To get to **Santa Claus Village** by public transport catch local bus number 8 or the seasonal Santa Claus Bus (*santaclausbus.fi*), or the bus running to the airport.

Reindeer Encounters
Meet them, feed them, ride with them

Rovaniemi's Santa Claus Village is often the first chance for people arriving from the south to see reindeer. **Santa Claus Safari** (*santaclausreindeer.fi*), based inside the village and managed by friendly Antti Körkkö and his family, can organise safaris of all lengths of time, from short one-hour trips to overnight journeys in search of the northern lights. To truly experience Rovaniemi's winter breeze (in winter it can be as cold as -30°C; the coldest recorded local temperature is -45.3°C) you can book a night in a traditional wooden *laavu* open cabin on the Porovaara Hill (*porovaara.fi*), and sleep by the fire surrounded by nature as reindeer herders used to do in the old days.

A Mausoleum for German Soldiers
The hidden cemetery by Lake Norvajärvi

On the shore of **Lake Norvajärvi**, a 15-minute drive north of Rovaniemi's city centre, sits a **monumental cemetery** housing the remains of over 2500 German soldiers who died in Lapland during WWII. While the Wehrmacht burned much of region to the ground during the Lapland War of 1944, Finland was allied with Nazi Germany in fighting the Soviet Union in the previous stage of the war, known as the Continuation War. The impressive red granite mausoleum is found at the end of a 500m path through the forest and is open for visitors from April to September.

Some Steam & a Dip in the River
Summer relaxation in the KesäRafla Sauna

Overlooking the Kemijoki River with its wide open terrace, the **KesäRafla Restaurant & Sauna** is a favourite

DRINKING IN ROVANIEMI: BEST BARS & PUBS

Paha Kurki: Dark but friendly rock bar. Try a Lapland Red Ale or two. *4pm-3.15am Mon-Thu, to 4.15am Fri & Sat; 6pm-3.15am Sun*

Uitto: For a pub with good beer, and maybe TV sport, head for wood-panelled Uitto. *5pm-12.30am Tue-Thu, to 2.30am Fri; 10am-2.30am Sat*

Loft Cocktail Lounge: Lapland-inspired cocktails are served in this child-free bar in Santa Claus Village. *10am-5.30pm*

Lapland Brewery: A short distance from the city centre, Finland's northernmost brewery has a tap room. *9am-6pm Mon-Thu, to 8pm Fri, noon-8pm Sat*

meeting point for locals during the warmer months of the year and a prime spot to recharge after your Lapland exploration. Get your sweat going in the wood-fuelled unisex sauna (adults €5), then take a dip in the river to cool off before ordering some fish from the grill. Open from mid-June to mid-August.

A Taste of Arctic Wilderness
Hike across rapids in the Arctic Circle Hiking Area

Continue driving 10 minutes past the Santa Claus Village on the E75 to reach Napapiirin Retkeilyalue, the **Arctic Circle Hiking Area**, a great spot to effortlessly immerse yourself in Lapland's nature. Suspension bridges cross the mighty rapids of the Raudanjoki River, running through the thick forests on the outskirts of the urban centre. The circular Könkäänsaari Nature Trail, stretching for 1.5km, is accessible to wheelchair users (with an assistant) thanks to a metre-wide boardwalk, while the 7km Vianaapa Mire Nature Trail takes you through bogs and mires where thousands of waterbirds come to breed in spring, after the snow melts.

Bridge over Raudanjoki River, Arctic Circle Hiking Area

LAPLAND'S FAVOURITE FOODS

Reindeer: The most common meat here – in fillets, sausages, soup, sautéed or as a great hunk of shoulder roasted over an open fire.

Elk: Also known as moose, hunted in Lapland's forests; it tastes like venison. Especially good from the Tenojoki in the far north.

Whitefish: A tender treat from Inarijärvi.

Berries: Cranberries, lingonberries, blueberries, and the beloved cloudberries. Laplanders love late-summer foraging then turning berries into jams, juices and desserts. Ranua is Lapland's unofficial cloudberry capital and holds a cloudberry festival in August.

Wild mushrooms: Another foragers' favourite.

Leipäjuusto: 'Bread cheese', also known as squeaky cheese.

Beyond Rovaniemi

Almost everyone goes to Santa's village, then there's a world of diverse experiences to enjoy year-round in the countryside beyond.

Places
Kemi p214
Kukkola p217
Ranua p218
Kemijärvi p218
Posio p219
Salla p220
Pyhä-Luosto p221
Sodankylä p221

GETTING AROUND

As ever, having your own transport is most convenient here, though you can get out to Santa Claus Village from Rovaniemi by city bus 8 and the privately operated Santa Claus Bus, and many activity operators offer transport to their locations. There are several buses daily to/from Ranua zoo, and several Kemijärvi- or Sodankylä-bound buses from Rovaniemi will stop at the Köngästie stop, a 500m walk from the start of the Vaattunkivaara walking trail. Some tour companies offer trips to Auttiköngäs.

Lapland's diversity isn't just a matter of season. Southern Lapland (Peräpohjola in Finnish), the area extending roughly from the Gulf of Bothnia in the west to the Salla region in the east, features vast forested areas, rivers and lakes, and much lower altitudes compared to its northern counterpart. Historically, this area belonged to the Oulu county in Nordbotten (Northern Ostrobothnia) – only in 1936 was it officially made part of Lapland. There are cultural and geographical peculiarities that you won't encounter elsewhere in the region. From the industrial centre of Kemi, for instance, you can reach the Bothnian Sea National Park or take a trip on an icebreaker. A little further north, you can hear the old Meänkieli Finnish dialect being spoken on the Swedish side of the Tornio River; go inland in search of precious stones at an Amethyst Mine; or reach Finland's newest national park in Salla to hike amid old-growth forests.

Kemi
TIME FROM ROVANIEMI: **1HR 20MINS**

Through the Bothnian Bay on the Sampo Icebreaker

The career of **Sampo** started in 1961, when the Finnish-built icebreaker began cutting through the thick layers of ice that formed on the Gulf of Bothnia to allow the larger commercial vessels to continue travelling across the sea during winter time. After nearly 30 years of diligent activity, the ship was purchased by the city of Kemi. Instead of retiring, it has been turned into a one-of-a-kind experience – between December and April, you can jump onboard *Sampo* and set off for a four-hour cruise between the ice sheets. At €400 tickets are not exactly cheap (*experience365.fi*), but this is the only existing icebreaker in Finland repurposed for tourism.

Lost Laitakari

The sprawling forests surrounding Kemi (Giepma in Northern Sámi), and the direct access to the Gulf of Bothnia, have made timber the main driver of Kemi's economy since the town's inception. Accessible in summer with the **M/S Leila** (*merike.fi; adult/child €20/10*), departing from Kemi's harbour, the fascinating site of industrial archeology that is the island of **Laitakari** tells the story of Kemi's origins. Here,

Icebreaker *Sampo*

the region's first steam sawmill was established in 1862, seven years before Kemi was founded on the mainland. A community of over 300 people lived on the island at its peak, operating one of Europe's largest steam sawmills. Dozens of tugboats carried hundreds of logs for processing to Laitakari along the Kemijoki River until 1939, when the company's owners decided to move operations to the mainland after a major fire damaged the sawmill. A few families continued to live on the island until 1966, when it was abandoned. In recent years Swiss-Dutch Kemi resident Oskar van Leperen has taken up the task of bringing back Laitakari's history to light, installing signs and historic photographs on the island to show what it looked like before it was reclaimed by nature. You can spend a few hours roaming through the foundations of the former sawmill and the partially submerged wooden piers, and looking through traces of the past. To learn more about Laitakari, you can also visit Kemi's **History Museum**, located in the local culture centre on Marina Takalon Katu, where a model of the island during its heyday is on display.

Ice & steam by the sea

Kemi's favorite public sauna is found inside a historic wooden house overlooking the island-dotted bay. Wear your swimsuit and step into the steam room, then cool down by jumping in the sea from the floating platform. During winter, when temperatures can go as low as -35°C, **Satamakonttori** welcomes brave ice-bathers for regenerative dips in nearly frozen water.

Handmade ritualistic crafts

In ancient times, Sámi healers – known as *noaidi* in Northern Sámi language – used a drum made of wood and reindeer hide to produce rhythms that allowed them to enter a trance to gain information from spirits and predict future events. While such rituals are hardly practised these days, the

WILDERNESS HUTS

Metsähallitus, the forest administration, operates a marvellous network of several hundred hikers'/skiers'/canoeists' huts in Finland's national parks and other protected areas.

Open wilderness huts: Unlocked huts with bunks or boards for sleeping, wood stove, cooking equipment, dry toilet and firewood. Often sociable places, in peak seasons some can fill up. Last arrivals have priority.

Day-trip huts: Like open wilderness huts, without sleeping space.

Campfire huts: Day huts with benches around a fireplace.

Reservable huts: Like open wilderness huts but locked; you pay to reserve an overnight place and get a key.

Rental huts: Pay to rent the whole thing.

For further information see Metsähallitus info centres and *nationalparks.fi*.

THE LAST MEÄNKIELI SPEAKERS

If you cross the Tornio River in Kukkola, you may be surprised to hear that Finnish is still spoken on the Swedish side of the town as well. This is not standard Finnish, however, but Meänkieli, an old dialect recognised as a minority language in Sweden. The Tornio River Valley was historically a Finnish-speaking region, but when Finland became a Grand Duchy of the Russian Empire in the early 19th century, Finnish speakers left outside the newly established border developed separately from a linguistic perspective, maintaining terms and idioms that have disappeared in modern Finland. There are approximately 30,000 people who undestand Meänkieli in Sweden today.

Kemi Lumilinna

Maahisen Tyvär shop located steps away from Kemi's town hall keeps pre-Christian Sámi traditions alive. Enter to find drums once used for celebratory rituals decorated with painted landscapes, jewellery made from stones collected around Lapland's forests, and wooden signs ironically recalling the times when Sámi women healers were believed to be witches – all made by hand by owner Annuka Ovaska.

Ice sculptures

Started as an exhibition for Kemi's Winter Park, this collection of large-scale ice sculptures is now visible year round inside what looks like a massive fridge, part of the city-owned **Kemi Lumilinna** (Snow Castle) hotel. While the actual snow castle that used to be built every winter on Kemi's waterfront is no longer part of the city's winter park, a fortress made of ice blocks stands together with animals, knights and igloos, in this kid-friendly frozen museum just outside the town's centre.

Reindeer rides

A 20-minute drive from Kemi's town centre, in the village of Simo, is the family-run **Arkadia Reindeer Farm**, a space immersed in the nature of southern Lapland where you'll have a chance to get close and personal with reindeer. Owners Päivi and Samuli will welcome you with some *munkki* donuts and coffee served around the fire in their impressive

 EATING IN KEMI: OUR PICKS

Sataman Krouwi: Enjoy a big tasty burger with a side of waterfront views. Veg options available. *10.30am-3pm Mon-Wed, to 9pm Th & Fri, noon-9pm Sat* €

Limihiutale: The restaurant of Kemi's Snow Castle hotel is one of the city's best fine-dining destinations. *5-8pm Wed-Sat* €€€

Pursiseura: With a large open terrace overlooking the marina, Pursiseura makes for a great lunch spot. *11am-2pm Mon-Fri summer* €

Satamakaffila Nuotta: This summer cafe along Kemi's seaside promenade has burgers, beers and light bites. *9am-midnight Mon-Fri, from 11am Sun* €€

teepee-like wooden headquarters – entirely built by Samuli himself – then guide you through the farm to meet the animals and tell you all the secrets of reindeer-keeping. Feed and sleigh-ride the reindeer on the snow-covered grounds in the winter, or visit the cafe and animal park in the summer.

Protecting the sailors

A miniature sailing vessel hangs from the ceiling in **Kemi's Church**, a neo-gothic pink building marking the heart of the town. Dating back to 1902 (but renovated multiple times over the course of the past century), this landmark structure designed by Finnish church architect Josef Stenbäck is among the largest in the Sea Lapland region. Guides will show you around free of charge, and point to the sea-related symbols decorating the church, a tradition typical of coastal places of worship, to protect sailors crossing the Gulf of Bothnia.

Cruise the Bothnian Bay National Park

The islands emerging within the boundaries of the 157 sq km **Bothnian Bay National Park** off the coast of Kemi and Tornio are the result of the post-glacial uplift that characterises much of the northern Nordics. This pristine area is best explored in the summer on board of the faux-historic **Jähti** ship departing regularly from Kemi's port. Built in 2007 following an 1850s design, the vessel runs full-day trips to the islands of Pensaskari and Selkä-Sarvi, both sitting near the Swedish border, between June and August. Check the season's schedule on *satamankrouwi.fi/jahti*

Kukkola

TIME FROM ROVANIEMI: 1½HR

United by a river

The mighty Tornionjoki River marks the border between Finland and Sweden in the northwestern part of the country. The twin towns of Kukkola, a name shared by the Finnish and Swedish hamlets split by the never-freezing rapids 18km north of Tornio, are two settlements historically united by their traditional fishing method, nominated for UNESCO's Intangible Cultural Heritage list. Thanks to the abundance of white fish (and salmon, to a lesser extent) migrating to the seas through the moving waters of the Tornionjoki, the two Kukkolas flourished in the Middle Ages – 19th-century red storehouses, smokehouses and mills still furnish the coastline on both sides, although the population is dwindling.

In summer, fisherman can still be seen using hand-held dipnets attached to a long pole to catch fish, with mirroring clock towers marking the workday, with a one-hour difference due to mismatching time zones. There is no bridge connecting the two Kukkolas – to visit the Swedish side you'll have to drive south to Tornio, cross to Haparanda and then drive back up to Swedish Kukkola. To place Kukkula in its historical context it's worth joining one of the cultural tours to the region run by LappOne (*lappone.com*), the Tornio-based operator run by former Nokia engineer Alessandro Maccari, specialising in the less-publicised corners of Lapland.

LAPLAND'S ELUSIVE FAUNA

Heini Niinimäki, zoological director at Ranua Wildlife Park, presents five rare creatures living in the big north.

Wolverine (*Gulo gulo*): The smallest of Finland's four large predators, the wolverine boasts a bite stronger than that of the brown bear.

Finnish Forest Reindeer (*Rangifer tarandus fennicus*): Unlike the domesticated reindeer, these native creatures have remained wild in Finland's untouched wilderness.

Least Weasel (*Mustela nivalis*): The smallest carnivore in the world can catch prey larger than itself.

Great Grey Owl (*Strix nebulosa*): Also known as lapinpöllö (Lapland owl), this owl can detect the faintest movement beneath half a metre of snow.

Arctic Fox (*Vulpes lagopus*): In 2022, Finland's most endangered mammal bred in Lapland for the first time since 1996, offering hope for its survival.

> **SNOWMOBILING IN SOUTHERN LAPLAND**
>
> **Arja Filén**, coordinator at Visit Kemijärvi, tells us about travelling through Lapland's icy grounds in winter, using a typically Nordic mode of transport.
>
> During winter, it's time to ride a snowmobile! In Lapland these vehicles are essential for different purposes, such as trail and backcountry riding, racing and utility work. Snowmobiling offers a unique way to explore remote landscapes that are otherwise inaccessible. Last winter, I did a 600km solo trip around southeast Lapland, passing through Luosto, Pyhä, Salla and Suomu. One of the highlights was taking a break in the middle of a vast frozen swamp, enjoying homemade pizza surrounded by a pristine white winter wonderland. In that moment, I felt a deep sense of peace, freedom and happiness.

Old-style cooking

Photos of celebrity chef Gordon Ramsay adorn the walls of **Myllyn Pirtti Café** in Kukkola, a cottage located on the banks of the Tornionjoki River. The cafe is known for preserving an ancient cooking tradition. It's not just the fishing method that reflects local heritage, but also the way whitefish is prepared. The fish is skewered and barbecued upright by the fire, then eaten by hand, scraping the tender flesh from the sides.

Ranua

TIME FROM ROVANIEMI: **1HR**

Arctic creatures at Ranua's Wildlife Park

Venus, Finland's only polar bear, is often the main draw for the visitors of **Ranua's Wildlife Park** (*ranuaresort.com/en/wildlife-park; adult/child €23.50/19; open year-round*), but it's the 50 species of animals indigenous to Lapland that offer an opportunity to learn more about Nordic ecosystem. Located in the coniferous forests steps away from the Ranua Resort, the wildlife park hosts wolverines, brown bears, reindeer and, if you're lucky, even an elusive Boreal owl. The wooden pathway that twists and turns inside the park was expanded in 2019 to connect to the *Seven Steps to Save the Ocean* installation by artist Maija Kovari – walk above the field of rocks that was once a seabed to encounter a series of messages embedded in the landscape inviting you to take action to save the environment.

Kemijärvi

TIME FROM ROVANIEMI: **1HR**

World wooden wonders

For 19 years starting from 1985, Kemijärvi hosted the locally celebrated Kemijärvi Woodsculpting Week, an event organised by local artist Upi Kärri where talented sculptors from different corners of the world gathered to present a variety of woodcarving styles and techniques. The legacy of the Woodsculpting Week is now a permanent show hosted at the **Puustelli art center**, a former boat shed transformed into a rustic exhibition hall that displays some of the most prominent works produced during previous editions of this one-of-a-kind festival. The space is open between June and September – if you are lucky you might even meet Upi, who'll tell you the stories of the people who created these often abstract artworks.

Fishing with the pros

During the long summer evenings when the wind quiets down, Lake Kemijärvi is a flat mirror reflecting the colours of the sky and the islands. Set out with fishermen Sámi Savolain-

EATING & DRINKING IN RANUA & KEMIJARVI: OUR PICKS

Book Bar: Former library in Ranua repurposed as a live-music pub hosting regular shows and karaoke nights. *4pm-2am Fri & Sat €*

Wild Arctic Restaurant: The menu changes seasonally at Ranua Resort's restaurant, with lunch buffet menus starting at €15. *10am-6pm €*

Jauri Resort: The restaurant of the homonymous Kemijärvi hotel (p237) sits right by the lake, serving freshly caught fish. *11am-3pm €€*

Susa's Bistro: In the heart of Kemijärvi, Susa's little restaurant is a safe bet for local fare, homemade cakes and coffee. *9am-3pm Mon-Fri €*

Brown bear, Ranua Wildlife Park

en and Antti Kumpula to the heart of this large body of water to pick up the nets as the midnight sun reaches its lowest point. Learn about small-scale pike fishing with certified professionals as you immerse yourself in the peaceful atmosphere of southern Lapland's nature. In winter, when the lake freezes, it is also possible to organise ice-fishing trips on foot. All excursions can be booked via the **Jauri Resort** (p237) (*jauriresort.com*) on the shore of the lake.

Kemijärvi views

See the Kemijärvi area from above by climbing the three-storey **Kotavaara Observation Tower**, located on top of Kotavaara Hill east of the city centre. On a sunny day, this privileged lookout spot offers exceptional views of the lakes and forests embracing this urban centre of 7000 inhabitants, the largest of eastern Lapland. The 400m uphill hike to the tower starts at Kotavaara's parking lot.

Posio

TIME FROM ROVANIEMI: **1HR 35MINS**

Finnish design icon

Fans of Finnish design should make a beeline 65km west from Ruka to the small town of Posio, home base of the outstanding interior-design house **Pentik**, founded here in 1971 by ceramic artist Anu Pentik and her husband Topi Pentikäinen. Pentik's readily appealing, never overcomplicated homewares, with designs often inspired by northern Finnish nature, are now sold in the company's nearly 50 shops (and many others) around Finland. Pentik's ceramics (some still designed by Anu) and candles are still made here in Posio.

Besides the Pentik shop, the **Kulttuurikeskus Pentik-Mäki** (Pentik Hill Culture Centre) houses a number of museums. The **Pentik Home Museum**, established in 1973, tells the story of Pentik's founder, showcasing the evolution of the brand over the decades. A small room below ground hosts the

ROVANIEMI ACTIVITY OPERATORS

Safartica: Quality local outfit offering a huge range, from berry foraging to gasoline-free electric-snowmobile safaris.

Lapland Welcome: Has a strong nature focus on trips, including elk (moose) spotting and wilderness wildlife photography.

Beyond Arctic Adventures: Experts in aurora borealis photography tours; carefully chosen locations up to 100km out of town.

Nordic Unique Travels: Wide-ranging operator with offerings from a midnight-sun sauna boat to ice fishing and cross-country skiing.

Roll Outdoors: Mountain bike, fatbike and e-fatbike rentals, route ideas and guided rides.

Lapland Safaris: The largest of Rovaniemi's tour operators, a very professional operation with a vast activities range.

THE 2032 SALLA OLYMPICS

In 2021, as cities around the world were making their bids to hold the 2032 summer Olympics, an unexpected contender joined the race. The town of Salla (population 3300) announced that it was going to apply to become the next Olympic city, as rising temperatures resulting from global warming were going to make the Arctic town a suitable location for summer sports within a decade. According to recent research, the Arctic has warmed nearly four times faster than the rest of the globe in the past 40 years, a trend that is bound to alter Lapland's climate drastically in the future. While Salla didn't end up submitting its bid to the Olympics committee, the stunt went viral and put the town self-branded as 'in the middle of nowhere' on the map.

Pyhä-Luosto National Park

International Cup Museum, where about 2000 ceramic cups from all around the world are exhibited behind glass. The **Anu Pentik Galleria**, with its stunning 20m-wide mosaic facade, hosts contemporary Finnish design exhibitions. All museums are free to access.

Salla

TIME FROM ROVANIEMI: 2HR

Finland's youngest National Park

Self-identifying as 'in the middle of nowhere', the town of Salla, in the southeastern corner of Lapland just above the Arctic Circle, offers a chance to immerse yourself in the protected old-growth forests. **Salla National Park**, Finland's newest national park, established in 2022, extends for nearly 100 sq km along the Russian border and provides many opportunities for exploring in both winter and summer. Hike up to **Iso Pyhätunturi**, the park's highest point peaking at 479m, through the 5km circular trail that starts behind the Salla Ski Resort. Climb the observation tower to admire endless forests stretching into Russian territory. The **Sallatunturin Tuvat** hotel and restaurant rents mountain bikes (€25/day) and the **Salla Ski Resort** rents electric fatbikes (starting at €50 for three hours) to ride on the snowy trails during winter time. Trail maps are available at the Visitor Centre.

A town divided

The world's oldest ski, dating back to 3245 BCE, was found in Salla in 1938. The archaeological artefact (conserved in the National Museum of Finland) testifies to human presence in the region since ancient times. Yet Salla has largely been shaped by 20th-century events. The town was ceded to the Soviet Union as part of the terms of the Moscow Peace Treaty, signed on 13 March 1940, at the end of the Winter War. A new border cut through the settlement, forming an 'old Salla' on the Soviet side, and a reconstructed Salla on the Finnish side. The story of Salla's transformation in the past century is told at the **Museum of** the War and Reconstruction (*adult €5*). Guides Samuli Attila and Annina Luostarinen are extremely knowledgeable and can point you in the right direction if the intricacies of the war get too complicated. Spot the leather jacket allegedly gifted by none other than Elvis to Captain Olavi Alakulppi, a Lapland native who escaped a conviction for arms smuggling and joined the military in the US when the King of Rock and Roll was in service.

Reindeer encounters
Thirteen kilometres south of Salla's town centre, find the state-of-the-art visitor centre of the **Salla Wilderness Park** (*sallareindeerpark.fi*), your point of access to the 200-hectare park that extends around the Tammakkolampi Lake, populated by about 60 reindeer. Both summer and winter activities are available – you can take a walk along the 5km trail that runs through the pine and spruce forest, join one of the daily feeding trips, or go for a sleigh ride on the snow. It's worth checking out the museum inside the visitor centre as well, to get a better understanding of the environment surrounding you.

Pyhä-Luosto
TIME FROM ROVANIEMI: 1½HR

Searching for amethysts
The **Pyhä-Luosto National Park**, a one-hour drive from Kemijärvi, is home to one of the few amethyst mines accessible to the public, the **Lampivaara Amethyst Mine** (*amethystmine.fi*). A symbol of Lapland, amethyst is a purple variety of quartz, used as a gemstone in jewellery for its stunning colour, which can vary from pale lilac to deep violet. Between June and September guided tours of the mine (*adult €25, no need to book in advance*) start multiple times a day from the Lampivaara cafe, a 2.5km hike from the Ukko-Luosto parking lot, and include the chance of digging up your own amethyst. In winter, you can hop on the Amethyst Pendolino snow train from the Pyhä-Luosto Visitor and Culture Center Naava and effortlessly reach the mine.

Summiting Ukko-Luosto
Hiking the **Ukko-Luosto** fell in Pyhä-Luosto National Park offers exceptional views of the vast forests covering the region's fells. The moderately challenging 6.5km circular trail includes the Ukko-Luosto 575-step staircase leading to the weather station at the top. The route passes through old-growth forests, and once at the top, you'll find a scenic platform with stunning vistas. The route continues towards the Ukko-Luosto scenic hut, where you can take a break before returning to your starting point.

Sodankylä
TIME FROM ROVANIEMI: 1½HR

Arctic naïve art
Steps away from Sodankylä's reindeer statue is the **Museum-Gallery Alariesto**, exhibiting over 100 paintings by 20th-century artist Andreas Alariesto. Alariesto's naïve style art depicting scenes of everyday life in Lapland reached national fame only at the end of his career, and he is now celebrated for his candid portrayals of animals, log houses and communities living above the Arctic Circle.

MIDNIGHT SUN FILM FESTIVAL

Film-lovers will want to stop in Sodankylä in mid-June, when the town's Midnight Sun Film Festival takes place, usually in the days leading up to the summer solstice. Running since 1986, the event has drawn a long list of international directors to this typically quiet town, from Mario Monicelli to Alice Rohrwacher and most recently Alfonso Cuaron. As the sun does not set at this time of the year, films are screened around the clock. During the five days of the event, Sodankylä's population doubles, or even triples, with thousands of people coming for screenings and workshops. Check this year's program at *msfilmfestival.fi*.

WALKING TOUR

Korouma Canyon

This 5km looping trail around a section of the Korouma Canyon takes you through three of the 14 waterfalls that line up along the 30km valley. The path is open year-round (although it can be extremely slippery in winter) and offers an entirely different scenery depending on when you visit – from frozen waterfalls dropping into the river to forested cliffs soaring above the canyon.

❶ Korouma Parking
On Rovaniementie, the road linking Rovaniemi to Posio, turn right onto the Koppelojärventie road and continue until you reach Saukkovaarantie road leading to the Kouroma Parking, where the 5km Koronjää Trail begins. Here you'll find the cafe Korouoma Eräkahvila, where you can fuel up on caffeine before setting out to tackle the trail.

The Hike: Take the old horse path used by loggers in the early 20th century, marked by green ribbons and yellow reflectors, and head south, following the trail clockwise with the river on your right.

❷ Jaska Jokusen
After approximately 1.8km you'll spot the the 50m-tall waterfall known as Jaska Jokusen (Charlie Brown) due to the dark colour it acquires when frozen as a

Korouoma Canyon

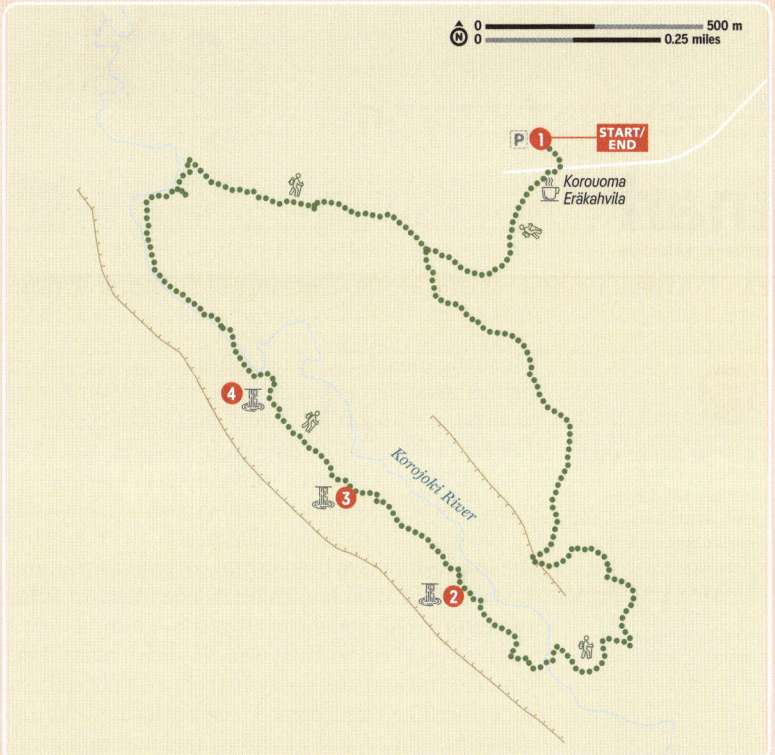

result of the minerals found in the rocky surface it crosses.

The Hike: After crossing the stream on the wooden bridge, turn around and start walking north towards the other two waterfalls found on the path.

❸ Mammuttiputous

Continue hiking until you find the multilevel Mammut Waterfall, less than 1km from Jaska Jokusen. Mammuttiputous reaches up to 40m in width during the period of maximum expansion and climbers can be spotted hacking into the monumental block of ice during winter.

The Hike: The trail stretches for 1.8km on the western side of the Korojoki River. Continue walking in the same direction until Riskea Virta.

❹ Riskea Virta

The last of the three waterfalls found along the Koronjää Trail is also the largest. Riskea Virta drops into the canyon from its majestic 60m in height, reaching the Korojoki River with its iron-rich reddish waters. Next to the waterfall, you'll find a fireplace where you can stop to warm or make some tea before returning to the starting point.

The Hike: Cross the river again through the bridge found below Riskea Virta to take the final leg of the itinerary and complete the hike by returning to the Korouma Parking lot.

❶ Korouma Parking

Leave the river behind and walk back into the forest for about 1km to close the loop and get back to the beginning of the trail. On the way, you will see a shelter hut shortly after Riskea Virta – here you have the option to extend your hike by taking the 5km Piippukallion Pihaus Trail, accessible only during summer months.

Inari

SÁMI CULTURAL CAPITAL | ARCTIC NATURAL WONDERS | OUTDOOR ACTION

GETTING AROUND

Inari is a small place and easy to walk around. Most lodgings can rent or lend you a bicycle if you wish. Many people get here by flying to Ivalo Airport, 49km south of Inari. The airport has car-hire desks. Buses run from Ivalos bus station to Inari multiple times a day, taking approximately 40 mintes to cover the route. Buy tickets online (*matkahuolto.fi*). Private transfers can also be organised through Visit Inari (*visitinari.fi*).

☑ TOP TIP

The centre of the village is effectively the K-Market supermarket, with a large parking area around it, some shops nearby and Hotel Inari across the main road. Sajos and Siida are to the northwest; a few places to stay are dotted along the lakeshore for 2km or 3km to the southeast.

The small, spread-out village of Inari (Anár in Northern Sámi, Aanaar in Inari Sámi, Aanar in Skolt Sámi) occupies a big and important place in the Lapland picture as the seat of the Sámi Parliament in Finland, and effectively the Sámi people's cultural capital in Finland. The village is strung along the shore of Inarijärvi, Lapland's very beautiful, island-studded biggest lake (1084 sq km). The Inari Sámi have been fishing and hunting around the lake since time immemorial. The excellent **Siida museum** (p226) and the nearby Sámi Cultural Centre Sajos are excellent starting places to learn more about Sámi culture and life. Today Inari is a hub of tourism in northern Lapland, a good base for local walks and lake trips, winter husky sledding and aurora borealis viewing, and for access to the outstanding Lemmenjoki and Urho Kekkonen national parks. It remains an agreeably low-key place, far from overwhelmed by visitors.

A Cruise on Lake Inari

Sail to a sacred island

A great way to experience Inarijärvi, Finland's third-largest lake, is to take a summer cruise from the dock at the Siida car park in the 120-seat catamaran operated by **Visit Inari**. The boat sails to (but does not land on) Ukko (Ukonsaari) Island, an old Sámi sacred site. Departures are at 1pm from mid-June to mid-September, and 5pm in July. On request the 1pm cruise will drop you at Pielpavuono, from where you can walk back to Inari via **Pielpajärvi Wilderness Church** (p225). Visit Inari, with an office next to Hotel Inari, offers a range of other summer, autumn and winter activities, such as reindeer- and husky-farm visits, snowmobiling and aurora borealis outings.

Sámi Cultural Home

Visit the Sámi Parliament building

The curved wooden structure housing the **Sámi Cultural Centre Sajos** (*sajos.fi*) is an impressive landmark building in

HIGHLIGHTS
1. Sámi Cultural Centre Sajos
2. Siida

ACTIVITIES, COURSES & TOURS
3. Visit Inari

SLEEPING
4. Hotel Inari
5. Lomakylä Inari
6. Villa Lanca

EATING
7. Aanaar
- Café Čaiju (see 1)
8. PaPaNa
- Restaurant Aurora (see 4)

SHOPPING
9. Inarin Hopea
10. Samekki
- Sámi Duodji Ry (see 1)
- Siida Museum Shop (see 2)

the heart of Inari. The Sámi Parliament in Finland operates from the oval meeting hall at the heart of Sajos, while a Sámi library, the Café Čaiju and a crafts store are found in other rooms. To learn about the functioning of the Sámi Parliament you can book a 45-minute guided tour of Sajos (€300 per group), although the building is publicly accessible free of charge.

Hike to a Wilderness Church
Follow the forest path to Pielpajärvi

Several well-marked trails invite you to explore the Inari countryside. One delightful walk, through mossy, boulder-strewn forests and past several lakes, leads to the handsome wooden **Pielpajärven Erämaakirkko** (Pielpajärvi Wilderness Church), built in the 1750s in a now-vanished Sámi winter village. The route starts along Sarviniementie running northeast from Siida: it's 2.5km along roads to a parking area (you can drive this far if you have a vehicle), then about 5km by forest paths to the church (total if walking the whole way: about 4½ hours there and back, plus stops). The church is always open, and you can open its shutters (just close everything behind you when leaving). Nowadays services are held there at Easter and midsummer. Retrace your steps to return to Inari. This walk can be done in winter with snowshoes.

BEST SÁMI CRAFTS IN INARI

Look for the Duodji certification that signals authenticity.

Sámi Duodji Ry: Sámi handicrafts association's shop, inside Sajos.

Siida Museum Shop: The museum shop has a good range of Sámi-made crafts.

Inarin Hopea: Matti Qvick crafts superb silver and gold jewellery.

Samekki: Finely worked silver jewellery and traditional Sámi crafts, including knives.

EATING IN INARI: BEST CAFES & RESTAURANTS

Café Čaiju: The cafe in Sajos does great organic coffee, cinnamon rolls and good-value set lunches. *9am-3pm Mon-Fri* €

Aanaar: Seasonal local produce in deliciously original preparations at the restaurant in Wilderness Hotel Juutua. *5-10pm* €€€

Restaurant Aurora: Hotel Inari's panoramic restaurant; satisfying menu, including white fish from the lake and roast reindeer. *noon-10pm* €€€

PaPaNa: Pine-panelled PaPaNa, with an outdoor terrace, serves thin-crust pizzas – it's also the village pub. *11am-midnight Sun-Thu, to 2am Fri* €

TOP EXPERIENCE

Siida

Fully renovated in 2022, Siida, a Sámi term referring to a traditional community or village system, offers a comprehensive introduction to Sámi culture through superbly displayed Sámi artefacts and northern Lapland nature. Learn about Sámi history and the holistic connection between livelihoods and nature, and the language of Europe's only recognised indigenous peoples.

TOP TIPS

- From June to September the museum is open from 9am to 6pm, while from October to May hours are 10am to 5pm.

- Guided tours are available on request for groups, for both the museum's permanent exhibition and the open-air museum.

- In 2023 Sámi director Suvi West released the documentary *Mácchan* (Homecoming), which tells the story of the repatriation of the Sámi collection from the National Museum of Finland.

PRACTICALITIES

Scan the QR code for information on tickets and exhibitions.

Nature & Nurture

The permanent exhibition combines huge, beautiful photo panels that illustrate the region's different ecosystems and the cycle of the seasons, with displays of artefacts and archeological findings that purposely blend to show how the relationship to Arctic nature continues to influence Sámi culture to this day. From clothing to hunting and cooking tools, geography has historically shaped the Sámi way of life – how climate change will affect future generations is a question the museum leaves open.

The Return of Sámi Artefacts

In 2021 the National Museum of Finland returned thousands of objects belonging to its Sámi collection to Siida, in an exemplary government-backed repatriation project that aimed to bring back heritage artefacts to their homeland and reconnect communities. Since 2024, a glass case displays part of these returned objects – many are still being studied as their origin is unknown – providing, for the first time, a new context for artefacts that have been tied to Finland's colonial history for the past century.

Open-Air Museum

Behind the main building the Open-Air Museum offers a glimpse into the architectural heritage of the Sámi people. Explore nearly 50 structures, including traditional Sámi pole tents, storage buildings and traps, along an 800m trail. The museum also showcases Sámi livelihoods and lifestyles, dating back 10,000 years, through artefacts, dwellings and archaeological findings.

Beyond Inari

Vast expanses of unspoiled Arctic nature await your explorations – by car, bike or boat, on foot or on skis.

Inari sits amid some of Finland's most spectacular and least populated territory, where lakes, rivers, forests and fells present endless scenic beauty and scope for active adventures. The country's two biggest national parks, Lemmenjoki and Urho Kekkonen, can both be reached in less than an hour's drive. To the north the valley of the beautiful Tenojoki, forming 140km of Finland's border with Norway, makes for a great road trip. Seasonal variations are extreme up here, presenting different activity options for different times of year. September is an ideal month for hiking, with autumn colours and few insects. March is good for cross-country skiing because of its reasonably long days and relatively moderate temperatures.

Places
Tulvalahti p227
Sevettijärvi p227
Lemmenjoki National Park p228
Saariselkä p229
Kiilopää p229
Tankavaara p230
Vuotso p231
Ivalo p232
Karigasniemi p232
Utsjoki p232

Tulvalahti
TIME FROM INARI: **20MINS**
Visit a Sámi home
Learn about Sámi life first-hand on a visit to the friendly lakeside home of **Tuula Airamo** (*tuulasreindeer.weebly.com*), at Tulvalahti, a 20-minute drive northwest of Inari (off the Angeli road). In a three-hour visit you get to feed Tuula's reindeer, see how reindeer-hide shoes are made and wool dyed from natural plants, and learn about local folklore and history over coffee and home-baked goodies. Shorter options are also possible; booking ahead is essential.

Sevettijärvi
TIME FROM INARI: **1½HR**
Skolt Sámi heritage
The Skolt Sámi are one of the Sámi groups living in Finland, primarily residing in the remote northeastern parts of the country. They haven't always been based around Sevettijärvi (Če'vetjäu'rr in Skolt Sámi, Čeavetjávri in Northern Sámi) – until 1944 the Skolt Sámi were mostly residing in the area of Petsamo (Pachenga in Russian), but relocated to Sevettijärvi after WWII when Finland ceded the Petsamo region to the Soviet Union. In northern Finland, the Skolt Sámi maintained their traditional livelihoods, particularly reindeer herding and fishing in the thousands of lakes that dot the region.

GETTING AROUND

Your own wheels are most convenient. Eskelisen Lapin Linjat buses depart Ivalo airport for Saariselkä and Kiilopää 20 minutes after flight arrivals. Returning, they leave Kiilopää 2½ hours before flight departures. Heading north, buses depart Kiilopää and Saariselka in the afternoons. A ski bus shuttles around Saariselkä during the season. There's no public transport to Lemmenjoki National Park.

BEST INARI AREA FESTIVALS

Poro-Kuninkuusajot: Inari's 'Royal Reindeer Race' (late March/early April): animals and skiing 'jockeys' on frozen Inarijärvi.

Ijahis Idja: Two-day 'Nightless Night' indigenous music festival (August) focuses on the multiple genres of Sámi music.

Inari Viikot: 'Inari Weeks' (late July): concerts, markets, parties and more in Inari, Saariselkä, Lemmenjoki and elsewhere.

Skábmagovat: Indigenous peoples' film festival (late January) includes films in English, with some open-air screenings.

Kaamosjazz: The 'world's darkest jazz festival' brightens up Saariselkä winter nights with a January weekend of gigs.

Lemmenjoki National Park

The Skolt Sámi have their own language, which has been partly influenced by Russian and is spoken by less than 300 people today. Next to the Sevettijärvi Orthodox Church, find the tiny **Skolt Sámi Heritage House** (Kolttien Perinnetalo) tracing the history of the Skolt Sámi through photographs, panels and a few artefacts. The museum is freely accessible, and worth a stop if you are driving to Norway.

Lemmenjoki National Park   TIME FROM INARI: **40MINS**
Finland's biggest national park

Finland's biggest national park, **Lemmenjoki**, stretches over 2860 sq km of virtually uninhabited forests, fells, river valleys and wetlands southwest of Inari. It's an excellent summer hiking area, with a helpful scheduled summer boat service along the river. Most of the marked walking trails are within the park's 'recreation zone', a strip about 40km long and up to 12km wide embracing the Lemmenjoki valley and the old-growth forests and fells either side of it.

Accommodation and services are concentrated around the small, scattered Sámi village of **Njurgulahti**, on the national park's eastern fringe, a 45-minute drive from Inari. The most popular route is along the river from Njurgulahti to Ravadasköngäs, where the Ravadasjoki tumbles into the Lemmenjoki in 10m-high falls (17km from Njurgulahti by boat, slightly less on foot), and a further 6km to Kultahamina. The boat service run by **Ahkun Tupa** from Njurgulahti operates from early June to mid-September. From mid-June to mid-August there's a morning and an evening service in each direction; otherwise it's evening only. Journey time to Ravadasköngäs (€25 one way) is about an hour, to Kultahamina (*€30*) it's 1½ hours.

The forest-lined river sometimes broadens to around 300m wide in stretches that the locals call lakes; at other times it passes through cliff-lined narrows. A good day-trip plan is to walk up to Ravadasköngäs then take the boat back. When there are two sailings each day, you could boat up and walk back, or boat up to Kultahamina then walk to Ravadasköngäs and catch the evening boat back from there. The marked walking trails start from a parking area about 1.5km south of the middle of Njurgulahti. From here it's about 14.5km along the river valley to a wilderness hut at Ravadasjärvi, then a further 700m to Ravadasköngäs. The trail spends a lot of its time on ridges above the river, but you have to descend to cross the river on a cable boat at either Searitniva or Härkäkoski. Another good trail from the parking area is the 16km circuit via the top of Joenkielinen fell (535m), with great panoramas rewarding a 300m ascent (and descent).

Kultahamina (meaning 'Gold Harbour') is the gateway to an area where much of the prospecting and panning happened during the 1940s and '50s Lemmenjoki gold rush. It's a 1.6km walk to the site of the first gold find, next to the Morgamoja stream. If you're up for an overnight trip with some steepish parts, the **Kultareitti** (Gold Trail) is a 25km loop from Kultahamina up through the pine and birch forests on to the open fells then back down to Ravadasjärvi. There are wilderness huts for sleeping at both ends of the route and at **Morgamoja** (after 4.5km). You can also camp.

Saariselkä

TIME FROM INARI: 1HR

Europe's most northerly ski resort

Saariselkä, an hour's drive south of Inari along Rd 4, is a pleasant, scattered settlement, far bigger than its permanent population of around 300 might suggest – because so many of its buildings are holiday cottages and hotels. It is busiest (and looks prettiest) in winter. **Ski Saariselkä**, as the ski resort calls itself, comprises 20 slopes on two hills, Kaunispää and Isisakkipää, rising either side of the same valley. The season here can last from mid-November to the beginning of May. The longest run is 2km with a vertical drop of 180m. You can also career down Finland's longest toboggan run (1.3km). Over 150km of maintained cross-country skiing tracks roam the fells and valleys around Saariselkä. Bikers, hikers and snowshoers aren't allowed to use these – but never fear, plenty of bike and walking trails are maintained in winter too. Drop into the helpful Kieninen information centre for trail maps and answers to any questions.

Kiilopää

TIME FROM INARI: 1¼HR

Urho Kekkonen trekking

A 2550 sq km expanse of forests, open fells, ridges and valleys, **Urho Kekkonen National Park** rolls more than 40km east from Saariselkä to the Russian border and even further to the south. It's a perfect canvas for anyone who likes vast expanses of pristine nature. You can walk into the park's northwest

EIGHT SEASONS

It's often said that northern Lapland has not just four seasons, but eight. Siida in Inari characterises them as follows (we've added approximate Gregorian-month equivalents):

Spring-winter (March–April): Migratory birds start arriving; sunlight combined with low nighttime temperatures forms a walkable crust on the snow.

Spring (May): Snow and ice melt; reindeer calves are born.

Spring-summer (June): Nightless night starts.

Summer (late June and July): The insect season, good for birds, bad for reindeer and humans.

Autumn-summer (August): Berry- and mushroom-collecting time.

Autumn (September–October): Glorious autumn colours (*ruska*), then first snowfalls.

Autumn-winter (November–December): Lakes freeze, snow settles, polar night starts.

Winter (January–February): Very low temperatures; once the sun reappears, daylight hours increase rapidly.

THE SALMON FISHING BAN

The Teno River (Tenojoki in Finnish, Deatnu in North Sámi, Tana in Norwegian), running for 361km along the border between Finland and Norway, has long been known as prime spot for Atlantic salmon fishing, drawing enthusiasts from all over the country to its banks for decades.

With the decline of salmon in the river's water, the Finnish and Norwegian governments restricted salmon fishing in 2017 and banned it completely in 2021.

The effort to preserve the dwindling salmon population halted the tourism industry and altering the traditional livelihoods of the Sámi communities living along the Teno.

The reason behind the decline is unclear – a combination of warming waters and overfishing could be causing the near disappearance of the fish.

corner at the edge of Saariselkä village, or reach deeper into the park from **Kiilopää**, about 1½ hours' drive from Inari at the end of a 6km road from Kakslauttanen, which is 11km south of Saariselkä on Rd 4. Kiilopää consists almost solely of the buildings of Suomen Latu Kiilopää, an excellent base with accommodation at various prices, a cafe, two restaurants and rental of bikes, skis and camping gear.

Numerous trails start at Kiilopää. The 6km Kiirunapolku loop takes you to the top of **Kiilopää fell** (546m) with superb panoramas. The hill is home to the poor Kiilopää birch, a type of tree which instead of growing upwards like normal trees creeps along the ground to survive the ferocious winter winds and temperatures up here. You can extend this walk by switching to the **Luulampi trail** on the way down for a total circuit of about 10km. A classic, more demanding route is the 22km **Rautulampi circuit**, over superb fell scenery. It's only partly marked so requires navigation skills. Serious fit trekkers can head out for days on end, using the park's numerous wilderness huts for overnighting. One of the most popular unmarked routes is the four- to six-day loop (70km to 80km) from Kiilopää to Luirojärvi via Suomuruoktu and Tuiskukuru and back via Lankojärvi. From Luirojärvi you can spend an extra day climbing up and down the park's highest peak, **Sokosti** (718m). There's comprehensive information on the national park at nationalparks.fi/urhokekkonennp.

Tankavaara

TIME FROM INARI: 1¼HR

Rushing for gold

Gold was first discovered in Lapland in 1836, when traces of the precious metal were found in the area of Kemi. A proper gold rush, however, didn't take off until the 1870s, after Norwegian geologist Tellef Dahll found larger deposits in the Teno River, leading to a series of expeditions in the border area and the Ivalo River Valley. As the presence of gold became public, Emperor Alexander II signed a declaration allowing every citizen of Finland and Russia (excluding Jews) to prospect for gold in the area. Hundreds of people reached the Ivalo River Valley hoping for a life-changing find. The area was panned dry within a few years, but a second rush started in Tankavaara in the 1930s, drawing a new generation of gold hunters to the edge of the Urho Kekkonen National Park.

The **Kultamuseo** (*kultamuseo.fi; adult/child €12/7*) compares the Lapland Gold Rush with other major gold rushes

---

 EATING IN SAARISELKÄ: OUR PICKS

Laanilan Kievari: 2.5km south of Saariselkä with well-prepared game, fish and veggie options; reservations advised. *4-10pm Mon-Sat* €€

Petronella: Artfully presented northern favourites – elk, snow grouse, lake fish – in an attractive dining room. *5-9pm Thu-Sat* €€€

Restaurant Kaltio: Lapland specialities, from salmon soup to grilled reindeer, at Santa's Hotel Tunturi. *4-10pm Mon-Sat* €€€

Pirkon Pirtti: Try the bouillabaisse and fish dishes in this bright, well-spaced dining room. *3-9pm* €€€

Sampion Arja

TRAIL RUNNING IN THE ARCTIC HIGHLANDS

Sonja Hyppänen, trail running guide in Utsjoki and winner of the 2024 Kaldoaivi Ultra Trail, the world's northernmost ultramarathon held in the Kaldoaivi Wilderness Area in July, tells us her favourite running spots. @sonja_mirjami

Skállovárri to Utsjoki: From the reindeer roundup fence take the westernmost trail to get stunning views of the big fells in Finnmark, Norway.

Njállavárri: Running all the way to old Njuohkarjávri reindeer village and back will give you solid elevation gain and a sense of true wilderness.

Heargevárri to Utsjoki: Fun technical trails. My absolute favourite descent in the area is from Vuolleseavttetvárri towards the village.

around the world in the area formerly used by prospectors to seek nuggets. The circular main hall takes you through a global journey of gold history (with a wall of fame dedicated to Finnish Goldpanning Champions) while the open-air museum outside offers a glimpse into the lifestyle of the prospectors who settled in this remote corner of Lapland. Upon request, it is possible to join a kid-friendly panning workshop to learn the tricks of this nearly disappeared trade – book ahead.

Vuotso

TIME FROM INARI: **1HR 20MINS**

Sámi crafts

As you drive through Vuotso, 40km south of Saariselkä, notice the wall of bicycles and reindeer antlers on the side of the road. Behind this installation find the shop of local artist Arja Kustula, a Sámi artisan specialising in artefacts, clothing and jewellery made from skins, bones and antlers of Lapland's most famous animal. The colours of the Sámi flag cover her shop, **Sampion Arja**, a *wunderkammer* of thousands of handmade objects. Arja speaks little English, but you are free to browse around.

 EATING IN KARIGASINIEMI, UTSJOKI & NUORGAM: OUR PICKS

Guossi: Serves salmon and reindeer dishes, plus pizzas and burgers. *11am-10pm Sun-Thu, to 11pm Fri & Sat* €€

Cafe Saivu: In a red wooden house near the river, Saivu makes for a great waffle stop during long summer drives. *9am-5pm Mon-Fri* €

Restaurant Aurora Holidays: Vegan and gluten-free options next to the traditional Lapland dishes. *4-9pm Thu-Sat* €€

Restaurant Suvanto: Part of the Nuorgam Holiday Village; expect Finnish dishes made with local ingredients. *10am-7pm Mon-Sat* €€

THE EU'S NORTHERNMOST POINT

While Utsjoki is Finland's northernmost municipality, to reach the country's northernmost geographical point you'll need to drive a little further east to Nuorgam, Finland's northernmost village.

At its far end you reach the Norwegian border and a roadside rock labelled 'The Northernmost Point in EU and Finland'. Maps indicate the real northernmost point is in the river, about 400m north of here, but let's not quibble.

The busiest place in town, when open, is Nuorgamin Lomakeskus, which has a good cafe-restaurant where you can stop for lunch on your way to Norway, plus comfortable cabins and apartments to break the trip and try to spot the aurora borealis (northern lights – when the season allows).

Ivalo

TIME FROM INARI: **30MINS**

Modernist place of worship

Hosting the northernmost airport in Finland, sleepy Ivalo is for many a gateway to more tourist-friendly destinations, such as Inari and Saariselkä. Before leaving this town of 3000, it's worth making a stop at the local **church**, a modernist temple of brick and iron on the banks of the Ivalo River. The angular structure is one of the earliest examples of post-war modernist architecture in Finland, completed in 1966.

Karigasniemi

TIME FROM INARI: **1HR 20MINS**

Remote contemporary art gallery

One the most beautiful roads you can drive in Finland begins in the area of Karigasniemi and runs along the Teno River parallel to the Norwegian border all the way to Nuorgam. Shortly after passing Karigasniemi's town centre, spot the sign pointing to the **Manna B&B**, a small guesthouse nestled in the woods on the left side of the main road. Here, curator Matti Sirvio has set up the EU's northernmost art gallery hosting works of about 20 contemporary painters from around the world in the hall of a wooden building opposite the guesthouse, with spectacular views of the river valley from the balcony.

Long-distance canyon hikes

The northern part of Lapland offers a scenery starkly different from the relatively flat landscapes of the southern areas of the region, with fells turning into highlands and rivers snaking through rocky cliffs. Entering the **Kevo Strict Nature Reserve** is an immersion in the pristine nature of this corner of the country. The 63km Kevo Canyon Trail begins at the parking lot in Sulaoja, 10km east of Karigasniemi, and runs along the Kevo River to Lake Kenesjärvi through the rock formations reaching up to 80m in height. The trek is doable only in the summer, taking three to five days. It's well signposted but there are no wilderness huts along the way and the route includes a few river crossings.

Utsjoki

TIME FROM INARI: **1½HR**

Historic church huts

The 14 **wooden huts** overlooking Lake Mantojärvi date back to the 18th and 19th centuries and were used until the 1940s by Sámi families attending the church here. Besides the picturesque setting, these log buildings are the most important

---

 EATING IN LAPLAND: BEST ROADSIDE CAFES

Café Harianna: Overlooking Lake Vajonen north of Sodankylä. Has souvenirs next to sandwiches and cakes. *9am-6pm (summer only)* €

Zippi & Suhaus: Legendary sweet and savoury waffles served with salmon or cloudberry ice cream, 40 minutes south of Saariselkä. *9am-9pm* €

Café Vuopio: In the tiny village of Kairala, this historic wooden house has homemade cakes and coffee. Try the blueberry pie. *10am-6pm Wed-Sun* €

Sannan Putiikki: The 50-cent *munkki* (sugar donuts) ensure everyone stops at this store and cafe on the road to Kilpisjärvi. *9am-9pm* €

example of historic architecture in Finland's sparsely populated far north. The site is freely accessible and the Ulrika Trail leads south from the huts to the area of the old church. During the summer months, a crafts shop and cafe opens in the area. The existing church, uphill, was built in 1853 to replace an earlier wooden one that had crumbled into disrepair. The Ulrika Trail leads south from the huts to the area of the old church.

Polar nights & northern lights

As the northernmost municipality in Finland (and the EU), the Utsjoki region is the area where polar nights (*kaamos* in Finnish) begin first and finish last. The length of the period when the sun does not rise above the horizon at any point varies slightly each year, but it lasts around 50 days in Utsjoki, more than anywhere else in the country. The abundance of darkness provides the highest chances of spotting the northern lights. The aurora borealis can be seen independently on a good day, but joining a five-day tour by **Aurora Holidays** (p237) you'll have professional help, accommodation and transport from Ivalo Airport. LGBTIQ+ friendly Aurora Holidays, run by a welcoming Finnish-Sámi local family, has modern cabins with a sauna overlooking the Teno River and will track the sun's activity during your stay to make sure you are in the right place at the right time.

Wooden huts, Utsjoki

A REINDEER YEAR

Almost all reindeer in Finland are semi-domesticated and are husbanded mainly for their meat. A typical reindeer year goes something like this:

April/May: Move to calving areas.

May: Calves are born. Females drop their antlers about two weeks later.

Late June/early July: Roundup for earmarking of calves.

October: The mating season (rut). Afterwards, male reindeer drop their antlers (antlers of both sexes grow back each summer).

End October/ November/ December: Roundup, and slaughter of selected animals.

24 December: A very lucky few fly off with Santa Claus to circumnavigate the globe.

December–March/ April: Reindeer stay on winter pastures, often close to their owner's homestead.

To learn much more about reindeer visit *paliskunnat.fi* (Finland's Reindeer Herders' Association).

Kilpisjärvi

HIGHLAND HIKING | REMOTE WILDERNESS | SCENIC DRIVES

GETTING AROUND

If you don't have your own transport you can get here by two daily buses from Rovaniemi via Muonio. In this case, staying at the Kilpisjärven Retkeilykeskus is the convenient option for M/S *Malla* and hiking trails. If you stay in the main part of the village you've got a long walk up to the north end unless you can rent or borrow a bicycle. It is, however, possible to access the Saanajärvi circuit path at its south end by a 2.3km trail from the main part of the village.

✓ TOP TIP

The main section of the village includes most accommodation and restaurants, the useful visitor centre of Metsähallitus (the forestry administration), a small shopping centre and a petrol station. Five kilometres up the road towards Norway is the Kilpisjärven Retkeilykeskus accommodation, and 2km beyond that is the main hiking trailhead.

If you like remote places, come to the village of Kilpisjärvi (Gilbbesjávri in Northern Sámi), right up at the top of Finland's northwest arm. There's only one settlement of any size (the small village of Karesuvanto) along the entire 200km road leading up here from Muonio. Kilpisjärvi sits under the stern gaze of Saana fell, on the east side of beautiful Kilpisjärvi (lake), looking across to northern Swedish hills on the far shore. The Norwegian border is just a few kilometres north, and Skibotn on Norway's Lyngen fjord is just 50km away. Kilpisjärvi is also the highest village in Finland, at 490m above sea level, situated as it is on the fringe of the northern end of the Scandinavian Mountains. It's a great spot for some wilderness hiking in the snow-free season (typically early June to early/mid-October), and that, along with transit to/from Norway, is why most visitors come here.

Summiting Saana
To the roof of Kilpisjärvi

Cliff-girt **Saana**, looming above Kilpisjärvi, looks distinctly forbidding when it's wreathed in cloud. But in decent weather this 1029m fell rewards a climb with spectacular panoramas. The main trail to its summit starts 2km along the main road past the **Kilpisjärven Retkeilykeskus**. After 1.5km the trail crosses a path coming from the Retkeilykeskus, which continues eastward round to Saanajärvi (5km). Head straight on over this up the treeless hillside. A flight of 200 steps surmounts the steepest part, then the often rocky path continues upward, with the gradient easing near the summit (4.3km from the start). Head down the way you came up. To make a full day of it, turn east towards Saanajärvi along the path you crossed earlier. This makes an 11km circuit right round the base of Saana, via Saanajärvi (with campfire huts) and the Retkeilykeskus. Some streams en route may have strong currents when they're running high.

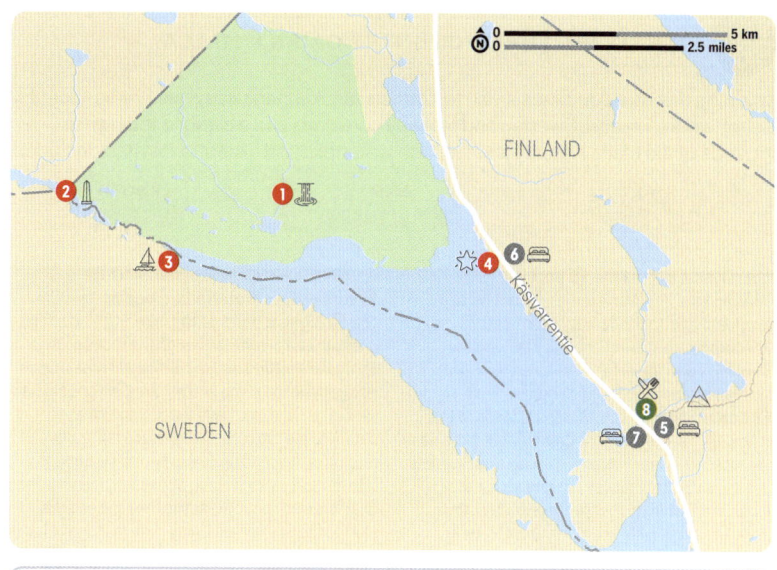

SIGHTS
1. Kitsiputous Waterfalls
2. Three-Country Cairn

ACTIVITIES, COURSES & TOURS
3. Koltaluokta

4. M/S Malla

SLEEPING
5. Cahkal Hotel
6. Kilpisjärven Retkeilykeskus
7. Tundrea

EATING
- Cahkal Hotel (see 5)
- Kilpisjärven Retkeilykeskus (see 6)
8. Restaurant Kilpis
- Tundrea (see 7)

Finland's Highest Point

A week-long expedition to Halti

Finland's highest point (1324m), on **Halti** fell on the Norwegian border, is a 55km trek of about four days (one way) from Kilpisjärvi, practicable July to mid-September. Both open and reservable wilderness huts dot the route from Kilpisjärvi to Halti, so you can plan your route based on the shelter options found along the way. With open huts, the first people to arrive should be the first to leave once it's full, according to custom. The Kilpisjärvi Visitor Centre has maps and can help you book reservable huts. For a quicker expedition, some Kilpisjärvi hotels and tour firms offer day-trips including transport to/from Guolasjávri in Norway and a quite strenuous hike up and down the hill from there (7km each way). The hill's actual summit, Ráisduattarháldi (1361m), is in Norway, 2km north of Finland's highest point.

EATING IN KILPISJÄRVI: OUR PICKS

Tundrea: Hotel restaurant good for northern favourites (salmon soup, reindeer steak) and pizza and pasta. *4-10pm* €€

Cahkal Hotel: Panoramic hotel restaurant with creative preparations (pike ceviche and reindeer sausages). *5.30-9.30pm* €€€

Kilpisjärven Retkeilykeskus: Good-value restaurant doing a buffet lunch, plus waffles, salads, pizzas and burgers. *8am-10pm Mar-Oct* €€

Restaurant Kilpis: Burgers, pizza, steaks and more in this modern pub-like restaurant. *noon-7pm Mon-Thu, to 9pm Fri & Sat, to 6pm Sun* €€

HIKE TO THE THREE-COUNTRY CAIRN & MALLA

This long day hike combines a visit to Kolmen valtakunnan rajapyykki (Three-Country Cairn), where Finland, Sweden and Norway converge, and a climb to the higher grounds of the Malla Nature Reserve, with waterfalls and exceptional vistas included.

START	END	LENGTH
Start M/S Malla port	End M/S Malla port	16km; 6 hours

Park your car by the little ❶ **port** where the M/S *Malla* and the M/S *Maria* ferries depart twice a day (*10am and 3pm, one way/return €40/60, pay on board*) to Koltalahti/Koltaluokta. Take the 10am ferry and travel for 30 minutes through the inlet forming the Swedish border. From ❷ **Koltaluokta**, an easy 3km path leads to the yellow ❸ **Three-Country Cairn** marking the point of contact between Finland, Norway and Sweden. Get there via the walkway running above the water, then return to the trail and walk northwest along the border into the Malla Strict Nature Reserve. Hike along the reindeer fence and tackle approximately 150m of elevation to reach the higher part of the reserve. After about 9km from Koltaluokta you'll find yourself under the ❹ **Kitsiputous Waterfalls**, dropping for 100m. The ❺ **highest point of the hike**, at 730m altitude, is less than 1km away, although the rocky ground can make spotting the trail difficult at times. Once you've done the climb and admired the spectacular view all around, you have the option to make a detour to the top of the Pikku-Malla fell (2.8km return), or descend back into Kilpisjärvi through a lake-dotted valley sloping above the tree line. The final forested section leads to the road and the start to the Saana trail. Unless you manage to hitch a ride, you'll have to walk along the road for 20 to 25 minutes to get back to your car at the ❶ **port** and complete the loop.

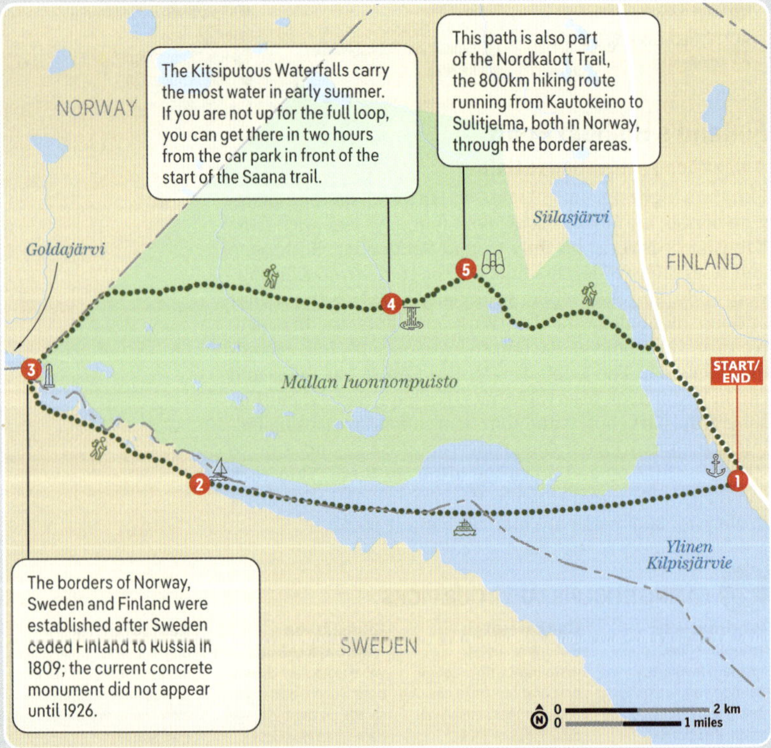
NORWAY
The Kitsiputous Waterfalls carry the most water in early summer. If you are not up for the full loop, you can get there in two hours from the car park in front of the start of the Saana trail.
This path is also part of the Nordkalott Trail, the 800km hiking route running from Kautokeino to Sulitjelma, both in Norway, through the border areas.
Siilasjärvi
Goldajärvi
FINLAND
START/ END
Mallan luonnonpuisto
Ylinen Kilpisjärvie
The borders of Norway, Sweden and Finland were established after Sweden ceded Finland to Russia in 1809; the current concrete monument did not appear until 1926.
SWEDEN
0 2 km
0 1 miles

Places We Love to Stay

€ Budget €€ Midrange €€€ Top End

Rovaniemi MAP p209

Hostel Cafe Koti €€ Centrally located, popular hostel with 24 rooms and two dorms in neat, clean Nordic style.

Arctic City Hotel €€ Rooms are compact but plush fabrics give them an intimate feel; location is super-central.

Santa Claus Holiday Village €€€ Least-expensive option in the expensive Santa Claus Village, with well-kept standard cottages and large rooms.

Glass Resort €€€ Luxurious two-floor 'glass apartments': glass bedroom ceilings and full-wall glass windows for comfortable aurora viewing.

Ranua

Ranua Resort €€ Watch the aurora from a glass igloo, or stay in one of the modern holiday villas near the wildlife park.

Arctic Guesthouse & Igloos €€ Choose between the cozy rooms of the red wooden guesthouse or stay in one of igloos floating on the lake.

Kemijärvi

Jauri Resort €€ Run by friendly Päivi and Mikko, this quiet resort right by the lake features a set of newly built family cottages with private saunas and balconies.

Salla

Sallatunturin Tuvat €€ Close to the town's centre, the reindeer park and the trails, this holiday village has budget-friendly cottages, bike rentals and the best restaurant in Salla.

Inari MAP p225

Hotel Inari €€ Well-run, comfortable, medium-sized lakeside hotel in the middle of town; great views from the restaurant.

Villa Lanca €€ Friendly, relatively economical, centrally located place. The Sámi owner has a husky farm outside Inari.

Holiday Village Inari (Lomakylä Inari) €€€ Comfy and modern two- to four-person cabins 1km from the village centre. Some right by lakeshore with a glass ceiling for aurora spotting, others with a private sauna.

Wilderness Hotel Inari €€€ Inari's classiest rooms, at the lakeside Wilderness Hotel Inari and the riverside Wilderness Hotel Juutua.

Lemmenjoki National Park

Ahkun Tupa € Sámi-owned Njurgulahti accommodation, from shared-bathroom rooms to log cottages with private sauna. Runs Lemmenjoki boat service.

Lomakylä Valkeaporo € Sámi-owned campground with good-quality cabins beside Menesjärvi on the Njurgulahti approach road. Does river trips; rents canoes.

Lemmenjoen Lumo € HI-affiliated summer campground at Njurgulahti with basic rooms and cabins and a cafe.

Karigasniemi

Manna B&B € Rustic and welcoming, this artist-run wooden B&B is a great budget option for solo travellers, with basic, semi-private rooms, generous breakfast and views of the Teno River.

Guossi Hotel €€€ The largest hotel in town, offering modern rooms and a good restaurant, near the Norwegian border.

Utsjoki

Aurora Holidays €€ Besides the comfortable cottages of Aurora, this family-run resort by the Teno River can help you plan all your outdoor adventures, including northern lights hunting.

Saariselkä

Suomen Latu Kiilopää €€ Excellent establishment at the Kiilopää trailheads, with hotel rooms, hostel, cabins, apartments and equipment rentals.

Star Arctic Hotel €€€ Classy, panoramic, Scandi-style hotel with suites and aurora-view glass-roofed cabins up on Kaunispää hill.

Kilpisjärvi MAP p235

Tundrea €€ Range of attractive apartments, chalets and cottages, some with private sauna; a good seasonal restaurant.

Kilpisjärven Retkeilykeskus €€ Well-kept, no-frills rooms and campground close to M/S *Malla* and hiking trailheads.

Cahkal Hotel €€€ Classy, contemporary-styled, 23-room boutique hotel in a panoramic position, opened in 2022.

TOOLKIT

Santa Claus Village, Rovaniemi (p211)
SMELOV/SHUTTERSTOCK ©

TOOLKIT

The chapters in this section cover the most important topics you'll need to know about in Finland. They're full of nuts-and-bolts information and valuable insights to help you understand and navigate Finland and get the most out of your trip.

Arriving p240

Getting Around p241

Money p242

Accommodation p243

Family Travel p244

Health & Safe Travel p245

Food, Drink & Nightlife p246

Responsible Travel p248

LGBTIQ+ Travellers p250

Accessible Travel p251

Finding Santa p252

Chasing Northern Lights p253

Sauna Etiquette p254

Nuts & Bolts p255

Language p256

Arriving

Helsinki-Vantaa Airport is the primary point of entry for most visitors arriving in Finland. The airport, with a railway station underneath, is located 28km from central Helsinki. Renovated in 2021, it now has one terminal for both arrivals and departures, plus lots of cafes, restaurants and shops. Regional hubs are located in Turku, Rovaniemi and elsewhere.

Visas
EU and Nordic nationals don't need a visa to enter Finland. Those from the UK, Canada, Australia, New Zealand, the US and South America can stay for up to 90 days.

SIM Cards
Prepaid SIM cards can be purchased at the airport R-kiosks; one is located in the arrivals terminal and the other by gate 50 in the non-Schengen area. WHSmith stores also sell SIM cards.

Border Crossing
When entering Finland by ferry, standard passport and visa requirements apply. Foreign nationals arriving from outside Schengen countries by land must use official border crossings, such as in Tornio/Utsjoki.

Wi-fi
Free 100 Mbps wi-fi is available in the airport without requiring a password. Wi-fi in Finland is typically fast and access is widespread.

Public Transport from Airports to City Centres

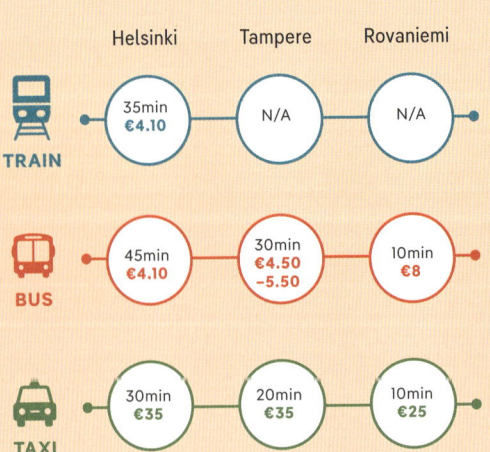

	Helsinki	Tampere	Rovaniemi
TRAIN	35min €4.10	N/A	N/A
BUS	45min €4.10	30min €4.50–5.50	10min €8
TAXI	30min €35	20min €35	10min €25

AIRPORTS IN FINLAND

Finland's busiest airport is Helsinki-Vantaa Airport, but international flights from European countries also use smaller airports, especially the Rovaniemi airport in Lapland. From Helsinki, it takes approximately 1½ hours to fly to Rovaniemi. But at half the price, you'll get there in about eight to nine hours by train, or the 11- to 12-hour night train.

Apart from Rovaniemi, Lapland's airports in Kemi-Tornio, Kittilä and Ivalo are mainly used for domestic flights. After Helsinki, Tampere-Pirkkala Airport has the biggest number of international flights, with planes landing mainly from the Netherlands, Denmark, Spain, Latvia and Estonia.

Accommodation

Rental Cottages

Finland is a nation of cottages and there is a good supply in the rental markets. Lomarengas *(lomarengas.fi)* has the biggest selection. Many cottages are located by lakes or the seaside and come with a sauna. Traditionally, Finnish cottages have been very modest places (with outdoor toilets) but recently, more luxurious cottages with electricity and showers have been built.

Camp Out

Freedom to roam guarantees that camping is allowed almost everywhere, especially if you pitch your tent for a day or two, and not on cultivated land. In nature reserves and national parks camping is allowed in designated areas. Some beaches have restricted camping possibilities. A landowner's permission is always needed before you make a fire. Leave no trace of your visit.

Glass Igloos & the Ice Hotel

Glass igloos are a fabulous way to see the aurora borealis, especially in Lapland where you can find many options, from Rovaniemi all the way to the northernmost parts of Saariselkä. In southern Finland, glass igloos are normally located by lakes and seashores. Or sleep in temperatures below zero (0°C to -5°C) in Rovaniemi's Arctic SnowHotel made of snow and ice.

Manor Houses

Finland doesn't have a big B&B culture but in more remote areas there are some charming guesthouses transformed from old manor and farm houses. The manor houses normally offer a feast of local produce, too. The range of manor houses varies from swish stays with spas to more modest, yet equally enchanting, settings, typically outside bigger cities.

HOW MUCH FOR A NIGHT IN...

a rustic lakeside cottage
€150

a hostel dorm
€30

a manor house
€150

Budget Sleeps

Hostel dorms start from around €30 in high season, although (especially in Helsinki) a bed in a dorm can be as expensive as €70. Hostellit.fi is a good resource for searching budget spots around Finland. You can also find budget hotels for around €70. Some guesthouses can be more budget-friendly, too, offering private rooms with shared bathrooms.

SUSTAINABLE STAYS

Nolla ('zero' in Finnish) cabins are modest huts with a design twist, located at Helsinki's seaside and the Archipelago Sea near Turku. The A-shaped cabins are based on a zero-waste ethos and part of the profits go to the Finnish Association for Nature Conservation. Ollero has sustainable glass igloos in Lapland, and Rovaniemi's Arctic TreeHouse has won sustainability awards, as has the Solo Sokos Hotel Seurahuone in Lahti. Look for the Green Key and the Sustainable Travel Finland labels when booking a sustainable stay: there are plenty around Finland.

Family Travel

Finland is incredibly child friendly, and a terrific place to holiday with kids. A trip with kids to this outdoorsy destination could include splashing about in lakes and rivers, hikes in national parks, cycling and open-air theme parks. In winter, the reliable snow opens up a world of outdoor possibilities, and there's a year-round seat on Santa's knee.

Getting Around

In Helsinki, children age seven and under travel free on all public transport and ferries. If a child is in a stroller, the adult with them travels free as well. Most other transport tickets for children tend to be around 60% of the adult charge. At car-hire firms, child safety seats must be booked in advance and cost about €45 a day; consider bringing one with you.

Sights

School holidays run from June to early August, and many child-oriented activities are closed outside this period. This is when campgrounds are buzzing with Finnish families, and temperatures are usually reliably warm. If your kids are older and you want to get active in the snow, March or April are the months to go to Lapland: there's plenty of daylight, better snow and the cold isn't so extreme.

KID-FRIENDLY PICKS

Muumimaailma (Moominworld) (p91)

Moomin theme-park extravaganza.

Santa Claus Village (p211)

Visit the big man in red and his post office year-round.

Arkadia Reindeer Farm (p216)

Feed and sleigh-ride reindeer on this family-run farm.

Särkänniemi (p135)

Amusement park with roller coasters and a rotating restaurant.

Children's Town (p53)

Helsinki's history experienced through imaginative playtime.

Rauma Maritime Museum (p176)

Learn how to navigate a ship with the Jenny simulator.

Going Out

Most museums in Helsinki have free admission for kids. High chairs are standard in many restaurants, but numbers may be limited. Most resort hotels have family-friendly restaurants with a kids' menu, or deals where children eat free if accompanied by adults.

Accommodation

Rental cabins, apartments and cottages make excellent family bases. Campgrounds are also good, often have a lake beach and playground, and rent out boats and bikes. Most hotels will provide an extra bed for little added cost. Kids under 12 often sleep free.

PARENTING IN FINLAND

Finland's parenting culture typically places a high importance on independent, outdoor play. Children are encouraged to explore nature freely. In the forests of regions such as Lapland, they may learn to build fires and use certain tools from a young age. Children's activities are sometimes less structured than in many other countries, and leave space for wandering, yet this approach also leads to a high focus on interactive, educational and fun museums. It's typical for such attractions to have plenty of summer demonstrations and activities, making visits interesting for grown-ups and kids alike.

Health & Safe Travel

BEAR ENCOUNTERS

Bear encounters are extremely unlikely as bears generally want to avoid human contact. Should you see one, back away quietly without eye contact: running won't help as they will always win. Bears are also good climbers and swimmers. If a bear starts chasing you, lie down on the ground covering your head and neck with your hands and pretend to be dead.

Mosquitos

Around June and July, mosquitos are everywhere in Finland, but especially in rural areas and Lapland. In cities you will barely see them; they are at their worst in forests when there's no breeze. Wear clothing that covers you from head to toe, including a mosquito head net, and use repellents. Apart from the itching bites, Finland's mosquitos are harmless.

Winter

In winter, Finland is a true wonderland, but it comes with a price: the cold. Dress in layers, as the air between the clothing works as insulation. When the temperature drops below -15°C, cover your face with a scarf or a commando hat and avoid using products with water on your face. These can include foundation and certain moisturisers.

SOLO TRAVEL

Finland is a relatively safe country for women travelling alone. Taking the same precautions, as when travelling everywhere, is advised.

ROAD SIGNS

Danger of moose on the road | Danger of reindeer on the road | Danger of deer on the road | Railroad crossing without a safety barrier | Forest fire warning: lighting a fire in nature forbidden

Theft

Finland is pretty safe when it comes to pickpocketing, but there are some incidences reported, especially in crowded city spots such as on public transport and in shops. If you happen to drop your phone, wallet or other valuables, contact Löytötavaratoimisto (lost and found, phone +358600 41006, available 24/7) or the local police – chances are you will get it back.

NIGHTLIFE

In general, Finns are a bit reserved but polite. Open aggression is most typically encountered during nighttime in bars, clubs and city streets when alcohol has been consumed, but the nightlife scene is still safe. For visitors, Finns' alcohol consumption might seem excessive, although in recent years more and more people are opting for mocktails instead of cocktails.

Food, Drink & Nightlife

When to Eat

Aamiainen (breakfast, 7am to 10am) is a simple affair, with filter coffee or tea and bread, yogurt or porridge.

Lounas (lunch, 11am to 1pm) is often a buffet, including salads, warm main course options (meat and vegetarian) and dessert.

Illallinen (dinner, 5pm to 6pm) normally consists of slightly pricier dishes and can be eaten later, especially when celebrating or meeting with friends.

Where to Eat

Ravintola (restaurant) Can vary from a lunch buffet or corner shop bar to fine dining.

Leipomo or **leipomo-kahvila** (bakery or coffee shop and bakery) Normally artisanal or traditional Finnish bakeries with a small eating area.

Panimoravintola (brewery restaurant) Typically you will find one or two in the biggest cities. Food can vary from street food and gastropub dishes to German-influenced plates.

Baari (a bar) Includes swish spots with classy cocktails as well as more relaxed neighbourhood joints.

MENU DECODER

Ruokalista: Menu
Alkuruoka: Starters
Pääruoka: Mains
Jälkiruoka: Dessert
Brunssi: Brunch
Lasten lista: Kids' menu
Sesongin menu: Seasonal menu
Maistelumenu: Tasting menu
Kasvismenu: Vegetarian menu
Kasvisvaihtoehto: Vegetarian option
Kala: Fish
Kana: Chicken
Liha: Meat
Naudanliha: Beef
Lammas: Lamb
Possu: Pork
Pihvi: Steak
Keitto: Soup
Salaatti: Salad

Ranskanperunat: French fries
Voileipä: Sandwich
Juomat: Drinks
Tuoppi: A pint
Pullo: A bottle
Lasi: A glass
Limonadi: Soft drink
Mehu: Juice
Viini: Wine
Punaviini: Red wine
Valkoviini: White wine
Rosé-viini: Rosé wine
Kuiva: Dry
Makea: Sweet
Siideri: Cider
Olut: Beer
Kuohuviini: Sparkling wine
Kahvi: Coffee
Noutopöytä: Buffet
Itsepalvelu: Self service

HOW TO... Order (& Clear Your Table)

Normally coffee shops have counter service where you order and pay by the till. Some cafes will bring your orders to the table, in others you are supposed to carry them yourself. It is also fairly normal that you are expected to clear your own table; check if there is a trolley where you are to place your dishes. If not, the staff will clear after you are finished. Lunch restaurants, especially the budget-friendly ones, are often buffets where you pay first and then proceed to collect your food and drinks. Normally there are salads, soups, and meat and vegetarian options available, as well as gluten- and lactose-free products. Buffets also include coffee/tea and dessert.
Dinner and à la carte lunch restaurants have table service, the same as almost everywhere in the world: sit down, and the staff will take care of you.

HOW MUCH FOR A...

Cinnamon bun
€2–4

Filter coffee
€2.50–5
(third-wave coffee shops are the priciest)

Lunch at a buffet
€9–13

Pizza
€13–16

Dinner at a Michelin-star restaurant
€200

Beer
€7–10

Wine
€8–15

HOW TO... Drink your Coffee

Finns drink the most coffee in the world per capita (12kg per person to be exact, according to the International Coffee Association), so you might find it odd that much of the coffee here is light-roasted filter coffee instead of the strong espressos or creamy cappuccinos found in many other coffee-obsessed countries. Typically, Finns start their mornings with a big mug (or three) of coffee. In the work environment, there are scheduled coffee breaks in place based on employment contracts, and sometimes people even have a special cup of coffee after their evening saunas.

In coffee shops, people normally order filter coffee – as sometimes *santsikuppi* (a second cup/refill) is included in the price – or cappuccinos. For more than a decade Finland has also enjoyed the rise of third-wave cafes, with beans roasted in artisan roasteries and smooth flat whites available. Purists still have their coffees black, the daring ones with a dash of milk – and the modern radicals with oat milk.

If you want to befriend a Finn, invite them for coffee – they'll find it hard to refuse. Enjoying a cup of coffee and a chat is also oddly reassuring to the Finns, as many have fond memories associated with the ritual, so apart from having a sauna with them, a shared coffee moment might turn out to be a true icebreaker.

No small talk, no offence taken

The Finnish language doesn't have a specific word for 'please' when ordering and there is no culture of small talk. Short sentences may not be a sign of rudeness, but just the way of the Finns.

GOING OUT

For a long time, Finns have been known for their heavy use of alcohol, but in recent years, the tendency has been easing up, especially among the younger generations: friends can meet up for dinner and a few cocktails or mocktails, and be home by midnight.

On the other hand, as alcohol is expensive in restaurants and bars, many Finns still prefer gathering at home parties before heading out, typically around midnight. In the summertime, gatherings also take place in parks and on beaches. In winter, it is common to go to fancier clubs in winter-ready shoes but change into heels by the cloakroom.

Pubs normally close at 2am on weekdays and 3am or 4am on Fridays and Saturdays, whereas clubs and bars stay open till 4am. After closing time, there are snack trucks or pizzerias open to cater to the party people in bigger cities and towns.

Karaoke is popular throughout the country and it is easy to partake in the fun; the crowds, normally a bit tipsy, are welcoming and there's much good cheer.

When ordering a pint of beer, don't expect the glass to be full: Finland has strict alcohol laws and measurements apply to all drinks, from wines to cocktails. A glass of wine is sold in three sizes, 12cL, 16cL and 24cL. In food stores, you will find alcohol products that are less than 8% alcohol – for heavier drinks, such as wine and spirits, head to Alko, Finland's national alcoholic beverage retailing monopoly.

Responsible Travel

Climate Change & Travel

It's impossible to ignore the impact we have when travelling; Lonely Planet urges all travellers to engage with their travel carbon footprint, which will mainly come from air travel. While there often isn't an alternative, travellers can look to minimise the number of flights they take, opt for newer aircrafts and use cleaner ground transport, such as trains. One proposed solution—purchasing carbon offsets—unfortunately does not cancel out the impact of individual flights. While most destinations will depend on air travel for the foreseeable future, for now, pursuing ground-based travel where possible is the best course of action.

The **UN Carbon Offset Calculator** shows how flying impacts a household's emissions.

The **ICAO's carbon emissions calculator** allows visitors to analyse the CO2 generated by point-to-point journeys.

Everyone's Right

Jokaisenoikeus ('everyone's right') is a Finnish code that allows people to walk, ski or cycle anywhere in wilderness – even on private lands – so long as they act responsibly.

Trekking

Enjoy a multiday adventure, hiking the nature trails of **Koli National Park** (p165). The longest hike, winding around Herajärvi lake, is 60km long and takes four days (although a shorter, 35km version is also possible).

Visit Finland's first zero-waste pizzeria: the slices at **YLP!** (p192) are made entirely with local produce.

Finland's favourite forest fruit is the cloudberry. Pick them yourself in **Ranua** (p218), Lapland's unofficial cloudberry capital.

Cycling Tour

Indulge in emissions-free island-hopping on the **Archipelago Trail** (p92). The 230km circular cycling route starts and ends in Turku, winding through lush southern countryside and over bridges connecting tiny islands and their unique maritime communities.

Sámi Handicrafts

Look for products with the colourful Sámi Duodji (Sámi handicrafts association) logo, guaranteeing authentic Sámi craftsmanship and proceeds for indigenous northern communities. The association also runs a shop in the **Sajos** (p225) in Inari.

Wildlife-spotting

The rugged, untouched forests of Kuhmo are home to thriving numbers of bears, wolves and wolverines. Grab some binoculars and observe them ethically from a wilderness hut in June and July, when the sun never sets.

Seal Conservation

Consider donating to conservation efforts for the endangered **Saimaa ringed seal** (p144). Over recent years, campaigns from WWF Suomi *(wwf.fi)* and others have helped numbers rise from only dozens to 400.

Circular Shopping

In Turku, shop at stores supporting a circular economy. Discover local boutiques and designers using natural fabrics, upcycling and selling vintage. Many antique shops give furniture and decorations a new chance at life.

Northern Lights Chasing

In Lapland, skip the tour buses and go looking for the aurora borealis yourself on a pair of snowshoes. Resources such as the 'My Aurora Forecast & Alerts' app can help.

Lake Bathing

You won't lack swimming options in this land of some 188,000 lakes – drive or cycle around Saimaa Lakeland, stopping wherever you fancy a dip. In winter, book a hotel with a sauna and ice swimming possibility.

Finland's forest administration operates well-maintained wilderness huts across national parks and protected areas. Be sure to leave the hut as you found it – replenish the firewood and take away your rubbish.

Take home a Lappish souvenir made from recycled natural materials such as dropped reindeer antlers and fish leather. At shops such as **Sampion Arja** (p231) and **Kangasniemi Hornwork** (p29), you can even watch the artisans at work.

Sustainability

Finland is an excellent responsible-travel destination. The 2024 Environmental Performance Index (EPI) ranked Finland in fourth place worldwide for overall sustainability, and first for protected area effectiveness. The country has also been recognised for ethical wildlife tourism.

RESOURCES

ymparisto.fi
Understand everyone's rights via Finland's environmental administration.

luomumatkailu.fi
Organic, sustainable farm stays.

metsa.fi
Well-maintained huts in national parks and protected wilderness areas.

LGBTIQ+ Travellers

In 2024, Spartacus Gay Travel index ranked Finland the world's 13th most LGBTIQ+ friendly place, leaving the country far behind its more progressive Nordic neighbours, Denmark, Iceland and Norway. Same-sex marriage was legalised in 2017, and same-sex adoption a year earlier. Generally speaking, Finns are friendly to all, though underlying prejudice still lingers.

Biggest Parties

The home of Tom of Finland (see below), Helsinki throws Finland's biggest LGBTIQ+ party in June, when the **Helsinki Pride** *(pride.fi)* celebrations last for a week. There has been an annual Helsinki Pride since 2006, but its history dates back to the 1970s, when organised activities to improve the status of sexual minorities in Finland began. Another event is the cinema festival Vinokino *(vinokino.fi)* held in five cities – including Helsinki, Turku and Tampere – in October and November. The festival showcases international queer cinema, from documentaries to films.

GAY-FRIENDLY DISTRICTS & BARS

Kallio is Helsinki's bohemian gay-friendly district, with a pub such as the classic, yet small, **Fairytale**. For a bigger party head to the city centre **Hercules**, with live music and a summertime terrace. Near Kallio in Vallila, you can experience Finland's only gay sauna **Vogue**. The more upscale/bohemian **Punavuori district** is also favoured by Helsinki's gay population. Tampere's – and Finland's – only gay bar is **Mixei**. In Turku, check out Bar **Suxes**.

Tourism

Gay Travel Finland *(gaytravelfinland.com)* is a member of IGLTA, the International LGBTQ+ Travel Association, and a great resource page for gay travels in Finland. The tips vary, from hotels and restaurants to events and LGTBQ rights. The international Gaily Tour *(gailytour.com)* also organises LGTBIQ+ themed tours in and around Helsinki.

SETA FOR SEXUAL MINORITIES

Seta ry *(seta.fi; from Finnish for 'sexual equality')* is Finland's main LGBT rights organisation, established in 1974 to advance equality in Finland, and successful with many legal battles, such as equal marriage and adoption laws. Seta's most notable chairperson is Tarja Halonen, Finland's first female president (2000–12).

Tom of Finland

Tom of Finland is the country's most celebrated gay icon and artist. His art adorns everything from T-shirts to sheets, and you can also taste his namesake vodka. In Helsinki, book a Tom of Finland walking tour from the Happy guide Helsinki *(happyguidehelsinki.com)*.

MINDSETS

In general, Finns won't show their approval or disapproval of other people's comings and goings, especially in bigger cities, but some negative attitudes can still be picked up. This manifests especially when alcohol is consumed, as some might get rowdier and more outspoken about their personal views. Some conservative priests may also refuse to hold a ceremony for a same-sex marriage.

Accessible Travel

Finland's public infrastructure, from offices to transport, takes into account accessibility, and work is being done to make nature and sights more accessible to all, too.

Accessible Nature

The National Parks website *(nationalparks.fi)* features a searchable map for accessible destinations. These include 57 different types of accessible locations (for example, boardwalks and accessible toilets), from Helsinki to the top of Lapland.

Airport

Helsinki airport was renovated in 2021 and offers wheelchairs and other assistance for people with reduced mobility. There are helpdesks at the airport, but calling prior to arrival is advised to guarantee assistance.

Accommodation

Chain hotels in particular have worked to improve accessibility in their facilities, but there are more and more smaller and family-owned hotels getting on board, too. The easiest way to check your accommodation's accessibility is to call in advance.

HELSINKI'S BEACHES

Helsinki's Hietaranta beach has a floating bathing chair as well as a Mobi-mat® carpet to make travelling easier on the sand. These services are handled by the lifeguard on duty.

Transport

Helsinki's public transport is free for people with vision impairment and for people using wheelchairs or mobility scooters (only allowed on metros). The EU Disability Card is a valid method to prove various types of disabilities.

Accessibility Award

Helsinki came second in ENAT's (European Network for Accessible Tourism) Accessible Cities Awards in 2022 in recognition of the city's long-term efforts.

HELSINKI'S STREETS

Helsinki's Senate Sq and Market Sq areas have cobblestoned streets. Traffic lights have little assistance for people with vision impairments, especially around the Market Sq and Mannerheimintie St. Winter makes the streets snowy.

RESOURCES

Respecta *(respecta.fi)* Provides the largest variety of assistive devices and related services in Finland. Contact it to reserve equipment.
The Finnish Association of People with Physical Disabilities *(invalidiliitto.fi)* Dedicated to advocacy and service provision for people with physical disabilities or functional impairment.
The Finnish Federation of the Visually Impaired *(Näkövammaisten liitto; nkl.fi)* Has accessible hotel rooms and a museum of visual impairment in its Iiris Centre in Helsinki's Itäkeskus neighbourhood.

Ekevent.johku.com organises accessible tours in and around Lohja, 60km from Helsinki. **Adventureapes.fi** provides nature-driven accessible expeditions and is a leader in accessible travel for the visually impaired. The **Palmuasema.fi** blog has tips for accessible hotels, spas and nature spots around Finland.

🎁 Finding Santa

You want to take the family for a treat to see Father Christmas, in the Arctic, where he lives. You've heard that Rovaniemi in Finnish Lapland is his 'official hometown'. But you've found that a three-night package for a family of four from the UK (for example) can cost £3500 or more – with no guarantee that you'll visit the actual Santa Claus Village. Well, it's not hard to set it all up independently and, if you book far enough ahead, probably save a chunk of money. For starters, several airlines offer direct scheduled flights to Rovaniemi from around Europe, especially in winter, among them Easyjet, Ryanair, Air France, KLM and Eurowings.

Where to Stay

Rovaniemi town has plenty of accommodation, from hostels and self-catering apartments to luxury hotels. At the budget end, a family room in winter high season can cost in the region of €200 a night. The hotels at Santa Claus Village itself tend to be luxurious, and expensive, but the well-kept standard cottages at Santa Claus Holiday Village are more moderately priced.

What to Do

Santa Claus Village, a sort of Christmas theme park scattered around the forest edge, is 8km from Rovaniemi town, easily reached by bus. There, you can visit a genial Santa in his 'office' any day of the year for free (you might have to queue a bit at busy times) and, for mostly reasonable prices, take a sleigh ride with his reindeer and have a go at snowmobiling or husky sledding. The Village can be magical in deep winter. With another day, try some skiing at Ounasvaara, visit the Arktikum or Pilke museums, look for the aurora borealis, or head out for a longer sled/sleigh ride at Bearhill Husky or Konttaniemen Porotila reindeer farm (book these in advance).

When to Go

If you're not dead set on Christmas, consider March. There's still plenty of snow, plus more daylight and not-quite-so-low temperatures, and accommodation can be cheaper. In summer? Well, there's no snow, but there is midnight sun, lower room rates, and Santa is still there!

HOW MANY SANTAS?

Santa Claus is magical of course, so it's perfectly reasonable that he can be in two, or four, or six places at once. But his tendency to pop up at unexpected times and places can cause puzzlement for people of any age. He even has a second manifestation in Santa Claus Village itself – in 'Christmas House', which is near the Santa Claus Holiday Village reception building. He has another office in central Rovaniemi as well. And he makes special appearances at other locations for some tour groups. Some parents try to avoid too many Santa appearances to avert overdose and confusion!

 Chasing Northern Lights

Imagine a firefox running across a snowy landscape under a dark winter sky. As it goes, its furry tail keeps hitting the snow, creating sparkles that illuminate the sky. These are *revontulet* (fires of the fox), or the aurora borealis (Northern Lights). In reality, the phenomenon is less poetic, and more scientific, caused by particles coming from the sun and slamming against Earth's protective, upper atmosphere at speeds of up to 72 million km/h, causing them to emit light of varying colours. Still, when you see the Northern Lights in Finland, you might just start believing in the firefox.

When to Spot

The best time to see the aurora borealis is March, when the skies are at their clearest. In winter, the snowy landscapes will also make the experience even more magical. September is another good time to chase the lights, as nights are dark enough by then for the phenomenon to be visible.
The best time of night to see the aurora is from 11pm to 1am.

Where to Spot

With its vast open areas and darkness, Lapland is the best place to see the aurora borealis – in its most northernmost parts you can see them up to three nights out of four, whereas roughly in the middle of Lapland, it comes down to 60% of nights. It's possible to see the lights as far south as Helsinki, where in dark months they light up the sky approximately once a month. Bear in mind that they're harder to see around light pollution.

Hotels for Spotting

Many hotels around Finland offer glass igloos and glass-walled hotel rooms to see the aurora comfortably from your bed. For example, the Arctic Snow Hotel, northwest of Rovaniemi, has lines of glass-walled rooms designed specifically for aurora viewing. There are also glass igloos in and around many of Lapland's skiing centres.

Gear for Spotting

Layers, layers, layers! That's the mantra if heading outdoors on cold winter nights, especially in Lapland, where the temperatures can drop as low as -40°C . Remember gloves or mittens, hat and warm shoes with enough space in them for thick woollen socks.

APPS TO ASSIST

There are many apps and websites that can assist when on a hunt for the aurora borealis. For example, My Aurora Forecast sends phone alerts if there's a chance of seeing the lights in your area. It also helps you to predict when and where are the best chances to see them. There's no point looking for the lights when the sky is covered with clouds, so it's also worth checking the Finnish Meteorological Institute's cloud map (*ilmatieteenlaitos.fi/pilvet-pohjoismaat*). Other good sources include the USA-based NOAA (*National Oceanic and Atmospheric Administration; swpc.noaa.gov*) with 30-minute and three-day forecasts, and *gi.alaska.edu/monitors/aurora-forecast*.

Sauna Etiquette

Sisu, Sibelius and sauna: this is the holy trinity Finns learn from an early age as representative of the nation. *Sisu* (perseverance): just enough to survive the long and dark winter months. The composer Sibelius is renowned all over the world. And sauna, well, maybe the institution has given the nation a less complicated attitude towards nudity. But it is the one thing Finns miss the most when living abroad.

How Common Is a Sauna?

There are over three million saunas in Finland, which makes saunas more common than cars in the country. Most private homes and apartments have their own saunas, and if not, there is a sauna in the block of flats for the residents to use. Summer cottages also have saunas, normally close to the water. Note the Finnish pronunciation of sauna, which sounds something like 'sour-na'.

Where to Have a Sauna

Almost all hotels have saunas for their guests. There are also historic and public neighbourhood saunas in bigger cities, such as Tampere and Helsinki. And then there are the leisure centres you can visit for a couple of euro, and have a swim and a sauna. Some cities also have modern sauna complexes lining the lakes and seashores, such as in Jyväskylä.

How to Have a Sauna

A sauna should be a simple affair, so don't stress about it. First, in public saunas, the locker and shower rooms are separate for men and women. Second, always have a shower before the sauna. When you go into a public unisex sauna, you should wear a swimsuit – unless it is specifically pointed out that it is optional. If so, you can still wear your bathing suit. Some Finns go naked, others don't, and both ways are fine. Lastly, remember to drink water.

What Not to Do in a Sauna

Avoid engaging in too-loud behaviour. It is totally fine to exchange words with others in the sauna – in fact, this might be the one environment where Finns are at their most chatty – but in general, sauna is for quiet enjoyment.

HOW TO MAKE & TAKE THE HEAT

In public saunas, the person closest to the stove normally throws water on the stones. The heat should be tolerable for all, so if you are in charge of the 'sauna ladle', don't go crazy with throwing the water: ask if people want more heat. For some Finns, it is a matter of pride to be able to take the heat no matter what, but should the sauna be too hot, it is normal to go and sit down on the lower benches – the top bench is the hottest. The steam is known as *löyly*. If you enjoy your sauna, you can say that the *löyly* was good.

Nuts & Bolts

OPENING HOURS

Opening hours vary between weekdays and weekends. Rural areas offer fewer services. Typical hours in bigger cities:

Banks 10am–4.30pm weekdays

Bars 3pm–2am weekdays, some to 4am Friday and Saturday

Cafes 8am–7pm weekdays, 9am–8pm Saturday, 10am–5pm Sunday

Clubs to 2am Monday and Tuesday, to 4am Wednesday to Saturday

Restaurants 11am–9.30pm

Shopping malls 10am–8pm

Shops 10am–6pm Monday to Friday, 11am–5pm Saturday and Sunday

Smoking

Smoking is not allowed inside public buildings. Most restaurants and cafes don't have smoking sections. Cigarette packets are sold by cashiers in shops.

GOOD TO KNOW

Time zone
GMT/UTC plus two hours

Country calling code
358

Emergency number
112

Population
5.5 million

PUBLIC HOLIDAYS

There are 13 public holidays in Finland. Some businesses and nonessential services are closed or operate with restricted opening hours.

New Year's Day 1 January

Epiphany 6 January

Good Friday The Friday preceding Easter

Easter March/April

Easter Monday The Monday following Easter Sunday

Labour Day 1 May

Feast of the Ascension 40 days after Easter (Thursday)

Pentecost Seventh Sunday after Easter

Midsummer Saturday between 20 and 26 June

All Saints' Day Saturday between 31 October and 6 November

Independence Day 6 December

Christmas Day 25 December

St Stephen's Day 26 December

Tap Water

Tap water is safe to drink and is of a high quality throughout Finland.

Weights & Measures

Finland uses the metric system. Decimals are indicated with commas. Thousands are marked with commas, eg 2,000.

Electricity
220V/50Hz; 230V/50Hz

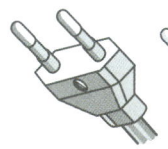

Type C
220V/50Hz

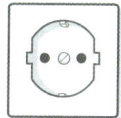

Type F
230V/50Hz

Language

NUMBERS

1 **yksi** *ük-si*
2 **kaksi** *kuhk-si*
3 **kolme** *kol-meh*
4 **neljä** *nehl-ya*
5 **viisi** *vee-si*
6 **kuusi** *koo-si*
7 **seitsemän** *sayt-seh-man*
8 **kahdeksan** *kuhkh-dehk-suhn*
9 **yhdeksän** *ükh-dehk-san*
10 **kymmenen** *küm-meh-nehn*

Basics

Hello. Hei/Terve (pol) Moi (inf) *hay/tehrr-veh/moy*
Goodbye. Näkemiin (pol)/Moi (inf). *na-keh-meen/moy*
Yes. Kyllä (pol)/Joo (inf). *kül-lah/yoo*
No. Ei. *ay*
Please. There's no frequently used word for 'please' in Finnish. Often kiitos (thank you) is used.
Thank you. Kiitos/Kiitti (inf). *kee-toss/keet-ti*
Excuse me. Anteeksi. *uhn-teehk-si*
Sorry. Olen pahoillani/Sori (inf). *o-lehn puh-hoyl-luh-ni/so-rri*
What's your name? Mikä teidän nimenne on?/Mikä sun nimi on? (inf). *mi-ka tay-dan ni-mehn-neh on?/mi-ka sun ni-mi on?*
My name is ... Minun nimeni on .../Mun nimi on ... (inf). *mi-nun ni-mehn-ni on .../mun ni-mi on...*
Do you speak English? Puhutko englantia? *pu-hut-ko ehng-luhn-ti-uh?*
I don't understand. En ymmärrä. *ehn üm-marr-rra*

Directions

Where's ...(train station)? Missä on ...? *mis-sa on ...?* (juna-asema (inf)/rautatie-asema *yu-nuh-uh-se-muh/row-tuh-ti-eh-uh-se-muh*)
I'm looking for...? Etsin....? *et sin...?*

Can you show me (on the map)? Voitko näyttää minulle (kartasta)? *voyt-ko na-üt-taa mi-nul-leh (kuhrr-tuhs-tuh)?*

Time

What time is it? Paljonko kello on? *puhl-yon-ko kehl-lo on?*
It's (one) o'clock. Kello on (yksi). *kehl-lo on (ük-si)*
morning aamu. *ah-mu*
afternoon iltapäivä. *il-tuh-pa-i-va*
evening/night ilta. *il-tuh*
today tänään. *ta-naan*
tomorrow huomenna. *hu-o-mehn-nuh*

Emergencies

Help! Apua! *uh-pu-uh!*
Go away! Mene pois!/Häivy! (inf). *meh-neh poys!/ha-i-vü!*
I'm ill. Minä olen sairas. *mi-na o-lehn sai-rruhs*
Call the police Soittakaa poliisi! *soyt-tuh-kah po-lee-si!*

Eating & drinking

What would you recommend? Mitä suosittelisit? *mi-ta su-o-sit-teh-li-sit?*
Can I see the menu please? Saisinko ruokalistan? *sai-sin-ko-ru-o-kuh-lis-tuhn?*

Phrases to sound like a local

Cool! Siistiä! *sees-ti-ah*
No worries. Ei se mitään. *ay seh mi-taan*
Sure. Toki. *to-ki*
No way! Eikä! *ay-kah*
Just joking! Ei nyt sentään! *ay nüt sehn-taan*
Too bad. Ikävää *i-ka-vaa*
What a shame. Sääli. *saa-li*
What's up? Mitä kuuluu? *mi-ta koo-loo?*
Well done! Hyvin tehty! *hü-vin teh-tü*
Not bad. Ei hassumpaa. *ay huhs-sum-pah*

DONATIONS TO ENGLISH
The most commonly used Finnish word in English is **sauna**.

UNIQUE LANGUAGE

Finnish is not closely related to any language other than Estonian and Karelian and a handful of other rare languages. There is also a notable Swedish-speaking minority in Finland, and all Finns learn Swedish in school, so you may need your Swedish vocabulary in Finland from time to time.

Must-Know Grammar

The main difficulties with Finnish are the endings added to noun and verb roots, which often alter in this process, and the habit of building long words by putting several small words together.

Sounds Familiar

Finnish isn't related to any Indo-European languages. There are, however, many loan words from Baltic, Slavonic and Germanic languages, and many words deriving from French and, especially, English.

Sámi Languages

There are nine different Sámi languages, of which three are spoken in Finland. It's estimated about one-third of Sámi people in Finland today speak a Sámi language.

bures - *pu res* - u is a long vowel - is how you say 'how are you, hello' when shaking hands in Northern Sámi.

oaidnaleapmái *oa y-dna-leap-may* means 'see you'.

giitu *ki y-htu* is how you say 'thank you'.

boazu *po a-tsu* is 'reindeer' in Northern Sámi; it's **poro** *po ro* in Finnish.

guovssahasat *ku ovs sa ha-saht* is 'Northern Lights' in Northern Sámi; it's *revontulet re von tu let* in Finnish.

Juovlastállu *juo v-la-stal-lu* is Santa Claus in Northern Sámi and **Joulupukki** *yo loo pu ki* in Finnish.

WHO SPEAKS FINNISH?

There are around six million Finnish speakers in Finland, Sweden, Norway and Russian Karelia. In Finnish, Finland is known as Suomi and the language itself as suomi.

STORYBOOK

THE FINLAND
STORYBOOK

Our writers delve deep into different aspects of Finland life

A History of Finland in 15 Places

Defining moments in Finland's past, from prehistoric art to today

Paula Hotti

p260

Meet the Finns

The relatively icy surface of the Finns might be hard to crack – but once you are in, you are in for a lifetime

Paula Hotti

p264

The Sámi

Meet the only recognised indigenous people within the European Union area

John Noble

p266

The Many Sides of Finnishness

Bold lines, strong statements and striking melodies are omnipresent in the Finnish art world

Paula Hotti

p268

Triumphs & Tragedies

How Finland is fighting to win the race against losing its most valuable asset – the natural realm

Paula Hotti

p270

Sámi man with reindeer

A HISTORY OF FINLAND IN
15 PLACES

For centuries, Finland's destiny was decided by its two neighbours Sweden and Russia, battling over lands and possessions. Both countries left their mark in architecture, food, language and culture. But the Finns have also always been characteristically their own people. By Paula Hotti

AS A REMOTE country tucked away in the northern corner of Europe, Finland's history doesn't often appear in schoolbooks around the world. Yet the small nation of some five million people has pushed through harsh environments and even harsher times during conquests from the East and West.

Finland's earliest written history, which started around the 12th century, is a tale of a nation stuck between two rivals, Sweden and Russia. As battles were fought and borders were drawn and redrawn, the people continued with their own lives as much as they could. Finland's borders were last defined in 1940 and 1945, as the country lost some of its eastern territories to the Soviet Union. The nation also had to pay hefty reparations in money and equipment to the Soviet Union, boosting further the Soviets' already developed metal industries. In fact, Finland became a modern welfare state quite swiftly after coming out of WWII. In politics, the nation got used to balancing between East and West, but in ideology, the West prevailed: in 1995, Finland became part of the EU and replaced its currency, the *markka*, with the euro in 2002. Following Russia's invasion of Ukraine, Finland took a step further and is now a member of NATO as well.

1. Astuvansalmi Rock Paintings
PREHISTORIC ART

Located in Mikkeli, Astuvansalmi's prehistoric rock paintings, the oldest ones dating from 3000 to 2500 BCE, are among Northern Europe's biggest. The 65 paintings depict human and animal figures, most notably moose, an animal the ancient Finns believed to be the centre of the universe. The images were painted with a mixture of red ochre and oil or blood, and it is thought that they were done from a boat or standing on the frozen lake when Saimaa's waters were 4m to 9m higher than they are now. The site is still today best approached by boat.

For more on Mikkeli, see p146

2. Sammallahdenmäki
BRONZE AGE BURIAL MOUNDS

These 36 mysterious stone burial cairns from 1500 to 500 BCE stand near the coastal city of Rauma (Raumo), forming a remarkable UNESCO World Heritage site. The walk to the group of rock mounds feels like a step back in time, as the path winds through the forest, floored with the ethereal-looking reindeer lichen. Originally the mounds stood on rocky islets just above the sea, as there was no forest in the area. The coastline has since receded 20km west, leaving the site on dry ground, revealing snippets on how the Finns lived and died in the Bronze and Iron Ages.

For more on Sammallahdenmäki, see p180

3. Siida & Sajos
AN INTRODUCTION TO LAPLAND'S SÁMI CULTURE

Around 1600 BCE, the Sámi people used to live all around Central Finland, before reaching and settling down in Lapland around the beginning of the Common Era. Siida (the Sámi Museum and Northern Lapland Nature Centre), with its permanent exhibition showcasing how nature and culture are closely linked in the Sámi concept of cultural environment, and Sajos (Sámi Parliament in Finland) are good spots to get to know the Sámi people's past and present. Both Siida and Sajos are easily visited in one day, and are very worthwhile to see while in Inari, as they are located about 500m apart.

For more on Siida & Sajos, see p224

4. Häme Castle
HIGHS & LOWS

One of Finland's medieval castles, Häme Castle dates from the late 13th century when it was built to solidify Swedish rule in the area. During its centuries-old history, the castle has witnessed highs and lows. The former, for example, in the hands of the mighty Lady Ingeborg, the de facto queen consort of Sweden and the fief holder of Häme Castle. The latter were the many fires and conquests the castle experienced during its heyday. From 1881 to 1972, a women's prison was located here, and now, you can visit both castle and prison museums as well as the neighbouring military museum.

For more on Häme Castle, see p160

5. Turun Linna
MEDIEVAL SPLENDOUR IN STONE

Turun Linna (Turku Castle) showcases Turku's importance as Finland's medieval capital. The castle dates from the 13th century, when southern parts of Finland became part of Sweden. In the 1560s Catherine Jagiellon, a Polish princess who married John III of Sweden, lived in the castle, upgrading its interiors – and introducing Finland to forks. Later the castle suffered damages and was used mainly as barracks – first for Swedish troops, and from 1809 onward for Russian troops. The final blow came from Russian bombings during WWII, but after the war, long-awaited restoration work began. Now visitors can sense the castle's medieval history in its whitewashed vaulted rooms and cobblestoned courtyard.

For more on Turku Castle, see p85

6. Suomenlinna Sea Fortress
FORTRESS TURNED IDYLL

A 15-minute ferry ride from Helsinki's city centre, Suomenlinna (Sveaborg in Swedish) has a long history. From the 1740s it was under Swedish rule, then under Russian rule from 1808, until finally it belonged to Finland, following the country's independence in 1917. This is also when the fortress, formerly known as Viaborg, got its present Finnish name 'Suomenlinna', Castle of Finland. Today, the fortress island is Helsinki's only UNESCO World Heritage site and hosts 800 inhabitants, 6km of walls, 100 cannons, tunnels, as well as museums, beautiful parks and seaside coves, which make Suomenlinna a thrilling day trip.

For more on Suomenlinna, see p52

Turun Linna (p85)

7. Vanha Rauma
WOODEN HOUSES & COBBLESTONE STREETS

Walk the streets of Old Rauma, one of Finland's seven UNESCO World Heritage sites and home to the Nordic countries' largest and most well-preserved wooden house quarters, dating from medieval times. You can also find small boutiques, cafes and restaurants here, which makes the historic site even more pleasant to visit. The oldest building is the Church of the Holy Cross, dating from the 16th century, whereas the wooden private homes are from the beginning of the 18th century. Strolling the streets, you can really get the feel of how the bourgeois of the city might have lived a few hundred years ago.

For more on Vanha Rauma, see p174

8. Koli National Park
PAINTINGS & PEAKS

When the mainly upper-class Finnish and Swedish-Finnish populace started to talk about the 'Finnish identity' in the 19th century, some with Swedish origins even changed their names into Finnish ones, and dozens of artists set across Finland to document – and invent – the country's ethos. One was Eero Järnefelt who, like many during his days, climbed Koli's peaks, took out his easel and brushes and started to paint. Today, Järnefelt's Koli paintings are renowned in Finland, making Koli's bare quartzite peaks and twisted tree trunks, pine-covered slopes and Lake Pielinen views Finland's most familiar national landscape.

For more on Koli National Park, see p165

9. Uspenski Cathedral
RUSSIAN INFLUENCES

The Eastern Orthodox Uspenski Cathedral, rising on top of a little cliff near Helsinki Market Sq in Katajanokka district, is one of the city's most photographed sights. The cathedral is also the biggest orthodox church in Western Europe. Built in 1868, some 50 years after Finland's annexation to Russia, the cathedral's red bricks were shipped in barges from the Bomarsund Fortress, which had been demolished in the Crimean War (1853–56). On top, 13 gold cupolas create an opulent feel, which is continued in the Byzantine-inspired interior, making the church one of the most visible statements of Russia's effect on Helsinki's cityscape.

For more on Uspenski Cathedral, see p52

10. Minna Canth's Salon
PROGRESSIVE THINKER

With the country full of famous residences turned into museums, it is a shame that Minna Canth (1844–97), the first woman in Finland who made a career out of writing and journalism, hasn't got a museum dedicated to her – especially as her home, Kanttila, is still standing opposite Kuopio's VB Museum and is actively promoted and protected by a dedicated group of activists. Still, you can visit Kuopion korttelimuseo, where Canth's progressive salon's setting has been recreated, partly using furniture that belonged to this groundbreaking writer and feminist. Luckily, at least Minna Canth's statue has a prominent spot in Jyväskylä's Kirkkopuisto (Church Park).

For more on Minna Canth's Salon, see p157

11. Hanko (Hango)
EASY BREEZES

Finland's history hasn't just been scuffles over borders and great men and women dedicated to hard work. There have also been leisurely moments and celebrations. One of the most famous spa spots in the early 20th century was Finland's southernmost city, Hanko (Hango), where the bourgeois flocked in hordes since the 1880s, and the military leader CG Mannerheim even owned a cafe. Hanko (Hango) also had its casino and fabulous wooden villas, which still adorn the city. Today, people head to Hanko to enjoy the summer breeze on multiple little beaches and the beautiful seaside setting.

For more on Hanko, see p103

12. Senate Square
ASSASSINATION & ARCHITECTURE

The Senate Square is Helsinki's empire-styled heart designed by the German-born architect Carl Ludwig Engel. Engel didn't enjoy moving to Helsinki, but couldn't resist the task given by Tsar Alexander I, of designing a new city. Helsinki Cathedral is the obvious eye-catcher here, but many intriguing historic events have taken place around the square, such as Finland's most notorious political assassination when the Russian General-Governor Nikolay Bobrikov was shot in

Oodi Library (p54)

1904 in the yellow Government Palace, opposite the University of Helsinki's main building. By the square, there is also the National Library of Finland, considered Engel's true masterpiece.

For more on Senate Square, see p48

13. Vapriikki
TAMPERE'S BLOODY SPRING IN 1918

After gaining independence from Russia in 1917, Finland went through possibly the most traumatising period of its history, a civil war. The bloodiest events were witnessed in Tampere between March and April. Here, the inexperienced 'reds' led by the amateur actor Hugo Salmela collided with the 'whites', led by the then-already-experienced CG Mannerheim, who later became the president of Finland. Over 2000 reds lost their lives, half of them executed, the rest in battle or in prison camps. On the white side, casualties amounted to 700. Tampere's Vapriikki museum, in the Finlayson area, dedicated a permanent exhibition to the bloody events of spring 1918.

For more on Vapriikki, see p132

14. Olympic Stadium
SPORTS, ARCHITECTURE & LONKERO

Helsinki's prime example of functionalist-style architecture is the Töölö Olympic Stadium. The 1952 Summer Olympics were a turning point in the city's urban lifestyle; WWII had destroyed the nation's leisure opportunities and infrastructure had to be upgraded to host the event. This included, for example, a new airport, now Finland's main entry point; traffic lights; and the city-centre Tennispalatsi ('tennis palace'), another functionalist-style masterpiece now hosting HAM (Helsinki Art Museum) and a cinema. But perhaps the most beloved innovation for the Olympics was Lonkero, a readymade long-drink mix of gin and grape, which eased the lives of inexperienced bar staff who served thirsty sports enthusiasts.

For more on the Olympic Stadium, see p71

15. Oodi Library
AN ODE TO LEARNING

Finland's first library was established in Vaasa in 1794, but the institution as it is now only arose in the early 20th century. The library system, where everyone can borrow books, films and music – and nowadays games, tools and even rowing boats or sewing machines – evolved hand in hand with the country's inclusive and free-for-all education system. Both are now valued as key aspects of Finland's success in international surveys on education and reading-skill levels. Although some smaller, remote libraries have had to close their doors in recent decades, libraries are still valued here. One example is the Oodi Library in Helsinki city centre, awarded for its architecture.

For more on the Oodi Library, see p54

MEET THE FINNS

The relatively icy surface of the Finns might be hard to crack – but once you are in, you are in for a lifetime. Paula Hotti introduces her people.

THE FINNS ARE a trusting bunch, and this trust is extended not just to friendships but also toward the media and government. In fact, according to a 2023 report by the OECD, 47% of the Finnish population trusts the government, compared to the OECD average of 39%. One reason behind this is considered to be the Finns' media literacy skills, scoring 74 points in the 2024 Media Literacy Index, followed closely behind by other Nordic nations. This skill is learned from an early age, as pupils learn to assess critically the information they are given. This affects everyone going through the school system here, as equal and free education has been one of Finland's core values for over a century.

In reality, a Finn may not come forth as a particularly trusting person: normally, there is a touch of reserve when meeting a Finn. It might take some time to break the somewhat cold surface and get an invitation to a local's home for a simple cup of coffee. But when you do achieve this, you have most likely got a loyal, kind and trustworthy friend for a lifetime.

This reserve is at least partly due to the fact that Finns value their private space, and they value it a lot, extending the same respect for privacy to others. Don't expect a Finn to sit next to you on the bus or share a spontaneous smile on the street.

Who & How Many

Finland has a population of just over 5.5 million. The majority (86.5%) has Finnish as mother tongue, then Swedish (5.2%). Sámi is spoken by about 2000 individuals. There are some 469,000 foreign nationals living in the country.

Finnish humour is often described as dry, or even sarcastic, and jokes can be delivered with a straight face: it might take a short moment to realise that you were actually just told a joke. A good introduction to the Finnish way of life, humour and personal space is the comic strip *Finnish Nightmares* by Karoliina Korhonen.

But it's not just quiet coffee moments here, as Finns do enjoy rowdy parties and lively conversations too. The attitudes have also been changing for the past couple of decades, and the younger generations are typically more open, and even hug each other if they happen to meet on the streets.

In general, Finns are also a very modest nation, with many proverbs to prove the dangers of bragging, from 'Silence is gold' to 'If you reach for the spruce you will fall onto the juniper', pointing out that high aspirations end up in lousy results. And then there is the oft-quoted line from one of Finland's most treasured poets, Eino Leino: 'Whoever is happy should hide it'. Which doesn't make sense for a country continuously hailed as the happiest nation on Earth.

But maybe that's the Finnish way: a modest nation with a solid education system and a trusting attitude towards life, with no need to go shouting about it.

Pictured clockwise from top left: Jasper Pääkkönen owner of Löyly (p59); Lakeside couple, Lapland (p202); Sámi couple, Saariselkä (p229); cyclist, Urho Kekkonen National Park (p229)

A VERY FINNISH CASE

I type this in my current home in Helsinki, but I was born in South Savo, where my 1990s childhood was a typical one: building tree huts in the forest, spending summer days on the city-centre beach, and cycling to school in -20°C.

This might sound a bit extreme, but it was a very typical Finnish childhood. But even then, I was dreaming of foreign lands and hoped that I'd have a little drop of some exotic blood. However, my sister recently did a DNA test, and we turned out to be of 100% Finnish descent. This also is very typical here, as for centuries the country has been quite a homogeneous one – a state of affairs which in recent decades has luckily been changing.

And, just when I had admitted my defeat in lacking diversity in my roots, my sister was contacted because of a connection to a clan in the Scottish Highlands – a drop of information that I happily cling to.

THE SÁMI
TRADITIONS AND CULTURE

The only recognised indigenous people within the European Union area.
By John Noble

THE SÁMI ARE spread across Norway, Sweden, Finland and Russia's Kola Peninsula. Historically they have lived mostly in the northern parts of those countries. There are approximately 40,000 to 45,000 Sámi in Norway, 15,000 to 25,000 in Sweden, 11,000 in Finland and 2000 in Russia.

In Finland, Lapland's three northernmost municipalities (Inari, Utsjoki, Enontekiö), along with the Vuotso area further south, are considered the Sámi Homeland – 30,000 sq km of forests, fells and lakes with just over 10,000 inhabitants, about one-third of whom are Sámi. Today more than 60% of Sámi in Finland live outside this area. There are nine different Sámi languages, of which three are spoken in Finland. It's estimated that about one-third of Sámi people in Finland today speak a Sámi language. Since 1996, the Sámi in Finland have had constitutional self-government in the Sámi Homeland in the spheres of language and culture. This self-government is managed by the Sámi Parliament in Finland, situated in Inari village.

The Sámi are famously associated with reindeer herding, which is an important cornerstone of their culture. The animals are used for meat, clothes, crafts and transport. Although many Sámi no longer earn their livelihood from reindeer herding – many pursue the same professions and occupations as the rest of society – reindeer herding retains a high cultural value, as do the other traditional Sámi livelihoods of fishing, gathering, handicrafts and hunting.

Today these activities are often modernised to make them more practical and cost-efficient. For example, Sámi reindeer herders use snowmobiles, ATVs, GPS collars, drones and helicopters in the tending and locating of their animals, just as Sámi artisans, while still working with natural materials, often employ modern tools in the making of Sámi handicrafts (duodji) – practical, handmade objects based on old traditions. Sámi who work in other professions often continue to make traditional handicrafts for their own use, or fish and forage to supplement their diets.

The Sámi today want the world to see them as the modern people they are, not as relics of bygone ages. One thing that is not part of their modern culture is the animistic religion that was replaced by Christianity several centuries ago. Touristic shamanism by non-Sámi distorts the cultural heritage with invented traditions.

The colourful traditional Sámi dress *does* remain an important part of Sámi culture. It not only identifies its wearer as Sámi, but its decorations, and the way it is worn, indicate which area the wearer comes from and can even reveal their family and marital status. Today it is worn mainly on special occasions. Sámi feel that they should be accorded due respect and privacy when wearing it, and especially that religious events like weddings, confirmations and funerals should be left in peace.

VIEW FROM THE SÁMI PARLIAMENT

Tuomas Aslak Juuso was elected in 2019 for a four-year term (2020 to 2023) as President of the Sámi Parliament in Finland, which is the official representative of the 11,000 Sámi who live in the country.

There are three Sámi languages spoken in Finland: North Sámi, Inari Sámi and Skolt Sámi, of which the latter two are most endangered. Many Sámi lost their language in assimilation processes during the 20th century, but through language nest projects and active work, more people can regain the language of their families and continue to strengthen Sámi culture and arts. More than half of the Sámi live outside the traditional Sámi area, which has created challenges in ensuring the right to learn Sámi languages and receive services in Sámi languages everywhere in Finland, not just the Sámi Homeland.

Despite many advancements in the past decades, there are still serious issues with Sámi self-determination in Finland. The Sámi are recognised in the Finnish Constitution as Indigenous People, but both the UN Human Rights Committee and the Committee on the Elimination of Racial Discrimination have found Finland in violation of Sámi rights in recent years. Despite several attempts, Finland had at the time of writing failed to make the necessary amendments to the Act on the Sámi Parliament and the Sámi's right for FPIC – free, prior, informed consent on matters relating to Sámi culture was not fulfilled. The Sámi have often not been properly consulted when deciding on activities affecting the Sámi livelihoods and culture, like mining and other land use projects. The latest attempt to amend the Act was expected to be resolved during the year 2023. The Finnish government has also appointed a Truth and Reconciliation Commission to increase dialogue and trust between the Sámi and the state.

Traditional livelihoods remain crucial to the Sámi culture. In addition to reindeer herding, fishing, gathering, hunting and handicrafts, Sámi are also somewhat involved in other modern livelihoods, like Sámi tourism. Unfortunately, the ethical guidelines created by us for the tourism industry in 2018 – a step forward in ensuring a sustainable and respectful treatment of the Sámi and their culture – and our visitor guidance for travelling in Sámi Homeland (published in 2022) are not followed by all companies operating in Finland, and for example fake Sámi traditions and imagery are still widely used.

Above all, the climate crisis remains a major challenge to Indigenous Peoples around the world, and its implications are already frighteningly visible in the Arctic. Preserving our nature while also creating socially sustainable solutions to combat climate change is a priority for us all – and for that, the Sámi people need to be heard.

THE MANY SIDES OF FINNISHNESS

Bold lines, strong statements and striking melodies are omnipresent in the Finnish art world. By Paula Hotti

FINNISH ART DIDN'T only evolve in synchronicity with other aspects of society over time – it was also an essential building material in creating the notion of 'Finnishness' in the wake of the country's independence in 1917.

From Cave Paintings to Russian Censorship

Naturally, where there are people, there is art. In Finland, travellers can visit the sites of prehistoric cave paintings, such as the drawings in red on the Astuvansalmi cliffside near Mikkeli (pictured); medieval churches with beautiful decor (prime examples are located in Turku, Hollola and Hattula); and castles full of artsy artefacts in Turku, Hämeenlinna and Savonlinna.

Finland's medieval period lasted roughly from the 12th to the 16th centuries. Around this time the Finnish language got its alphabet when, in the 1540s, the reformist Mikael Agricola sat down to work with his quill and translated the New Testament into Finnish and published the first book written in Finland, the *Abckirja* (ABC book). But the first novels in Finnish, alongside institutionalised art in other fields, only came into existence during the 19th century, when authors and artists set out to create the Finnish identity, looking through their romantic goggles at Finnish landscapes and folklore. The project lasted from around the 1840s till the early 20th century. This period produced artists such as Akseli Gallen-Kallela, known for his scenes from *Kalevala* (1835), Finland's national epic written by Elias Lönnrot, who travelled around what is today Karelia (both in eastern Finland and on the Russian side), collected oral

Pictured clockwise from top left: Astuvansalmi prehistoric rock paintings (p260); Helsinki train station; Relief of Eero Järnefelt, Koli National Park; An Alvar Aalto building, Helsinki

poetry and composed a consistent work from it. Another influential painter from the time is Eero Järnefelt (pictured), renowned for scenes from the top of Koli peaks, which are now celebrated as a national park and a symbolic part of Finland's landscape. In music, Jean Sibelius set the tone for Finland's emancipation project with his *Finlandia, Op 26*, which includes the often-performed Finlandia hymn. The hymn, originally without words, was also part of a campaign against Russia's censorship and ever-tightening grip on Finland.

The Finnishness these artists created on their canvasses, words and melodies had a clear focus: depicting an idealised image of the nation, with wild forests and high viewpoints. Factories and cities were left outside the frames, although both modern phenomena were already found all over Finland towards the end of the 20th century.

20th-Century Finnishness – and the Moomins

Apart from these solemn works, there has been another influence in the Finnish art world. When many were painting austere landscapes, Helene Schjerfbeck held a more delicate brush. Having spent her early career studying, painting and travelling in Paris and other parts of Europe, in later life, she relocated mainly to small-town Hyvinkää and is now one of Finland's most esteemed modern painters, known for her still-life works and haunting self-portraits.

During the rest of the 20th century, the young nation's art scene kept diversifying. In architecture, Eliel Saarinen and Alvar Aalto opened the doors of Finnish architecture and design to the world, Aalto accompanied by his first wife, the designer and architect Aino Aalto – with many stating that the work of the two is often inseparable – and, after Aino's death, Elissa Aalto, also an architect. Aalto became a forerunner of mid-20th-century modernism, with his buildings relying heavily on functional details and also with his invention of bent plywood furniture, influencing the aesthetics of international designers. Saarinen's extraordinary railway station designed with Emil Wikström's stately statues will greet anyone arriving in Helsinki by train (pictured), whereas Aalto's work can be found in churches as well as in private and official architecture around Finland. Today, you will find neighbourhoods with sombre and pastel-coloured 1950s blocks of flats anywhere in Finland as well as public buildings with bold straight lines combined with airy and wavy structures, such as the award-winning Oodi Library. Finland has been in synch with the minimalist Scandi-style, too, sometimes adding a playful twist, as Eero Aarnio has shown with his Ball and Bubble Chairs.

Towards the latter part of the 20th century, Tove Jansson's moody and philosophical Moomin comic strips morphed into books and animated TV series, capturing the imagination of old and young throughout the world. Tom of Finland's gay erotica first found its audience in the underground queer world – first abroad (homosexuality was illegal in Finland till 1971), but later also in Finland, ending up adorning official stamps in 2014. Today, you can also buy duvets and pillow covers and other interior fabrics carrying his striking drawings.

The Big Stories in Books, Music & Cinema

Another success story of the late 20th and early 21st century is Finnish cinema and literature. On the big screen, Aki Kaurismäki and his beautifully melancholic and near-monosyllabic films depict the margins of city life. Many hail his cinematic genius, gaining him many awards from Cannes, Berlin and elsewhere with films such as *The Man Without a Past* (2002), *Le Havre* (2011) and *Fallen Leaves* (2023).

Also Finnish literature is lauded worldwide, with authors such as Sofi Oksanen (her most-famed work *Purge* (2008) investigating the legacies of Soviet rule in Estonia); Johanna Sinisalo (a master of science fiction and fantasy); and Pajtim Statovci, a Kosovo-born Finn writing powerful stories of cultural conflicts, family relations, identity and self-discovery leading the way.

Contemporary Finnish music goes beyond the realm of grand symphonies. Composers like Kaija Saariaho have gained international acclaim for her ethereal, innovative classical works that often incorporate electronic elements, while the Finnish music festivals, particularly in the summer, showcase the nation's rich musical diversity.

Today, Finland's artistic identity is as varied as the music it produces, reflecting a blend of tradition and modern innovation across genres.

TRIUMPHS & TRAGEDIES
NATURE CONSERVATION IN FINLAND

How Finland is fighting to win the race against losing its most valuable asset – nature. By Paula Hotti

ACCORDING TO A study in the summer of 2022 by the Ministry of Environment and the Finnish Environment Institute, Finns' concern about the state of Finland's nature has increased by 15% since 2020. Almost half of the participants also acknowledged that they now know more about biodiversity than before. The study also concluded that the COVID-19 pandemic deepened people's attachment to nature: now, 92% of the respondents think that nature is an integral part of Finnish identity.

This may not sound surprising, given that nature engulfs Finland, even its cities: Finland has 187,888 lakes over 500 sq metres in size, and over 75% of the land is covered by forests. Yet the country is not without its environmental challenges. Every ninth species in Finland is endangered, due to the lack of biodiversity and the ever-narrowing living spaces. Outdated mining laws make Finland seem like the Wild West, where land is up for grabs, regardless of the environmental costs. Finland's marshes are also under threat, half of them on the verge of being lost, affecting up to 120 endangered species that call these landscapes their home. Fortunately, Finland is historically a proactive country, at least on the NGO level, in tackling conservation and other environmental issues – even if it takes a little while to put any tangible structures into play.

The Roots of Finnish Nature Conservation

Finnish nature conservation has its roots in the 19th century, when the Finnish-Swedish Arctic explorer AE Nordenskjöld and the author and historian Zacharias Topelius spoke and wrote on the topic. Yet it took until 1938 when Finland's first society to protect the environment was officially established as Suomen luonnonsuojeluliitto (the Finnish Association for Nature Conservation; FANC) before the country had a dedicated force to campaign for the environment. In the 1930s, Finland also

got its first national parks established on government-owned lands to protect the environment – exactly as Nordenskjöld had hoped some 50 years before.

Since the 1930s, the FANC has had many triumphs: more national parks – such as Linnansaari, Oulanka and Lemmenjoki – and nature reserves were established in the 1950s. During the 20th century, the association also reacted to many international developments, such as informing people about the dangers of the insecticide DDT in the 1960s and the limits of what was considered infinite growth in the following decade. An important shift in nature conservation and awareness came about in the 1990s, as climate change and the limits of natural resources became evident.

Triumphs on Land & the Waters

More recently, in the autumn of 2022, the fells of Lapland witnessed the first successful nesting of the Arctic fox in Finland since 1996. And the year before, over 170 fishers in the Saimaa Lakeland region received wire fish traps that are safe for the area's endangered seals, Saimaa ringed seals, to prevent the frequency of young seal pups dying in the fishing nets used here. Much of Finland's marshes have also been protected, due to vigorous campaigning by political parties, NGOs and actively participating private people, whereas in Lapland, the Finnish state-owned enterprise Metsähallitus (Forest Administration) oversees 12 wilderness areas to protect their uniqueness.

In 2022, Finland also got its 41st national park, Salla in Lapland, to give more species a fighting chance of survival. The year was also to witness a much-needed rewriting of Finland's 25-year-old law on environmental protection, but the final drafts were watered down, as the Central party lined up with the opposition, demanding changes to key aspects of protecting endangered species. In 2022 the FANC and Finnish Greenpeace also sued the Finnish Government – a first-time occurrence in Finland's history – as its actions are not in accordance with Finland's climate laws that aim for carbon neutrality by 2035. A year later, the then Prime Minister Sanna Marin's government protected 30,000 hectares of the government's land.

Marshlands in Focus

In the summer of 2024, Finland's nature conservation efforts received a significant boost when the EU finalised its ambitious nature restoration goals. Under these guidelines, member countries are required to restore at least 30% of degraded habitats by 2030, 60% by 2040 and 90% by 2050. For Finland, this translates to placing approximately one-third of the nation's land under targeted conservation initiatives. Particularly critical are the country's marshlands, where current restoration efforts fall dramatically short – with an estimated need for eight times more protective work on wetland areas than is currently being undertaken.

In addition to marshlands, other wetland areas are receiving closer attention. For instance, old dams and constructed barriers are being removed to restore the natural flow of water and support endangered migratory fish populations. While these efforts are commendable, it must be noted that the scale of the task is immense: Finland has over 100,000km of streams and more than 20,000km of rivers. In Central Finland alone, only 1% of streams are in their natural state.

Meanwhile, in Lapland, over 3000km of the Tornio River and its tributaries, heavily used for log-floating in the past, are being restored in what is one of Europe's largest nature restoration projects. This initiative, known as the Torne River International Watershed LIFE (Triwa LIFE), not only benefits fish populations but also helps mitigate the impacts of climate change, including reducing flood risks. Further south, in Helsinki, the city is investing in the restoration of an underwater 'meadow' on the seabed by planting eelgrass (*Zostera marina*), a vital seagrass known for enhancing marine biodiversity.

With these developments in mind, it might be justified to say that all species living in this country of thousands of lakes still have hope – with a lot of help from their human friends.

INDEX

A

Aalto, Aino 93, 269
Aalto, Alvar 73, 93, 110-11, 152, 188, 269
accessible travel 251
 Könkäänsaari Nature Trail 213
accommodation 125, 201, 237, 243
activities 28-9, 36-9, **38-9**, *see also individual activities, individual locations, family travel*
 Huikee Adventure Park 178
 Lampivaara Amethyst Mine 221
 Medieval Fair 159
 Nallikari Safaris 192
 Pilke Science Centre 210-11
 wilderness huts 215
Agricola, Mikael 65-6
airports 240, 241
Alajärvi 188
Åland Archipelago 79-125, **80-1**, *see also* Hanko, Mariehamn, Porvoo, South Coast, Turku
 accommodation 125
 activities 82-3
 autonomy 94-6, 101
 drinking 100
 eating 100, 101, 102
 events 82-3
 islands of 102
 itineraries 82-3
 navigation 80-1
 travel within 80-1
amethysts 221
archaeology 195, *see also* history
archery 195
architecture 16-17, *see also individual architects*
 Aalto Centre 188
 Art Nouveau 52, 57, 105, 162
 Hanko walking tour 109, **109**
 modernist 93
 National Romanticism 109
 Nordic classicism 74
 Torni Hotel 67
Arctic, the, *see also* Lapland
 Arctic naïve art 221
 geography 212
 history 208-10
art 268-9, *see also* museums & galleries
 Arctic naïve art 221
 avant-garde 115
 Edelfelt, Albert 115
 Hildén, Sara 136
 Iittala Naïve Art Exhibition 161
 interior design 219-20
 Mäntän kuvataideviikot 139
 Pikisaari Art Trail 193
 Porvoo Triennale 115
 Posankka 88
aurora borealis 38-9, 219, 233, 249, 253, **38-9**

B

B&Bs 243
beaches 251
 Eiran Ranta 60
 Hanko 108
 Hietaranta 75
 Nallikari 192
 Viikinsaari 136
 Yyteri 37, 178
bears 165, 199, 245, *see also* Ranua Wildlife Park
 safety 245
beer, *see* breweries & distilleries
Bengtskär Lighthouse 108
bird-watching 123, 178, 180, 213
boat tours 154
boat trips 88-9
 Jähti 217
 JL Runeberg 113
 Kuopio's harbour 156-7
 M/S *Kerttu* 180
 M/S *Klippan* 120
 M/S *Leila* 214
 M/S *Tiira* 187
 Puumala 145
 Saimaa Lakeland 146-7
Nordic classicism 74
Torni Hotel 67
Sampo (icebreaker) 214
Savonlinna 143
Bonk Museum 181
books 31, 52, 111, 269, *see also* Jansson, Tove
 Vinhan Kirjakauppa 139-40
 walking tours 54, **54**
border crossings 240
bowling, *see Mölkky*
breweries & distilleries
 Åland Distillery 99
 Bock's Corner Brewery 185
 Hailouto Organic Brewery 196
 Hanko Brewing Company 107
 Kakola Brewing Company 89
 Malmgård Manor 83, 118
 Schinebrykoff 71
 Sinebrychoff 64
 Stallhagen Brewery 101
 Takatalo & Tompuri 122
budget 241, 242, 243, 247
Bulevardi 66
burial grounds,
 see cemeteries & burial grounds
bus travel 241
business hours 255

C

camping 243
canals
 Saimaa Canal 151
 Vääksy's Canal 150
canoeing, *see* kayaking
Canth, Minna 157, 262
car travel 241, 245
castles & fortifications
 Bomarsund Fortress 99-100
 Häme Castle 158, 160, 261
 Kastelholm Slott 98
 Linnoitus 145
 Olavinlinna castle 141, 145
 Raseborg Castle 110
 Suomenlinna sea fortress 46, 51, 52, 261
 Turun Linna 85-6, 261
cemeteries & burial grounds
 Hietaniemi Cemetery 75
 Rovaniemi 212
 Sammallahdenmäki 260
children, travel with, *see* family travel
churches & cathedrals
 Agricola 65-6
 Alajärvi Church 188
 Church of St Nicholas 120
 Helsinki Cathedral 46, 48
 Holy Trinity Church 183
 Johanneksenkirkko 66
 Kampin Kappeli 67
 Kemi Church 217
 Kuopio Cathedral 156
 Lakeuden Risti Kirkko 188
 Naantalin Kirkko 92
 Närpes Church 189
 Pielpajärven Erämaakirkko 225
 Pyhän Kolminaisuuden Kirkko 176
 Pyhän Ristin Kirkko 174-6
 Ruotsinpyhtää church 119
 Sankt Görans Kyrka 96
 Sankt Johannes Kyrka 100
 Sankt Mikael Kyrka 101
 Sankt Olof Kyrka 100
 Sankta Anna Kyrka 102
 Taidekappeli 88
 Temppeliaukion Kirkko 47, 73-4
 Tuomiokirkko (Porvoo) 83, 113
 Tuomiokirkko (Turku) 84
 Turku Cathedral 86-7
 Ulrika Eleonora Kyrka 189
 Uspenski Cathedral 262
cinemas, *see* films
climate 28-9, 248
climate change 248
climbing 91
 Olhavinvuori 150-1
coffee 52, 108, 247
 Pystökaffe 177
conservation 270-2
cottages, *see mökki*
courses cookery 98-9

273

crafts 149, 177, 215-16, 225, 231
 Craft Museum of Finland 155, 231
 Lace Week 176
 Luostarinmäen Käsityöläismuseo 89-90
 Salt 96
credit cards 242
crime 245
culture
 Finnish 31, 166, 264-5
 Sámi 266-7
currency 242
cycling 154, 178, 211, 248, *see also* cycling tours
 bike hire 69, 151, 152, 220
 Puumala archipelago 141
 Saimaa archipelago 141
 Töölö Bay 72
cycling tours
 Hanko 106
 Helsinki 58-9, **59**
 Oulu 193, **193**

design 14
dialling code 255
disabilities, travellers with 251
 Könkäänsaari Nature Trail 213
discounts 242
distilleries, *see* breweries & distilleries
drinking 246-7, *see also* breweries & distilleries, coffee
 language 256
 lonkero 74
 SpåraKoff (tram-bar) 71
drinking water 255
driving, *see* car travel
driving tours
 Hailuoto 196, **196**
 Saimaa Lakeland 148, **148**

Eira 55-60, **56**
 accommodation 76
 food 60
Ekberg 47, 66
Ekenäs Archipelago National Park 111-1
electricity 255
emergencies 255, 256
 language 256
Engel, Carl Ludwig 262-3
Erikssonin osteribaari 51
etiquette 30, 254
events, *see* festivals & events

family travel 154, 244
 activities 37
 Doghill Fairytale Farm 135
 rafting & kayaking 198
 Rosa & Rudolf Family Park 200
Father Christmas, *see* Santa Claus
ferry travel 53, 60, 91, 241
 Föri 82
 Hailuoto 194
 Sea Oulu Water Taxi 190
 Summersea 108
 Viikinsaari 135
 Vikla Ferry 121
festivals & events 28-9, *see also* films, music
 Hanko Regatta 107
 harvest celebrations 33
 Hillamarkkinat 33
 Inari 228
 Lace Week (Rauma) 176
 Mäntän kuvataideviikot 139
 Midsommar (Mariehamn) 96
 National Sleepyhead Day 29
 Porvoo Triennale 115
 Skábmagovat 29
 Vappu (May Day) 29
 Vappuaatto (May Day Eve) 29
films 31, 269
 Finlayson Centre (cinema) 132
 Lahti International Film Festival 150
 Midnight Sun Film Festival 221
 Orion cinema 68
 Skábmagovat (film festival) 228
 Vera Film Festival 96
Finnish Association for Nature Conservation (FANC) 270-2
Finnjävel Salonki and Sali 47
Finström 100-1
fishing 164, 199, 218-19
Fiskars 83, 112
 accommodation 125
Flatiron House 58
Föglö 83, 102
food 32-5, 246-7
 Ålandspannkak 97
 apples 100
 Arctic Food Lab 192
 festivals 33
 language 256
 Lapland specialities 213
 liquorice 34, 117, 154
 Michelin-starred 51, 60, 72
 organic 98-9
 vendace 35
forestry 210-11
 Metsähallitus 215

gardens, *see* parks & gardens
gay travellers 250
 Aurora Holidays 233
geology 187, 217
 eskers 150
glasswork 161-2

Hailuoto 196
 accommodation 201
Halkolaituri Pier 52
Hämeenlinna 27, 158-62, **159**
 accommodation 167
 beyond Hämeenlinna 161-2, *see also indivdual locations*
 eating 160
 travel within 158, 161
Hamina 121-2
 eating 121
 tours 124, **124**
Hanko 26, 83, 103-9, **104**
 accommodation 103, 125
 beyond Hanko 110-12, *see also individual locations*
 drinking 106, 107
 eating 105, 108
 shopping 111
 tours 109, **109**
 travel within 103, 110
Hauensuoli 108
health 245
Helsinki 22, 26, 42-77, **44-5**, **49**, **56**, *see also* Eira, Hietalahti, Kaivopuisto, Kamppi, Katajanokka, Kruununhaka, Punavuori, Ullanlinna
 accommodation 76-7
 city centre 48-54, **49**
 drinking 52, 64, 74
 food 50, 51, 64, 67
 itineraries 46-7
 navigation 44
 shopping 50, 51, 53, 57
 tours 54, 58-9, **54**, **59**
 travel within 44, 48, 55, 61, 69
Helsinki Cathedral 46
Helsinki Central railway station 54
Helvetinjärvi National Park 139
Hietalahden Kauppahalli 47, 65
Hietalahti 61-8, **62**
 food 64-5
highlights 8-19
hiking 36-7, 39, 178, 211, 248, **39**, *see also* walking
 Arctic Circle Hiking Area 213
 Huippujen kierros trail 163
 Iso Pyhätunturi 220
 Kanjonin 198
 Karhunkierros 197
 Kevo Strict Nature Reserve 232
 Kiirunapolku loop 230
 Kilpisjärven Retkeilykeskus 234
 Koli National Park 163-4
 Könkään keino 198
 Kultareitti (Gold Trail) 229
 Lemmenjoki National Park 228-9
 Luulampi trai 230
 Pieni Karhunkierros 197-8
 Rautalampi circuit 230
 Three-Country Cairn 236, **236**
 Ukko-Luosto fell 221
historic buildings & sites
 Appelgrenintie 109
 Capitolium 152
 Finlandia-talo 72
 Holm House 115
 Iso Linnämaki Castle Hill 116
 Jyväskylä Workers' Club 153
 Kierikkikeskus 195
 Langinkoski Imperial Fishing Lodge 121
 Lasipalatsi 61
 Laukko Manor 140
 Malmgård Manor 83, 118
 Marela 176
 Monument of Liberty 107
 Muuratsalon Koetalo 153
 Neljän Tuulen Tupa 105-6
 Neristan 187
 Ostrobothnian Acropolis 188
 Paimio Sanatorium 93
 Palanderin Talo 160
 presidential villa (Helsinki) 55
 Qwensel House 88
 Säynätsalon Kunnantalo 153
 Verla Groundwood and Board Mill 122
 Villa Mairea 179

Map Pages **000**

Villa Skeppet 111
Villa Väinölä 188
World Heritage Gateway Visitor Centre 186
history 65, 66, 208-10, 260-1, 268-9, see also historic buildings & sites, Olympic Games
Åland 94-6
Astuvansalmi Rock Paintings 260
Bronze Age 99, 180, 260-1
civil war 263
conservation 270-2
Continuation War 71, 108
emigration 105
gold rush 230-1
Häme Castle 261
Hanko (Hango) 262
homosexuality 269
industrial 112, 119, 122-3, 134, 137, 179, 214
Iron Age 99
Koli National Park 262
maritime 119, 176-7
Minna Canth's Salo 262
national parks 272
Olympic Stadium 263
Oodi Library 263
prehistoric 115, 150, 195, 220, 260-1
Russia/Soviet Union 103-4, 106, 116, 134, 216, 260
Sammallahdenmäki 260
Senate Square 262
Suomenlinna sea fortress 261
Turku
Turun Linna (Turku) 261
Uspenski Cathedral 262
Vanha Rauma 262
Vapriikki 263
Winter War 103-4, 106, 107, 166
WWII 55, 67, 103, 122, 210, 212
hitchhiking 241
Houtskari 93

ice swimming 57, see also swimming
igloos 216, 243
Iittala 161-2
  shopping 162
Inari 25, 224-33, **225**
  accommodation 237
  beyond Inari 227-34, see also individual locations
  eating 225
  festivals 228
  travel within 224, 227
Iniö 93
internet 240
islands, see also Åland
  Archipelago, Ekenäs
Archipelago National Park
  Bothnian Bay 217
  Brändö 102
  Föglö 102
  Hailuoto 196
  Kökar 102
  Kumlinge 102
  Kvarken Archipelago 186-7
  Laitakari 214
  Oulujoki River, island of 194
  Turku archipelago 84
  Uunisaari 57
  Vårdö 102
Iso Roobertinkatu 47, 63
itineraries 22-7, 46-7, 82-3, 130, 172-3, 206-7, see also individual locations
Ivalo 232

Jakobstad 187-8
Jansson, Tove 67, 92, 269, see also Moomins
Jomala 100
Jugendstil 73, 109
Juhannus Midsommar (midsummer) 29
Jyväskylä 152-8, **153**
  accommodation 167
  beyond Jyväskylä 156-7, see also individual locations
  eating 154
  habour 154
  shopping 155
  tours 155, **155**
  travel within 152, 156

Kaisaniemi 69-75, **70**
  accommodation 77
  food 72
Kaivopuisto 55-60, **56**
  accommodation 76
  food 58-9
Kalevala (poem) 71, 140, 166
Kallio 69-75, **70**
  accommodation 77
  drinking 71
  food 71, 72
Kamppi 61-8, **62**
  accommodation 76-7
  drinking 68
Kansalliskirjasto (National Library of Finland) 52, 54
Kappeli 46, 50
Karelia 126-67, **128-9**, see also, Jyväskylä, Koli National Park, Saimaa Lakeland, Tampere
  accommodation 167
  activities 130-1
  events 130-1
  itineraries 130-1
  navigation 128-9
  travel within 128-9
Karigasiniemi 232
  accommodation 237
  eating 231
Katajanokka 48-54, **49**
  accommodation 76
  food 51
  shopping 53
Kauppatori (Helsinki market square) 53
kayaking 69, 136, 151, 192, 198
Kelvenne 150
Kemi 214-16
  eating 216
  shopping 216
Kemi Lumilinna (Snow Castle) 216
Kemijärvi 218-19
  accommodation 237
  eating 218
Kiilopää 229-30
Kilpisjärvi 25, 234-5, **235**
  accommodation 237
  eating 235
  tours 236, **236**
  travel within 234
Kökar 83, 102
Kokkola 187
  eating 188
Koli National Park 24, 163-4
  accommodation 167
  beyond Koli National Park 165-6, see also individual locations
  eating 164
  travel within 163, 165
Konepaja 47, 74
Korkeavuorenkatu 57
Korppoo 93
Kotka 83
  eating 121
Kouvola 122-3
  accommodation 125
Kristinestad 188-9
  accommodation 201
  eating 189
Kruununhaka 48-54, **49**
  accommodation 76
  food 51
  shopping 53
Kuhmo 24, 165-6
Kukkola 217-18
Kultahamina 229
Kumlinge 101-2
Kuopio 156-7
  accommodation 167
  eating 157
Kuusamo 199
Kvarken Archipelago 186-7
  eating 187

lace-making 177
Lahti 149-50
  accommodation 167
  eating 149, 151
Laitakari 214-15
lake bathing 249, see also swimming
Lake Norvajärvi 212
language 31, 246, 256-7
  Finnish 216
  Sámi 267
  Swedish 111, 187, 189
Lapland 202-37, **204-5**, see also, Inari, Kilpisjärvi, Rovaniemi
  accommodation 237
  activities 219
  eating 232
  itineraries 206-7
  navigation 204-5
  travel seasons 206-7, 229
  travel within 204-5
  weather 206-7
Lappo 102
Laukko Manor 140
Lemmenjoki National Park 228-9
  accommodation 228, 237
  boat service 228
lesbian travellers 250
  Aurora Holidays 233
LGBTIQ+ travellers 250
  Aurora Holidays 233
Loi Loi 47
Loviisa 118-19

Mannerheim, CG 55, 105-6, 263
manors, see historic buildings & sites
Mänttä-Vilppula 138
Mariehamn 83, 94-7, **95**
  beyond Mariehamn 98-101, see also individual locations
  drinking 95, 100
  eating 100, 101
  festivals 96
  food 96
  shopping 96
  travel within 94, 98
markets
  Christmas markets 29
  Herring Market 33
  Hietalahden kirpputori 65
  Kauppahalli (Turku) 82, 87
  Market Hall (Oulu) 190
  Medieval Market (Turku) 90
  Vanha Kauppahalli 51
measures 255
Merisatamanranta 57

M–O

mobile phones 240
mökki 19, 243
Mölkky 136
money 242
Moomins 92, 134-5, 269
 Muumimaailma 91
mosquitos 245
mountains, *see* peaks & mountains
museums & galleries 53
 Aboa Vetus & Ars Nova 82, 84
 Åland Art Museum 96
 Ålands Fotografiska Museum 100-1, 135
 Ålands Kulturhistoriska & Konstmuseum 96
 Alvar Aalto Museo 152
 Amos Rex 47, 61
 Amuri Working Class Quarters 137
 Archipelago Museum 102
 Arktikum 208-9
 Artillery, Engineer, & Signals Museum of Finland 159
 Ateneum Art Museum 47, 50, 51
 B-Galleria 90
 Birthplace of Jean Sibelius museum 160
 Bonk Museum 181
 Bunker Museum 122
 Cavalry Museum 145
 Chappe Museum 111
 Craft Museum of Finland 155
 Design Museum (Helsinki) 63-4
 Fängelsemuseet Vita Björn 98
 Finnish Hockey Hall of Fame 132-3
 Finnish Labour Museum Werstas 134
 Finnish Museum of Games 132-3
 Finnish Museum of Natural History 65
 Fiskars Museum 112
 Galerie Anhava 68
 Galerie Forsblom 68
 Galleria Halmetoja 68
 Gallery Vanha Kappalaisentalo 115
 HAM 67
 Hämeenlinna Art Museum 160
 Helsinki City Museum 53
 Helsinki Contemporary 68
 History Museum (Kemi) 215
 Iittala Glass Museum 161
 Jan Karlsgårdens 99
 Jyväskylä Art Museum 155
 Keski-Suomen Museo 152
 KH Renlund Museum 187
 Kiasma (Museum of Contemporary Art) 47, 51
 Kieppi Natural History Museum 187
 Kultamuseo 230
 Kulttuurikeskus Pentik-Mäki 219
 Kuopio Art Museum 156
 Kuopio Museum 156
 Kuopion Korttelimuseo 156
 Lahti Ski Museum 150
 Lappeenranta Art Museum 145
 Mariehamnsmuseet 96-7
 Maritime Museum 176-7
 Mental Museum 75
 Merikeskus Vellamo 83, 119
 Moomin Museum 134-5
 Museo Skogster 160
 Museum Nootti 134
 Museum of Hanko 108
 Museum of the War & Reconstruction 220-1
 Museum of Visual Arts 149
 Museum Shop Sparvin 155
 Museum-Gallery Alariesto 221
 Muumimaailma 91
 Naantali Museum 92
 Nanoq Arctic Museum 188
 Natural History Museum of Central Finland 155
 Pharmacy Museum 88
 Pohjanmaan Museo 184
 Porvoon Museo 115
 Pro Puu 149
 Puustelli art center 218
 Rintama Museo 83, 107
 Rosenlew Museo 179
 Rovaniemi Art Museum 211
 Salpa Line Museum 122
 Satakunnan Museo 179
 Savonlinna Museum 141-3
 Serlachius Museums Gösta 138
 Serlachius Museums Gustaf 138
 Sibelius Museum 90
 Siida 226, 261
 Sinebrychoff Art Museum 64
 Sjöfartsmuseum 94
 Suomenlinna-Museo 52
 Tahto (sports musuem) 72
 Taidehalli 74
 Taidemuseo 177
 Talvisotamuseo (Winter War Museum) 166
 Tampere Art Museum 137
 Tikanoja Art Museum 185
 Turkansaari Open Air Museum 194
 Vaasa Museum of Labour 185
 Vankilamuseo (prison wing) 158
 Verla Groundwood and Board Mill 122
 Zetterberg Gallery 68
music 18, 31, 153, 269, *see also* Sibelius, Jean
 Air Guitar World Championships 192
 Åland Sea Jazz 96
 Hamina Tattoo 122
 Ijahis Idja 228
 Jazztori 150
 Kaamosjazz 228
 Kuhmon Kamarimusiikki 166
 Lahti Organ Festival 150
 Lahti Sibelius Festival 150
 Manserock 132
 Olavinlinna opera festival 141
 opera 29
 Pori Jazz festival 179
 punk 66
 Qstock Music Festival 192
 Rockoff 96
 Ruisrock festival 29, 87
 Sibelius experience 106
 Soundfest 150
 Tavastia 64

N

Naantali 91-2
 food 92
Närpes 189
National Library of Finland 52, 54
national parks & reserves 38-9, **38-9**, *see also* Koli National Park, Lemmenjoki National Park, Oulanka National Park
 Aulanka Nature Reserve 159-60
 Bothnian Bay National Park 217
 Ekenäs Archipelago National Park 111-12
 Helvetinjärvi National Park 139
 Kevo Strict Nature Reserve 232
 Kolovesi National Park 143
 Linnansaari National Park 143
 Nuuksio National Park 53
 Päijänne National Park 150
 Pyhä-Luosto National Park 221
 Rapovesi National Park 119
 Repovesi National Park 150-1
 Salla National Park 220
 Salla Wilderness Park 221
 Siikakoski Rapids Park & Arboretum 119
 Urho Kekkonen National Park 229
 Valkmusa National Park 119
nature 270-2
Nauvo 93
nightlife 245, 246-7
Njurgulahti 228
Nolla 46
northern lights, *see* aurora borealis
Northern Ostrobothnia 169-201, **170-1**, *see also* Oullanka National Park, Oulu, Rauma, Vaasa, West Coast
 accommodation 201
 activities 172-3
 events 172-3
 itineraries 172-3
 navigation 170-1
 travel witin 170-1

O

Observatory Hill Park 47, 58
Ollinkivi 139
Olympic Games 65, 67, 72
Olympic Stadium 71-2, 263
Oodi Library 54, 263
opening hours 255
organic 249
Oulanka National Park 24, 197-200, **198**
 accommodation 201
 beyond Oulanka National Park 199-200, *see also individual locations*
 eating 198
 travel within 197, 199
Oulu 190-6, **191**
 beyond Oulu 194-6, *see also individual locations*
 drinking 192
 eating 192
 European Capital of Culture (2026) 190

Toripolliisi 190
tours 190, 193, 196, **193, 196**
travel within 190

Paimio 93
Parainen 93
Pargas 92
parks & gardens
  Arboretum Mustila 123
  Eiranpuisto 59
  Esplanadi Park 46, 50
  Isopuisto 120
  Kaisaniemen botanic gardens 71
  Kaivopuisto 55
  Nuuksio National Park 53
  Observatory Hill Park 47, 58
  Snellmanninpuisto 156
  Talvipuutarha 71
  Vanha kirkkopuisto 67
peaks & mountains
  Akka-Koli 163
  Halti 235
  Kiilopää fell 230
  Paha-Koli 163
  Saana 234
  Sokosti 230
  Ukko-Koli 163
people
  Finnish 264-5
  Finnish emigration 105
  Nanoq 188
  population 255, 264-5
  Sámi 266-7
photography 219
Pitkäluoto 180
planning
  clothes 30
  etiquette 30
  Finland basics 30-1
podcasts 31
population 255, 264-5
Pori 178-9
  accommodation 201
  eating 179
Porvoo 22, 27, 113-17, **114**
  accommodation 125
  beyond Porvoo 118-24, see also individual locations
  eating 115, 116
  old town 83
  tours 117, **117**
  travel within 113, 118
  Tuomiokirkko 83
Posio 219-20
public holidays 255
Pulkkilanharju 150
Punavuori 47, 61-8, **62**
  accommodation 76-7
  drinking 68
  food 63, 67
Pyhä-Luosto 221
Pyhamaa 180

Pyynikki Hill 137

rafting 198
Ranua 218
  accommodation 237
Ranua Wildlife Park 217, 218
Raseborg 110-12
  accommodation 125
  eating 112
Rauma 23, 27, 174-81, **175**
  accommodation 201
  beyond Rauma 178-81
  eating 177
  island-hopping 180
  shopping 177
  travel within 174, 178
Rauna 218
  eating 218
reindeer 221, 233, 267
  Arkadia Reindeer Farm 216-17
  Royal Reindeer Race 29, 228
  Salla Wilderness Park 221
  Tuula Airamo 227
responsible travel 248-9
Riihisaari 141-3
rivers
  Aura 89
  Kemijoki 212-13
  Kitkajoki 198
  Kymi 123
  Oulankajoki 198
  Oulujoki 192, 194
  Raudanjoki 213
  River Oulu Delta 192
  Teno 230
  Tornio 272
  Tornionjoki 217
road trips, see driving tours
Rovaniemi 25, 208-23, **209**
  accommodation 237
  beyond Rovaniemi 214-23, see also individual locations
  drinking 212
  eating 210-11
  tours 222-3
  travel within 208, 214
Ruka 200
  accommodation 201
  eating 200
Runeberg, Johan Ludvig 116
Ruovesi 139-40

S

Saariselkä 229
  accommodation 237
  eating 230
safe travel 245
sailing
  Hanko Regatta 107
Saimaa Lakeland 22, 126-67, **128-9, 142**, see

also Hämeenlinna, Jyväskylä, Karelia, Koli National Park, Tampere
  accommodation 167
  activities 130-1
  beyond Saimaa Lakeland 149-51, see also individual locations
  boat trips 146-7
  eating 143, 144, 145
  events 130-1
  itineraries 130-1
  navigation 128-9
  tours 148, **148**
  travel within 128-9, 141, 149
Sajos (Sámi Parliament) 225, 261, 267
Salla 220-1
  accommodation 237
Salpausselkä Geopark 150
Sámi 227-8, 266-7
  crafts 225, 248
  culture 226, 228, 261, 266-7
  languages 257, 266, 267
  parliament (Sajos) 225, 261, 267
  people 8-9
  tourism 267
Sámi Cultural Centre Sajos 224-5
Sammallahdenmäki 180, 260
Santa Claus 252
  origins of 211
  Santa Claus Post Office 212
  Santa Claus Village 211-12
  Santa's Lapland 15
saunas 11, 120, 254
  Allas Sea Pool 51
  Jätkänkämppä 157
  Kesän Sauna 192
  KesäRafla 212
  Kotiharjun Sauna 47, 75
  Löyly 59
  Rajaportin 137
  Satamakonttori 215
  Serlachius Art Sauna 138
  Tampere, saunas in 134
  Viilu 154
Savonlinna 141-3
  eating 143
seal-spotting 144-5, 180
Seinäjoki 188
Sevettijärvi 227-8
shopping 63, 117, see also books
  antiques 89
  ceramics 162
  crafts 89-90, 96, 149, 196, 225, 231
  Finlayson Centre 132
  Iittala outlet 162
  Iso Roobertinkatu 47, 63
  jewellery 96, 112, 177

pottery 112
Tampere 135
Toivolan vanha piha 155
Vanha Kauppahalli 51
vintage 53, 57, 63, 111
Sibelius, Jean 90, 106, 159, 160, 269
Sibelius Monument 71
Siida 226
Siikaneva 139
sisu 31, 113, 166, 254
Sisu (film) 166
skating 154
skiing 154, 157, 164, 219
  Lahti Ski Museum 150
  ski jumping 149-50
smoking 255
snow activities 10, 37, 38-9, 218, 219, **38-9**, see also individual activities
  Ounasvaara Ski Resort 211
  Ruka ski slopes 200
  Ski Saariselkä 229
snowshoeing 157, 164
Sodankylä 221
Sokosti 230
solo travel 245
South Coast 79-125, **80-1**, see also Åland Archipelago, Hanko, Mariehamn, Turku
  accommodation 125
  activities 82-3
  events 82-3
  itineraries 82-3
  navigation 80-1
  travel within 80-1
spas
  Regatta Spa 105
  Spa Hotel Peurunka 154
  Spa Hotel Scandic Laajavuori 154
sports, see also Olympic Games
  Finnish Hockey Hall of Fame 132-3
standup paddle boarding 69, 136
Story (restuarant) 46, 51
Strömfors Ironworks 119
Sund 98-100
  food 98-9
Suomenlinna Sea Fortress 261
SUPs 69, 136
sustainability 230, 249
sustainable travel 210-11, 243
swimming 57, 136, 164, 215, 249
  Allas Sea Pool 51

Taidehalli 47
Tammio 121

Tampere 23, 126-67, 132-41, **128-9**, **133**, see also Hämeenlinna, Jyväskylä, Karelia, Koli National Park, Saimaa Lakeland
  accommodation 167
  beyond Tampere 138-40, see also individual locations
  drinking 135
  eating 132-4, 136
  itineraries 130-1
  navigation 128-9
  shopping 132-4, 135
  tours 137, **137**
  travel within 128-9, 132, 138
Tankavaara 230-1
Tavastia 64
taxes 242
Tennispalatsi 67
theatres
  Jyväskylä City Theatre 152-3
theme parks
  Linnanmäki 47, 74-5
  Särkänniemi 135
time zone 255
  language 256
tipping 242
Töölö 69-75, **70**
  accommodation 77
  drinking 71
  food 69, 71, 72
Torikorttelit 46, 50
tours, see cycling tours, driving tours, walking tours
trail running 231
trains 241
travel seasons 28-9
  northern Lapland 229
travel to/from Finland 240
travel within Finland 241
Trillby & Chadwick 47, 50
Tulvalahti 227
Turkansaari 194-5
Turku 23, 26, 79-125, **80-1**, **85**, see also Åland Archipelago, Hanko, Mariehamn, Porvoo, South Coast
  activities 82-3
  beyond Turku 91-3, see also individual locations
  drinking 82, 87, 90
  events 82-3
  food 86
  island hopping 84, 93
  itineraries 82-3
  medieval market 90
  navigation 80-1
  nightlife 89
  shopping 89
  travel within 80-1, 82, 84, 91
Turun Linna 261
Turku Cathedral 86-7

Ullanlinna 55-60, **56**
  accommodation 76
  food 57, 58-9, 60
UNESCO recognised sites
  Kuhmo 166
  Kvarken Archipelago 186-7
  Rajaportin 134
  Salpausselkä 150
  Sammallahdenmäki 180
  Suomenlinna sea fortress 52-3
  Vanha Rauma 174-7
  Verla Groundwood & Board Mill 122-3
Utsjoki 232-3
  accommodation 237
  eating 231
Uunisaari 57
Uusikaupunki 180
  accommodation 201
  eating 180

V

Vääksy 150
  eating 150
Vaasa 182-9, **183**
  accommodation 201
  beyond Vaasa 186-9, see also individual locations
  eating 184
  travel within 182, 186
Vallila 74
Vanha Kauppahalli 51
Vanha Raatihuone (Rauma) 174
Vanha Rauma 174-7, 262
Vanha Vaasa 183
Vappu (May Day) 29
Vappuaatto (May Day Eve) 29
Vapriikki 132-3
Vårdö 102
Varissaari 120
Väski Adventure Island 91
viewpoints 71
  Bengtskär Lighthouse 108
  Hanko Water Tower 103
  Kotavaara Observation Tower 219
  Lahti ski towers 150
  Linnanvuori 143
  Näsinneula 135
  Puijo viewing tower 156
  Pyynikki Observation Tower 137
  Vesilinna observation tower 155
Viikinsaari 135-6
Vjrolahti 122
visas 240
Visavuori 162
Vuotso 231

walking 106, 119, 154, 180, 211, 221, 225, see also hiking, national parks & reserves, walking tours
  Bodvattnet nature trail 186
  Könkäänsaari Nature Trail 213
  Korouma Canyon 222
  Kumlinge åttan 101-2
  Lemmenjoki National Park 228-9
  Merisatamanranta promenade 57, 60
  Puistovuoret Cape 109
  Töölö Bay 72
  Vianaapa Mire Nature Trail 213
walking tours
  Hamina 124, **124**
  Hanko 106, 109, **109**
  Helsinki 54, 58-9, **54**, **59**
  Jyväskylä 155, **155**
  Lapland 236, **236**
  Porvoo 117, **117**
  Rovaniemi 222-3, **223**
  Tampere 137, **137**
water activities 37, 39, **39**, see also individual activities
waterfalls
  Jyrävä 198
  Kitsiputous 236
  Kiutaköngäs 198
  Korouma Canyon 222-3
weather 28-9
weights 255
West Coast 169-201, **170-1**, see also Northern Ostrobothnia, Oulanka National Park, Rauma, Vaasa
  accommodation 201
  activities 172-3
  events 172-3
  itineraries 172-3
  navigation 170-1
  travel witin 170-1
wi-fi 240
Wikström, Emil 162, 269
wildlife-watching 12-13, 165-6, 217, 219, 249, see also Rauna Wildlife Park, individual species
wooden buildings
  Falu red houses 195
  Kahvila Saima 143
  Kirsti 176
  Kristinestad 188-9
  Öjskogsparken 189
  Pielpajärven Erämaakirkko 225
  Utsjoki 232
  Vanha Rauma 174-7, 262

zip lining 91

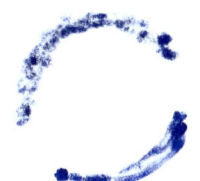

NOTES

The best way to survive and thrive in subzero conditions? Bundle up and get busy outdoors (p36)! Hiking, snowsports, and watersports will all get you out and warmed up.

Nothing is more integral to Finnish culture, psyche and wellbeing than the sauna (p11). With over three million around the country, you shouldn't struggle to find one.

All rights reserved. No part of this publication may be copied, stored in a retrieval system, or transmitted in any form by any means, electronic, mechanical, recording or otherwise, except brief extracts for the purpose of review, and no part of this publication may be sold or hired, without the written permission of the publisher. Lonely Planet and the Lonely Planet logo are trademarks of Lonely Planet and are registered in the US Patent and Trademark Office and in other countries. Lonely Planet does not allow its name or logo to be appropriated by commercial establishments, such as retailers, restaurants or hotels. Please let us know of any misuses: lonelyplanet.com/legal/intellectual-property.

Mapping data sources:
© Lonely Planet
© OpenStreetMap http://openstreetmap.org/copyright

THIS BOOK

Destination Editor
Amy Lynch

Production Editor
Jeremy Toynbee

Book Designer
Dominic Allen

Cartographer
Anthony Phelan

Assisting Editors
Andrea Dobbin,
Natalie Jayne Butler,
Charles Rawlings-Way

Cover Researcher
Kat Marsh

Thanks Ronan Abayawickrema, Fergal Condon, Melanie Dankel, Alison Killilea

Paper in this book is certified against the Forest Stewardship Council™ standards. FSC™ promotes environmentally responsible, socially beneficial and economically viable management of the world's forests.

Published by Lonely Planet Global Limited
CRN 554153
11th edition – Jul 2025
ISBN 978 1 83758 365 2
© Lonely Planet 2025 Photographs © as indicated 2025
10 9 8 7 6 5 4 3 2 1
Printed in China